NATIONAL INTELLIGENCE SYSTEMS
Current Research and Future Prospects

A series of investigations, especially in the United States and Britain, has focused attention on the performance of national intelligence services. At the same time, the onset of an era of terrorism and a broad span of transnational security challenges have highlighted the crucial role of intelligence. This book takes stock of the underlying intellectual substructure of intelligence. For intelligence – as for other areas of policy – serious intellectual inquiry is the basis for improving the performance of real-world institutions. This volume explores intelligence from an intellectual rather than an organizational perspective. Instead, the aim of the book is to identify themes that run through these applications, such as the lack of comprehensive theories, the unclear relationships between providers and users of intelligence, and the predominance of bureaucratic organizations driven by collection. A key element is the development – or, rather, nondevelopment – of intelligence toward an established set of methods and standards and, above all, an ongoing scientific discourse. Here, in the transformation from an experience-based protoscience to a science of intelligence in-being, the book argues, lies perhaps the most fundamental challenge for a field of immense impact on the international community, on nations, and on individuals.

Gregory F. Treverton is Director of the RAND Corporation's Center for Global Risk and Security. He previously directed RAND's Intelligence Policy Center and its International Security and Defense Policy Center, and he was associate dean of the Pardee RAND Graduate School. His recent work has examined terrorism, intelligence, and law enforcement, with a special interest in new forms of public–private partnership. He has served in government for the first Senate Select Committee on Intelligence, handling Europe for the National Security Council and, most recently, as vice chair of the National Intelligence Council, overseeing the writing of America's National Intelligence Estimates. He holds an A.B. *summa cum laude* from Princeton University and a master's in public policy and a Ph.D. in economics and politics from Harvard. His most recent books are *Intelligence for an Age of Terror* (Cambridge University Press, 2009); *Reshaping National Intelligence for an Age of Information* (Cambridge University Press, 2001); and *New Challenges, New Tools for Defense Decisionmaking* (2003).

Wilhelm Agrell is Professor in Intelligence Analysis at Lund University, Sweden, and visiting professor at the Swedish National Defence College, Stockholm. His background is in Swedish intelligence and military service in the Middle East. As an academic scholar, with a Ph.D. in history from Lund University in 1985, he has written more than 20 books that deal mainly with Cold War history and Swedish security, including an account of the aborted Swedish nuclear and chemical weapons programs in the 1950s and 1960s. He has been active in establishing intelligence analysis as an academic field and became the first professor in the subject in Scandinavia in 2006. He has also written nine novels, some of which have been translated into other Scandinavian languages, Finnish, and German.

National Intelligence Systems

Current Research and Future Prospects

Edited by

GREGORY F. TREVERTON

RAND Corporation, Santa Monica, CA

WILHELM AGRELL

Lund University, Sweden

CAMBRIDGE
UNIVERSITY PRESS

CAMBRIDGE UNIVERSITY PRESS
Cambridge, New York, Melbourne, Madrid, Cape Town, Singapore, São Paulo, Delhi

Cambridge University Press
32 Avenue of the Americas, New York, NY 10013-2473, USA

www.cambridge.org
Information on this title: www.cambridge.org/9780521518574

First published 2009

Printed in the United States of America

A catalog record for this publication is available from the British Library.

Library of Congress Cataloging in Publication data

National intelligence systems : current research and future prospects /
edited by Gregory F. Treverton, Wilhelm Agrell.
p.   cm.
Includes bibliographical references and index.
ISBN 978-0-521-51857-4 (hardback)
1. Intelligence service.   2. Military intelligence.   I. Treverton, Gregory F.   II. Agrell, Wilhelm.
JF1525.I6N38   2009
327.12 – dc22   2009000037

ISBN   978-0-521-51857-4 hardback

Contents

Preface

This book was part of a project of the Centre for Asymmetric Threat Studies (CATS) at the Swedish National Defence College. It was sponsored by the Swedish Emergency Management Agencies (SEMA), which in 2008 were combined with another agency to form the Swedish Civil Contingencies Agency (MSB). SEMA and MSB had the wisdom, from our perspective, to see benefit for their operations in asking deeper questions about what is required of intelligence for homeland security and the fight against terrorism.

In this portion of the project, we sought to ask about the state of serious, academic research on intelligence. Our purpose was, first, to improve understanding and lay out suggestions for where additional research might fill gaps or enrich our understanding. To that end, we assembled a distinguished set of experts on various facets of intelligence, and in particular sought to reach beyond the native English speakers that dominate so much of the literature on intelligence. The result is a book that is different from many other recent volumes on intelligence. It is a little more academic in style and international in composition.

Yet, our second purpose was to build better understanding in the hope of improving the practice of intelligence. A theme that runs through the entire book, and is turned to explicitly in the conclusions, is where intelligence stands as a profession. Is it an experience-based activity or a science, or something in between? How might better understanding of its current practice, along with suggestions from relevant adjacent lines of intellectual activity, enable its conduct to become more professional, if not more scientific, in methods?

Our primary debt is to the distinguished authors who did drafts, convened in Stockholm to work through them in the presence of interested Swedish thinkers and practitioners, then revised their chapters more than once in response to comments – for which we thank our anonymous reviewers. CATS and the Defence College have been both a happy sometime home for Gregory Treverton, during his stints as a visiting Fellow, and a venue that makes it easier to attract an impressive international group for discussions of intelligence issues. We express our thanks to all the people at CATS and the College who have made this possible, especially our immediate colleagues Lars Nicander, the director of CATS, Jan Leijonhielm, and Magnus Ranstorp, and finally Catharina Jönsson, who solved all practical problems as they appeared. We are also grateful for both the financial support from SEMA and MSB, and for the collegiality of their officers.

To be sure, the usual caveat remains: we are responsible for any remaining errors or gremlins in what follows.

Gregory F. Treverton
Wilhelm Agrell
May 2009

ONE

Introduction

Gregory F. Treverton and Wilhelm Agrell

A series of investigations, especially in the United States and Britain, has focused attention on the performance of national intelligence services.[1] At the same time, the onset of an era of terrorism has highlighted the role of intelligence in trying to detect and prevent possible terrorist acts. In many countries, intelligence services have expanded and been reorganized, or both, and new training programs for intelligence have sprung up around the world.

In these circumstances, it seemed propitious to take stock of the underlying intellectual substructure of intelligence. What is the current state of research on and relevant to intelligence? This is the question addressed by this book. The project that spawned it was conducted by the Centre for Asymmetric Threat Studies at the Swedish National Defence College, with funding from the Swedish Emergency Management Agency. The purpose of the book is primarily to assess the state of research. However, that purpose runs beyond pure understanding because the book's premise is that for intelligence, as for other areas of policy, serious intellectual inquiry is the basis for improving the performance of real-world institutions. The volume explores intelligence from an intellectual rather than an organizational perspective. Our ambitions do not run to systematically covering the various applications or "subdisciplines" of intelligence (e.g., foreign, domestic, counterespionage, counterterrorism, and covert operations) in the way that

---

[1] The two most detailed in the United States are those of the 9/11 Commission and the Weapons of Mass Destruction Commission. Formally, they are, respectively, the National Commission on Terrorist Attacks Upon the United States, *The 9/11 Commission Report* (Washington, 2004), available at www.9-11commission.gov; and *Final Report of the Commission on the Intelligence Capabilities of the United States Regarding Weapons of Mass Destruction* (Washington, 2005), available at www.wmd.gov/report. Britain's inquiry into pre–Iraq war intelligence, the Butler report, is *Review of Intelligence on Weapons of Mass Destruction* (London, 2004), available at www.butlerreview.org.uk/index.asp.

Table 1.1. *Intelligence: From the Cold War to an era of terror*

	Old: Cold War	New: Era of terror
Target	States, primarily the Soviet Union	Transnational actors, also some states
"Story" about target	Story: States are geographic, hierarchical, bureaucratic	Not much story: Nonstates come in many sizes, shapes
"Boundedness"	Relatively bounded: Soviet Union ponderous	Much less bounded: Terrorists patient but new groups and attack modes
Information	Too little: Dominated by secret sources	Too much: Broader range of sources, although secrets still matter
Interaction with target	Relatively little: Soviet Union would do what it would do	Intense: Terrorists as the ultimate asymmetric threat

most traditional accounts of intelligence do. Instead, our aim is to identify themes that run through these applications, including the lack of comprehensive theories, the unclear relationships between providers and users of intelligence, and the predominance of bureaucratic organizations driven by collection.

FROM THE OLD WORLD OF INTELLIGENCE TO THE NEW

With the end of the Cold War and then, a decade later, the onset of Muslim extremist terrorism, the task of intelligence changed dramatically. Table 1.1 summarizes the major differences.

As an analytic challenge, transnational targets, like terrorists, differ from traditional state targets in four main ways. First, although the current Islamic extremist terrorists hardly act quickly but instead plan their attacks carefully over years, transnational targets are less bounded than states. There will be discontinuities in targets and attack modes, and new groups will emerge unpredictably. Second, the new targets deprive intelligence and policy of a shared story that would facilitate analysis and communication. We knew what states were like, even very different states like the Soviet Union: they were geographical, hierarchical, and bureaucratic. There is no comparable story for nonstates, which come in many sizes and shapes.

Third, as former U.S. Secretary of Defense Harold Brown quipped to Congress about the U.S.–Soviet nuclear competition, "When we build, they build. When we cut, they build."[2] Although various countries, especially

[2] From Suzy Platt (ed.), *Respectfully Quoted: A Dictionary of Quotations Requested from the Congressional Research Service* (Washington: Library of Congress, 1989), p. 80.

the United States, hoped that their policies would influence Moscow, as a first approximation, intelligence analysts could presume that they would not. The Soviet Union would do what it would do. The challenge, in the first instance, was figuring out its likely course, not calibrating influence that other nations might have over that course.

The terrorist target, however, is utterly different. It is the ultimate asymmetric threat, shaping its capabilities to our vulnerabilities. The September 11, 2001, suicide bombers did not conceive of their attack plan because they were airline buffs. They knew that fuel-filled jets in flight were a vulnerable asset and that defensive passenger-clearance procedures were weak, and the scheme obviated the need to face a more effective defense against procuring or importing ordnance. Similarly, the London, Madrid, and other suicide bombers conducted enough tactical reconnaissance to shape their plans to the vulnerabilities of their targets. To a great extent, we shape the threat to us; it reflects our vulnerable assets and weak defenses. As military planners would characterize it, it is impossible to understand red (potential foes) without knowing a lot about blue (ourselves).

That fact has awkward implications for intelligence, especially foreign intelligence that, in many countries, has been enjoined from examining the home front and, less formally, is worried that getting too close to "policy" is to risk becoming politicized. Moreover, to the extent that intelligence now becomes the net assessment of red against blue, that too is something that has been the province of military, not civilian, agencies.

Finally, given that most Cold War adversaries of the Western nations were closed societies, Cold War intelligence, analysis included, gave pride of place to secrets – information gathered by human and technical means that intelligence "owned." Terrorists are hardly open, but an avalanche of open data is relevant to them: witness the September 11 hijackers whose true addresses were available in California motor vehicle records. Then, the problem was too little information; now, it is too much. Then, intelligence's secrets were deemed reliable; now, the torrents on the Web are a stew of fact, fancy, and disinformation.

These changes frame all the chapters that follow, and a number of common themes run through them. One is risk. Intelligence always has been a hedge against risk but now, as the nature of the threat has changed, so has the nature of the risk. Terrorists willing to die for their cause as suicide bombers, for example, cannot be deterred from acting in any way similar to the way that states could. Thus, there is all the more pressure on intelligence, which now has to be not merely good enough to structure deterrent threats but also must reach deeply enough into small groups – their proclivities and capabilities – to prevent them from acting.

A second theme throughout the chapters of this book is the corresponding expansion in the consumers of intelligence. National intelligence used to be primarily of use to a relatively small set of political and military leaders of states. Now, in principle, it would be of use to a huge number of consumers, extending to police officers on the beat and private-sector managers of major infrastructure. Intelligence has moved, as the catchphrase goes, from "need to know" to "need to share."

A third theme is the increased number of needs for – hence, kinds of – intelligence, across a variety of time horizons from immediate warning to longer term understanding. Much of Cold War intelligence was puzzle-solving: looking for additional pieces to fill in a mosaic of understanding whose broad shape was a given.[3] Those puzzles – for example, how many warheads did a Soviet missile carry? – could be answered with certainty if only we had access to information that, in principle, is available. Puzzle-solving is inductive. Mysteries are different; no evidence can settle them definitively because, typically, they are about people, not things. They are contingent. Mystery-framing is deductive: the analysis begins where the evidence ends. There were mysteries during the Cold War, but the era of terrorism seems especially rife with them. For instance, many of the national military capabilities could be treated as a puzzle during the Cold War, but now even the capabilities of terrorists are a mystery: those capabilities depend, not least, on us.

A final overarching theme is boundaries, of both law and organization. During the Cold War, democratic societies drew boundaries, with varying degrees of sharpness, between intelligence and law enforcement, between home and abroad, and between public and private. The first two boundaries, in particular, were drawn to protect the privacy and civil liberties of a nation's citizens. In the circumstances of the Cold War, those boundaries made sense. However, they set up nations to fail against a terrorist foe who respected none of those boundaries. Now, the balance between security and civil liberties is being struck anew and, in the process, the organizational distinctions, like that between intelligence and law enforcement, are being erased.

[3] On the distinction between puzzles and mysteries, see Gregory F. Treverton, "Estimating Beyond the Cold War," *Defense Intelligence Journal*, 3, 2 (Fall 1994); and Joseph S. Nye, Jr., "Peering into the Future," *Foreign Affairs*, 77, 4 (July/August 1994), 82–93.

FROM DEFINITIONS AND HISTORY TO POLITICS AND OVERSIGHT

Intelligence first must be defined, and that is Michael Warner's task in Chapter Two. Although common usages of the word *intelligence* have not changed much since Shakespeare's time, the fault line also remains: Is intelligence support for a decision maker and thus composed of anything that will help, or is it the quiet or secret component that leaders deploy in dealing with their adversaries, both foreign and domestic? Intelligence has to be defined before it can be compared across countries. Warner focuses on intelligence systems, not – as most comparative analyses do – on either the characteristics of agencies or how those agencies approach particular challenges, such as early warning of attack. Warner argues that three main factors – strategy, regime, and technology – determine the nature of a regime's intelligence system. They do so from the perspective of sovereigns, where "state" is synonymous with sovereignty; however, not all sovereigns are states and, thus, nongovernmental groups also have intelligence systems.

By far, most of the writing on intelligence, if not the serious research, is history. Chapter Three, by the eminent historian of intelligence, Christopher Andrew, reflects on the state of historiography of intelligence. It is not surprising that most of that history deals with operations, especially what is called *covert action* – that is, operations intended to influence foreign politics, not merely penetrate them for espionage purposes. However, because American investigations into intelligence produced massive amounts of material, most accounts of the Cold War are the "intelligence equivalent of one hand clapping" – devoting considerable attention to the covert operations of the U.S. Central Intelligence Agency (CIA) but virtually none to those of the CIA's Soviet counterpart, the KGB.

Similarly, although the breaking of the German code during World War II captured the imagination of both historians and the public when it was revealed in 1973, the interest "usually ceases at V-J Day." The implications of postwar signals intelligence (SIGINT) for either the United States or the Soviet Union have been neglected; what history there is on Soviet intelligence treats neither covert action nor SIGINT but instead focuses on Moscow's espionage, or human intelligence (HUMINT). In setting out principles for official histories of intelligence, Andrew emphasizes that they must include interactions with policy makers because it is in the use of intelligence that Andrew locates the greatest weakness of postwar U.S. intelligence.[4]

---

[4] See Andrew, *For the President's Eyes Only: Secret Intelligence and the American Presidency from Washington to Bush* (New York: HarperCollins, 1995).

In Chapter Four, Jennifer Sims turns to theory, picking up the central themes of both Warner and Andrew. If, as Warner argues, scholars have not developed techniques for assessing the relative intelligence capabilities of states and other actions, neither have they asked whether and how those capabilities matter in international politics. On that score, what exists is from histories – thus, anecdotal and, as Andrew underscores, partial. If intelligence is about power, international-relations theory should have explored it in detail. Sims defines *intelligence* as a means of seeking comparative advantage; indeed, "intelligence failure may be less about inaccuracy than about losing advantage." She then seeks to measure that advantage across four critical intelligence functions: collecting information on competitors, anticipating new competitions, transmitting information across the divide between intelligence and decision makers, and degrading competitors' efforts to do all of these. About each function, she asks what work is relevant to each and what are the obvious gaps (and opportunities).

Chapter Five, by Wilhelm Agrell, forms a bridge between the first two parts of the book. The second part focuses on the major change in intelligence after the Cold War – which is the change after September 11, July 7, 2005, and March 3, 2004 – from a primary focus on states to a strong focus on nonstate transnational groups. His chapter begins with his own experience, as a young Swedish military analyst, of the institutional "failure to comprehend new knowledge." Agrell applies Thomas Kuhn's pathbreaking insights about the structure of science to understand intelligence. Like Kuhn's "normal science," intelligence too is often puzzle-solving, where new information is incorporated into an established frame of reference and results that do not fit are rejected. For Agrell, the canonical notion of an intelligence cycle from collection to analysis to dissemination ratifies that failing in a compartmented and hierarchical structure. Intelligence was slow to absorb the changes of the 1990s, and Agrell is skeptical that even the dramatic shocks of terrorist attacks can inspire the required creativity and imagination within existing – and traditional – intelligence organizations. For him, the fundamental problem is not how intelligence is directed or organized; rather, it is how intelligence *thinks*.

Terrorism is not only a nonstate threat; it is also the ultimate asymmetric threat, adjusting its capacity to its targets' vulnerabilities. It thus represents a very different challenge from the nation-states of the Cold War; Chapter Six, by Neal Pollard, surveys research that is relevant to understanding that challenge. This threat is not only abroad but rather both at home and abroad. It is less bounded than the threat posed by states, and it comes with no "story" comparable to the story about states, shared in the minds of intelligence and policy personnel. Although secrets still matter, so do a plethora of credit-card transactions, motor-vehicle records, and the like. Perhaps most uncomfortable for intelligence because the threat is so asymmetric, it is impossible to understand without significant knowledge about the home country – something that cuts across preexisting boundaries between foreign and domestic intelligence. All these factors bear directly not only on how intelligence does its work but also on how it relates to policy – in Pollard's opinion, especially to strategic planning.

The change in targets has also reconfigured intelligence collection, including by technical means, and those changes are the subject of Chapter Seven by Jeffrey Richelson. For most countries, especially the larger ones but also including Sweden, technical collection consumes most of the national resources for intelligence. In Chapter Seven, Richelson primarily examines research relevant to the technical issues confronted by collection, but he also comments on the legal issues at play. For imagery, the main question is relevance: Imagery was critical in understanding nation-states that had addresses, but how important can it be now against terrorist targets that lack addresses – all the more so because imagery's methods are well known? SIGINT is more relevant and more critical. The technical issues run into legal ones: If SIGINT needs to both get closer to the signals of interest and collect more domestic signals, how does it do so both technically and legally? What research is relevant to the answers to these questions?

The third part of the book turns to the politics on intelligence in democratic societies, starting with Olav Riste's overview in Chapter Eight. Like it or not, intelligence in democracies is increasingly the subject of political debate. The specific concern is *politicization* – that is, the risk that intelligence will be under pressure, usually more implicit than explicit, to produce assessments that suit the preferences of national administrations. That concern ran through the American and British investigations of intelligence assessments in the run-up to the 2003 war in Iraq. Yet, protection against politicization needs to be balanced against its opposite: intelligence that is not relevant to any policy question at issue. These issues are the subject of Chapter Eight. Riste also considers the larger public – and political – debate about intelligence. Using intelligence to defend the homeland has necessarily opened up intelligence. What can be learned from research on the state of that debate and its boundaries?

The change in intelligence's targets and the consequent need to expand surveillance at home is stretching democratic oversight of intelligence, as public debates over the boundaries of SIGINT in both Sweden and the United States testify. In Chapter Nine, Wolfgang Krieger surveys research on intelligence oversight or democratic control of intelligence services. He does so in an explicitly comparative perspective, suggesting how different practices and experiences are reflections of the different national ways of dealing with intelligence. In fact, they reflect different political cultures, different relationships between elites and the public (because intelligence services are a most exclusive part of national governments), and different ways of defining and managing power. For example, consider the contrast between Britain and France, which still believe they are global powers, and countries like Germany and the Netherlands, which do not. Thus, it is not surprising that the attitudes toward intelligence, particularly to covert action, are very different. In Europe's case, there is the specific issue of over-coming the legacy of communist regimes and their intelligence personnel, a task that has only just begun in Russia.

The change in intelligence's targets also raises ethical issues, and Chapter Ten, by the distinguished former practitioner, Sir David Omand, assesses relevant research. The campaign against terrorism not only is mixing mil-itary force and intelligence in new ways, it is also straining the limits of both – from the limits of preemption to the use of covert action away from the battlefield. Intelligence is expanding dramatically, in both expense and breadth of activity, some of which is controversial. At the same time that intelligence is seeking and being given new powers, technology is providing new opportunities to survey major amounts of information about individ-uals. The irony is that intelligence will be more effective the less terrorists understand of its scope and methods – which constrains the scope of the public debate.

Finally, the concluding Chapter Eleven, by the editors, sums up the vol-ume by drawing together key themes of the various chapters, focusing on the development – or, rather, nondevelopment – of intelligence toward an established set of methods and standards and, above all, an ongoing sci-entific discourse. Here, in the transformation from an experience-based protoscience to a science of intelligence in-being, the authors argue, lies perhaps the most fundamental challenge for a field of immense impact on the international community, on nations, and on individuals.

PART 1

DEFINING THE FIELD, ITS THEORY, HISTORIOGRAPHY, AND CHANGES AFTER THE COLD WAR

TWO

Building a Theory of Intelligence Systems

Michael Warner

From a hobby of kings and a staple of lurid tales, intelligence has gradually become a proper topic of scholarship. During the last generation, various scholars have voiced impatience with the insightful but ad hoc pattern of studies in this new field and have called for research agendas oriented around cross-national comparisons. Such agendas, however, have not yet emerged. Various well-known factors help to explain this deficit of truly comparative analyses: the paucity of reliable, declassified data to analyze; the general lack of interest among government agencies in sponsoring such studies by in-house experts with access to the files; and the methodological divide between the academic historians (and their official counterparts) mining the available documents and their colleagues trained in political science who draw generalizations from the historical findings. Unfortunately, these perennial obstacles seem immune to quick or easy solutions. Another reason for the lack of comparative studies, however, is closer to home and perhaps easier to address: the lack of agreement, among both scholars and practitioners, of just what would be compared in a comparative approach to intelligence studies.

A great amount of writing, and some excellent research, has been done on intelligence activities and personalities. Not so much has been done on the *collective* authorities, resources, oversight, and missions assigned to parties officially assembled to perform intelligence duties of particular nations. Still less has been done to compare these collectivities across nations, cultures, or eras. What has been written is not comprehensive. Researchers use conflicting concepts and definitions, do not mine other disciplines for insights, and rarely regard the "literary record." Furthermore, little has been done to build taxonomies of intelligence-related variables and to chart their relationships.

Actually doing such work might open up several profitable lines for comparison. The key to comparative analyses is a grasp of intelligence *systems* (as opposed to the agencies, functions, and capabilities that are simply the component parts of those systems). When the overall systems are understood, then the agencies, functions, and capabilities of those systems could be compared in terms of their purposes, their effectiveness, and their governance, to name only three likely areas of inquiry. Tools that could perform comparisons across cultures and epochs would be truly useful to scholars. Tools that sharp might also help intelligence practitioners by providing diagnostic insight and a better understanding of entire intelligence enterprises, as well as of the individual agencies that comprise them.

COMPARATIVE BEGINNINGS

Glenn Hastedt was not the first to call for comparative studies of intelligence, but his 1992 survey of the field and his description of the work to be done in it remains a touchstone for researchers. Hastedt noted two principal ways in which intelligence activities had previously been compared: (1) by the characteristics of agencies employed by several countries, and/or (2) by how those agencies approached certain types of events or activities (e.g., the perennial problem of surprise). He proposed the following four additional planes of comparison that could encourage the development of testable hypotheses and theories of intelligence[1]:

- the "role orientations" of intelligence officers (on the idea that similarly placed individuals in different services ordinarily will act in similar fashions)
- the institutional aspects of various intelligence organizations (i.e., their "standard operating procedures, grants of authority and jurisdiction, and . . . bureaucratic culture")
- the social contexts for national intelligence efforts (i.e., "the manner in which intelligence is shaped by the societal values, norms, political structures, and the amount of power exercised by the state")
- the respective international contexts of a nation's intelligence ("the distribution of power in the international system; its level of stability; the presence or absence of war; or the rate and direction [of power shifts]").

[1] Glenn P. Hastedt, "Towards the Comparative Study of Intelligence," *Conflict Quarterly*, 11, 3 (Summer 1991), 60–4.

Hastedt offered several strategies for comparing these topics and urged his colleagues to cast their research along lines that would allow meaningful, verifiable, and generalizable findings. He might have explicitly posited the previous "aspects" and "contexts" as independent variables, but he did not do so, perhaps because (as he hinted) the field had not yet defined a true dependent variable to appose to them. The comparative study of intelligence was compromised, in his view, by "the absence of a shared definition or perspective on intelligence."[2] Hastedt thus stepped up to the verge of offering a theory of intelligence and a framework for testing it through comparative observations – and then stepped back when confronted by the challenge of specifying what exactly should be compared.

Since Hastedt's call for systematic comparative studies, the number of books, articles, theses, movies, and exhibits on intelligence seems to have grown significantly each year and (with exceptions) to become more sophisticated in its methodologies and insights. Scholars have continued producing examples of the two main types of protocomparisons that he described: (1) publishing more side-by-side descriptions of intelligence agencies and operations, and (2) examining more events and episodes (especially "warning failures"). Much of this work has been valuable, to be sure; however, in the aggregate, it nonetheless has not amounted to a true compendium of rigorous studies grouped around defined research topics. Without a clear sense of the dependent variable in the equation, we find it difficult to understand which independent factors cause and affect intelligence phenomena. Nevertheless, there have been signs of progress in the direction that Hastedt envisioned.

Recent work has brought us closer to defining the dependent variable that eluded Hastedt. Much effort has been devoted to debates about the meaning of the term *intelligence*, as is discussed herein. At the same time, scholars have sought knowledge of that dependent variable from several angles – in effect, specifying more than one object of study. David Kahn described the ways in which intelligence, in war, is a tool that optimizes a commander's resources (and also benefits the defense more than the offense).[3] Loch Johnson listed a set of independent variables affecting the amount or scope of *resources* that states expend on strategic intelligence. He identified the chief factors in this equation as "a nation's foreign policy objectives, its sense of danger at home and abroad, and its affluence."[4] In a second essay published almost

---

[2] Hastedt, "Towards the Comparative Study of Intelligence," 61.
[3] David Kahn, "An Historical Theory of Intelligence," *Intelligence and National Security, 16*, 3 (Autumn 2001), 84–5.
[4] Loch K. Johnson, "Preface to a Theory of Strategic Intelligence," *International Journal of Intelligence and Counterintelligence, 16*, 4 (2003), 657.

concurrently, Johnson offered 37 propositions about the factors affecting the *efficacy* of overall national-intelligence efforts. Effective intelligence, he averred, is largely a function of national wealth, although other factors also play a role in determining the relative effectiveness of a nation's specific intelligence functions.[5]

These insights may hold lasting value for intelligence studies, but their value may not be fully appreciated without an intervening stage of analysis. To wit, we need to explain why one international power organizes and tasks its intelligence capability in one way whereas another does so in a different way – and to account for the differences and commonalities of those two establishments over time. Efforts to explore national intelligence "styles" hold promise for filling this gap. Michael Turner looked to insights adduced by students of national strategic cultures in his explanation of the distinctive U.S. intelligence "identity" as the product of a series of norms rooted in America's strategic culture.[6] Rob Johnston did something similar in a more systematic way, building a taxonomy of variables to explain "analytic cultures" in American intelligence agencies.[7] Although neither Turner nor Johnston took the next step and showed how to compare such identities, either across nations or eras, their taxonomies for American intelligence presumably could inspire examinations and comparisons of other nations as well.

Kevin O'Connell took the next step and proposed comparing national-intelligence services or "systems." He posed a series of questions relating to intelligence establishments under study and suggested that systematically answering such questions could enable categorization of a nation's political, diplomatic, and military contexts, as well as the organizational factors affecting its intelligence organs and even the varied emphases on security and cooperation within the services under scrutiny.[8]

---

[5] Loch K. Johnson, "Bricks and Mortar for a Theory of Intelligence," *Comparative Strategy* 22 (2003), 22–3. Effective collection and analysis, for example, "is above all, a function of national wealth; but it also depends on focused targeting, all-source synergism, and good liaison ties between intelligence officers and policymakers." Other factors also affect the efficacy of a nation's covert action and counterintelligence work, Johnson explained, although national wealth is an important factor for both of these activities as well.

[6] Michael A. Turner, "A Distinctive U.S. Intelligence Identity," *International Journal of Intelligence and Counterintelligence, 17* (2004), 42–5.

[7] Rob Johnston, *Analytic Culture in the U.S. Intelligence Community: An Ethnographic Study* (Washington: Central Intelligence Agency, 2005), p. 37.

[8] Kevin M. O'Connell, "Thinking about Intelligence Comparatively," *Brown Journal of World Affairs, 11* (Summer/Fall 2004), 193–7.

It is clear that there are overarching similarities in the demands and structures of intelligence systems across the world. However, it is the differences that require our close attention because they reveal different possibilities for various intelligence services.

The data collected and sorted according to this framework could provide "some basis within which to assess performance, relevance, patterns of innovation, and variation within norms and standards."[9]

O'Connell's insight suggests how to compare intelligence systems across national and temporal boundaries; if followed, it could open a way for more policy-prescriptive comparisons like those proposed by Johnson. Yet, even if we take up O'Connell's challenge and focus our efforts on comparing intelligence systems – that is, on the ways in which a nation has organized, authorized, funded, and tasked its intelligence agencies to serve decision makers – we soon hit an obstacle: the sharp divide over exactly what it is that intelligence "does" when it serves decision makers.

Indeed, in scholarly parlance, *intelligence* has assumed two fairly specialized – and rival – significations. One camp follows 20th-century American military nomenclature and holds that intelligence is *information for decision makers*: anything from any source (and possibly the activities that acquire such information) that helps leaders decide what to do about their surroundings.[10] The second camp defines intelligence as *warfare by quieter means*.[11] In summary, one definition emphasizes intelligence as something that informs decision making; the second sees intelligence as activity (often conducted in secret) that assists both the informing and executing of decisions.[12]

The argument between these camps might seem esoteric, but it has almost immediate policy and institutional implications. If an "intelligence system" can be thought of as the collective authorities, resources, oversight, and missions assigned to parties officially assembled to perform intelligence

---

[9] O'Connell, p. 197.

[10] See, for instance, Kristan J. Wheaton and Michael T. Beerbower, "Towards a New Definition of Intelligence," *Stanford Law & Policy Review*, 17, 2 (2006), 329.

[11] James Der Derian called intelligence "the continuation of war by the clandestine interference of one power into the affairs of another." *Antidiplomacy: Spies, Terror, Speed, and War* (Cambridge, MA: Blackwell, 1992), p. 21.

[12] Michael Warner, "Wanted: A Definition of Intelligence," *Studies in Intelligence*, 46, 3 (2002). Abram N. Shulsky and Gary J. Schmitt called these the "traditional" and "American" views; *Silent Warfare: Understanding the World of Intelligence* (Washington: Potomac Books, 2002 [1991]), pp. 159–67. See also Peter Jackson, "Historical Reflections on the Uses and Limits of Intelligence," in Peter Jackson and Jennifer Siegel (eds.), *Intelligence and Statecraft: The Use and Limits of Intelligence in International Society* (Westport, CT: Praeger, 2005), pp. 12–13.

duties, then the question immediately arises: What are intelligence *duties*? Scholars and practitioners who do not agree on what intelligence does will hardly reach agreement on the proper functions, organizations, and authorities for the institution.

Each camp would dictate the placement of various legal and oversight markers bounding a state's intelligence system, but each would place those markers differently. Adherents of the former definition tend to view intelligence as a form of information, which only *informs* policy – and never *executes* it – thus, they would keep intelligence distinct from what they see as the corrupting influence of "policy execution."[13] Proponents of the latter view, conversely, tend to view activities such as covert action and clandestine diplomacy as well within the fold of "secret intelligence services." Their argument could (but need not) support an insistence that intelligence services confine themselves to secret means and activities while leaving "merely informational" tasks to the more open agencies of government.[14] We are not likely to make much progress in comparing intelligence systems without settling, or transcending, this definitional argument.

WHAT DOES INTELLIGENCE DO?

Which of these two schools is right? Surely some overlap exists between them. Indeed, these rival definitions of intelligence might yield an interesting area of agreement. Both camps would seem to agree, whether or not explicitly, that intelligence is a service or interaction with decision makers to help them manage – by some private or privileged means – the hazards they face in dealing with rival powers.[15] Both camps, moreover, seem to agree that intelligence helps leaders act to know or shape the world around them.

[13] William W. Kennedy, for example, lamented that the intelligence function has been besmirched by activities that have nothing to do with intelligence, as such.... To the extent to which they have any legitimacy at all, such functions are properly described under the heading of political and military "operations." The mischief lies in failing to maintain a distinct organizational boundary. In short, intelligence is one thing: operations are something else. See *Intelligence Warfare: Penetrating the Secret World of Today's Advanced Technology Conflict* (New York: Crescent Books, 1987), p. 16.

[14] Len Scott, "Secret Intelligence, Covert Action and Clandestine Diplomacy," in L. V. Scott and P. D. Jackson (eds.), *Understanding Intelligence in the Twenty-First Century: Journeys in Shadows* (London: Routledge, 2004), pp. 162–3.

[15] I explain this at greater length in exploring the notion that intelligence is a means for managing risk and uncertainty in "Intelligence as Risk Shifting," in Peter R. Gill, Mark Phythian, and Stephen Marrin (eds.), *Intelligence Theory: Key Questions and Debates* (London: Routledge, 2008).

The divide is over the status of the *action*. Indeed, either contending side could attempt to craft a dependent variable for use in comparative studies of intelligence systems.

We need some help in thinking through this problem. Happily, the field of international relations could offer some assistance here. Intelligence is essentially a "Realist" enterprise, presupposing eternal rivalry and potential conflict between essentially atomistic state actors. In Chapter Four, Jennifer E. Sims looks to international-relations theory (specifically, Neo-Realism) for insights that emphasize intelligence as a common if not inevitable facet of interstate competition. Where there is such competition, there is intelligence, which is not simply a process for serving senior officials. It is more accurately seen as the interaction between decision makers and their subordinates that helps them collectively to best their opponents. Sims emphasizes that intelligence enhances the effectiveness of decisions made by actors who are working in opposition to other actors (who may well be employing their own intelligence assets). Thus, "If politics involves the competition for power, 'intelligence' may be best understood as a process by which competitors improve their decision-making relative to their opponents."[16] She is well aware that many states cooperate with other states quite productively and even amicably in the intelligence field, but she recognizes that such covert cooperation is based on shared interests in working against common rivals and, therefore, is ultimately a derivative of international competition.[17] It provides "decision advantage," either by making our decisions better or theirs worse. "Success is not getting everything right, it is getting enough right to beat the other side." Intelligence methods can foster decision advantage by stealing opponents' secrets or adulterating the information available to rivals – or both.[18]

At this point, we need to clarify who these rival leaders are. Adda Bozeman observed in 1988 that the state "is not the decisive working unit in intelligence studies." Rather, she noted, "[i]nternationally relevant decision making ... emanates increasingly from scattered, often dissimulated

---

[16] See also Jennifer E. Sims, "Understanding Friends and Enemies: The Context for American Intelligence Reform," in Jennifer E. Sims and Burton Gerber (eds.), *Transforming U.S. Intelligence* (Washington: Georgetown University Press, 2005), pp. 15–16.

[17] Jennifer E. Sims, "Foreign Intelligence Liaison: Devils, Deals, and Details," *International Journal of Intelligence and Counterintelligence*, *19*, 2 (Fall 2005), 196–201.

[18] Office of the Director of National Intelligence (Strategy, Plans, and Policy Office), "Exploring the Doctrinal Principle of Integration," proceedings of a workshop in Washington, DC, 12 October 2006, p. 19. The quoted passage paraphrases a remark by Dr. Sims at that event.

command posts of liberation fronts, terrorist brigades, provisional governments, or international Communist parties."[19] Bozeman's insight showed
us a way to understand why and how a multiplicity of actors – and not just
states – uses intelligence methods.

These actors, including the Westphalian states with which they interact,
may all be understood as *sovereignties*, distinguishable and divided from
another by their competitive willingness to use violence to hold or gain
control over people, resources, and (where possible) territory. That addition of lethal force as a factor raises their competition to a qualitatively
different plane from the rivalry between corporations striving for market
share or sports clubs that might want to steal one another's signs. Indeed,
the potential lethality of the stakes convinces some leaders that they need to
act in dangerous and provocative ways to protect themselves and, ultimately,
to prevail – and that they must do all they can to cloak their provocative
ways from other actors who could neutralize them.

The mechanism by which sovereignties use such ways, however, is not
something that the international-relations specialists or other scholars have
explained. The naming and explaining of that mechanism was instead done
by another species of social theorists, who called it *surveillance*. The word,
in this case, is French; it does not mean what its cognate does in English
(i.e., watching people or spaces or following suspicious characters). As
employed by Michel Foucault and others, *surveillance* denotes something
larger. Peter R. Gill and Mark Phythian explained that *surveillance* has two
components: "[F]irst, the gathering and storing of information and, second,
the supervision of people's behaviour. In other words, it is concerned with
knowledge and power."[20] Surveillance is thus a characteristic dimension of
political order that encapsulates the way in which governing bodies (both
democratic and autocratic) employ knowledge of their constituents and
their rivals in ways to preserve and extend their power.

Gill and Phythian viewed intelligence as just one of several forms of
surveillance. In accord with Bozeman, they also acknowledged that nonstate actors wield surveillance for purposes similar to those that animate
many states. Both forms of sovereignties – states and nonstates – pursue power and knowledge to protect and advance their interests, however
defined; the notion of surveillance transcends questions of whether leaders

---

[19] Adda Bozeman, "Political Intelligence in Non-Western Societies: Suggestions for Comparative Research," in Roy Godson (ed.), *Comparing Foreign Intelligence: The US, the USSR,
the UK, and the Third World* (Washington: Pergamon-Brassey's, 1988), p. 135.

[20] Peter R. Gill, "Theories of Intelligence: The Next Steps?," paper presented at the International Studies Association Conference, Chicago, 28 February 2007.

have properly understood those interests. For sovereignties, intelligence is that special mode of surveillance that addresses security, secrecy, and resistance; that is, it seeks to protect and extend the sovereign's interests by secret means employed against subjects who do not want to be watched or manipulated (and who might well have the power to resist that watching and manipulation). Intelligence, therefore, for Gill and Phythian consists of the range of activities – from planning to information collection to analysis and dissemination – conducted in secret and aimed at maintaining or enhancing relative security by providing forewarning of threats in a manner that allows for the timely implementation of a preventive policy or strategy – including, where deemed desirable, covert activities.[21] Intelligence here does more than provide forewarning; often, it serves to establish conditions in which threats are eliminated or kept at a distance.

What follows are several insights from Bozeman, Sims, and Gill and Phythian. Viewing intelligence (as Gill and Phythian did) from the vantage point of the concept of surveillance both complements Sims's emphasis on competition and bridges any lingering domestic–foreign divide: intelligence is both a domestic bulwark and a foreign policy tool, protecting regimes from internal as well as external threats.[22] Bozeman implied that we must expand our focus beyond states to include sovereignties. In addition, Gill and Phythian, like Sims, understood that the security purchased via intelligence is only relative, depending as it does on an adversary's reactions (and vice versa). Thus, they place intelligence in a dynamic system of complex actions and reactions, where cause and effect cannot be clearly discerned, where impacts may be disproportionate to intentions, and where consequences can rarely be calibrated.

THE RECORD OF HISTORY

These collective insights into secrecy, institutions, sovereignty, and statecraft help explain why sovereign powers build intelligence systems, but do these findings correspond with anything in the historical record? One place to look is in the most distant sources available to us. Ancient history is more literary than scientific and, in that sense, it hardly seems a fitting test for modern

---

[21] Peter R. Gill and Mark Phythian, *Intelligence in an Insecure World* (Cambridge, England: Polity, 2006), pp. 7, 29.

[22] The foreign/domestic divide can be found in the thinking of many authors. Gill and Phythian (*Intelligence in an Insecure World*, p. 29) cited Sherman Kent's seminal treatise on analysis, *Strategic Intelligence for American World Policy* (Princeton, NJ: Princeton University Press, 1949), p. 3.

conceptions of intelligence. Yet, for just that reason, it represents a necessary benchmark because principles of intelligence systems must transcend times and cultures if they really are principles.

At least two ancient Eastern writings treat espionage in enough detail for our purpose. Sun Tzu's famous *The Art of War*, composed in the third century BC, teaches a ruler to conquer by reducing his own risks and increasing his opponent's (although Sun Tzu did not write in quite those terms). It is not surprising that Sun Tzu had much to say about spies. *The Art of War*'s rhetorical climax is its final chapter, on their use; it concludes with the thought that spies "are essential in war; upon them the army depends to make its every move."[23] A century or so after Sun Tzu, the Indian author Kautilya explained the domestic uses of intelligence. Spies perform many functions for the wise and ruthless king in Kautilya's monumental treatise on governance, the *Arthashastra*. Mostly, however, spies form a variegated internal secret service that watches everyone and stifles plots and dissensions by fair means and foul.[24] This is surveillance indeed – and what spymasters have aspired to do for most of history.

Reflecting on these classics can help us understand how intelligence was and is performed by states and "nonstates" before and during our Westphalian era. Sun Tzu and Kautilya described the actions of principalities, clans, and even armed bands that acquired and defended territory by force. These authors depicted sovereignties rather than true states. They also suggested why it is that nonstates employ intelligence in many ways similar to the ways in which modern states employ it. Since ancient times, intelligence has promised to help sovereignties manage risk and uncertainty by reducing the probability of setbacks, controlling their impact, or both. In practical terms, intelligence informs and executes decision; it helps to make leaders more confident in their understanding of the hazards surrounding them and their regimes; and it helps them to reassure their friends, make new allies, and confuse or injure their enemies.

Sun Tzu and Kautilya never read another's thoughts on espionage, but they nevertheless arrived at the same conclusion: spies must be carefully

[23] Michael Warner, "The Divine Skein: Sun Tzu on Intelligence," *Intelligence and National Security*, 17, 4 (August 2006). David Kahn seemingly disagreed with Sun Tzu's point that intelligence is essential to the army's every move when he argued that intelligence "is an auxiliary, not a primary, element in war"; see "An Historical Theory of Intelligence," p. 84.

[24] The *Arthashastra* has several English translations. R. Shamasastry's 1915 version is available online; see Kautilya's *Arthashastra* (Mysore: Sri Raghuveer, 1956), particularly Book I, Chapter XII, at www.mssu.edu/projectsouthasia/history/primarydocs/Arthashastra/index.htm4. A more recent translation is by L. N. Rangarajan (ed.), *Kautilya: The Arthashastra* (New Delhi, India: Penguin Classics, 1992).

managed. It is not enough for the sagacious prince or cunning general to hire an occasional secret agent; such agents, if amateurishly directed, are apt to cause more harm than good for their employers. Both authors urged rulers and generals to introduce true method into their direction of spies by ruthlessly vetting agents, keeping them and their assignments widely separated from one another, weighing their reports, and using their information and access sparingly but to maximum effect. This introduction of method into what had hitherto been almost an occult craft amounted to the dawn of the intelligence system. Sun Tzu had his own name for it: he called it the "Divine Skein" and counted it among the ruler's treasures. Kautilya listed an "Institute of Spies" among the principal offices of any well-run kingdom. Both authors agreed that espionage, methodically conducted, gave princes and commanders a command over events that would seem godlike to their ignorant contemporaries.

Intelligence systems changed little between the ancient world and the dawn of the modern era. The modern state had begun its long emergence from feudalism around five hundred years ago and, eventually, the new states – at least in the West – would tame and supplant the feudal baronies and virtually monopolize the legitimate use of force. As the feudal order eroded, kings and princes vied for power with proud barons and their private armies. The new states organized their intelligence functions in their own way, as we shall see, but the missions that they gave their secret operatives – to understand and influence rivals and enemies – paralleled those that Sun Tzu and Kautilya had described hundreds of years earlier. Yet change was coming. Even before the Industrial Revolution, modernizing states had emerged and found a durable *modus vivendi* with one another in the "inter-national" order imposed by the Treaty of Westphalia in 1648. Indeed, the supplanting of feudal quasi-sovereignties by true states and national governments is a characteristic of modernity per se. In overawing the barons and monopolizing (and rationalizing) the functions of statecraft, the new nations reduced the power of the all-purpose but geographically localized "public services" that the barons had provided.

Moreover, in the Industrial Revolution, modern nations grew to depend on new, nationally distributed but functionally specialized professions (especially military-officer cadres, diplomatic corps, civil servants, and police). Intelligence changed at the same time and it is important to understand how. The barons, being minor sovereignties theoretically owing allegiance to a central authority, had surely employed their own spies to watch over rivals and local discontent. As the national state supplanted them and came to rely on the new professionals and their bureaus, the state's intelligence needs (and, consequently, its arrangements for meeting those needs) grew more complex. Napoleon was one of the last figures to serve simultaneously and successfully (for a time) as head of state and command-ing general; he was also one of the last to operate as his own spymaster in a way that Sun Tzu would have recognized.[25] After him – indeed, beginning in his era with the revolution in military affairs occasioned by the *levee en masse* and interchangeable parts – specialization became indispensable. Each of the rapidly professionalizing functions serving the regime required increas-ingly more information for its own purposes.[26] A commander preparing for war or a minister executing his sovereign's mandate needed information, however gained, to help him make decisions in defending and implement-ing national policies. In the 19th century, these ministries – at least, in the major powers – built up their own ways of gaining and using privileged information.[27]

For the sovereign who made national policies (or his proconsuls in direct contact with the sovereign's enemies), however, intelligence remained what it had always been: an instrument to help him understand *and influence* others who were sources of risk and uncertainty for the state. Hence, intel-ligence was split between "national" and "departmental" needs, and intelli-gence systems changed as well. The case of the United States illustrates the point (albeit on an exaggerated scale). Its departmental services grew up haphazardly in the World Wars with no central direction. Presidents, mean-while, continued to gather secrets by their own private (and sometimes comic) means. The whole congeries of offices was confederated in a formal system in 1946 under a Director of Central Intelligence (DCI) (revised in 2005 under a Director of National Intelligence [DNI]), with long-running debates about who controls scarce "national" collection assets (which, by definition, cannot be acquired and employed in numbers sufficient to satisfy simultaneously both national and departmental demands).

This detour through international-relations theory, constructivist social thought, and certain Eastern classics has presumably clarified what it is that we might posit as a dependent variable for use in comparing intelligence

[25] Jay Luvaas, "Napoleon's Use of Intelligence: The Jena Campaign of 1805," in Michael I. Handel (ed.), *Leaders and Intelligence* (London: Frank Cass, 1989), pp. 48–52.

[26] Peter Jackson, "Historical Reflections on the Uses and Limits of Intelligence," in Peter Jack-son and Jennifer Siegel (eds.), *Intelligence and Statecraft: The Use and Limits of Intelligence in International Society* (Westport, CT: Praeger, 2005), pp. 19–26.

[27] Olivier Forcade and Sebastien Laurent, *Secrets d'Etat: Pouvoir et renseignement dans le monde contemporain* (Paris: Armand Colin, 2005), pp. 53–64.

systems. The "silent warfare" school suggests that intelligence duties are those undertaken by stealth to understand or manipulate other sovereignties. By this description, an intelligence system would be constituted by the organizations and officers who work by stealth to divine or shape the plans and activities of powers outside their sovereign's control. The "information for decision" school, conversely, would seem to suggest that an intelligence system is that which provides information to decision makers. This is problematic on the face, however, at least for the purpose of positing a dependent variable for comparing intelligence systems. Every government office, for instance, provides information to decision makers. Comparative intelligence studies, if pursued according to this logic, would thus take on the dimensions of the entire field of comparative government. Narrowing intelligence studies to cover only "information for decision making against competitors," or even "information for decision making against other sovereignties," does not seem to help.[28] It may ultimately prove possible to craft a dependent variable that will allow comparisons of how sovereignties harness and process privileged information for use against other sovereignties (i.e., the narrowest and most modest of the possible definitions following from the assumption that intelligence is simply information for decision making). Such a dependent variable, however, would seemingly have to include a wide range of services for the sovereign that have not been historically or commonly understood as "intelligence" (e.g., privileged legal counsel), while excluding other services that, as we have seen, have long been performed by spies and secret services (e.g., covert action and clandestine liaison).

ORGANIZING AND TASKING INTELLIGENCE

What all this discussion means is that "intelligence" cannot be fully understood without reference to "intelligence systems." Every sovereignty works to understand and influence risks and uncertainties arising from the world outside the span of control of its regime and, therefore, has – by plan or by default – mechanisms for dealing with the larger world. That sphere of

---

[28] Wilhelm Agrell would seem to reach this same impasse from another direction when he lamented the widespread "application of the *concept* or perhaps the *illusion* of intelligence analysis to various information-processing activities that are not really intelligence in the professional sense of the word." See "When Everything Is Intelligence – Nothing Is Intelligence," Central Intelligence Agency (Sherman Kent Center for Intelligence Analysis), Occasional Papers: Volume 1, Number 4, 2002, p. 4. Emphases in original.

activity (i.e., understanding and influencing) is not intelligence per se; it is commerce, diplomacy, security, defense, strategy, and many other things. For some sovereignties, however, some portion of that sphere deals in secrets, and this is the realm of intelligence. How these quiet dealings are organized, treated, and exercised, by plan or by default, is what we call *intelligence systems.*

With a firmer grasp of the nature of the work that "intelligence systems" perform, we can take on O'Connell's challenge and search for ways to compare them. Two documents from early 1946 inadvertently suggested a method for doing this; when read in conjunction, they point toward the variables that affect how governments organize and task their secret activities. Although written and implemented half a world apart, by men working with no knowledge of one another's efforts, they have uncanny similarities. The contrasts between the two documents are also instructive for understanding intelligence at large and intelligence systems in particular.

The first document drafted is comparatively well known to historians of American intelligence. On 22 January 1946, President Harry S. Truman signed a directive creating the post of DCI. This new officer was to curtail the inefficiencies that had marred the nation's intelligence effort in World War II. First, the DCI's office would serve as a clearinghouse for "the correlation and evaluation of intelligence relating to the national security." This function, in theory, would prevent another strategic surprise like Pearl Harbor. Second, the DCI would know about all clandestine activities conducted abroad by agents of the U.S. government, thereby ensuring that those agents did not cross one another's operational paths.[29] The new DCI, according to President Truman's directive, would also be strictly limited to intelligence matters concerning *foreign* subjects and would have no domestic security role.[30]

Another president in another land signed the second document barely a month later. On 21 February 1946, Ho Chi Minh, of the Provisional Government of Vietnam, directed the creation a single bureau, the Public Security Department, housed in the Interior Ministry and authorized to "centralize" all information – both foreign and domestic – relating to national security. The new bureau would both suggest and implement measures "to protect against all actions which could disrupt national order and the maintenance

---

[29] Ibid., p. 4.
[30] Harry S. Truman to the Secretaries of State, War, and Navy, 22 January 1946, reprinted in Michael Warner, *The CIA under Harry Truman* (Washington: Central Intelligence Agency, 1994), pp. 29–32.

of order." It would also investigate "all actions that violate the law" and track those who break it so they might be tried and punished.[31]

The two documents resembled one another in affecting major changes in their respective national intelligence system. Both did so because the leaders who signed them perceived significant and potentially deadly challenges in their respective environment. Finally, both documents spoke to how intelligence would address challenges in both the foreign and domestic realms – that is, how it would posture itself against adversaries inside and outside their ruler's sphere of sovereignty. The similarities of these documents reflect a fundamental "sameness" of intelligence across two very different regimes: the one a nuclear-armed state feeling its way toward a role as guarantor of global order and the other a revolutionary movement tenuously holding a small territory but cherishing bold ambitions.

The differences between the two documents speak volumes as well. If each reflected the outlook and structure of its parent regime, then it is clear that two rather different regimes were involved here. In the American example, the intelligence establishment was sharply divided between the foreign and domestic realms, with the new DCI's writ restricted to the former – and the latter implicitly left to the Federal Bureau of Investigation. His foreign intelligence authorities, President Truman decreed, would perform no "police, law enforcement, or internal security functions." By contrast, the new Vietnamese security service would monitor both foreign and domestic threats and, most emphatically, would combine intelligence and law enforcement powers and methods.

Comparing the two documents prompts a range of speculation about why two independent governing structures, acting in essentially the same historical moment but with vastly different cultures and material endowments, chose parallel mechanisms to create such different intelligence systems. The obvious answer – the variance across the American and Vietnamese regimes – does not fully satisfy, for it cannot explain why the same U.S. institutions that codified and implemented President Truman's 1946 directive (in the parallel intelligence provisions of the National Security Act of 1947) could and did make sweeping changes to those same provisions in 2004. The United States had not adopted a new political system in the intervening decades, but the technology of mass destruction had changed by 2004, as had the cast of enemies wielding such weapons; hence, a new

---

[31] Decree No. 23-SL, 21 February 1946, translated by Christopher E. Goscha and reprinted in "Three Documents on Early Vietnamese Intelligence and Security Services," *Intelligence and National Security*, 22, 1 (February 2007), 139–40.

strategic posture seemed warranted against those perils. Indeed, where the DCI had been banned from any domestic intelligence role in 1946, the officer who replaced him – the DNI – was granted important (if still limited) authorities to oversee intelligence in the homeland, a significant blurring of the foreign–domestic boundary that Truman had prescribed.[32]

We cannot explain why structures "built" in the same year should be constructed so differently in one place compared to another – and why one of those regimes would modify its own system so sharply in later decades – until we catalogue and analyze the variables that shape intelligence systems. The American and Vietnamese examples are illustrative in that they should enable at least two research strategies. In one sense, the dependent variable remained constant across the two cases (in that both nations saw fit to rationalize the major components of their intelligence systems at the same moment in time), thus inviting us to search for attributes of the independent variables in both cases that also remained fixed. In another sense, however, the intelligence systems resulting from these reforms diverged enough to illuminate the variations in the independent variables affecting the reform of intelligence systems in the United States and Vietnam. Such intellectual spadework along these two courses should uncover the interplay between the dependent and independent variables, thereby explaining the ways in which sovereign powers task, orient, and organize the secret means they employ to protect themselves and expand their interests.

In this example of the United States and Vietnam, the types of intelligence systems that sovereignties construct would seem to depend on three main independent but interlocking variables.

Strategy

The first and foremost variable to consider is the sovereignty's "grand strategy," or its policies regarding other sovereignties.[33] As Johnson suggested, the posture that a state assumes (by choice or compulsion) toward its neighbors, allies, and rivals largely determines the intelligence needs of its leaders and their lieutenants.[34] If A is that regime's strategy and B its intelligence

---

[32] The Intelligence Reform and Terrorism Prevention Act of 2004 replaced the DCI with a DNI wielding expanded powers and authorized to collect "national" intelligence both at home and abroad.

[33] The attempts at theorizing here follow Stephen Van Evera, *Guide to Methods for Students of Political Science* (Ithaca, NY: Cornell University Press, 1997), pp. 7–21.

[34] "The starting point for determining the extent of a nation's allocation of scarce resources for intelligence activities is a clear demarcation of its international objectives and its adversaries." Loch K. Johnson, "Preface to a Theory of Strategic Intelligence," *International Journal of Intelligence and Counterintelligence*, 16, 4 (2003), 639. Diplomatic

system – including the ministerial and departmental subcomponents of that system – then intelligence is the dependent variable in the relationship, and the variables can be plotted as follows:

$$A \rightarrow B$$

The aforementioned concept of *surveillance* suggests that sovereignties use intelligence to augment knowledge and power in order to protect themselves and advance their interests. In both augmenting knowledge and facilitating power, they employ intelligence to help manage the specific sets of risk and uncertainty that their own policies (whether passive or aggressive) generate for them. This is true of their information requirements and of their needs for secret activities (both in terms of clandestine activities and secret liaison ties). The policy context – that is, what the leadership is trying to accomplish or prevent – dictates the targets and tempo of intelligence collection and operations.

Our theory of the origin and evolution of intelligence systems seems to allow us to build a taxonomy of intelligence systems and structures and also shows us how and why they change across variant regimes and over time. Possible (but by no means all possible) values of the strategy variable are as follows:

- **Basic orientation:** The essential posture that a sovereignty presents vis-à-vis other sovereignties may be passive, aggressive, or a vigilant wariness without any overt steps to provoke antagonism.
- **Geopolitical:** A sovereignty's relative power vis-à-vis its neighbors will have a large effect on its posture toward them, as will the absolute power that it and its neighbors wield. In addition, sovereignties that are physically isolated from potential adversaries will have fewer needs for intelligence and fewer opportunities to employ it.
- **Motives:** Sovereignties act in the world from a variety and a mixture of motives. They may have mercantile, imperial, religious, or racial ambitions for persuading or forcing neighbors or other sovereignties to accept their goods or influence. They may want colonies as outlets for excess population or goods. They may wish to improve or legitimate dynastic claims to power through interrelationships with powerful families in other realms.

historian Richard E. Immerman recently came to this observation from another direction when he noted that intelligence, although it may well affect tactics, does not really seem to influence the strategic picture that policy makers employ in their leadership. "Telling the Emperor He Has No Clothes: The Psychology and Politics of Strategic Intelligence," presidential address to the annual conference of the Society for American Foreign Relations, Chantilly, Virginia, June 2007. I am also grateful to Stephen Marrin of Mercyhurst College for clarifying this larger point.

- **Objectives:** Motives are often closely related to objectives or goals. Every sovereignty, it may be assumed, ranks survival as its first objective, followed closely in priority by the defense of the sovereignty's interests and allies. Expansion of those interests may be an object as well, if the sovereignty can afford it. Such expansion may become an active campaign of conquest. A few towering egos have even glimpsed the possibility of regional or even world domination and turned their energies and their sovereignties toward achieving it.
- **Sources of support or mediation:** Sovereignties have their being among a web of mutual relationships – some friendly or allied, some hostile or antagonistic, and others neutral or simply uncaring. Allies and foes may be nominal, real, or potential. In certain times and places, extra-sovereign or multilateral institutions such as the Church or the League of Nations may have influence over sovereignties, restricting their freedom of action or even providing a degree of protection or assistance for them against antagonists.
- **Situational:** The severity of competition and conflict can be gauged across a continuum ranging from harmony to latent hostility to crisis to war (both declared and undeclared). War's intensity can be measured as well, although it often cannot be reliably calibrated by those engaged in it.
- **Strategic culture:** Much has been written about the ways in which a nation's "strategic culture" affects its conduct of military operations. The same would seem to apply in the intelligence realm as well. A sovereignty's historical context and collective perceptions of its place in the world, the shared ethical boundaries of its people and leaders, and the perhaps indefinable quality called "national character" will all affect its intelligence system.

The notion that strategy is the main or a major influence on intelligence systems seems broadly in harmony with the historical evidence. States with few foreign entanglements or threats may neglect external intelligence. Weaker states in conflict-ridden regions, like Poland between the World Wars, may concentrate on collecting against likely threats and honing their security organs to thwart subversion by their neighbors. Vigilant but essentially passive states, like the United States before Pearl Harbor, may branch out into limited foreign intelligence gathering. Expansionist powers like Hitler's Germany or Stalin's Soviet Union, conversely, will busily conduct covert operations abroad. Revolutionary movements like Ho Chi Minh's will need excellent intelligence-gathering capabilities based in the surrounding population and the agility and ruthlessness to run subversion and deception operations on a constant basis. These emphases are not mutually exclusive. Stalin, for instance, was both aggressive and paranoid, sending his operatives to work on foreign soil as far away as America and building unprecedented monitoring capabilities at home.

Strategy also determines alliances and, hence, intelligence liaison relationships. All intelligence may be about competition, as Sims suggests, but competition loves company, and a great deal of intelligence work is accomplished in quiet cooperation with other sovereignties against shared adversaries. This applies to narrow and fleeting commonalities of interest as well as to long-lasting "special relationships."[35]

Regime

Carl von Clausewitz noted that the French revolutionary state in the 1790s fought very differently from the monarchies opposed to it.[36] We can infer a similar contrast among the intelligence systems of various regime types. In short, the type of intelligence system that a sovereignty constructs depends in part on its regime type, defined in the Aristotelian fashion as the *politeia*, or the "arrangement of a city with respect to its offices, particularly the one that has authority over all."[37] The type and structure of the regime (r) thus affects the intelligence system directly, as shown here:

$$r \rightarrow$$
$$A \rightarrow B$$

Possible values of the regime variable seem to include the following:

- **Type of sovereignty:** Whether a sovereignty is a city-state, a Westphalian nation, an empire, a nonstate actor, or an international institution may well affect the type of intelligence system it builds. All of these sovereign entities undertake activities that we can regard as intelligence work, and it stands to reason that similar entities – other factors being equal – may structure, task, and orient intelligence activities in similar ways.
- **Form of government:** Whether a sovereignty was representative, aristocratic, or tyrannical was an important question for Aristotle in

---

[35] Sims, "Foreign Intelligence Liaison," pp. 196–203.

[36] Note his discussion on "War Is an Instrument of Policy" in Book Eight; Carl von Clausewitz, *On War*, edited and translated by Michael Howard and Peter Paret (Princeton, NJ: Princeton University Press, 1984 [1976]), pp. 605–10.

[37] Aristotle, *The Politics*, Book III, 6:1. This uses the Carnes Lord translation (Chicago: University of Chicago Press, 1984).

considering its behavior, and we can infer that it matters for our purposes as well. Each of these three categories admits to several gradations that may be significant for intelligence; for example, parliamentary systems may exercise oversight differently than republican neighbors. Aristocratic or monarchical systems have their own ways of doing things. Tyrannies come in several stripes, although the ideological systems of the 20th century (i.e., communism and fascism) were unprecedented in important ways.

- **Oversight:** All sovereignties exercise some form of oversight over their intelligence systems, whether by a single ruler or commander, a council of ministers, or a team of professional civil servants. Where the executive and legislative functions are fairly distinct, the lawmakers may or may not play a role in advising the intelligence function. Oversight may be exercised by long-standing, expert officials or by a rotating cast of political or military decision makers. Partisan political motives may intrude on the oversight function because parties or groups out-of-power use influence over intelligence to affect the ruling coalition. In some sovereignties, judicial, media, or public actions or attitudes may well shape the circumstances in which an intelligence system operates.

- **Ministerial/departmental structure:** The assortment of tasks and offices created to conduct the sovereignty's affairs will have a significant effect on an intelligence system, which – after all – exists in large part to inform and execute the decisions of those offices. Ministries, departments, and bureaus have attributes that are both tangible (e.g., size, resources, and legal authorities) and intangible (e.g., tradition, clout, and degree of professionalism).

- **Internal challenges:** Many sovereignties endure some degree of internal friction, opposition, and even conflict for much of their existence. This may range from passive resistance to armed insurrection, and its motives may be based in differences of class, race, creed, ethnicity, or ideology. Dynastic struggles have afflicted countless regimes. Internal opposition may be "homegrown" or foreign-inspired (or, at least, externally subsidized). All are targets of intelligence and therefore potential "influences" on an intelligence system that must devote to them a share of its attention.

Totalitarian, authoritarian, imperial, and democratic regimes have their characteristic types of intelligence systems, built first to protect the rulers at home and then to help them function abroad. Nonstate sovereignties like the Vietnamese revolutionary movement in 1946 have their own systems of governance that also may be considered regimes for this purpose.

Democracies, being built by definition on a broad base of popular consent, may have the luxury of focusing a smaller (but never insignificant) portion of their intelligence efforts at home than abroad, and they tend to build comparatively confederal intelligence systems on the theory that such are less apt and able to abuse the liberties of their citizens. For both reasons, democracies tend to be less proficient at counterintelligence. Authoritarian states, in contrast, will spend more attention at home than abroad, monitoring pretenders to the throne and potential instigators of coups.[38] Imperial regimes, to continue in this vein, may have large intelligence efforts concentrated on monitoring the communications of their rivals and watching factions and potential threats just inside and outside the empire.

Regime type and structure also affect the strategy variable. The totalitarian regimes – fascist, communist, and otherwise – merit special note in this regard. These regimes believe themselves beset by enemies from rival classes, races, or creeds, and they build *counterintelligence states* (Dziak's term) to defend themselves from wreckers, saboteurs, *kulaks*, or non-Aryans.[39] Indeed, argues Christopher Andrew, such one-party states themselves have "depended on the creation of new intelligence agencies with an unprecedented ability to monitor and suppress dissent."[40] The Party leads the fight against ideological enemies – real or imagined, at home and abroad – and the institutions of the state become servants of the Party, which reduces the ministries to corrupt vestiges.

Where the Party still needs certain state organs – for instance, a professional military – it laces them with spies to guard its political purity; thus it was that parallel intelligence services grew up together. In such instances – as with the Gestapo and the *Abwehr* under Hitler and the KGB and GRU in the USSR – the Party-controlled intelligence element will be the larger and more powerful, collecting and acting against threats to the regime at home and abroad; the military service will be the smaller and more narrowly focused. Thus, our relationship among the variables affecting intelligence systems must be refined to show that the regime affects an intelligence system directly and indirectly (through its effect on strategy), as shown here:

$$r \rightarrow$$

$$x$$

$$A \rightarrow B$$

[38] Bozeman, "Political Intelligence in Non-Western Societies," p. 149.
[39] John J. Dziak, *Chekisty: A History of the KGB* (Lexington, MA: Lexington Books, 1988), p. 2.
[40] Christopher Andrew, "Intelligence, International Relations and 'Under-theorisation'," in Scott and Jackson (eds.), *Understanding Intelligence in the Twenty-First Century*, pp. 34–7.

Technology

The way in which a sovereignty tasks and organizes its intelligence system will also have much to do with its technological environment. By altering threats to the regime as well as opportunities available to it, changes in technology have direct and indirect effects on a regime's intelligence work. Therefore, technology helps to determine the objects of intelligence *and* the means that intelligence employs. It also helps to determine the numbers and sorts of intelligence officers hired to collect and analyze data as well as to disseminate the resulting reports to decision makers. Returning to the chart of variables, technology (t) thus helps shape strategy and directly shapes the intelligence system, as shown here:

$$r \rightarrow$$
$$x$$
$$A \rightarrow B$$
$$x$$
$$t \rightarrow$$

Possible values of the technology variable seem to include the following:

- **Information:** Much of intelligence work is learning what others know or think they know. How those others acquire, store, transmit, and secure such information, therefore, is of fundamental importance to intelligence in all eras – indeed, it will dictate at a basic level the tactics and techniques of intelligence, which – in that sense – can be thought of as a function of the changes in "information technology."
- **Production:** How a society manages the available "means of production" to shape its physical environment and accumulate wealth will provide the foundation of resources and capabilities on which the intelligence system stands. It also may suggest that system's targets; for example, intelligence efforts in a society based on restive slave labor will be directed differently than the work of an intelligence system charged with preventing industrial espionage.
- **Resources:** Over and above the resources made available for intelligence work by the prevailing means of production, the endowment of agricultural wealth, mineral stocks, and human capital of the sovereignty and its rivals will affect the target lists for intelligence activities. Water and energy stocks are two obvious concerns for intelligence today and in the future.
- **Social and institutional forms:** One does not have to be a Marxian to see links between technological levels and social structures.

Sovereignties composed primarily of wandering tribes, feudal de-mesnes, or urban professionals will have different intelligence needs and capabilities.

- **Military:** Because much intelligence work is devoted to managing competition or winning conflicts, the way in which a sovereignty applies violence in an organized manner to achieve its objectives will shape, in important ways, its intelligence system. The organization, mobility, and lethality of a sovereignty's military – and those of its adversaries – will dictate (among other factors) the timeliness and precision demanded of intelligence work, the analytical expertise that must be devoted to understanding what intelligence collects, and possibly the relative importance of human versus technical means of collection and dissemination.

Technology's influence, of course, will be felt first by those sovereignties striving – for offensive or defensive purposes – to catch technology's leading wave. Intelligence history has seen two technological revolutions. First was the "analog revolution," beginning in World War I and continuing well into the Cold War. Second was the "digital revolution" that began with the dawn of the Internet age in the 1990s and is still sweeping the world and the intelligence profession. Both revolutions caused profound effects on the means and ends of intelligence.

In the analog revolution, the major European powers exploited electronic signals and the maturing techniques of organization to create intelligence disciplines and bureaucracies, supplanting the amateur spies and Black Chambers that had operated since ancient times and forcing other world powers to follow suit for their own protection. In that first revolution, beginning in 1914, intelligence arose from being a secret annex to the state's security, diplomatic, and reconnaissance functions and matured into its own quasi-profession, populated with specialists laboring in bureaus custom-organized for intelligence work. The disciplines of signals intelligence and imagery intelligence, with their corps of analysts and technicians, developed complex, late–industrial-age procedures to process data and disseminate their products to their patrons and "customers."

Higher up the production ladder, "all-source analysis," an intelligence discipline unto itself, harnessed academic skills to build – out of fragments of information – mosaic pictures of the intentions and capabilities of opponents. As the central problem of intelligence turned from gleaning scarce clues to coping with the glut of data, the analog revolution empowered the richer states that could afford the mass-production intelligence systems that it made possible, giving them distinct (if sometimes fleeting) diplomatic and military advantages over more backward allies and competitors.

The effects of the digital revolution are still emerging and the outcome is difficult to predict, although evidence of their significance is all around us. Its impetus is the tectonic confluence of three developments: (1) the inter-linking of mankind via cheap and instant mass communications, (2) the shift of humanity's collective memory into increasingly accessible electronic archives, and (3) the "democratization" of weapons that can kill indiscrimi-nately. Since the early 1990s, these developments have given all nations – and even angry and determined groups and individuals – suites of capabilities that had been long virtually monopolized by the richer and more advanced states. Concepts and doctrines that intelligence services had shaped for the analog age – security, cover, and dissemination, to name only three – now have to be revised "on the fly." The organization, tasking, and oversight of intelligence systems are changing to suit. Every government and intelligence system is feeling the effects of this digital storm, but its ultimate vector and results remain uncertain.

Intelligence Systems

The three independent variables discussed here – strategy, regime, and tech-nology – coexist in a dynamic interrelationship. Their "values" differ from place to place, and the differences explain the variations – and similari-ties – among the intelligence systems that sovereignties build. Those values shift over time as well, sometimes dramatically, as sovereignties evolve and respond to new threats and opportunities. National intelligence systems change as a consequence, both in particular and in the aggregate.

This conception of intelligence systems offers us a tool for drawing con-ceptual bounds around the secret activities of various countries, kingdoms, and nonstate actors, thereby specifying what it is that we seek to explain as a product of related independent variables. If we think of intelligence in this way, then we have fashioned a true dependent variable to explain as the resultant of other factors. Indeed, we can make logical and verifiable surmises about how leaders organize and task the secret means they employ to shift risk to adversaries.

Which values might we expect to see in our dependent variable? The effects of strategy, regime, and technology will always be present but may not always be quantifiable, just as the proposition "greater wealth leads to increased happiness" is not strictly or directly measurable in quantitative terms. Anyone seeking to prove such a proposition would have to seek measures that somehow substitute for or change in proportion to the ambiguous and subjective term *happiness.* Longevity, education, health, living arrangements, and emotional stability might be a few eligible proxies for happiness, especially if viewed in conjunction with one another. Even a comprehensive set of such variables, however, cannot yield a precise index proving that wealth makes some people happier than their neighbor, but they may well allow comparisons of the probability that they might describe themselves as content – and suggest why.

Characterizing an intelligence system and comparing it with another intelligence system is a chore of similar complexity. Nonetheless, changes in strategy, regime, and technology can be expected to affect the following characteristics of an intelligence system:

- structure and subordination of agencies
- budget
- physical size and layout
- targets and requirements
- technological prowess
- nature and extent of liaison with foreign services
- access to consumers and quality of relationships
- quality and vision of leadership
- professionalism of the workforce
- management acumen
- quality of internal communications
- quality of internal consultation
- quality of security procedures and equipment
- presence or absence of corruption
- sanctions for misconduct

Next Steps: An Agenda for Research

Examination of the dependent and independent variables of intelligence systems allows intelligence scholarship to partake of the insights and methods developed by and for the larger field of comparative government. Much work remains to be done to describe the variables involved with intelligence systems, provide proper taxonomies for them, craft hypotheses about how they relate to one another, and test cases on a comparative basis. However, by isolating strategy, regime, and technology as variables and the key determinants of how sovereignties build, resource, deploy, and task their intelligence systems, we can at least begin this process. We can also seek ways in which the theory of intelligence systems might be falsified. At least three potential developments suggest that the theory is untenable, as follows:

- First, one could potentially show that O'Connell was wrong and that an "intelligence system" is a meaningless, trivial, or ill-conceived concept not worthy of consideration as a dependent variable.
- Second, it could be demonstrated that one or more factors not considered in this survey actually hold more influence over the shape and orientation of intelligence systems.
- Third, one could find that this chapter's characterization and weighting of the strategy, regime, and technology variables were incorrect; that is, that technology is more important than strategy or that there are only two fundamental types of regimes that matter for intelligence systems.

The third possibility would seem the most likely way of falsifying the theory. O'Connell's observation about the fundamental sameness of intelligence arrangements and the possibilities for explaining their differences seems intuitively sound in the light of the admittedly unsystematic but nonetheless broad literature on intelligence agencies and activities. As for the second possibility, it is difficult to think of additional variables of significance at this juncture, which is why none were included. It is quite probable, however, that some adjustment could be made to the sorting of the three key variables in light of unexpected and inexplicable results. For instance, were we to find a passive democracy with peaceful neighbors building a massive internal-security service to monitor its own citizens, we might suspect the accuracy of the hypothesis about the relationship between regime structure and intelligence systems.

None of these tests can be applied without additional exploration of the relationships among strategy, regime, and technology and their effects on intelligence systems. That exploration can progress along two paths: (1) the historical literature and the growing number of careful case studies could be mined for supporting and disproving examples; and (2) a new research agenda could be shaped around the posited variables and relationships to yield knowledge of national intelligence systems that is truly comparable with the methodologically analogous findings on other systems.

The previous discussion seeks to explain the factors *outside* an intelligence system that influence conditions *inside* it. Little has been discussed so far about how that influence is exerted – about how the mechanisms internal to intelligence systems determine how the external influences mesh together to result in changes to the work performed by them. That is an entire field of inquiry destined for future exploration by historians, political scientists, and students of organizational behavior; however, the methods developed by these disciplines have not yet found full scope for employment given the limited public availability of intelligence records.

One final caution: intelligence systems can be studied as dependent variables, but they must also be recognized – in some places and times – as contributing factors in determining the trajectories of their respective regimes. Several examples – none of them encouraging from a democratic standpoint – could be cited here. Let it suffice to say that a greater understanding of the factors that influence intelligence systems could almost certainly help to ensure that intelligence systems do not become powers unto themselves.

THREE

Reflections on Intelligence Historiography
since 1939

Christopher Andrew

Sherman Kent, the founding father of U.S. intelligence analysis, complained in 1955 that intelligence was the only profession which lacked a serious literature:

From my point of view this is a matter of greatest importance. As long as this discipline lacks a literature, its methods, its vocabulary, its body of doctrine, and even its fundamental theory run the risk of never reaching full maturity.[1]

Practicing economists and politicians, among others, are rightly critical of the remoteness of some academic research from the real world in which they operate. However, economics without economic theory and economic history, politics without political history and political science, would be what Kent forecasted intelligence would remain without an intelligence literature: immature disciplines.

The public space left vacant by the slow growth of intelligence studies as an academic discipline was invaded by a generation of fantasists and conspiracy theorists. Intelligence thus became the only profession in which a fictional character is still many times better known than any real intelligence officer, alive or dead. That character, of course, is James Bond, who made his first appearance in *Casino Royal* two years before Kent's article on "The Need for an Intelligence Literature." Bond films have since been seen and mostly enjoyed by a majority of the world's population.

THE ABSENCE OF SIGINT, OR "NO SUCH AGENCY"

Until the 1970s, the majority of the world's modern historians, political scientists, and international-relations specialists was so bemused by

[1] Sherman Kent, "The Need for an Intelligence Literature", in Donald P Steury (ed.), *Sherman Kent and the Board of National Estimates: Collected Essays* (Washington: CIA Center for the Study of Intelligence, 1994).

intelligence that it was ignored altogether. Take signals intelligence, or SIGINT, for example. At the end of World War II, Government Communications Headquarters (GCHQ) (i.e., the British SIGINT agency) wanted to keep secret indefinitely the wartime ULTRA intelligence derived from breaking Enigma and other high-grade enemy ciphers but expected the secret to be uncovered within a few years. The clues to ULTRA, GCHQ believed, were too obvious for historians to miss: "[T]he comparing of the German and British documents is bound to arouse suspicion in [historians'] minds that we succeeded in reading the enemy ciphers".[2] For almost 30 years after the war, however, most historians suspected no such thing. Some of the clues which they overlooked now seem obvious. The fact that American cryptanalysts had broken the main Japanese diplomatic cipher in 1940 (known to the Americans as PURPLE) was extensively publicized during the postwar congressional inquiry into Pearl Harbor. It was also common knowledge that British cryptanalysts had broken German ciphers during World War I; indeed, one well-publicized German decrypt – the Zimmermann telegram – may even have hastened American entry into the war. However, until the revelation of ULTRA in 1973, almost no historian considered the possibility that German ciphers had been extensively broken during World War II as well as World War I.

Modern intelligence studies owe their origins to two major revelations in the 1970s which captured the public imagination. The first was ULTRA, which generated a large literature on the role of SIGINT in World War II which, in turn, attracted a large literature. The second was the sensational disclosure during 1975, the "Year of Intelligence," of Central Intelligence Agency (CIA) "dirty tricks" – among them, assassination plots against foreign statesmen, notably Fidel Castro, and illegal spying on U.S. citizens during Operation CHAOS – which inspired an equally large literature on covert action.

The subsequent historiography of both SIGINT and covert action, however, has been curiously lopsided. Although most historians nowadays acknowledge the wartime significance of SIGINT, their interest in it usually ceases at V-J Day. Its surprising absence from the postwar historiographical landscape has produced a series of eccentric anomalies even in some of the leading studies of Cold War policy makers and international relations. Sir Martin Gilbert's epic nine-volume biography of Sir Winston Churchill,

---

[2] COS (45), confidential annexe, 31 July 1945, CAB 76/36; Special Order by Sir Edward Travis (Director GCHQ), 7 May 1945, FO 371/39171, U.K. National Archives, Kew. Both cited by Richard J. Aldrich, *The Hidden Hand: Britain, America, and Cold War Secret Intelligence* (London: John Murray, 2001), pp. 1–3.

for example, rightly makes much of Churchill's passion for ULTRA as war leader but neglects entirely his interest in SIGINT as peacetime prime minister from 1951 to 1955. Neither does it contain a single reference to GCHQ, then (as now) the biggest and the most expensive of the British intelligence agencies. The reader is left to infer – improbably – that Churchill's enormous enthusiasm for SIGINT, which had remained constant since 1914, had inexplicably disappeared.

There are similar startling lacunae in many of the best studies of U.S. policy in the early Cold War. General Dwight D. Eisenhower, briefed personally by Churchill on ULTRA soon after his arrival in England in June 1942, quickly became a SIGINT enthusiast. In July 1945, Eisenhower wrote to GCHQ that ULTRA had been "of priceless value" to his conduct of the war and sent to "each and everyone" of the cryptanalysts at Bletchley Park "my heartfelt admiration and sincere thanks for their very decisive contribution to the Allied war effort". Although Ike's enthusiasm for SIGINT continued into the Cold War,[3] there is no mention of it in Stephen Ambrose's otherwise excellent biography of Eisenhower as president – or in almost any other studies of his or any succeeding administration. Similarly, none of Harry S. Truman's biographers mention that he was so impressed by the wartime British–American SIGINT alliance that in September 1945 he approved its peacetime continuation – thereby profoundly influencing the development of the "special relationship".[4] Ever since, the United States and Britain have shared more secrets than any two independent powers had ever shared before. The British–American SIGINT accords of March 1946 and June 1948 (the latter known as the UKUSA agreement), also involving Australia, Canada, and New Zealand, still lack their rightful place in the historiography of the Cold War.[5] Although studies of Cold War U.S. foreign policy invariably mention the CIA, there is rarely any reference to the National Security Agency (NSA) – despite the public acknowledgment by George H. W. Bush that SIGINT was a "prime factor" in his foreign policy.[6] The small circle of those "in the know" in Washington used to joke that

---

[3] Christopher Andrew, *For the President's Eyes Only: Secret Intelligence and the American Presidency from Washington to Bush* (London/New York: HarperCollins, 1995), ch. 6.

[4] Truman, "Memorandum for the Secretaries of State, War, and the Navy", 12 September 1945, Naval Aide Files, box 10, file 1, Harry S. Truman Library. Bradley J. Smith, *The Ultra-Magic Deals* (Novato, CA: Presidio, 1993), p. 212.

[5] Christopher Andrew, "The Making of the Anglo-American SIGINT Alliance, 1940–1948", in James E. Dillard and Walter T. Hitchcock (eds.), *The Intelligence Revolution and Modern Warfare* (Chicago: Imprint Publications, 1996).

[6] Andrew, *For the President's Eyes Only*, p. 5 and ch. 13. This volume, *inter alia*, attempts an assessment, on the fragmentary evidence available, of varying presidential attitudes towards SIGINT.

"NSA" stood for "No Such Agency". Most histories of the Cold War reflect a similar amnesia.

DISTORTED HISTORY

The virtual exclusion of SIGINT from the history of postwar international relations has distorted understanding of the Cold War in significant ways. That point is illustrated by the very first Cold War SIGINT to be declassified: the approximately three thousand intercepted Soviet intelligence and other telegrams (ultimately codenamed VENONA) for the period 1939–48, partially decrypted by American and British code breakers in the late 1940s and early 1950s. The decrypts have large implications for American political history as well as for Soviet–American relations. The outrageous exaggerations and inventions of Senator Joseph McCarthy's self-serving anti-communist witch-hunt in the early 1950s made U.S. liberal opinion skeptical for the remainder of the Cold War about the significance of the Soviet intelligence offensive.

McCarthy thus became, albeit unconsciously, arguably the KGB's most successful Cold War agent of influence. The evidence of Elizabeth Bentley and Whittaker Chambers, who had worked as couriers for Soviet intelligence, was widely but mistakenly ridiculed; VENONA provides compelling corroboration for both. From Los Alamos to the Office of Strategic Services (OSS), the wartime Roosevelt administration was penetrated by Soviet intelligence.[7] The revelation of that penetration in the VENONA decrypts helped to prevent most of it continuing into the Cold War. Although declassification of the VENONA decrypts began only in 1995, their existence had been known since the early 1980s, and some of their contents had leaked out during that decade. VENONA, however, was ignored by most U.S. historians until the late 1990s. Its implications for both U.S. history and farther afield have still to be fully absorbed.[8] As Wilhelm Agrell, Desmond Ball, and David Horner have shown, the historiographical significance of VENONA extends from Scandinavia to Australia.[9]

---

[7] Roger Louis Benson and Michael Warner (eds.), *VENONA: Soviet Espionage and the American Response, 1939–1957* (Washington: National Security Agency/Central Intelligence Agency, 1996). John Earl Haynes and Harvey Klehr, *VENONA: Decoding Soviet Espionage in America* (New Haven, CT: Yale University Press, 1999).

[8] On the controversies aroused by the VENONA declassification, far greater in the U.S. than in the U.K., see John Earl Haynes and Harvey Klehr, *In Denial: Historians, Communism, and Espionage* (San Francisco, CA: Encounter, 2003).

[9] Wilhelm Agrell, *VENONA: Spåren från ett underrättelsekrig* (Lund: Historiska Media, 2003). Desmond Ball and David Horner, *Breaking the Codes: Australia's KGB Network 1944–1950* (St. Leonard's, NSW: Allen & Unwin, 1998).

The VENONA revelations cast unexpected new light on both the handling of top-secret intelligence in the United States and the functioning of the British–American intelligence alliance at the beginning of the Cold War. The VENONA secret was shared with Clement Attlee, the British prime minister, and with all three British intelligence agencies but – chiefly due to J. Edgar Hoover – not with President Truman or, until late 1952, the CIA. When Kim Philby was posted to Washington as the representative of the Secret Intelligence Service (SIS) in 1949, he was thus told that he could discuss VENONA with the Federal Bureau of Investigation (FBI) but not with the CIA. Philby obeyed instructions not to mention the decrypts to the CIA but revealed them to his KGB case officer. Thanks to Philby and William Weisband, a Soviet agent in U.S. SIGINT, Stalin was thus better informed than Truman about the early Cold War successes of American code breakers.[10]

The study of the role of SIGINT since World War II is still in its infancy. Recent case studies, however, have demonstrated the importance of Western SIGINT in the Korean War and the Falklands Conflict.[11] Several intriguing studies also demonstrate the deep interest in domestic eavesdropping shown by political leaders as different as Nikolai Ceausescu[12] and François Mitterrand. While in opposition in the 1970s, Mitterrand complained of being bugged and called those responsible "idiots": "What do they actually do with these thousands of stolen words?" As president, however, he had a secret office in the Elysée Palace responsible for bugging a wide variety of people in public life, ranging from political opponents to the wife of one of his prime ministers.[13]

Although the continued classification of most of the Cold War SIGINT archive usually renders detailed research impossible, two major conclusions emerge from recent historiography. First, although high-grade cipher systems of the Cold War were less vulnerable than those of World War II, the total volume of SIGINT generated by both Soviet intelligence and the UKUSA alliance greatly increased. Second, much of the diplomatic traffic

---

[10] Christopher Andrew, "The VENONA Secret", in K. G. Robertson (ed.), *War, Resistance, and Intelligence: Essays in Honour of M. R. D. Foot* (Barnsley: Pen and Sword, 1999).

[11] Matthew Aid and Cees Wiebes (eds.), *Secrets of Signals Intelligence during the Cold War and Beyond* (London and Portland, OR: Frank Cass, 2001). Sir Lawrence Freedman, *The Official History of the Falklands*, 2 vols. (London: Routledge, 2005).

[12] Ion Mihai Pacepa, *Red Horizons* (Washington: Regnery Gateway, 1987).

[13] The first detailed account, with some documentary evidence, of the bugging carried out from the Elysée in the Mitterrand era was Jean-Marie Pontaut and Jérome Dupuis, *Les Oreilles du Président – suivi de la liste des 2000 personnes "écoutées" par François Mitterrand* (Paris: Fayard, 1996); quotation from p. 215.

of Third World states was vulnerable to cryptanalysts in both East and West. On the eve of the 1956 Suez Crisis, for example, the British Foreign Secretary Selwyn Lloyd formally congratulated the director of the U.K. SIGINT agency, GCHQ, on both the "volume" and the "excellence" of the decrypts he had supplied to the Foreign Office "relating to all the countries of the Middle East. I am writing to let you know how valuable we have found this material...".[14] Although Selwyn Lloyd did not mention it, the decrypts were the product of joint GCHQ/NSA operations under the terms of the UKUSA agreement. Soviet cryptanalysts probably enjoyed a similar level of success against Middle Eastern diplomatic traffic. There was probably never a year during the Cold War, at least from the 1950s onwards, when the KGB sent fewer than 100,000 diplomatic decrypts to the Central Committee (chiefly, no doubt, to its International Department). By 1967, the KGB was able to decrypt 152 cipher systems employed by a total of 72 states.[15]

The historiography of the KGB has so far concentrated overwhelmingly on its human intelligence (HUMINT) operations, often to the virtual exclusion of SIGINT. There is now, however, ample published evidence of the extent to which KGB SIGINT successes were made possible by HUMINT operations – chief among them the recruitment of foreign cipher clerks and other diplomatic personnel. Few if any embassies in Moscow escaped some degree of KGB penetration. The U.S. Embassy was penetrated virtually continuously from the beginning of Soviet–American diplomatic relations in 1933 until at least the mid-1960s.[16] Remarkably, most studies of U.S.–Soviet relations continue to take no account of the hemorrhage of diplomatic secrets from the Moscow Embassy for more than 30 years. Although security at the U.S. Embassy in Moscow improved after the mid-1960s, security at many other embassies did not. According to Admiral Fulvio Martini, head of SISMI (i.e., the Italian foreign intelligence) from 1984 to 1991, the attitude towards security in Italian embassies in the Soviet Bloc frequently continued to be characterized by *"legerezza e superficilità"*.[17] Soviet SIGINT throughout the Cold War was also assisted by the penetration of foreign ministries in the West and the Third World. In 1945, the KGB's Paris residency recruited a 23-year-old cipher officer, codenamed JOUR, in the Quai d'Orsay who

---

[14] Selwyn Lloyd to E. M. Jones (Director, GCHQ), 30 September 1956, AIR 20/10621, U.K. National Archives, Kew.

[15] Raymond L. Garthoff, "The KGB Reports to Gorbachev", *Intelligence and National Security*, 11, 2 (1996), p. 228.

[16] Christopher Andrew and Vasili Mitrokhin, *The Mitrokhin Archive: The KGB in Europe and the West* (London: Allen Lane/Penguin, 1999; published in the U.S. as *The Sword and the Shield* by Basic Books, NY), ch. 21.

[17] Admiral Fulvio Martini, *Nome in codice: ULISSE* (Milan: Rizzoli, 1999), pp. 19–20.

was still active in the early 1980s. In the Italian Foreign Ministry, DARIO had an almost equally long career as both KGB agent and talent-spotter.[18]

Recently published research suggests that at a number of periods during the Cold War, France and Italy – like much of the Third World – were unconsciously conducting towards the Soviet Union something akin to open diplomacy. In 1983, for example, the French Embassy in Moscow discovered that bugs in its teleprinters had been relaying all incoming and outgoing telegrams to the KGB for the past six years. According to Viktor Makarov, who served in the KGB Sixteenth (SIGINT) Directorate from 1980 to 1986, the European states whose diplomatic traffic was decrypted with varying frequency during those years included Denmark, Finland, France, Greece, Italy, Sweden, Switzerland, and West Germany.[19] An inner circle within the Politburo – consisting in 1980 of Brezhnev, Andropov, Gromyko, Kirilenko, Suslov, and Ustinov – were sent a daily selection of the most important intercepts. A larger selection went to the heads of the KGB First (Foreign Intelligence) and Second (Internal Security and Counter-Intelligence) Chief Directorates.[20] Although none of this material is yet available for research, it will one day be a source of major importance for historians of the Cold War and Soviet foreign policy.

CIA DIRTY TRICKS: FACT AND FANCY

Thanks to the sensational disclosures of CIA "dirty tricks" in the mid-1970s, shortly after the revelation of the ULTRA secret, far more has been published on covert action during the Cold War than on SIGINT.[21] The Director of Central Intelligence (DCI) William Colby claimed (probably correctly) that in the aftermath of the revelations, "... The CIA came under the closest and harshest public scrutiny that any such service has ever experienced not only in this country but anywhere in the world". Senator Frank Church, chairman of the Senate Select Committee set up to investigate the abuses, declared: "The Agency may have been behaving like a rogue elephant on the rampage". A later congressional report concluded more accurately that

---

[18] Andrew and Mitrokhin, *The Mitrokhin Archive: The KGB in Europe and the West*, pp. 200, 361–2, 459, 601, 603, 608–9, 621, 628, 630, 718. On DARIO, see the additional information in the Italian edition, *L'Archivio Mitrokhin* (Milan: Rizzoli, 1999), pp. 693–4.

[19] Andrew and Mitrokhin, *The Mitrokhin Archive: The KGB in Europe and the West*, pp. 458–9, 625–6.

[20] David Kahn, "Soviet COMINT in the Cold War", *Cryptologia*, 22 (1998).

[21] On the U.S. side, the best introduction remains Gregory F. Treverton, *Covert Action: The Limits of Intervention in the Postwar World* (New York: Basic Books, 1987). Andrew, *For the President's Eyes Only*, analyses changing presidential interest in covert action.

"far from being out of control", the CIA had been "utterly responsive to the instructions of the President and the Assistant to the President for National Security Affairs".[22] Echoes of Church's "rogue elephant" analogy, however, commonly recur in the global literature on covert action.

Alongside the accurate revelations of U.S. covert action there emerged during the 1970s other ill-founded allegations of CIA dirty tricks which, by dint of frequent repetition, became conventional wisdom and still appear in otherwise reliable Cold War histories. President Nixon infamously told the CIA in 1970 to try to prevent the election of Chile's Marxist president, Salvador Allende, and to make the Chilean economy "scream". However, as recent research by Kristian Gustafson demonstrates, the regularly repeated claims that the CIA orchestrated Allende's overthrow (and even his death) in 1973 and the rise of his successor, General Augusto Pinochet, are mistaken:

> ... The Chilean military junta was desperate not to be associated with the U.S.... A post-coup CIA intelligence bulletin reported Pinochet's private comment that "he and his colleagues, as a matter of policy, had not given any hints to the U.S. as to their developing resolve to act".... The Chilean military's *amour propre* would have been offended by the notion that they needed the U.S. to run the coup for them. It was best and simplest, from the Chilean point of view, to keep the CIA on a string with the occasional piece of intelligence, but otherwise to keep them shut out.[23]

Although the revelations of the "Year of Intelligence" exposed scandalous wrongdoing, they also gave rise to bestselling conspiracy theories – chief among them the unfounded claim, which a majority of Americans believed and the KGB did its best to encourage, that the CIA was responsible for the assassination of John F. Kennedy.[24] According to opinion polls in 1993 on the 30th anniversary of Kennedy's assassination, three quarters of Americans believed the Agency was responsible.[25] If the CIA had been involved in killing its own president, it was reasonable to conclude that there were no limits to which the Agency would go to subvert foreign regimes and assassinate other statesmen who had incurred its displeasure. Indian historiography

---

[22] Andrew, *For the President's Eyes Only*, pp. 402–4.

[23] Kristian Gustafson, "The CIA and Chile, 1964–1974", Ph.D. dissertation (University of Cambridge, 2005). An expanded version is to be published shortly in book form.

[24] Andrew and Mitrokhin, *The Mitrokhin Archive: The KGB in Europe and the West*, ch. 14. Max Holland, "The Lie That Linked CIA to the Kennedy Assassination", *Studies in Intelligence*, 11 (Fall/Winter 2001–2).

[25] Daniel Patrick Moynihan, *Secrecy: The American Experience* (New Haven, CT: Yale University Press, 1998), pp. 219–20. Oliver Stone's film version of the conspiracy theory, *JFK*, was enormously influential. One enthusiastic U.S. historian claimed that *JFK* probably "had a greater impact on public opinion than any other work of art in American history" except *Uncle Tom's Cabin*. Robert Brent Toplin (ed.), *Oliver Stone's U.S.A.: Film, History, and Controversy* (Lawrence, KN: University Press of Kansas, 2000), p. 174.

of the CIA is powerfully influenced by such beliefs.[26] KGB active measures successfully promoted the belief that the methods which the CIA had used to attempt to kill Castro and destabilize his regime were being routinely employed against "progressive" governments around the world. One Soviet active-measures operation in the Middle East in 1975 named 45 leading statesmen who, allegedly, had been the victims of successful or unsuccessful Agency assassination attempts during the past decade. Indira Gandhi was one of several Third World leaders influenced by disinformation fabricated by Service A of the First Chief Directorate (i.e., the KGB active-measures specialists) who became obsessed by supposed CIA plots against them.[27] In November 1973, she told Fidel Castro, "What they [the CIA] have done to Allende they want to do to me also. There are people here, connected with the same foreign forces that acted in Chile, who would like to eliminate me". The belief that Allende had been murdered in cold blood and that the Agency had marked her for the same fate became something of an obsession. Dismissing accurate American claims that, in reality, Allende had turned his gun on himself during the storming of his palace, Mrs. Gandhi declared, "When I am murdered, they will say I arranged it myself".[28] Tragically, Mrs. Gandhi paid more attention to the imaginary menace of a CIA-supported assassination attempt than to the real threat from her own bodyguards, who murdered her in 1984.

Just as the history of intelligence collection in the Cold War has been distorted by the neglect of SIGINT, so the history of covert action has been distorted by overconcentration on the U.S. experience. No account of American Cold War policy in the Third World omits the role of the CIA. By contrast, covert action by the KGB passes almost unmentioned in most histories of both Soviet foreign relations and developing countries. The result has been a curiously lopsided history of the secret Cold War in the Third World – the intelligence equivalent of the sound of one hand clapping. The admirable history of the Cold War by John Gaddis, for example, refers to CIA covert action in Chile, Cuba, and Iran but makes no reference to the extensive KGB operations in the same countries.[29]

---

[26] See, for example, Pandit Sheel Bhadra Yajee, *CIA: Manipulating Arm of U.S. Foreign Policy* (New Delhi: Criterion Publications, 1987).

[27] Christopher Andrew and Vasili Mitrokhin, *The Mitrokhin Archive II: The KGB and the World* (London: Allen Lane/Penguin, 2005; published in the U.S. as *The World Was Going Our Way* by Basic Books, New York), pp. 18, 326.

[28] Katherine Frank, *Indira: The Life of Indira Nehru Gandhi* (London: HarperCollins, 2001), pp. 368, 374–5.

[29] John Lewis Gaddis, *The Cold War* (London: Allen Lane, 2006).

COLD WAR IN THE THIRD WORLD: THE PRIMACY OF THE KGB

In reality, from at least the early 1960s onwards – as the material exfiltrated by Vasili Mitrokhin from KGB files demonstrates – the KGB played an even more active global role than the CIA. The belief that the Cold War could be won in the Third World transformed the agenda of Soviet intelligence. In 1961, the youthful and dynamic chairman of the KGB, Aleksandr Shelepin, won Khrushchev's support for the use of national liberation movements and other anti-imperialist forces in an aggressive new grand strategy against the "Main Adversary" (i.e., the United States) in the Third World.[30] Although Khrushchev was soon to replace Shelepin with the more compliant and less ambitious Vladimir Semichastny, the KGB's grand strategy survived. The memoirs of several senior KGB officers who made their reputations in Third Operations complement the revelations of *The Mitrokhin Archive*: among them, those of Nikolai Leonov, the Centre's leading Latin American expert (later head of KGB intelligence assessment); Vadim Kirpichenko, its chief Middle Eastern and African expert who became first deputy head of foreign intelligence; and Leonid Shebarshin, a specialist on the affairs of the Indian subcontinent who rose to become head of foreign intelligence.[31] As Leonov recalled:

Basically, of course, we were guided by the idea that the destiny of world confrontation between the United States and the Soviet Union, between Capitalism and Socialism, would be resolved in the Third World. This was the basic premise.[32]

After Khrushchev was forced to step down in 1964 and was succeeded by Leonid Brezhnev, the belief that the Cold War could be won in the Third World was held with greater conviction in the Centre than in the Kremlin or the Foreign Ministry. It was enthusiastically embraced by Yuri Andropov from the moment he succeeded Semichastny as KGB chairman in 1967. He told a meeting of the Second Chief Directorate (Internal Security and Counter-Intelligence) a year later:

One must understand that the struggle between the [Soviet] organs of state security and the special [intelligence] organs of the opponent in the present conditions

---

[30] Andrew and Mitrokhin, *The Mitrokhin Archive: The KGB in Europe and the West*, pp. 236–7. Andrew and Mitrokhin, *The Mitrokhin Archive II: The KGB and the World*, p. 40.

[31] S. Leonov, *Likholet'e* (Moscow: Mezhdunarodnye otnosheniia, 1995). Vadim Kirpichenko, *Iz arkhiva razvedchika* (Moscow: Mezhdunarodnoye otnosheniia, 1993); idem., *Razvedka: litsa i lichnosti* (Moscow: Geiia, 1998). Leonid Shebarshin, *Ruka Moskvy: Zapiski nachal'nika sovetskoi razvedki* (Moscow: Tsentr-100, 1992).

[32] Nikolai Leonov, Eugenia Fediakova, and Joaquín Fermandois, "El general Nikolai Leonov en el CEP", *Estudios Públicos*, no. 73 (1999).

reflect the present stage of a heightening of the class struggle. And this means that the struggle is more merciless. Today the same question is being decided as in the first days of Soviet power: who prevails over whom? Only today this question is being decided not within our country but within the framework of the whole world system, in a global struggle between two world systems.[33]

The initiative for the "global struggle" came from the KGB rather than the Foreign Ministry. The long-serving Soviet Foreign Minister Andrei Gromyko is remembered in the memoirs of his almost equally long-serving ambassador in Washington, Anatoli Dobrynin, as a man with little interest in the Third World.[34] According to Leonov's memoirs, much of the Foreign Ministry, as well as Gromyko, was "openly scornful" about it:

Andrei Andreyevich [Gromyko] visited and received his colleagues from small European states with greater pleasure than the disturbers of the peace from the countries of the "third world." Even the Politburo failed to convince him to visit the Near East, Africa, or Latin America. Trips to the countries of these regions were isolated incidents in his seemingly endless career as minister for foreign affairs.[35]

(i) The Soviet Union's forward policy in the Third World was thus led not by the Foreign Ministry but by the KGB with the support of the International Department of the CPSU Central Committee. Andropov was always careful not to appear to be treading on Gromyko's toes. The two men gradually became co-sponsors of the major foreign policy proposals put before Brezhnev's Politburo.[36]

As *The Mitrokhin Archive*, Soviet memoirs, and other published research since the end of the Cold War reveal, at most of the main moments of Soviet penetration of the Third World – from the alliance with the first communist "bridgehead" in the Western hemisphere (to quote the KGB's codename for Castro's Cuba)[37] to the final, disastrous defense of the communist regime in Afghanistan – the Centre had greater influence than the Foreign Ministry. Castro preferred the company of KGB officers to that of Soviet diplomats, telling the KGB resident in Havana, Aleksandr Alekseyev, that their meetings were a way of "bypassing the Ministry of Foreign Affairs and every rule of protocol". In 1962, largely at Castro's insistence, Alekseyev replaced the unpopular Soviet ambassador. Other prominent Latin American leaders who, like Castro, preferred KGB officers to Soviet diplomats included

[33] Andrew and Mitrokhin, *The Mitrokhin Archive II: The KGB and the World*, p. 10.

[34] Anatoly Dobrynin, *In Confidence* (New York: Times Books, 1995), pp. 404–5.

[35] Leonov, *Likholet'e*, p. 141.

[36] Dobrynin, *In Confidence*, pp. 209–10, 404–5, 408.

[37] On this subject, see the pathbreaking study by Alexander Fursenko and Timothy Naftali, *One Hell of a Gamble: Khrushchev, Kennedy, Castro, and the Cuban Missile Crisis, 1958–1964* (London: John Murray, 1997), based on unprecedented authorized access to closed Soviet archives as well as publicly available U.S. documents.

Salvador Allende in Chile, Juan José Torres in Bolivia, Omar Torrijos (not to be confused with his son) in Panama, and José Figueres in Costa Rica. The first Soviet contact with Juan and Isabel Perón before their return to Argentina in 1973 was also made by the KGB rather than by a diplomat. KGB support for the Sandinistas began almost two decades before their conquest of power in Nicaragua in 1979.[38]

In Asia, Africa, and the Middle East, as in Latin America, the main initiatives in Soviet policy during the 1960s and 1970s were more frequently taken by the KGB than by the Foreign Ministry. India, the world's largest democracy, is described in the memoirs of Oleg Kalugin – who, in the mid-1970s, was the youngest general in KGB foreign intelligence – as "a model of KGB infiltration of a Third World government".[39] The publicity generated by the detailed revelations of the KGB's Indian operations in *The Mitrokhin Archive II*, which became front-page news in India on its publication in 2005, is one sign of a developing awareness that covert action in the subcontinent was far from being – as much existing Indian historiography had supposed – something approaching a U.S. monopoly.

Several Indian historians have since drawn my attention to information on KGB active measures in India which had accumulated since the disintegration of the Soviet Union but had so far attracted little or no attention in Indian historiography.[40] Those who challenged the reliability of Mitrokhin's material from KGB archives on the regular secret Soviet subsidies to the Communist Party of India (CPI), for example, seemed unaware of the documents in the archives of the Central Committee of the Soviet Communist Party which corroborate Mitrokhin's evidence and record the annual totals of the subsidies. Although the information on payments to Western communist parties had been widely publicized and its authenticity generally accepted, the documents on subsidies to the CPI had previously attracted little attention.[41] The developing Indian historiography of the Cold War will doubtless produce a more balanced assessment of intelligence operations in the subcontinent than has previously been available. It is likely to conclude that despite the priority given by the KGB to India, its operations there – as

---

[38] Andrew and Mitrokhin, *The Mitrokhin Archive II: The KGB and the World*, ch. 2–6.

[39] Oleg Kalugin, *Spymaster: My 32 Years in Intelligence and Espionage against the West* (London: Smith Gryphon, 1994).

[40] See the introduction to the paperback edition of Andrew and Mitrokhin, *The Mitrokhin Archive II: The KGB and the World*, published in 2006.

[41] A selection of the Central Committee documents on secret Soviet subsidies to the CPI and other foreign communist parties is published in appendices to Valerio Riva, *Ora da Mosca* (Milan: Mondadori, 1999).

in many other developing countries – led to transitory successes rather than enduring influence.

THE UNEVEN GROWTH OF ACADEMIC STUDY

The growth in academic intelligence studies on both sides of the Atlantic, already apparent during the 1980s, has accelerated since the end of the Cold War – thanks to both increasing openness by intelligence communities and partial declassification of their historical archives. The transformation has been particularly marked in Britain, where even the existence of the Secret Intelligence Service (commonly referred to as MI6) was not officially acknowledged until 1992 and no peacetime intelligence files were declassified until 1996.

Although the growth of intelligence studies in universities is primarily a phenomenon of the English-speaking world, it is also expanding at a slower pace in other countries – most noticeably in Continental Europe. Sweden occupies a special place; intelligence studies began at the University of Lund earlier than in any other university in Europe (Britain included). Where undergraduate and postgraduate intelligence courses are available, they are almost invariably popular with students. In the last 15 years at Cambridge, for example, intelligence-history courses have more often than not been taken by more final-year undergraduate historians than any other of the numerous options available to them. Currently, 20 Cambridge postgraduates are writing Ph.D. or M.Phil. theses on intelligence topics.

The growth in intelligence studies in universities has had two striking consequences. The first is the normalization of a subject which had commonly been either ignored or sensationalized; the second is the emergence of a generational divide. Able postgraduates in history, political science, and international relations are now likely to have a better grasp of intelligence than most senior academics in their departments who entered the academic profession at a time when intelligence studies did not yet exist. The word SIGINT provides one striking example of the extent of the generational divide. Although commonly used in undergraduate essays by those taking intelligence courses, SIGINT does not appear at all in the publications and lectures by most tenured professors in their departments. The fact that many postgraduates have a greater understanding of intelligence than most senior academics gives them an interesting sense of intellectual empowerment.

As the workshop that led to this book demonstrated, intelligence communities show an increasing interest in the developing historiography of intelligence, although one which varies greatly among countries. In Britain, unlike the United States, retired intelligence officers rarely contribute publicly to the growth of intelligence studies. Although there is a growing body of memoirs by retired U.S. senior intelligence officers – among them, six former DCIs (i.e., Allen Dulles, Richard Helms, William Colby, Stansfield Turner, Robert Gates, and George Tenet)[42] – the only authorized peacetime intelligence memoir in Britain in the last half-century is *Open Secret* by Dame Stella Rimington (Director General of the Security Service from 1992 to 1996), published in 2001. *Open Secret*'s publication was so unwelcome in Whitehall that there is no prospect of any other authorized memoir in the foreseeable future.

In the last 20 years, however, a small number of unauthorized British intelligence memoirs (e.g., Peter Wright, Richard Tomlinson, and David Shayler) have caused anguish in Whitehall and excitement in the media. The British government's bungled attempts 20 years ago to ban the publication of Wright's *Spycatcher* turned it into a global best-seller, comfortably outselling any other book on intelligence ever published in the United States. Its conspiracy theories proved sadly influential: among them, the myths that Sir Roger Hollis (Director General of the Security Service from 1956 to 1965) was a Soviet agent and that the Security Service plotted to bring down the last government of Harold Wilson (1974–6). The myth of the "Wilson plot" has proved so enduring that it has acquired the status of conventional wisdom.

Although it is no longer possible to complain – as Sherman Kent did only a half-century ago – that there is no intelligence historiography, that historiography has so far had only a limited influence on neighboring fields of research. In 1996, the former Deputy Director for Intelligence (DDI) John Helgerson produced a pioneering study of the CIA's early briefings of incoming presidents from Truman to Clinton entitled *Getting to Know the President*, based on both unrestricted access to relevant CIA files and interviews with surviving presidents and their briefers. I wrote in a foreword to the unclassified version of Helgerson's study, "Until similar volumes are available on the briefing of, among others, British prime ministers, German chancellors, French and Russian presidents, and leading Asian statesmen, the use made of intelligence by world leaders will continue to be a major gap in our understanding of both modern government and international relations".[43] That major gap still remains. Even the most basic questions

---

[42] I have excluded Bill Casey from the list because his memoirs are confined to World War II.

[43] John L. Helgerson, *Getting to Know the President: CIA Briefings of Presidential Candidates, 1952–1992* (Washington: CIA Center for the Study of Intelligence, 1996).

about the attitude of most 20th-century world leaders towards intelligence have yet to be asked, let alone answered.

Why, for example, did Margaret Thatcher develop such an interest in – perhaps even a passion for – intelligence? (Her memoirs briefly put on record her "highest regard" for the former British agent inside the KGB, Oleg Gordievsky, and "his judgement about events in the USSR" after his defection in 1985[44] but say nothing about the impact on her of the extraordinary intelligence he had supplied before his defection.) Why, in contrast to Mrs. Thatcher, did Helmut Kohl take such a jaundiced view of his intelligence services, whom he still accuses of giving him "a lot of information that was quite simply false"?[45] Why was François Mitterrand more concerned than, apparently, any of his predecessors at the Élysée, with tapping the telephones of so many of his rivals and opponents?[46] Why did his successor, Jacques Chirac, sack the heads of both the Directorate of Territorial Security (DST) and the Directorate-General for External Security (DGSE) after his election victory in 2002? *Le Monde* claimed that "The Élysée is accusing the secret services of having carried out investigations into M. Chirac under the Jospin government".[47] The attitude to intelligence of most Third World leaders remains at least equally mysterious.

AGENDA FOR THE FUTURE

The future historiography of intelligence thus has a large research agenda. Intelligence communities, as Sherman Kent realized, have much to gain from it. They cannot learn from past experience until they understand – better than they are able to at present – their own past experience. Kent wrote in 1955:

As things stand, we of the intelligence profession possess practically no permanent institutional memory. Our principal fund of knowledge rests pretty largely in our heads; other funds of knowledge are scattered in bits through cubic miles of files.[48]

---

[44] Margaret Thatcher, *The Downing Street Years* (London: HarperCollins, 1993), p. 470.

[45] *Ten Years After. Reflections on the Decade since the Velvet Revolution: An International Conference Held at Prague Castle, November 17–18, 1999* (Prague: EastWest Institute, 2000), p. 17.

[46] Jean-Marie Pontaut and Jérôme Dupuis, *Les Oreilles du Président – suivi de la liste des 2000 personnes "écoutées" par François Mitterrand* (Paris: Fayard, 1996).

[47] "L'Elysée accuse les services secrets d'avoir enquêté sur M. Chirac sous le gouvernement de M. Jospin", *Le Monde*, 23 June 2002.

[48] Sherman Kent, "The Need for an Intelligence Literature", in Donald P Steury (ed.), *Sherman Kent and the Board of National Estimates: Collected Essays* (Washington: CIA Center for the Study of Intelligence, 1994).

Institutional memory cannot be assembled simply from unclassified and declassified material, however valuable individual studies based on those sources are. Although unofficial historians will continue to have a vital role, the nature of the intelligence archive will always render it impossible for any but official historians to have full access to material which remains classified in order to protect sources and methods. During the last generation, the development of intelligence history – in particular, the increasing emphasis on the relationship between intelligence and policy – has transformed the once narrow agenda of in-house histories of intelligence agencies, most of which (e.g., Arthur Darling's history of the early CIA[49]) used to resemble regimental histories primarily concerned with the minutiae of operations and organization. Both intelligence communities and intelligence services need official historians with broader perspectives than Darling to work on those parts of the archive which are not yet declassified. The example of the British official histories of intelligence during World War II demonstrate that official and unofficial historians can coexist to their mutual benefit. (At this point, I need to declare an interest as, since 2003, the official historian of the British Security Service, MI5.)[50]

The cautionary example of Russian official histories of intelligence shows, however, that unless the independence of the authors is rigorously protected, there is a danger that they may degenerate into official apologia. The Russian Foreign Intelligence Service (SVR) dates its own foundation from 20 December 1920, when the Cheka's Foreign Department was established. It celebrated its 75th anniversary in 1995 by publishing an uncritical eulogy of "the large number of glorious deeds" performed by Soviet intelligence officers "who have made an outstanding contribution to guaranteeing the security of our Homeland".[51] The more recent six-volume official history of Russian foreign intelligence initially edited by the former head of the SVR and Russian prime minister, Yevgeni Primakov, is similarly devoted to demonstrating that from the Cheka to the KGB, Soviet foreign intelligence "honourably and unselfishly did its patriotic duty to Motherland and people".[52]

---

[49] Arthur Darling, *The Central Intelligence Agency, An Instrument of Government, to 1950* (University Park: Pennsylvania University Press, 1990).

[50] Sir F. H. Hinsley et al., *British Intelligence during the Second World War*, 4 vols. (London: HMSO, 1979–89); Sir Michael Howard, *British Intelligence during the Second World War*, vol. V (London: HMSO, 1991); M. R. D. Foot, *SOE in France: An Account of the Work of the British Special Operations Executive in France, 1940–1944* (London: HMSO, 1966).

[51] T. V. Samolis (ed.), *Veterany vneshnei razvedki Rossii: Kratkii biograficheskii spravochnik* (Moscow: SVR, 1995).

[52] Y. E. Primakov et al., *Ocherkii Istorii Rossiyskoi Vneshnei Razvedki*, 6 vols. (Moscow: Mezhdunarodnoye otnosheniia, 1995–2005).

Official histories of intelligence should, in my view, fulfil the following three criteria:

(1) They should be based on full access to papers and persons. Although the need to protect sources and methods necessarily limits what can be published, the conclusions of official histories must be based on access to all relevant evidence. Sir F. H. Hinsley and his collaborators wrote in the foreword to their official history of intelligence in World War II:

> No restriction has been placed on us while carrying out our research. On the contrary, in obtaining access to archives and in consulting members of the wartime intelligence community we have received the full cooperation and prompt assistance from the Historical Section of the Cabinet Office and appropriate government departments.[53]

(2) Official historians must have complete freedom to reach whatever conclusions they believe are consistent with the evidence. That principle dates back to the very origins of British official histories. The official historians of Britain in World War I, Professors G. P. Gooch and Howard Temperley, memorably wrote – in grandiloquent terms – that if they had not been given independence to form their own opinions, they would have resigned their official positions.[54] My own contract as official historian of the Security Service contains a public guarantee that none of the judgements I arrive at can be changed in the published history. "My job", a British intelligence chief once told me, "was to tell the Prime Minister what the Prime Minister did not want to know." Official histories have to be free, on occasion, to tell intelligence agencies uncomfortable truths.

(3) The third principle is that official histories of intelligence should not be simply internal histories but rather address the whole of the intelligence cycle, including the interaction with policy makers. For 21st-century intelligence to improve on that of the 20th century, intelligence consumers as well as intelligence agencies will have to raise their game. On current evidence, for example, it seems likely that the weakest link in the 20th-century American intelligence process was not collection or analysis but rather the use made of intelligence by policy makers. The first of the measures proposed in 1996 by the Aspin–Brown Commission to improve "the performance of U.S.

---

[53] Hinsley et al., *British Intelligence during the Second World War*, vol. 1, p. vii.
[54] G. P. Gooch and Howard Temperley (eds.), *British Documents on the Origins of War* (London: HMSO, 1926), vol. IX, p. ix.

intelligence" was directed at policy makers rather than the intelligence agencies:

(i) Intelligence needs better direction from the policy level, regarding both the roles they perform and what they collect and analyze. Policy makers need to appreciate to a greater extent what intelligence can offer them and be more involved in how intelligence capabilities are used.

Public and academic awareness of the role of intelligence has been transformed by the international crises of the early 21st century – September 11, Iraq, and the "War on Terror" – and the official reports they have generated on both sides of the Atlantic. In the United States, the 9/11 Commission Report became a best seller.[55] The animated public debate provoked by these crises highlighted a curious contradiction. Few if any contemporary commentators doubt that the use and abuse of intelligence are central to an understanding of both counterterrorism and the war in Iraq. The fact that the role of intelligence is equally central to an understanding of international relations a half-century ago, however, has escaped most historians' attention. That contradiction between the interpretation of past and present cannot be long sustained.

There is one further sense in which 21st-century intelligence studies need to return to the past. Like much else, intelligence studies suffer "short-termism", the distinguishing intellectual vice of the late 20th and early 21st century. For the first time in recorded history, there is currently a widespread conviction that the experience of all previous generations except our own is irrelevant to present and future policy and intelligence analysis. Our political culture is dominated by an unprecedented malady: Historical Attention-Span Deficit Disorder, or HASDD (the only medical term and the only acronym I have ever invented). Little of real importance about future trends, however, can be deduced from the study of a mere generation of human experience. As my Cambridge colleague Quentin Skinner argues, only long-term historical perspective can "liberate us from the parochialism of our own forms of cultural analysis" – the type of intellectual parochialism which has, for example, led to the common belief that globalization is an offshoot of late 20th-century American capitalism rather than the product of a long and complex interaction between the West and other cultures. For intelligence analysts, the most effective antidote to HASDD is to follow Winston Churchill's celebrated (although nowadays

---

[55] *The 9/11 Commission Report: Final Report of the National Commission on Terrorist Attacks upon the United States* (New York: W. W. Norton, 2007).

neglected) advice: "The further backwards you look, the further forward you can see".[56]

Failure to heed the lessons of long-term past experience has done at least as much damage to intelligence analysis as the failure to realize how much the world has changed. In the quarter-century before September 11, much academic research actually *lessened* our understanding of terrorism by extrapolating from short-term late-20th-century trends, as embodied, for example, by the Irish Republican Army rather than the long-term threat posed by Holy Terror and other fanatical ideologically based terrorism which seeks to destroy its enemies rather than bomb them to the negotiating table. During that quarter-century, for example, the generally excellent *Journal of Strategic Studies*, the premier British journal in the field, had only three issues containing articles on terrorism, presumably because it did not regard transnational terrorism as a problem of real strategic significance. More remarkably still, during the decade before September 11, there was not a single article on terrorism in the journal *International Security*.[57]

Those who showed the most understanding of the threat of transnational terrorism before September 11 were those, like Bruce Hoffman, who took Churchill's advice to look a long way back. Those who got it most wrong were those who ignored it. That is not simply wisdom with hindsight after the event but rather an argument which I put forth for some years before September 11 – although the credit belongs mainly to Hoffman, whose long-term analysis of "Holy Terror" powerfully influenced my own views.[58] I wrote in February 2001:

The nature of the current terrorist threat has been widely misunderstood because it has been seen in too short-term a perspective. For the past generation the conventional wisdom has been that the terrorist's prime objective is publicity rather than victims, to terrify rather than to kill.... This [late-20th-century variety of terrorism, however,] is simply a short-term deviation from a much more dangerous longer-term terrorist tradition which is now reasserting itself.

As Bruce Hoffman has argued, historically, most terrorism has been far more concerned to kill than terrify. Until the nineteenth century terrorism was essentially Holy Terror....

Over the last 20 years there has been a resurgence of traditional religious and cult-based terrorism, whose aims are epitomized by words of the former Hezbollah

---

[56] Christopher Andrew, "Historical Attention-Span Deficit Disorder: Why Intelligence Analysis Needs to Look Back Before Looking Forward", Proceedings of New Frontiers 2004 Rome Conference.

[57] I owe these examples to Amelia Walker.

[58] Bruce Hoffman, *Inside Terrorism*, 2nd edition (New York: Columbia University Press, 2006).

leader, Hussein Massawi: "We are not fighting so the enemy will *offer* us something. We are fighting to *wipe out* the enemy". That was the ideology of the religious wars in early modern Europe. That is also the ideology of, among others, Usama bin Laden. . . . If . . . bin Laden . . . possessed WMD [weapons of mass destruction], [he] would probably already have used them. Indeed bin Laden declared in 1998 that acquiring WMD is a "religious duty".[59]

Intelligence studies in the 21st century must broaden both their chronological and thematic perspectives. Understanding bin Laden is impossible without understanding his deluded conviction that the "Jews and Crusaders" (us, that is to say) have been engaged in a thousand-year war of aggression against Islam. To take on that challenge, intelligence studies require a chronological perspective which goes back at least to the First Crusade and an understanding of theology. What counterterrorism most lacked at the beginning of the 21st century was, arguably, theologians.

[59] Andrew, "Historical Attention-Span Deficit Disorder".

FOUR

A Theory of Intelligence and International Politics

Jennifer E. Sims

(T)he standard depiction of the battle of Gettysburg as the accidental collision of two armies marching half blindly... (was) true only for the Confederates. Their 150-mile march from the Rappahannock River to Pennsylvania was penetrated by soldier-spies... Thus General Meade was able to foresee that the enemy would concentrate at or near Gettysburg. His forces seized commanding heights there and surprised the arriving Confederates, who never overcame the Federals' initial advantage of position.

> Edwin C. Fishel, *The Secret War for the Union*[1]

Intelligence has made a dramatic difference to the outcomes of battles.[2] Yet, scholars have not developed analytical techniques for assessing when

[1] Edwin C. Fishel, *The Secret War for the Union: The Untold Story of Military Intelligence in the Civil War* (New York: Houghton Mifflin, 1996), p. 1. Historians such as Fishel have been relatively more active in this field than political scientists. Just a sampling of the best known might include Ernest May (ed.), *Knowing One's Enemies: Intelligence Assessment Before the Two World Wars* (Princeton, NJ: Princeton University Press, 1984); David Kahn, The Code Breakers (New York: Scribner, 1996); Christopher Andrew, *For the President's Eyes Only: Secret Intelligence and the American Presidency from Washington to Bush* (New York: HarperCollins, 1995); Douglas Porch, *The French Secret Services: A History of French Intelligence from the Dreyfus Affair to the Gulf War* (New York: Farrar, Straus, and Giroux, 1995); Michael Warner, "Wanted: A Definition of 'Intelligence,'" *Studies in Intelligence*, 46, 3 (2002): 15–22; Michael Warner, "The Divine Skein: Sun Tzu on Intelligence," *Intelligence and National Security*, 21, 4 (August 2006), 483–92; Jeffrey T. Richelson, *A Century of Spies: Intelligence in the Twentieth Century* (New York: Oxford University Press, 1995); William B. Feis, *Grant's Secret Service: The Intelligence War from Belmont to Appomattox* (Lincoln, NE, and London: University of Nebraska Press, 2002); Nigel West, *Mask: MI5's Penetration of the Communist Party of Great Britain* (London and New York: Routledge, 2005); and Alexander Rose, *Washington's Spies: The Story of America's First Spy Ring* (New York: Bantam Dell, 2006). Of course, there are many others, including works by official historians.

[2] William B. Feis, *Grant's Secret Service: The Intelligence War from Belmont to Appomattox* (Lincoln, NE, and London: University of Nebraska Press, 2002); Nigel West, *Mask: MI5's Penetration of the Communist Party of Great Britain* (London and New York: Routledge, 2005); and Alexander Rose, *Washington's Spies: The Story of America's First Spy Ring* (New

intelligence matters in international politics, why it does, or the relative intelligence capabilities of states – a point that Michael Warner makes in Chapter Two. True, several political scientists have written important studies that have put surprise attacks, such as Pearl Harbor and September 11, 2001, in larger perspective.[3] Former intelligence officers have occasionally revealed their experiences in memoirs that suggest the causes of intelligence success and failure. In general, however, the two realms of theory and practice have not talked to one another. Practitioners seem uncomfortable encouraging inquiry in such a sensitive area; academics seem to have few theory-building objectives related to the field; and, with a few notable exceptions, political scientists have shunned intelligence – perhaps in part because they are so unfamiliar with its workings.[4]

Whatever the reason, the lack of scholarly attention to the discipline of intelligence seems odd. If intelligence were irrelevant to power, the

York: Bantam Dell, 2006). Of course, there are many others, including works by official historians.

[3] Roberta Wholstetter, *Pearl Harbor: Warning and Decision* (Stanford, CA: Stanford University Press, June 1962); and Lawrence Freedman, *U.S. Intelligence and the Soviet Threat* (Princeton, NJ: Princeton University Press, May 1987). Other scholars working intermittently in the field of intelligence include Richard Betts, "Analysis, War and Decision: Why Intelligence Failures Are Inevitable," *World Politics, 31,* 1 (October 1978), 61–89; Michael Handel, *War, Politics, and Intelligence* (New York: Routledge, 1989); Robert Jervis, *Perception and Misperception in International Politics* (Princeton, NJ: Princeton University Press, 1976); Roy Godson, *Dirty Tricks or Trump Cards: U.S. Covert Action and Counterintelligence* (New Brunswick, NJ, and London: Transaction Publishers, 2001); Amy Zegart, *Flawed by Design: The Evolution of the CIA, JCS, and NSC* (Stanford, CA: Stanford University Press, 2000); and Michael Herman, *Intelligence Power in Peace and War* (Cambridge: Cambridge University Press, 1996). Loch Johnson is perhaps the most prolific of all, writing numerous works on intelligence including *America's Secret Power: The CIA in a Democratic Society* (New York: Oxford University Press, 1989). This knowledge base has been amplified by psychologists, such as Daniel Kahneman, who work on a cross-disciplinary basis to discuss the role of cognitive frames in filtering information for decision making. Jeffrey Cooper applied Kahneman's insights to intelligence; see Jeffrey R. Cooper, *Curing Analytic Pathologies: Pathways to Improved Intelligence Analysis* (Washington: Center for the Study of Intelligence, CIA, December 2005).

[4] Scholarly books by former or current practitioners include, inter alia, Gregory F. Treverton, *Reshaping National Intelligence for an Age of Information* (Cambridge: Cambridge University Press/RAND, 2001); R. V. Jones, *The Wizard War: British Scientific Intelligence 1939–1945* (New York: Coward, McCann & Geoghegan, 1978); John C. Masterman, *The Double-Cross System in the War of 1939 to 1945* (New Haven, CT: Yale University Press, 1972); Abram Shulsky, *Silent Warfare: Understanding the World of Intelligence,* 2nd edition, revised by Gary Schmitt (New York: Brassey's, 1993); Richards J. Heuer, *Psychology of Intelligence Analysis* (Washington: Center for the Study of Intelligence, CIA, 1999); and Mark Lowenthal, *Intelligence: From Secrets to Policy,* 3rd edition (Washington: CQ Press, 2006). I am grateful to Andrew Sawka and Matthew Walker for their extensive contributions as research assistants during the preparation of this chapter.

continuing high levels of government spending on it should have prompted more systematic inquiry among political scientists than appears to have been the case. If, on the contrary, intelligence is related to power, one would have expected international-relations theorists to have developed a rich literature on how this might be so.[5]

That this latter effort lags is surprising. In addition to Fishel's findings on Gettysburg cited at the opening of this chapter, historians have shown that the success of Operation Overlord, which led to Hitler's defeat during World War II, turned on British signals intelligence (SIGINT) and double-agent operations – a point Christopher Andrew stresses in Chapter Three.[6] The United States won the Battle of Midway, the turning point of World War II in the Pacific, largely because of a SIGINT coup.[7] Queen Elizabeth I arguably owed her longevity to her chief spy, Sir Francis Walsingham, who caught Mary Queen of Scots' treachery and plotted the defeat of the Spanish Armada.[8] George Washington's troops arguably survived Valley Forge because of the general's artful deception campaigns.[9] It would seem almost self-evident that there is an element of power – perhaps first recognized by Sun Tzu in 6th-century BC – that involves the ability to achieve objectives through surprise, deceit, and directed force.[10]

Indeed, this chapter assumes that intelligence *does* make a difference to the outcome of conflict and that advantages in intelligence can cause

---

[5] Political scientists have considered communications as an aspect of the theory of games. See Thomas C. Schelling, *The Strategy of Conflict* (New York: Oxford University Press, 1960). They also studied information as an aspect of decision theory (see Richard Hybel, John Steinbruner, et al.). Stephen Van Evera discussed the role of "non-self-evaluation" in foolish foreign-policy decisions; Robert Powell argued that information available to states on the structure of the system may affect outcomes when states interact. However, none of these scholars sought to address systematically the relationship of intelligence to national power.

[6] John C. Masterman, *The Double-Cross System in the War of 1939 to 1945*.

[7] The U.S. ability to read Japanese codes was "...helpful in the Coral Sea battle and absolutely critical to the Battle of Midway." Stephen E. Ambrose and C. L. Sulzberger, *American Heritage New History of World War II* (New York: Viking/Penguin) 1997, p. 297.

[8] Stephen Budiansky, *Her Majesty's Spymaster: Elizabeth I, Sir Francis Walsingham, and the Birth of Modern Espionage* (New York: Viking/Penguin, 2005).

[9] "Washington prepared fake documents in his own hand, full of references to non-existent infantry and cavalry regiments, which were then passed on to the enemy by double agents. The British credited Washington with more than eight thousand troops he did not have and mistakenly concluded he was too strong to attack." Christopher Andrew, *For the President's Eyes Only*, pp. 9–10.

[10] See Michael Warner, "The Divine Skein: Sun Tzu on Intelligence," *Intelligence and National Security, 21*, 4 (August 2006): 483–92.

seemingly weak armies or states to prevail against seemingly stronger ones. In relating intelligence to national power and the workings of the international system,[11] this chapter considers intelligence as a form of support to decision making during competitions, including cooperative competitions in which both sides care more about securing relative gains than defeating one another. It offers an explanation of how intelligence succeeds in providing advantages to decision makers and how its performance can be measured before failure occurs.

The analysis begins with a set of propositions about the effects of intelligence on power at the structural level and continues with an outline of a theory of intelligence that suggests the latter's importance for politics more generally. In particular, the chapter suggests four attributes of intelligence that are the principal determinants of its performance and thus its contributions to state power. The analysis concludes with some implications for theories of international relations in general and U.S. intelligence reform in particular. Based on the framework offered here, analysts can assess and compare intelligence capabilities for the purpose of estimating the outcomes of conflict among states. Conducted correctly, such estimates will be better than more traditional assessments of power that exclude the intelligence dimension.

This effort to identify the characteristics of superior intelligence seems timely and warranted. How can intelligence be reformed if the causes of strength and weakness are unknown or, at best, anecdotal? Definitions and theory have lagged far behind the rise of intelligence power among states. The United States spends more than 40 billion dollars annually on intelligence systems employing sophisticated technologies for land, air, sea, and outer space. Efforts to harness such power to strategies for its use have been underway for years.[12] It is time for theory to catch up.

INITIAL PROPOSITIONS

If we are to understand the relationship among intelligence, threats, and power, a consensus on what intelligence is and terminology to describe

---

[11] My efforts were energized by Steven Walt, who noted that asking big questions is a good thing for political scientists to do and urged us to aim high. See Andrew K. Hanami (ed.), *Perspectives on Structural Realism* (New York: Palgrave Macmillan, 2003), p. xiii.

[12] The most recent U.S. national-intelligence strategy was issued in 2005. Mark Lowenthal noted elsewhere that there is little in this document that looks like a strategy – at least, not in the sense of a top-level guide to action. "What, at the end of the day, is intelligence being asked to do?" Personal communication with author; 12 October 2006.

its central characteristics is essential.[13] In fact, if theorists of comparative politics correctly observe that "he who knows only England, knows England not," then he who knows only American or British intelligence knows precious little about intelligence either.[14] It is therefore important to develop a simple, universally applicable definition that distinguishes intelligence from other related activities such as news, secret policy, or propaganda. The core attributes of intelligence can then be identified and its differing manifestations explained.

In this spirit, we may best understand *intelligence* as the collection, analysis, and dissemination of information for decision makers engaged in a competitive enterprise.[15] It is a process by which competitors improve their decision making relative to their opponents.[16] Whether in business, politics, or sports, the purpose of intelligence is the same: to obtain better information than opponents do about relevant plans, capabilities, rules, and terrain through directed and often secretive learning. In Chapter Two, Warner gives pride of place to the secret dimension; here, I stress the inherently competitive dimension of intelligence, which often makes secrecy an attribute of high-quality intelligence systems but which leaves open the possibility of trading off secrecy to gain speed or other forms of decisive advantage. Winning information delivered openly may be just as good as or better than that which arrives secretly. The test for intelligence is relevance and timeliness for the competition, not the covering with which it arrives. In any case, gaining "intelligence advantage" requires superior knowledge of the rules or of the capabilities, strategies, quirks, and proclivities of the other players. The purpose of having it is to gain "decision advantage" – an opportunity to score a tactical victory or win the game.

Viewed in this light, some admittedly controversial propositions arise: intelligence failure may be less about inaccuracy than about losing advantage; intelligence success may be less about getting everything right than

---

[13] Testing these propositions will require additional work involving case studies and plausibility probes. For the latter, see Alexander George, "Case Studies and Theory Development: The Method of Structured, Focused Comparison," in Paul G. Lauren (ed.), *Diplomacy: New Approaches in History, Theory, and Policy* (1979), pp. 43–68.

[14] This aphorism, used in the context of a discussion of comparative politics and its uses, comes from Bernard E. Brown, *Comparative Politics: Notes and Readings*, 9th edition (New York: Harcourt College Publishers, 2000), p. 1.

[15] Jennifer E. Sims, "Understanding Friends and Enemies: The Context for American Intelligence Reform," in Jennifer E. Sims and Burton Gerber (eds.), *Transforming U.S. Intelligence* (Washington: Georgetown University Press, 2005), p. 15.

[16] One key premise of the following analysis is that, all other things being equal, better intelligence leads to better decision making – that is, decision making more in keeping with the national interest than it would otherwise be.

about beating the other side; and speed and relevance can be more important in certain circumstances than secrecy, comprehensiveness, or even accuracy.[17] After all, information crucial to improving an adversary's decisions may be posted on the Internet, as the United States realized after the September 11 attacks when officials found online blueprints of potential terrorist targets, such as bridges and other critical infrastructure. Although intelligence is necessary for secret policy – known as *covert action* in the United States – this relationship does not mean that secret policy or covert action should be confused with intelligence, which is a distinct function.[18]

Of course, in international politics, an anarchic competition, there are no rule-setters and the competitions and players may overlap or shift abruptly. States' military capacities and the distribution of power among them limit what any single state can accomplish to gain security relative to others. Intelligence is used to *discover* these capacities and this limiting structure as well as to *estimate* other states' relative abilities to do likewise. With good intelligence, states make better projections of likely outcomes than they would if they operated in the dark. In fact, those states with the best intelligence or the best capability to degrade their opponents' intelligence can compensate for disadvantages they may have in weapons, money, and warriors. They do so by knowing how to apply diplomatic pressure or force in an efficient, tailored, and timely manner. With repeated advantages in intelligence, a state may outmaneuver or even beat an opponent despite contrary predictions based on standard measures of power.

If this opening set of propositions is reasonable, then there are interesting implications for the international system. For example, if intelligence capabilities could be maximized for all states, misperception and uncertainty should be minimized.[19] The number of wars caused by surprise and folly would be expected to decline because good intelligence would allow states to assess correctly the strategies and capabilities of adversaries and to adjust

---

[17] This rather provocative assertion is defended at length in the following discussion. The author thanks Michael Warner for the ongoing debate we have had on the role of secrecy in intelligence. I agree with Warner that intelligence employed by states almost always involves secrecy at some stage of the process because the stakes are so high.

[18] This is true even if secret policy is often executed by those within an intelligence establishment for purposes of security and efficiency.

[19] "Perfect" intelligence means the ideal situation in which there is complete situational awareness, including foreknowledge of relevant decisions taken by the opponent. Foreknowledge of intentions, absent decisions, is usually impossible to achieve. In this author's view, intelligence cannot eliminate misperception as a cause of war; cognitive blocks and natural predilections will always have a role to play in decision making, even given "perfect" information. See Robert Jervis, *Perception and Misperception in International Politics* (Princeton, NJ: Princeton University Press, 1976).

to them through negotiation and weapons-building instead of battle.[20] Although conflict is endemic in the international system, war – at least, theoretically – is not. It is simply an (inefficient) adjustment mechanism among states contending to secure their interests. With good situational awareness, states seeking security should be able to claim niches that reflect their best possible positions relative to others.[21]

Of course, in the real world, substantial uncertainty causes states to compete for knowledge, seeking "intelligence advantages" over others whose plans and capabilities seem threatening.[22] Governments create and exploit uncertainties, even when they know such actions may increase the risks of silly wars. A good theory of intelligence should be able to explain such choices – what the historian Barbara Tuchman famously labeled "marches of folly."[23] In fact, a central thesis of this chapter is that bizarre decisions – such as needless or ill-timed wars, provocative actions intended to convey pacific intent, and balancing against the wrong state – are predictable consequences of discernable imbalances in intelligence power. The Greeks, *knowing* the Trojans' veneration of the horse and their fear of the goddess Athena, constructed a device – a wooden horse dedicated to the goddess – that caused the Trojans to open their gates to an enemy that, until then, had been unable to defeat them.[24] The Trojans' gullibility was, as Tuchman observed, a breathtaking sort of wooden-headedness, but it was wooden-headedness *induced* by a wily opponent. The Greeks employed intelligence power and won.

It is obvious that intelligence dominance does not always dictate success. An advantage in weapons or rate of economic growth does not predict

---

[20] Conversely, bad information on competitors and allies often leads to poor strategies; poor decision making; and increases in the occurrence, length, and costs of war. Some alert readers may object that "ideal" intelligence would include ideal counterintelligence capabilities as well. This would suggest that deception and denial might dominate a world of steadily improving intelligence capabilities. However, as discussed later in this chapter, any system that tends toward equilibrium will also tend toward transparency, with sudden accretions of power countered by increased intelligence-sharing arrangements among powers seeking to balance it. Moreover, the larger the number of competing states, the less feasible deception of any one of them becomes. For these and other reasons, systems tending toward equilibrium will also tend toward transparency.

[21] This proposition assumes, of course, that states seek to maximize their security, not their power, in international politics. The assumption places this theoretical work firmly in the Neo-Realist literature.

[22] "Decision advantages" may also result, of course, from favorable terrain, better weapons systems, and so forth.

[23] See, for example, Barbara W. Tuchman, *The March of Folly: From Troy to Vietnam* (New York: Alfred A. Knopf, 1984).

[24] Ibid., 36–49.

victory either. The quality of political decision making will weigh as much in the wielding of the intelligence instrument as military art weighs in the wielding of arms. Intelligence in this sense, delivers "decision advantage;" outcomes will only be as good as the decision makers using it, and its purposes can be no better or worse than theirs. Intelligence theory is, therefore, more than of academic interest – particularly so if that theory offers ways to measure current performance relative to competitors and, therefore, ways to build power when other forms of it are less easily acquired.

This brief discussion of the impact of intelligence on international politics suggests that intelligence can "get it wrong" and still succeed in gaining advantage for decision makers as long as competitors make worse mistakes over time. Moreover, the nature of the competition and, therefore, the type of decision making involved will affect the intelligence system that supports it.[25] In Chapter Six, Neal Pollard makes this point strongly in the counterterrorism context. To be good, intelligence must be tightly bound to the nature of the decisions that competitors must make: whether to focus on a rising issue; whether to generate options and, if so, which ones; and how to monitor conflicts, engage, and ultimately end them. Fortunately, theoretical work on decision making runs deep; unfortunately, it barely covers aspects crucial to the intelligence enterprise.[26] Factors affecting discreet choices (cognitive bias for example) are better understood than are the ways in which decision makers come to recognize the competitive game and mobilize resources to win – processes during which intelligence plays its most influential and difficult roles.[27]

The next section explores these connections and offers ways to judge the effectiveness of any intelligence process. The key ingredient in optimized intelligence is comparative and contextual assessment: Is a competitor's intelligence system better than his adversary's, given the nature of the competition (bureaucratic, anarchic, multiparty, etc.) in which they are engaged? Of course, an intelligence system that can repeatedly warn while satisfying decision makers' desire to gauge and to control the competition is strong;

---

[25] For an introduction to the theory of decision making, see Jonathan Baron, *Thinking and Deciding*, 3rd edition (New York: Cambridge University Press, 2000).

[26] Exceptions include, of course, the works on perception and misperception by Robert Jervis and Richard Heuer and on decision theory in games. The latter, however, mostly assume conditions of uncertainty.

[27] Economics, with its focus on scarcity and choice, offers many useful insights that go beyond the scope of this chapter. For a discussion of current trends in decision theory in international relations and the application of one school to Latin American politics, see Alex Roberto Hybel, *How Leaders Reason: U.S. Intervention in the Caribbean Basin and Latin America* (Cambridge, MA: Basil Blackwell, 1990).

one that cannot is weak. This is true regardless of whether, in specific instances, these advantages are exploited or winning decisions are made. The degree to which a weakness is tolerable on one side is determined by the strength of the adversary's countervailing capabilities. As long as such comparisons are possible, relative intelligence power is possible to deduce.

Difficulties arise, however, when assessing intelligence power in the midst of conflict or based on information from only one side – as is frequently the case when contemplating current reforms. In the midst of battle, a competitor cannot reliably assess advantages, only the apparent strength of his own side. For example, if an opponent loses an intelligence advantage, was it because of intelligence failure or because the "losing" side purposefully forfeited intelligence for later strategic gain? During World War II, the British deferred opportunities for tactical success for years as they developed the bona fides of double agents, by allowing them to provide accurate intelligence to the Germans. The Allies eventually proved the worth of those investments when they used those agents to deceive the Nazis about the Normandy invasion.[28] However, prior to that point, before final outcomes were clear, the Germans apparently enjoyed repeated intelligence advantages.

How, then, does one assess the strength of an intelligence system in isolation from others and in a manner rigorous enough for comparative purposes, such as before reforms and after? A theory of intelligence must offer consistent causal explanations for intelligence success and failure so that those attempting to improve an intelligence system are not just tinkering based on trial, error, and anecdote.

To be useful, the theory also must be one that offers ways to measure the ingredients of success. "Operationalizing" theoretical propositions for such purposes is often difficult. The problem of metrics bedevils the world of intelligence in particular because few people believe that the quality of

[28] The costs of forfeiting decision advantages for later gain, in theory, can be extraordinarily high – higher than even the loss of double agents once their deceits are exposed. During the World War II Blitz, the British appear to have delayed Air Raid Precaution orders for the cities targeted by German bombers until the directional beams used to guide bombers to targets were turned on. This policy protected the secret of the British ability to read German code. See R. A. Ratcliff, *Delusions of Intelligence: Enigma, ULTRA, and the End of Secure Ciphers* (Cambridge: Cambridge University Press, 2006), p. 113. It led to the myth, which Ratcliff joins others in debunking, that Churchill decided to sacrifice Coventry for ULTRA; in fact, he made no such decision. However, the policy illustrates the point nonetheless: sometimes intelligence advantage may be so crucial to strategic or future decision making that it is worth delays and even potential losses in battle to preserve it for the present. For the definitive explanation of the Coventry issue, see F. H. Hinsley, *British Intelligence in the Second World War* (New York: Cambridge University Press, abridged edition, 1993).

a human intelligence (HUMINT) source can be judged by the quantity of what he says or the number of products his case officer generates. Even identifying and maximizing any one "good," such as security, can put other "goods" at risk, such as timely delivery of secrets to those who need them, rendering the whole system inefficient and risk averse. What, then, are the "goods" to be measured and how, realistically, can we do so?

MEASURING INTELLIGENCE ADVANTAGE

Arguably, an intelligence system's strength comes from the following four critical functions; that is, its ability to:

- *collect* information on competitors, including the essential structure of the competition in which all are engaged
- *anticipate* new competitions
- *transmit* information across the intelligence–decision maker divide (if it exists)
- *degrade* opponents' efforts to do all of the previous functions to achieve a competitive advantage.[29]

Competitors who are relatively weak in any one of these "measures" for quality intelligence must compensate by developing relative strengths in others if they are reliably and repeatedly to gain intelligence advantages over their adversaries. These factors also involve critical trade-offs: for example, a terrorist who does his own intelligence has no problem believing and using what he learns (i.e., the transmission factor), but he will be limited in what he can collect or anticipate. Degrading an opponent's intelligence may make that opponent more prone to misperception, thus complicating efforts to anticipate his future behavior. Comparing intelligence capabilities among states requires disaggregating and comparing their capacities in the four areas. In the absence of the ability to compare, each side must seek to maximize all four. For this reason, intelligence services pursue intelligence policy – decisions involving the allocation of resources among competing needs – which also invokes the need for intelligence.

The remainder of this chapter explains the four variables in greater detail, providing for illustration brief examples of the presence, absence, and

---

[29] Analysis, a critical ingredient of intelligence at all stages, is not mentioned here because it is, in and of itself, more a feature of the intelligence process than a means to measure its quality. Mistakes of this type lead to simplistic and fallacious metrics of intelligence performance, such as how many reports have been produced or assets recruited, rather than the effects that the reports or recruitments had on outcomes.

variance of each. Given the limitation of space, this discussion is not comprehensive but instead focuses on the elements of sound intelligence performance most obviously missing from modern discussions of intelligence reform.

COLLECTION

Collection power turns on three principal factors: the number of collection systems available, the range of their coverage, and the degree to which the components of those systems are reliably integrated and collectively managed.[30] Attempts to measure the quality of an intelligence system should begin with three questions: How many collection systems does the competitor have available? How extensive is their reach? How reliably integrated and controlled are they? To answer these questions, we must understand the concepts of collection and integration in more depth.

In theory, collecting data about a target requires a flexible way to "sense" the target, a vehicle to get the sensor within good range, a method for turning the sensor's data on the target into meaningful information, and then a means for getting this information safely back to users. In other words, at a minimum, a collection system needs five elements: command and control, platform, sensor, processing and exploitation, and data "exfiltration."[31]

The quality of intelligence against a given adversary or competitor will vary, other factors staying constant, not just according to the number of sensing systems available and their access but also the degree to which they are collectively and singly managed on behalf of the principal decision makers. Each of their five components must be optimized, integrated, and tailored to the competition and related targets as well as protected against disruption or degradation in certain circumstances.[32] Because achieving

---

[30] Protection of collection systems is also of importance, but it is not integral to the collection function itself, which may take place in a nonhostile environment. Collectors that increase protection without reference to threat and strategy will overinvest in it.

[31] The term *exfiltration* is used here to indicate that this need only be a one-way information flow.

[32] *Command and control* is the steering system for a collector. A collector's *platform* is the ship, building, bench, animal, or other structure on which one or more sensors ride. *Sensors*, such as cameras, antennae, or even human beings, provide data on the target. *Processing* employs the tools and skills (e.g., translation and decryption) for turning the sensor's collected data into understandable information for *exploitation* or interpretation. *Data exfiltration* is the system and technique for getting the exploited intelligence back to users. *Security* is designed to preserve its longevity. These components can interfere with one another. Collection management involves trade-offs optimizing productivity, efficiency,

these goals can involve difficult trade-offs among research and development goals or the elements of performance (imagery resolution versus aircraft altitude or satellite orbit), the first and most important indicator of high-quality collection is a locus for managing it. Thus, a new sensor may decrease net capabilities if it collects so much data that it overwhelms processors, stalls the platform, or reveals the location of the collector at a critical time. Only collection managers with good knowledge and control of all five components of each collector as well as across collection systems (such as human, signals, and imagery collection) can make the trade-offs that optimize the collector's performance against a shifting array of adversaries.

U.S. RB-45s and other reconnaissance aircraft deliberately flew over the boundaries of the Soviet Union in the 1950s to induce Soviet radars to reveal their locations, thus sacrificing security for sensor performance in a classic example of what has been called "ferreting."[33] If control during those missions had been divided between the owners of the sensors and the owners of the planes placed at risk, the missions might never have flown. Indeed, by the time of the Cuban Missile Crisis, lack of integrated management of U2s and other collection assets arguably delayed optimum intelligence on the deployment of Soviet medium-range missiles.

Achieving such vertical transparency and integration can be difficult when warring bureaucracies control different critical components – for example, the State Department generates the commands (e.g., monitoring an arms-control negotiation), the Department of Defense funds the platform (say, a ship), and the Department of Energy processes the data (say through its national laboratories). If the Department of State makes the negotiation a priority, while at the same time the Department of Defense schedules the ship for maintenance, and the Department of Energy cuts back personnel at the laboratories, the collection system as a whole will suffer and perhaps fail as a result of misaligned resources. In such circumstances, the system becomes dysfunctional as one piece ill-fits another or puts the whole at unrecognized risk.

"tunability" (i.e., the capacity to shift targets without loss of production), connectedness, usability, robustness, and boosting capacity (i.e., the ability to enhance the performance of other collectors).

[33] These flights were conducted by "...piston engined B-50s, all-jet RB-45s and – not well known – RB-47s. The British flew in borrowed RB-45s and Canberras...." Private communication from Wilhelm Agrell, Lund University. I am indebted to Agrell for his assistance in keeping my facts straight on air operations during the 1950s.

Given access to an entire collection system, managers can align research and development of communications, platforms, data management, encryption, and sensors to changing targets. In such a case, suboptimization in the performance of any one element of a collection system would be a deliberate effort to optimize security and the long-term performance of the system as a whole. This point holds true for horizontal integration among collectors as well. Stalin's *Rote Kapelle* (Red Orchestra), a World War II HUMINT system mentioned previously, was a "system of systems" in the sense that each cell was a collector in a larger network of cells. The network was largely managed by its chief "conductor" on the ground, Leopold Trepper. A deft judge of agents and manipulator of the platforms off of which they worked, Trepper ran a highly successful and deeply penetrating collection apparatus. He did not, however, control the separate cells' decisions on data exfiltration. The network's uncoordinated decisions to transmit heavily in 1941 to warn Stalin of Hitler's attack and subsequent advance toward Moscow cost it most of its cells.[34] The Red Orchestra's suicidal burst of communications was arguably a reasonable management decision for each individual cell but perhaps not for the network as a whole.[35]

It is interesting that the U.S. collection system involves much divided and uncoordinated management, leading the Department of Defense – a major platform owner – to seek as much control of the collection process as possible. Although the Pentagon's effort to gain such control frequently has been seen as bureaucratic warfare, its motivation may actually be driven by the more laudable desire to establish integrated collection management – albeit with the purpose of ensuring that its own needs are met. In the new era of transnational threats, military managers may not have knowledge of nondefense-related innovations and countermeasures available to private or commercial enterprises or may not be able to adopt those innovations as swiftly as private-sector competitors such as drug rings, organized crime, or terrorists.

---

[34] Because of the sensitivity of command and control, the *Rote Kapelle* used interesting nomenclature; its chiefs were known as conductors and its wireless radios were called pianos. See V. E. Tarrant, *The Red Orchestra: The Soviet Spy Network Inside Nazi Europe* (New York: John Wiley and Sons, Inc., 1995). See also Christopher Andrew and Vasili Mitrokhin, *The Sword and the Shield: The Mitrokhin Archive and the Secret History of the KGB* (New York: Basic Books, 1999), p. 102.

[35] This case illustrates another key point: those who manage collection, including those who construct new collection systems, need intelligence support themselves. See comments on the implications for analysis in Jeffrey Cooper, *Curing Analytic Pathologies: Pathways to Improved Intelligence Analysis* (Washington: Center for the Study of Intelligence, CIA, December 2005).

In any case, if decision makers delegate collection management to intelligence officers, they should recognize that they are also potentially delegating important choices, such as the one the Red Orchestra made in 1941. Ideally, the training of those who manage collection would emphasize that the decision maker's strategic interests in the overall competition are integral to finding the correct balance between loss and gain – whether the question is of the scale faced by the Red Orchestra or at lower levels involving the declassification of an intercept for use in negotiations. Because the purpose of intelligence is decision advantage, any slavish fixation on collection retention over critical use – or its converse, use over retention –is in error.[36]

Similar calculations hold when policy makers restrict the use of certain platforms for political reasons. An otherwise optimized collection system that creates or complicates a crisis by its very use may not be as attractive for intelligence as one that does not. For this reason, collection managers must not only be knowledgeable about the attributes of the systems they develop and employ but also knowledgeable about the operating environment that will constrain their operations. Sophisticated understanding of international politics and law is as important as engineering in developing and managing advanced collection systems – not least because knowledge of the legal and political terrain helps an intelligence service design good cover for its operations.

In summary, although the quality of collection management is difficult to measure, the existence of multiple, wide-ranging, and integrated collectors, as well as authoritative managers for each and for the system as a whole, is the critical indicator of the strength of an intelligence service.

ANTICIPATION

Without a way to anticipate competitions, to foresee related threats and opportunities, and to identify new, crucial decision makers – both one's own and the adversaries' – an intelligence service loses its sense of mission, risks irrelevance, and thus courts catastrophic failure. Identifying the appropriate recipients of intelligence may be the assigned responsibility of policy makers, but it is critical to the intelligence function and illustrates again how failures

---

[36] The Red Orchestra's impact on Soviet decision-making after the initial Nazi invasion of the Soviet Union was apparently and not surprisingly minimal. According to Christopher Andrew and Vasili Mitrokhin, the Germans captured most of the network by the end of 1942. Leopold Trepper, the "conductor," was apprehended in his dentist's chair in Paris on December 5 of that year. *The Sword and the Shield: The Mitrokhin Archive and the Secret History of the KGB*, (New York: Basic Books, 1999), 102.

on the policy side can implicate intelligence performance. Before September 11, 2001, U.S. intelligence institutions were faster at identifying emerging adversaries than they were at identifying those in the United States who would need to make the crucial decisions necessary for blocking them: law enforcement, border control, airline security, and first responders. This gap allowed Osama bin Laden's network to plan and carry out its attacks using an intelligence system far less sophisticated than that of the U.S. government.

In fact, the September 11 example suggests that the primary ingredients of surprise include four potential gaps: (1) not knowing who the adversary is (lack of strategic vision); (2) knowing who the adversary is but not seeing him coming (lack of tactical vision); (3) knowing who he is, seeing him coming, but not knowing who needs to know about it (lack of self-knowledge); and (4) knowing all the foregoing but not getting the information to the crucial decision makers in time for them to act. Arguably, September 11 involved the last three.[37] Recent research suggests that when circumstances close these gaps – as was the case before the millennium terrorist threat of January 2000 – intelligence institutions otherwise prone to failure can perform well. Crucial differences in the latter case were the limited boundaries of the threat (i.e., millennium-related venues) and the time it would peak, as well as who would play the decisive roles in countering the opponent: border security and local law enforcement.[38]

In any case, identifying new decision makers is a crucial intelligence function that requires cooperation among intelligence and policy officials and is put at risk by too deep a divide between them. In this sense, bureaucratic systems would seem to have advantages over chaotic, tribal, or feudal systems: new "customers" are routinely identified by their portfolios. Thus, an intelligence service has a script for knowing – at least, in theory – who incoming officials are, what decisions they will make, and whom they will engage when making them (i.e., their bureaucratic counterparts in other governments). Policy makers play fewer games seeking to limit access to bureaucratic competitors whose titles become their tickets. Unfortunately, bureaucratically organized decision making can also make adapting intelligence support to new, competitive environments sticky and dropping old customers difficult.

---

[37] Because intelligence is theoretically part of a decision-making process, this chapter includes decision makers in the intelligence cycle and attributes mistakes they make in exercising these responsibilities to failures in the national-intelligence function.

[38] Matthew Walker, "A Study of the Role of Intelligence–Policymaker Engagement in National Security Decision-Making," unpublished master's thesis, Georgetown University, May 2006.

The problem is more than one of red tape. Arguably, warning of new threats is an inescapable part of an intelligence provider's job; delivery to appropriate decision makers is integral to job completion. Intelligence efforts to bring in new customers to address new threats can, however, encounter bureaucratic resistance to shifts in agenda, players, and intelligence resources, given competitions already in play. Given that intelligence is a limited good, decision makers with good access to intelligence will resist losing priority or letting others compete for decision support. This entrepreneurial orientation becomes more evident the higher one goes in the decision-making bureaucracy. Officials want to be good at their jobs and intelligence is one way to help them succeed. Access to intelligence and the clearances that come with it can be an indicator of the national worth of the topic one works and the trajectory of one's career. Officials stand to lose much if a competing topic gains national attention at the expense of one's own, making success more difficult and risks higher.

The incentives and results of this process are brilliantly illustrated in Jack Davis's interview of former National Security Council (NSC) Director Robert Blackwill, published in the Central Intelligence Agency (CIA) journal *Studies in Intelligence*.[39] Recounting stories of the support he received from the intelligence community, Blackwill called the CIA intelligence team he created and nurtured his "analytic hogs," a reference to the Redskins' powerful front line that created space and time for the quarterback to decide among receivers and prevent sacks. The game, as he recounts it, was intensely bureaucratic:

... (T)he most heavily engaged and influential policy officials on any given issue spend 90 percent of their time assessing their policy competitors in Washington. I am talking here about getting ready to leverage competing Administration officials, not just congress.... Let me tell you, any policy official who can do his own research on all aspects of an issue, cannot be very important – because he is not fully engaged in the coalition building and power-leverage games essential for getting serious policy work done in Washington.[40]

Blackwill went on to suggest that even useful intelligence products may be properly withheld from colleagues in the policy-making community for bureaucratic reasons.

---

[39] Jack Davis, "A Policymaker's Perspective on Intelligence Analysis," *Studies in Intelligence*, 38, 5 (1995), 7–15.

[40] Ibid., 9.

Once a senior State Department colleague joined me for breakfast in Brussels as I was reading my very own newsletter (from CIA analysts). He studied it with great interest and asked me where it came from. I chose not to tell him.[41]

This dynamic, in which the national-intelligence function is not only cultivated to needs but also kept from others in the interest of bureaucratic politics, may be called the *privatization* of intelligence – a distortion possibly more prevalent and less understood than *politicization*, its better known sibling. The signal feature of this distortion is not close-up support to a policy maker; if all decision makers behaved in this aggressive way, bureaucratic decision making arguably would be better informed and options better understood. What makes privatization bad is the nondisclosure of product or process to others on one's own team because it would improve those teammates' effectiveness at the expense of one's own.

Privatization can lead to intelligence failure as alternative (better) points of view are less well supported or overlooked. In the run-up to the Iraq war, this would seem to have been the issue between Undersecretary of Defense Doug Feith and his intelligence-community critics: where those working in Feith's office saw themselves as bureaucratic black belts or "analytic hogs" legitimately mining intelligence to see if it supported a particular point of view, intelligence professionals saw cherry-picking of intelligence and distortion of the decision-making process.

If the national interest is served by optimizing a leader's choice, it is also served by the full fleshing out of options before that choice is made, regardless of the bureaucratic skills of those options' advocates. Because, inevitably, talent for the Machiavellian arts is inequitably distributed, institutional arrangements are often necessary to engineer balance. A little-known mission of the coordination division of the Bureau of Intelligence and Research (INR) at the U.S. Department of State is to ensure that all the relevant policy makers get the intelligence they need when supporting the Secretary.[42] This may simply involve briefing all products to the relevant bureaus or sharing as widely as possible the answers to questions asked by the intelligence community's most vigorous users. INR theoretically empowers all bureaus on the Secretary's behalf; in practice, it understands which ones will and will not be influential on a decision according to the Secretary's wishes and distributes intelligence accordingly. Indeed, recognition of this power

---

[41] Ibid., 11.

[42] Indeed, Robert Blackwill who, quoted previously, developed a special relationship with his team of analysts from the CIA, believed this was not possible in the State Department because INR was less able to meet his needs. As he stated it, INR worked "for the Secretary" – not, in other words, exclusively for him. Jack Davis, *A Policymaker's Perspective on Intelligence Analysis*, p. 9.

and, thus, INR's ability to disrupt bureaucratic strategies has sometimes led senior-level decision makers to try to exclude INR itself from certain intelligence compartments. If the Secretary of State does not intervene, balance in intelligence support to the department as a whole may be seriously compromised and effective warning – the ability of lower priority issues and decisions to become higher priority when necessary – may be compromised.

Special problems arise when senior policy makers want to deny intelligence support to senior officials holding outlying views – such as a "grenade-throwing" officer in the human rights bureau or a stickler for legalities in the intelligence bureau's office for coordinating covert action. In the United States, the tool most often hijacked for this purpose – at least, when done in a formal way – is classification and security: the senior official disinterested in dissent creates a compartment with a "bigot list" including only the names of the insiders.[43] Notwithstanding whether the original reason is benign or even positive – for instance, protecting sources and methods – the result is degraded intelligence for "need-to-know" outsiders, such as relevant analysts and intelligence advisors, with predictably distorting effects. Handicapped in performing the sensitive jobs for which they are accountable, officers may find themselves publicly responsible for failures in which they played no part and about which they have only incomplete knowledge. If an outsider's retribution for damaged influence and career takes the form of leaks or whistle-blowing, further damage may be done.[44] Thus, ironically, perfecting support at the *individual level* – where national interest may become harnessed to bureaucratic competition – can lead to systemic failure in the form of suboptimized *national* decision making and the compromise of sources and methods.

For these reasons, an intelligence service's ability to anticipate and warn depends on its capacity to distance itself from the users it supports and to select efficiently those with a "need to know." The intelligence service must be able to envision threats and opportunities that current policy makers discount and alert those who may be currently excluded from the inner circles of policy making.

It is not just the capacity to warn that is at stake with this type of independence; it is also the capacity to protect sources and methods by reducing vulnerabilities. This is because the hijacking of a national-intelligence process for bureaucratic purposes and the resulting damage to the policy

---

[43] This unfortunate term is nonetheless widely used in government to describe a compartment so closely held that those within it are selected and controlled by name.

[44] This point is not meant to suggest that vindictiveness is the only or even primary motivation for leaks or whistle-blowing – only that it may be one cause that flows directly from flaws in an intelligence system.

process exacerbates counterintelligence issues over the long term. Insider spies are made, not born. In hierarchically competitive environments in which winners succeed by partnering with intelligence to exclude the losers, resentments can develop among those consistently at the bottom of the bureaucratic pile.[45] Angry about a process apparently stacked against them, repeated losers can become vulnerable to foreign services interested in exploiting frustration, rewarding revenge, or demonstrating mastery of "the game." Arguably, Robert Hanssen, the Federal Bureau of Investigation (FBI) insider spy, was an example of such a case.[46]

Of course, bureaucratic winners may make good but difficult recruits for an adversarial intelligence service because of their excellent prospects for promotions and thus greater access to secrets in the future. Spies such as Britain's Kim Philby have successfully burrowed into bureaucracies and have risen swiftly and dangerously up the intelligence and foreign-policy establishment in part because they supplemented their innate skills as bureaucrats with help from their handlers. The Philby case illustrates that when legitimacy and access to intelligence come with a standard portfolio and career path, as it does in most hierarchically organized governments, the security and counterintelligence challenge becomes increasingly difficult as that career progresses. The point here is not to suggest that decision makers should always be suspect but rather to stress the value of an intelligence service that can operate independently of influential policy makers when necessary, such as when selecting who does and does not receive intelligence.

Thus arises the first paradox of intelligence optimization: a predictable process for identifying and ranking customers is crucial. However, once established, such a process may threaten the adaptability of the intelligence system to new threats and heightens the risks of deception by both adversaries and insider spies. It is not an unreasonable hypothesis that bureaucratic systems are likely to exemplify the best and worst of this paradox. Yet, these bureaucracies also may serve as the ultimate solution. If an optimized intelligence system must have a way of identifying new decision makers and distributing intelligence support equitably among them, creation of an office or bureau with this mission in each competing bureaucracy and protecting it from bureaucratic end-runs may help to solve the paradox.

In summary, a high-quality intelligence service must be able to anticipate competitions and competitors. To do this, it must establish mechanisms that

---

[45] Dr. David Charney also made this point in discussing the Hanssen case, among others. See "The Psychology of the Insider Spy" (lecture, CPASS Series on Intelligence, Georgetown University, Washington, February 23, 2006).

[46] Of course, Hanssen volunteered his services, but he did so because of frustrations of the type mentioned here.

maintain a certain independence from the preferences of decision makers: a willingness to collect against the possibility of policy failure or mistaken priorities, a readiness to include new decision makers at the expense of the old, and a dedication to ensuring that no single decision maker succeeds too well in establishing a protective line of analytic hogs.

Despite the importance of sustaining a certain distance from the policy makers in the interest of warning and balance, an intelligence system will fail if decision makers disconnect or become alienated as a result. This is the problem of engagement and the third measure of quality: transmission capacity.

ENGAGING THE DECISION MAKER:
THE PROBLEM OF TRANSMISSION

If intelligence systems can make or break their users, then engaging one's own users once they have been identified should not be particularly difficult. Yet, it often is, particularly in complex organizations. Some decision makers may learn to distrust their intelligence system because it has persuaded their bosses to reject their advice. For others, intelligence has overwhelmed them with information irrelevant to their mission. Some decision makers dislike reports of bad outcomes despite their own best efforts. Decision makers probably instinctively distrust sources of power that they do not control and are prohibited from influencing. After all, intelligence can unsettle, confuse, or disrupt preexisting strategies. Even if warning is expected and appreciated, recipients nonetheless may suspect disloyalty to the original plan and discount the message. Thus, success in the anticipatory function described previously can actually worsen levels of trust between intelligence providers and decision makers, thereby increasing tensions and the prospect for failure.

Trust between intelligence providers and decision makers is perhaps the most critical requirement of superior performance. The point has been made many times but bears repeating: intelligence is worthless without a decision maker to use it. Without a transmission to connect the engine of intelligence to the wheels of policy, the result is much revving with little traction. In democratic states, superior intelligence services have solved this problem by establishing oversight mechanisms to reassure the electorate of their loyalty.

Unfortunately, oversight is not always enough to solve the problem; even with it, policy makers need assurances that their intelligence service is on their side in the contests they are managing. In fact, that failures of trust persist in modern intelligence systems – including in democracies with strong traditions of oversight – is attributable to regulations preventing intimacy between decision makers and intelligence officials. For example, in the United States, intelligence officials cannot study U.S. vulnerabilities and are actively discouraged from walking in the shoes of the policy makers they serve lest they lose their objectivity.

To understand why these regulations are problematic, consider the scene from the movie *Raiders of the Lost Ark*, in which a sword-wielding adversary displays his astonishing technique before an apparently dazzled Indiana Jones. After pausing momentarily, the hero pulls out a gun and shoots the swordsman dead. Audiences are entertained because they identify with the human tendency to gauge strengths through simple comparisons – the skilled swordsman *should* confound the hopeless professor. Indiana Jones's brilliant decision turned the simple comparison on its head. Intelligence, done well, enables such action. Indeed, if intelligence is to make a pedestrian bureaucrat the Indiana Jones of his game, it should have one simple objective: help the decision maker to anticipate the adversary, demystify the razzle-dazzle, and – at the right time – find the trigger. This mission requires, in the first instance, knowing one's enemy well; however, it also requires knowing one's own side and the character (i.e., pace and location) of the conflict.

In fact, knowing the user is the essential prerequisite to engaging him; therefore, it lies at the heart of the transmission problem. If the intelligence analyst simply examines the adversary's best techniques, the quality and heft of his sword, and the artfulness of his footwork, he may produce a highly accurate and objective analysis at the expense of a useful one. He not only will miss his calling, he also will make the fight more confusing and thus fail to bring added value to the situation. This is the pitfall that emerged the first time that a military commander delegated intelligence analysis to someone else – that the professional analyst would lose his orientation to the nature of the battle and thus be unable to help the commander see it more clearly. In cases such as Indiana Jones's, analysis must discern from all the flash and blur that assessments of the swordsman's skills make little sense given that the client, not the adversary, has the gun.

If intelligence managers and analysts in particular do not understand the decision makers' context, decision makers will disengage; if analysts and producers do understand it, they can become indispensable to the competition. In superior intelligence services, producers vary products to ensure that meaning – not just content – is conveyed and that this happens in a way suitable to the decision makers' needs. On the cusp of battle with a superior swordsman, shouting out useful options may be better than handing over a 15-page paper or waiting for the availability of a secure room. To be useful, intelligence production must be supremely sensitive to all aspects of the decision maker's competitive situation.

In the U.S. intelligence system, the value added of this, what might be termed "framed choice," is important enough that analysts have become the primary interface between decision makers and the intelligence system. Indeed, this is true in most modern Western intelligence systems. Analysts are responsible for representing to the diversified intelligence system the context for decision and the best methods of production (i.e., format, location, and timing). To the extent that they are well connected to the managers of collection, analysts also alert decision makers to the possibilities for and risks of getting more intelligence in time to thwart the adversary. Yet, civilian analysts in particular are also trained to believe that a "red line" must exist between themselves and the policy makers. If asked by Professor Jones about what to do in the face of the swordsman, most would stay safely mute. They have been trained to do so.

This is in part because in the U.S. case, civil-liberties concerns properly prevent the theoretically optimal result: an intelligence capability in which those analysts with expertise on the adversary *also have expertise on the client's own capabilities.* The effort to ensure that intelligence power does not bleed into domestic politics has led the U.S. federal government to limit executive intelligence powers to national security. Intelligence officers do not analyze domestic police forces, create files on weaknesses within the Department of Homeland Security, or compare the capabilities of the U.S. military services. Such investigative powers would be anathema in a secret agency. However, this limitation leaves a crucial intelligence function – net assessment – outside the formal national intelligence system. In democracies such as the United States, policy makers therefore must function to some degree as intelligence analysts. At the same time, because policy makers are properly precluded from influencing U.S. intelligence analyses, the benefits of net assessment are rarely integrated into intelligence analyses. This characteristic, in theory, is a weakness of the U.S. system because net assessment is crucial to correcting flaws in an intelligence system itself.

The problem of net assessment can be compounded by one of Western culture's greatest gifts: the rigor of scientific method and the proofs it can generate. Imbued with the ethic of "speaking truth to power," analysts may forget that power and truth exist on both sides of the analyst–customer divide and that some truths – although objective and seemingly relevant – are nonetheless distinctly unhelpful.

Consider *Raiders* again: an enlightened Indiana Jones could decide to save his bullets by having his partner garrote the swordsman from behind. Whether this makes sense requires both net assessment and bias – a desire to help the professor win by generating new options for him. Indeed, good intelligence analysis, in this instance, should illuminate the hero's options by lifting his eyes from the otherwise mesmerizing quality of the adversary's threats in order to illuminate the locus of decision advantage. If intelligence analysis does this, then its "failure" to accurately assess the length and weight of the sword or the swordsman's skill does not matter. What does matter is an analyst's ability to imagine the confrontation and then help the decision maker understand his advantages in a broader context. Analysis not relevant to that advantage *whether or not accurate* is worse than useless – it can be incapacitating.

Here lies the problem with slavish adherence to objectivity in the intelligence profession: unmoored from a stake in the outcome of a choice and precluded from analyzing his own side's strengths and weaknesses, an analyst is forced to catalogue all the facts without a guide to which ones matter most at a given instant. Presented with too much data, a decision maker may or may not hesitate; however, he is unlikely to ask the analyst back to the battle. Objectivity is good only if it diminishes bias by noting facts (like the existence of the garrote) despite the hero's past preference for the gun. Objectivity is bad if it involves neutrality toward the policy maker, an unwillingness to consider all aspects of the contest, or resistance to the strategy that frames his decisions. Optimal intelligence is not neutral. It plays sides.[47]

It is obvious that these particular lessons about the relationship of relevance to objectivity and accuracy pertain to analysis in support of military engagement as well as diplomacy. For example, after the First Battle of Bull Run during the American Civil War, General McDowell noted that his scouts had reported the Run, a narrow stream, as fordable at several points. They had failed to point out that the known approaches to these fords were only suitable for a man on foot or horseback who could manage the narrow lanes – not an entire marching army. In fact, only a few approaches were

---

[47] That this is so complicates matters for parliamentary democracies in which the opposition may play an oversight function for intelligence. As crucial as oversight is to sustained quality of an intelligence service – largely because it enhances trust among elected leaders, secret information providers, and the electorate – oversight of performance often evolves into an expectation for policy support to the legislative agenda. When an intelligence service engages different power centers with different strategic preferences and strives to serve each, it risks losing effectiveness. This is because the loyalty of the service to the executive's strategy may become suspect. The U.S. system has solved this conundrum to the extent that its congressional oversight committees act in a bipartisan manner.

suitable for a stealthy army crossing, and it took days to subsequently find them. McDowell's scouts and engineers had answered the question accurately and objectively but also wrongly. By not reflecting on their general's particular dilemma, they failed in their mission.

Such problems persisted in the modern U.S. military of the 1990s. Returning from the First Gulf War, General Schwartzkoff noted that the highly sophisticated U.S. intelligence system had given him precise and accurate information that at times proved to be useless intelligence. When he once asked for an assessment of a certain bridge prior to sending his troops in that direction, he heard that a certain percentage of it was destroyed but nothing about whether it still functioned as a bridge. His concerns were reflected in Secretary of Defense Dick Cheney's summary of the Pentagon's report on the war:

During Operation Desert Storm, the national intelligence agencies produced numerous reports and special national intelligence estimates. Field commanders have criticized some of these products as being . . . too broad, and non-predictive.[48]

These complaints echoed those made more than a century earlier by the defeated U.S. general at First Bull Run. Successful intelligence in both cases required knowing for whom the intelligence was being generated and something about the decision maker's own forces (the weight and agility of heavy equipment, for example). Even if conducting such net assessments is determined to be beyond the proper mandate of intelligence professionals because of concerns related to civil liberties or security, net assessment remains part of the necessary business of intelligence, and its absence heightens the problems of keeping intelligence relevant and timely. Missions may fail if scouting is left to intelligence professionals privy only to foreign obstacles – the bridge or stream – without good knowledge of the forces required to cross them.

An optimized intelligence system will counteract these built-in problems, including analytic biases and the fetish for precision over relevance. It will include mechanisms for adjusting analytic tradecraft to customers' immediate needs while also ensuring that the larger context for the competition is not lost. This requires both proximity to and distance from the decision maker – the latter not so much for the sake of some type of academic objectivity about his policies than for the purpose of knowing him and his adversary in their larger milieus. Analysts need to know what makes decision makers tick and how they might use the terrain to their respective advantages. They also need to know, from a counterintelligence standpoint,

---

[48] Department of Defense, *Conduct of the Persian Gulf War: Final Report to Congress* (Washington: U.S. Government Printing Office, 1992), Appendix C-6.

what the adversary is thinking and doing to foil their own side and its strategy in order to avoid being deceived or manipulated. Divorced from counterintelligence information, analysis easily becomes unmoored from the competitive context it is meant to serve.

An analyst's purpose *is* favoritism: he wants the client to win. Although analysts do no favors by suggesting that a win is achievable or a bridge crossable when it is not, once a more negative judgment is rejected and a general marches in that direction, analysts should generally refrain from nagging and jump to the next critical decision.[49] Their role is to assess the effect on strategy, envisioning how the enemy will react and how the players will engage in round two. This is true even if the general cites collected data on the percentage of the bridge remaining or the width of a lane to support his call. A superior intelligence service will focus less on proving the general or president wrong than on discerning the next issue and looking for the next win. By staying ahead of the decision maker – indeed, preparing the groundwork for supporting the decision maker 15 minutes or 15 years hence – an intelligence service brings value added and, potentially, an opening for wiser moves.

Although trusted relationships between the users and producers of intelligence may be difficult to discern, the existence of its precursor – a strong system of executive and legislative oversight – is not. Institutionalized oversight can help policy makers evaluate the extent to which intelligence officers are supporting their strategies while also providing the latter recourse should they feel pressure from those same policy makers to forfeit their independence and thus their capacity to warn. A system of oversight is an important indicator of an intelligence system's strength: its ability to optimize and yet also balance the functions of anticipation and transmission. Because of its critical role in enabling the independence of an intelligence service by developing a polity's trust in it, oversight that is more restrictive than enabling will greatly damage an intelligence system and generate predictable failures.

DEGRADING THE ADVERSARY'S INTELLIGENCE CAPABILITIES

To achieve most complex goals, there are no silver bullets. To achieve intelligence advantage, some say there are two: denial and deception. According to this view, even if a competitor is desperately weak, he can achieve a competitive advantage by keeping secrets and controlling the intelligence

---

[49] This is provided, of course, that the nagging is not based on new information of an anticipatory nature.

service of his adversaries so that it underperforms his own. Besieged by insurrection and the machinations of outside powers in the aftermath of World War I, the Bolsheviks developed an underground counterintelligence network known as "the Trust," which deceived exiled monarchists and lured them to the homeland for execution.[50] The Bolsheviks' success against plotters backed by relatively strong state governments, demonstrates that counterintelligence can be a highly effective way of beating an adversary, even if that opponent is militarily superior. The opponent's strength can be deflected and wasted through baits and lures.

The two critical ingredients for gaining such advantages are, first, a healthy positive intelligence system and, second, an ability to manage secrets in the context of overall strategy. Critical to the latter is a capacity for selective secrecy: hiding and revealing information in ways designed to control what an enemy knows at critical moments. To be a decisive asset, counterintelligence must be married to excellent positive intelligence so that enemy probes and one's own efforts to block and deceive may be monitored and used for larger strategic purposes. A close examination of the Trust suggests that it succeeded with its deception campaign because the Cheka had a far-reaching positive intelligence apparatus supporting it. Because deception as successful as that performed by the Trust requires an initial phase of confidence-building with the enemy – often using double agents who must establish their bona fides – it can involve high risks and costs. Such counterintelligence games are played by many in international politics; it has aptly been called a game of smoke and mirrors.

Indeed, there is nothing in the world of intelligence and espionage as difficult and potentially dangerous as counterintelligence. Counterintelligence operations can be defensive, such as protecting oneself by blocking the intelligence collection of others, or offensive, such as gaining advantage for oneself by manipulating or skewing the intelligence capabilities of others.[51] Defensive counterintelligence may involve passive means, such as locks and classification procedures, or active means, such as surveillance, moles, defector debriefings, and "dangles." These sources can tell a competitor what the enemy intelligence service is up to so that steps can be taken

---

[50] For a thumbnail sketch of the Trust, see Jeffrey Richelson, *A Century of Spies: Intelligence in the Twentieth Century* (New York: Oxford University Press, 1995).

[51] This breakdown of offensive and defensive counterintelligence takes into account the strategic dimension of the competition. However, it is not universally accepted. For a different approach, see Stan A. Taylor, "Definitions and Theories of Counterintelligence," in Loch Johnson (ed.), *Strategic Intelligence: Counterintelligence and Counterterrorism, Defending the Nation Against Hostile Forces* (Westport, CT: Praeger Security Iternational, 2007), pp. 1–13.

to better protect intelligence processes – including sensitive decision mak-ing – from degradation or manipulation. Offensive operations are similarly divided into active and passive measures. The former may involve dou-ble agents and deception; the latter often involves dummy deployments or camouflage. In either case, offensive counterintelligence does not so much block the opponent's operations as it distorts his *thinking* to the perpetra-tor's advantage, whether or not the perpetrator's own intelligence assets are at risk from the opposing service. The better an intelligence service is, the greater will be others' temptation to control or manipulate it to their advantage because of the influence that may be gained over an opponent's decisions. That said, the better the targeted service, the more likely it is to catch these machinations and use them for its own purposes.[52] This makes counterintelligence a highly effective weapon but not a silver bullet.

Both active and passive defensive counterintelligence can be a bottomless pit for dollars and the source of great disadvantages as well. It is a pitfall, in particular, for the relatively powerful because they believe, often rightly, that their intelligence systems and associated secrets are vital targets for others. However, this is not always the case. First, what is important to one's own strategy may not always be crucial to the adversary's. The September 11 hijackers accomplished their mission without breaking any U.S. codes or stealing any of Washington's secrets. They frequently acted in the open, trusting the speed of their decision making and the secrecy of their tactical objectives to outpace the reaction times of U.S. counterintelligence agencies. This example has a parallel in business when established firms invest in protecting their proprietary information while overlooking innovations by startups that make such investments a waste.

Second, adding defenses can have unintended, magnetic effects. In a recently reported study of risk, Professor Ian Walker of the University of Bath has shown that putting on a helmet while bicycling leads British drivers to increase speed and proximity as compared to the results when cycling bare-headed.[53] Defenses that reduce vulnerability may increase boldness and aggressive tendencies that increase risk in unexpected ways. Good counter-intelligence choices require analysis of actions and reactions in the context of the strategies of all relevant parties. In some cases, such analysis may suggest that neither denial nor deception would be as effective as simple influence: discouraging an opponent from looking again at a vulnerability

[52] Counterintelligence, done well, provides information on the adversary that can be used by decision makers for strategic or tactical purposes.
[53] "Risk Averse Across the Atlantic," *The Economist*, February 28, 2008.

that he has discounted or encouraging him to recognize the fallacies that his intelligence service is generating and thus to distrust it.

These examples illustrate the dangerous fallacy of assuming that the rigorous protection of self-selected secrets secures intelligence advantages and that increases in security necessarily increase protection from threat. Some competitors do not care about gathering government secrets, thereby reducing the requirement to protect them; some are obsessed with collecting secrets, thereby leaving anything unprotected reasonably safe; others may not know what they need to protect to win; and still others hide in the open to deliberately mislead their adversaries. Confusion about the role of secrets in intelligence practice can dangerously damage and distort sound counter-intelligence policy. What is certain is that if counterintelligence managers focus on securing secrets as their principal mission, they are likely to gravely weaken the very intelligence enterprise that they seek to protect.

Passive defense is not the only problem; active defense can have its costs. Before the Battle of Trenton, Hessian troops defending the city were sent on frequent nighttime patrols and kept on alert against the threat of harassing attacks from the Continental Army. By the time the attack came, the guards had become too weary to struggle against the raging blizzard that was engulf-ing nearby roads. It was at that moment that General Washington attacked, achieving tactical surprise. Whereas Hessian patrols used defensive coun-terintelligence in the form of patrols, the Continental Army used offensive techniques: ferreting initiatives designed less to collect positive intelligence than to alarm Hessian patrols and influence their reporting. The Conti-nental Army succeeded in straining the Hessians' resources and, by beating hasty retreats, in encouraging assumptions of American incompetence.[54] The lessons here are clear: efforts to protect an intelligence system must increase as the quality of that system improves; but if taken as an absolute good, defensive counterintelligence can become excessive, thereby thwarting risk-taking, dulling collection, and draining resources.

Offensive counterintelligence, conversely, offers both greater advantages and greater risks than its defensive counterpart. It includes efforts to mislead or degrade the intelligence activities of the adversary – ideally so that his decisions are worse than they would have been without any intelligence at all. Saddam Hussein used passive offensive measures to great effect prior to the First Gulf War. As detailed by David Kay, those measures included housing nuclear-weapons activities in buildings designed to look benign and

---

[54] Fischer, *Washington's Crossing*, pp. 194–282.

using other sophisticated camouflage techniques.[55] Saddam's manipulation of U.S. decision making required understanding – not blocking – U.S. collection efforts. It required in-depth knowledge of the capabilities of U.S. imagery satellites and U.S. techniques for photo-interpretation.

Of course, the highest form of offensive counterintelligence is strategic deception – that is, convincing the adversary of a fiction that provides conflict-winning advantages to the perpetrator. Apart from the Trust, the most famous deception operation of modern times may have been the Double Cross System developed by Britain during World War II and used to great effect in the Normandy landings. As reported by John Masterman, who ran the highly secret committee in charge of Double Cross, the most crucial instruments for this deception were double agents and ULTRA, the highly secret intercepts of the German high command that showed that Hitler trusted the double agents under British control.[56] This latter capability is important because managing deception involves difficult trade-offs – the most difficult of which may be the decision to finally feed the adversary a fiction that cripples him at a crucial moment. Once this is accomplished, the double agent is likely to be exposed as the source of the disaster. The manager of double agents must therefore weigh the degree of exposure for each of his assets and be closely connected to policy makers to ensure that the timing and character of the planned deception truly will provide decision advantages. Given the need to prove their productivity without giving away too much, double agents are always at risk.[57]

Perhaps the most misunderstood aspect of counterintelligence, however, is the relationship of both passive and defensive forms to positive intelligence collection. A competitor who learns from his adversary's moves

---

[55] David Kay, "Denial and Deception: The Lessons of Iraq," 109–28.

[56] Double agents are spies, employed by one competitor, who are "turned" by the opponent and work secretly for him. Nested in their host's intelligence collection network, double agents can feed false information to the adversarial decision makers, thereby corrupting their options, timing, and choices. They differ from moles by function: double agents perform espionage on behalf of two services; moles burrow inside the intelligence superstructure, using their access to provide intelligence to their handlers.

[57] Offensive counterintelligence can involve the secret manipulation of political, economic, or military activities overseas – covert action – albeit for purposes of protecting one's own plans and operations. It is, therefore, a most difficult game for democracies to play. Covert action, by the definition of intelligence used here, is not properly considered part of an intelligence enterprise unless it is associated with this counterintelligence aspect. Covert action is secret policy that intelligence must support because it supports other forms of policy making; however, absent the counterintelligence function, covert action is a quite separate endeavor.

against him and incorporates that knowledge to expand his options or adapt his own offensive strategy will be able to gain decision advantages over a competitor who does not. Indeed, at this level of sophisticated intelligence management, counterintelligence becomes almost indistinguishable from positive foreign-intelligence collection because it reveals what the adversary is thinking. For example, if passive security identifies repeated attempts to break into a database about the Hoover Dam, this may be as valid an indicator of an opponent's intentions as HUMINT indications of adversary intent.[58] For these reasons, a counterintelligence service disconnected from or lacking intimacy with policy makers or one that delegates most of its work to security or law enforcement professionals will be of lesser quality than one that does not.[59]

CONCLUSION

Intelligence theory augments our understanding of power by explaining how power influences or fails to influence choices of both individuals and, ultimately, states. Those with better intelligence have a better understanding of power relationships and, therefore, superior means to adapt to the environment in which they operate. Well-equipped states can thus find their niche or optimize their decision making to fit what realism suggests is the "best" course of action in a particular circumstance, such as balancing or "bandwagoning." A sound intelligence system characterizes the nature and structure of international competition at all phases of decision – from the moment decision makers recognize a conflict through their design of strategy and tactics – to help states secure favorable outcomes. Intelligence systems thus generate a form of power that makes a difference in international politics.

For simplicity, this chapter has grouped the attributes of a sound intelligence system into four functions: collection, anticipation, transmission, and counterintelligence. Operationalizing the requirements of these functions in detail and testing their importance to outcomes in particular international conflicts are beyond the scope of this chapter. Still, a few tentative hypotheses about U.S. intelligence capabilities are possible using this theoretical approach. The intelligence power of a state is always best considered in a

---

[58] Example supplied by Matthew Walker, personal communication, October 2006.
[59] I elaborated on these ideas in a volume, co-edited with Burton Gerber, *Vaults, Mirrors, and Masks: Rediscovering U.S. Counterintelligence* (Washington: Georgetown University Press) 2009.

comparative context because the test of sufficiency is beating opponents. That said, as the dominant state in the international system, the United States can expect others, including friends, to seek to leverage power by exploiting U.S. weaknesses. It behooves us to find them before they do.

So, what of current U.S. intelligence capabilities? A brief list of impressions may guide future study. First, regarding collection, the United States seems both gifted and hobbled. On the one hand, the intelligence community has a close alliance with its industrial base – a collection system with sophisticated sensors; air-, sea-, and land-based platforms; and secure worldwide communications. On the other hand, for sound political reasons, these systems are largely prohibited from domestic operations against adversaries operating within U.S. borders. Inside the United States, official collection is in the hands of those charged with counterintelligence – principally the FBI, which does not (and arguably should not) consider itself an intelligence collector working on behalf of political interests and diplomacy as opposed to law enforcement and homeland security. Information held by businesses and airlines that could provide indications and warning of attack may not find its way to the government even during crises, especially now that telephone companies are being rebuked for having done so in the past. Yet, the development of protocols for the appropriate sharing of information from the private sector to the federal government is in its infancy at best. In the meantime, "fusions centers" – created by localities to build case files on suspicious domestic activity but operating without national consensus on their scope or oversight – are possibly transgressing legal boundaries, thus generating increased attention by the media. In these ways, the range of U.S. intelligence collection remains constrained against agile transnational adversaries as well as perceptive foreign services, such as the Chinese, who are increasingly engaged in industrial espionage.

The problem of domestic operations aside, the individual components of the collection systems seem only loosely integrated. Collection managers for human, technical, and open-source intelligence have little insight into or control over the platforms, sensors, processing, and communications integral to their work. This is because the system components are owned by competing bureaucracies, many of which lie outside the formal intelligence community. The problem here is not excessive hierarchical controls or "stovepipes" but rather just the reverse. Because of this lack of integrated management, U.S. collectors are probably less flexible than they should be in a world that demands agility more than ever.

Second, regarding the anticipatory function, the U.S. intelligence system also gets mixed marks. It has a well-established process for reading-in new bureaucrats and a capacity for secure, worldwide dissemination. However, its warning system is seriously flawed. Current, predominantly military decision makers dominate a requirements system that should be better balanced and is far too top-down in orientation. Civilian HUMINT, considered a risky collection system of last resort, tends to forgo opportunities that emerge unexpectedly in favor of responding to threats already perceived. Strategic analysis and collection are difficult to sustain, perhaps because they seem less exciting and immediately useful to current decision makers. Yet, strategic and tactical analysis should be both relevant to current policy and vice versa.[60] To study strategic trends productively, an intelligence system must be aware of how competitions are playing out; it must study its own side's expectations and priorities in order to remain alert to the unexpected. An intelligence system also must temper its preference for all-source over single-source strategic analysis. Human collectors embedded in foreign countries may sense trends in ways that current all-source analysts cannot. The long-held belief that analysis and collection are separate endeavors makes the problem worse. The processing and exploitation performed by collectors, although perhaps not "all-source," nonetheless can be actionable in certain circumstances. If collectors do not have the authority to collect unrequested information and act on the basis of their own analysis, policy makers undermine an intelligence service's ability to warn and forfeit their own opportunities for swift interdiction.

In fact, the problems in getting threat information to the U.S. Coast Guard, police, or first responders before September 11 suggest that the system – good at clearing those with known portfolios – is biased against new national-security decision makers. No one in the U.S. intelligence system appears to be equipped and directly responsible for linking strategic warning with timely changes in dissemination practices so that the right decision makers get the information in time. In addition, efforts to protect sensitive collection methods may skew debate in favor of the few who are granted access to certain highly restricted compartments – typically, those with the highest ranking, not with the greatest need. The system also seems inadvertently biased toward the national-security *policy* elite and only haphazardly serving those *managers* responsible for decisions related to collection platforms, buildings, communications, logistics, and so forth. In the Department of State, for example, INR has not traditionally provided regular support to management bureaus; it has worked only fitfully for

---

[60] The concept of "safe haven" presumes an uneducated decision maker; educated ones do not retaliate against those who warn about the unexpected.

diplomatic security and embassy administrators. Across the government, current policy makers dominate collection priorities at the expense of new or prospective ones or those responsible for intelligence management. An ombudsman, accountable to the Director of National Intelligence (DNI), is needed to identify critical emerging decision makers, expedite their entry into the intelligence system, and ensure that intelligence is properly balanced among all recipients.

Third, U.S. intelligence probably overemphasizes what has been called the "red line": the intelligence–decision maker divide. The result is loss of trust, intimacy, and discretion in the relationship. Decision makers seem not to recognize or value their critical roles in intelligence performance or their potential culpability for intelligence failures. At the same time, U.S. intelligence officers often do not seem to believe they are working *on behalf of* policy makers or as part of their team. They tend to see themselves as a check on an administration's power and the repository of truth in a system riddled with biases. Thus, "speaking truth to power" has become the mantra of an intelligence service juxtaposed to policy and intent on inoculating itself against the competitive world of which policy is a part. Although policy makers do want intelligence to provide facts or "ground-truth," other branches of government have the job of checking the power of those in office, not intelligence. The job of intelligence is to help the state succeed in securing national interests; this requires truth telling and power sharing across the intelligence–policy divide – a divide all the more dangerous in the U.S. case because the U.S. system does not integrate net assessments into the intelligence function.

This point is worth special emphasis: U.S. intelligence managers may not be sufficiently careful when urging "objectivity."[61] Objectivity is bad when it is translated as "neutral to policy," that is, as a willingness to entertain all questions equally, regardless of their relevance to strategy and decisions. Unrestrained subservience to "objectivity" in the latter sense may cause analysts to detach themselves from the policy contest, lose their creative edge (including the ability to imagine what information might be needed to win), or prove points past their moment of relevancy. All these effects can undermine the intimacy so necessary for a productive working relationship with the decision maker. Similarly, indiscriminate information

[61] See Kevin Russell, "The Subjectivity of Intelligence Analysis and Implications for the U.S. National Security Strategy," *SAIS Review*, 24, 1 (Winter/Spring 2004): 147–63; Harry Howe Ransom, "The Politicization of Intelligence," in Loch Johnson and James Wirtz, (eds.), *Strategic Intelligence: Windows into a Secret World* (Los Angeles: Roxbury Publishing), pp. 171–97.

sharing, disconnected from decision makers' needs, will lead to mistrust as well. Although sharing is necessarily emphasized in the post–September 11 context, too little importance is currently placed on ensuring that what is shared is useful to those receiving it – a judgment that requires good knowledge of one's own side.

Of course, privatizing or politicizing intelligence does not help the team beat an adversary either. Policy makers need unvarnished information – particularly when they are blind to the consequences of their policies. They will, however, discount information delivered by those persistently professing neutrality to the cause. In fact, as the problem of net assessment makes clear, intelligence officers have no more exclusive claim to truth than decision makers have exclusive grip on power. Intelligence analysts have jobs quite different from university scholars, whose work can be conducted in relative isolation and without regard to its eventual application to policy problems.[62] The evaluations and promotions of intelligence officers should reflect that difference.

Fourth, the U.S. system seems weak in its counterintelligence functions: much more is invested in passive denial than in active defensive and offensive capabilities and too little synergy exists between counterintelligence analysis and national-security strategy. Although U.S. intelligence is not perfect, opponents also are susceptible to analytic and operational pathologies; it is not clear that the United States is good at mapping and exploiting these to gain strategic advantage. Even if we were better at understanding opponents, insights derived from counterintelligence operations are better integrated into law enforcement than into national-security policy making. The flawed assumption persists that adversaries will always want to know what we hold most secret – namely, what we know from our collection systems – rather than what they need to know to gain decision advantage. Adversaries may not care if they are being watched as long as they succeed in blowing something up, acquiring nuclear-weapons technologies, or launching a preemptive strike against an ally before the U.S. system can respond effectively.

Whether these apparent problems with U.S. intelligence are grave or minor will require separate and more detailed study. However, the list inspires a concluding point: intelligence reform should do more than simply

---

[62] For important parallels with the role of universities and political science in national discourse – parallels that may explain the persistence in the United States of this notion that an analytic "ivory tower" constitutes sound intelligence practice – see John G. Gunnell, "The Founding of the American Political Science Association: Discipline, Profession, Political Theory, and Politics," *American Political Science Review, 100*, 4, November 2006.

register a reaction to one disaster, calamitous as it may have been. Reform should be based on a comprehensive review of strengths and weaknesses in light of present and coming competitions. Intelligence reform should be about sharpening and amplifying a form of power crucial to national security and, ultimately, international stability.

FIVE

Intelligence Analysis after the Cold War – New Paradigm or Old Anomalies?

Wilhelm Agrell

Intelligence organisations, in their modern 20th-century form, are not only providers of information acquired through what is traditionally described as special means. Intelligence organisations or communities are also increasingly expected to achieve some sort of comprehension of a general situation and the course of specific events. In the best of worlds, this comprehension can be transformed into useful background analysis or warning – whether early or late, specific or general – that something is or might be developing in the domain that the intelligence service is expected to monitor. In the real world, lack of comprehension and, thus, of foresight is a common phenomenon, so common that it now constitutes the dominating theme of intelligence studies. Remove the failures and little is left of what is written about intelligence analysis and its use during the Cold War and beyond. Huge efforts have thus been expended to investigate and ponder why intelligence has been unable to deliver what was rightfully or wrongfully expected from it and to find solutions in terms of intelligence reform, often focused on reorganisation. This failure–investigation–reorganisation cycle has become something of a malaise of early 21st-century Western intelligence.[1]

---

[1] The term *intelligence* is often used synonymously with *U.S. intelligence*. Although it is a gross oversimplification to regard intelligence as a homogeneous global phenomenon, U.S. intelligence and experience, for a number of obvious reasons, spill over to the intelligence organisations and cultures in other Western countries, most of which are formally or informally linked in liaison networks and alliances. Therefore, although all U.S. intelligence experiences are U.S.-specific, some of them have broader implications either because they concern general technical, cognitive, or intellectual aspects of intelligence or because of the implications of a U.S.-centric intelligence culture. Accordingly, other national experiences have a corresponding relevance for the general aspects of intelligence (the Yom Kippur War being one of the most commonly referred-to examples); however, they hardly have significance beyond this because of the structure and perspective of the international intelligence discourse.

A consensus has emerged on the necessity to transform intelligence and improve its ability to analyse and deliver foresight. However, neither reorganisation nor analytic training is a sufficient answer. The fundamental problem is the implicit model for knowledge production in intelligence systems that have been in place for more than a half-century. If the problem is the intellectual output, transformation has to address it – that is, with the way intelligence *thinks.*

Intelligence is not a science but rather something that could be called a protoscience: a field of intellectual problem-solving but thus far lacking a comprehensive set of theories, a scientific discourse, and self-reflection. During the Cold War, this protoscience flourished and established an intelligence paradigm so dominating that it was regarded not as a way to see the world but as the world itself. Anomalies – pieces not fitting into the giant puzzle – were routinely disregarded. The slow and reactive awareness of the process of breakup of the Cold War order was typical and constitutes one of the major analytic intelligence failures of the 20th century – fortunately, not accompanied by a corresponding security failure.

In this chapter, I discuss the underlying analytic problems facing intelligence in the transformation from the Cold War to a far more complex and rapidly changing intelligence environment. Are all the discovered problems, the failures, and the criticism a consequence of the adjustment – or, rather, lack of adjustment – to this transformation from a world order to a world with (assumed) increasing disorder? Or, is perhaps the critical question stated in the wrong way and the answer sought is under the streetlight and not where it might be located, in much the same way that the intelligence failures themselves seem to arise? Is there a more fundamental problem in intelligence that simply became more important and, hence, more visible in the post–Cold War context? Is there, to invoke Hamlet, something rotten in the state of intelligence as such? These questions are not new and have resulted in a growing literature.[2] However, I take my point of departure not in this recent discourse but rather in a personal experience from the Cold War period.

A BRIEF ENCOUNTER WITH THE UNTHINKABLE

I joined the Swedish Air Force intelligence in 1974 as a junior analyst at the air staff intelligence branch, a part of the central military intelligence

---

[2] For examples of this debate on the dominating modus operandi of Western intelligence, see Michael Herman, *Intelligence Power in Peace and War* (Cambridge: Cambridge University Press, 1996); and Gregory F. Treverton, *Reshaping National Intelligence in the Age of Information* (Cambridge: Cambridge University Press, 2001).

machinery. Working in the analytic section, by the autumn of 1975 I had been assigned the task of monitoring training and tactics of the Soviet *Frontovaya Aviatsiya*, primarily the units based in the Baltic Military District that were regarded as the main opponent of the Swedish Air Force in case of war. These were the years of détente, the signing of the Helsinki Treaty; war was far away mentally, a contingency safely deposited at the far end of the long-term planning process. Intelligence worked according to the procedures of a night watchman, checking that the Soviet forces conducted "normal activities" according to the pattern well known to our intelligence and logged in the periodic reports. There was even a secret handbook, a type of intelligence almanac, describing the cycle of normal activities of the Warsaw Pact forces in the Baltic area during the year. The watchmen simply had to check the almanac, log the current events, and all was well. The weekly intelligence summary always started with the phrase, "No signs of increased preparedness in foreign forces in neighboring areas". This mantra never changed, year after year, even when the Soviet forces, during a major summer maneuver in the Baltic, embarked elements of a motorised rifle division on landing crafts and ro-ro (roll-on/roll-off) ships and put to sea along the eastern coast. Ground-force units also embarked and in the Baltic Sea was the paramount warning indicator for a surprise attack. Yet, when the formulation of the infamous first sentence of the intelligence summary was raised at an intelligence briefing, it was like a joke to see if any subordinates would even notice. It was a humorous idea but, of course, nothing came out of it. War was unthinkable and so was surprise.[3]

Monday, 10 November 1975, was by any standard a typical working day in the intelligence community, or so it seemed at first. Sometime that morning, I met a colleague from the radar intelligence (RADINT) section in the corridor. The RADINT section screened and analysed the intelligence recorded by the radar network of the STRIL-60 air defence system. The raw intelligence was processed, interpreted, and passed on to other users, among them the analytic section. Because we shared the same premises and had morning coffee together, urgent intelligence and odd features were usually passed on in an informal way. Somewhat amused, my RADINT colleague greeted me with, "Your Brewers were out flying yesterday morning". By my "Brewers", he meant the strike regiments of the 30th Tactical Aviation Army

---

[3] However, normal precautions were taken in terms of intelligence-gathering and the Soviet armada was shadowed by Swedish reconnaissance planes. Photographs taken of the ro-ro ships were later published in a declassified report of the Soviet manoeuvre, *Sovjetiska Östersjömarinen – landstigningsövning*, 1978 (Soviet Baltic Fleet – landing manoeuvre 1978), Defence Staff information branch 1978-10-20.

in the Baltic Military District, which was still equipped with the aging Yak-28 Brewer light bombers. That they were out flying was nothing remarkable; the odd thing was the timing. Sunday mornings were typically a time of widespread inactivity in the Soviet Air Force, and November 7 was the Soviet revolutionary anniversary, after which it usually took a few days off for aircrews to recover to flying conditions.

As the intelligence material was more closely investigated, it turned out that the Brewers had not only been up flying; they obviously had also been engaged in bombing-run training. The strange thing was that they seemed to have practiced on a sea target, which was far more disturbing than the choice of day, which represented a break in the well-known postrevolution anniversary alcohol-induced blackout. The Soviet tactical air force was supposed to support the operations of the Soviet ground forces, and the navy had its own naval air force, one for each fleet.

This would have been a minor new occurrence among others had it not been for a previous request from one of the numerous defence-planning bodies demanding an intelligence assessment on the likelihood that the Soviet Union might use its tactical air power against the Swedish surface fleet. Because I did not know much about this – in fact, nothing – I asked my predecessor and got an unambiguous answer: the *Frontovaya Aviatsiya* did not do naval support, was not equipped for it, and had never trained for it. So, I wrote an answer accordingly. However, the Soviet units were obviously doing something they had never done before, and my firm assessment was perhaps not that firm after all or, even worse, a piece of unintentional disinformation fed into the machinery of the defence-planning process. I kept a close watch on the Brewers for some time to see if they would continue their naval training. To my relief, everything returned to normal, with the bombers dropping their loads over their familiar sandpit in Latvia, as prescribed by the "Big Book" of normal activity.

Several months later, a Swedish newspaper published an article about an attempted mutiny on what was described as a Soviet minesweeper in the harbour of Riga. According to the article, some crew members had seized the ship and attempted to defect; however, they were caught and brought to trial. Bells now started to ring here and there and various bodies of the intelligence community took a closer look at the "anomalies" in November 1975. The picture that emerged now was completely different.

Early on Sunday, November 9, in the prevailing postrevolution-anniversary lull, part of the crew of the modern Soviet Krivak-class destroyer *Storozevoy* mutinied, led by their political officer. The *Storozevoy* quietly left the naval harbour at Riga and set sail westward. In the Irben Strait, the coast watch started to sense that something was wrong and called the ship but received no answer. The entire command and control system of the Baltic fleet was on alert, the admiral went to the command center, and all available ships were sent out to chase the assumed defector. Around 8:30 p.m., the light bombers were alerted and were in the air heading for the ship that was now leaving Soviet territorial waters. As it turned out, our intelligence assessment had been correct: the Brewers performed poorly, hitting wide of the mark, and finally mistaking one of the chasing ships for the mutineer.

However, the renewed review of the raw intelligence also revealed something else far more disturbing than the Brewers that the RADINT analyst had spotted. An hour and a half hour later, at 10 p.m., the *Storozevoy* was roughly midway between Soviet and Swedish territorial waters at northern Gotland. A Tu-16 bomber of the Badger-C model from the Baltic Fleet Naval Aviation had taken off and was approaching from the south but was still some 35 to 40 nautical miles away. The Badger-C, typically equipped with an AS-3 Kipper anti-ship stand-off missile, locked the tracking radar on the *Storozevoy* and received orders from ground control to "launch the weapon", presumably the Kipper. As the crew prepared the launch, the plane reported that it had lost tracking of the target and had to abort the attack. Shortly thereafter, the plane was ordered to return to base because the *Storozevoy* had surrendered and the mutiny was over.[4]

The *Storozevoy* mutiny was a sudden close encounter with at least a serious military incident and perhaps with the improbable ghost of war by mistake. The destruction of a capital ship of whatever nationality by an air-to-surface missile on international waters was definitely not in accordance with the prevailing normality. However, from an intelligence perspective, the event – or, rather, nonevent – illustrates a number of limitations in the way intelligence analysis deals with problems in the surrounding world. Some of the limitations have a distinct local character; others are familiar from the international scene and literature. Some have an unmistaken Cold War touch; others are of a more general character, concerning an intelligence

---

[4] Little reliable information has been published on the *Storozevoy* or Krivak 500 drama, famous mainly for inspiring Tom Clancy to the plot in *The Hunt for Red October*. Some parts of Swedish raw intelligence on the incident were recently declassified. This material includes recordings from the Swedish Air Force radar station R-130 (now decommissioned) on eastern Gotland, a high-powered surveillance radar used primarily for early warning and intelligence collection. It has been claimed that the leader of the mutiny, the political officer Sabling, was a staunch communist and that his intention was not defection but rather to sail to Leningrad to protest the sloppy conditions in the fleet. Apart from being a rather bizarre purpose of an undertaking as deadly as a mutiny, the Leningrad version is clearly contradicted by the available radar intelligence.

heritage that is becoming increasingly problematic in the 21st century. The most fundamental of these problems can be summarised as the failure to comprehend new knowledge.

RESISTANCE TO NEW AND UNWANTED KNOWLEDGE
IN SCIENCE AND INTELLIGENCE

In 1962, the still mostly unknown philosopher and expert in the history of science Thomas S. Kuhn published an essay that would become an academic blockbuster, achieving – together with Kuhn himself – academic cult status and providing fuel for decades of debate about the nature of scientific knowledge.[5] "The Structure of Scientific Revolutions" was not only about revolutions in knowledge; it also was a revolution itself. What Kuhn delivered was an attack against the prevailing and, according to him, uncritical and unhistorical self-image of science in general and classical physics in particular – an image of continuously growing knowledge and discoveries leading to new discoveries. Kuhn introduced an element of relativity into the scientific claim for objectivity and absolute although incomplete knowledge: the truth was simply what everyone agreed to be true, not the Truth with a capital T.[6]

Employing a predominantly historical and sociological approach, Kuhn argued that scientific knowledge does not grow through a cumulative process, where new data, by definition, result in new theories. Instead, there is an inherent resistance within the scientific system that blocks the acceptance of new data that contradicts the dominating intellectual framework, the famous scientific paradigm. So, what Kuhn observed was that we cannot understand the development of interpretations, of theories, from the production and influx of new data. The development (or nondevelopment) must be understood in terms of the powerful intellectual, cognitive, and social mechanisms of the scientific community.

Here, "normal science" dominates, a puzzle-solving in which new research results are merged into an established frame of reference and those results (and research) that do not fit are rejected, which is perceived as

---

[5] Thomas S. Kuhn, *The Structure of Scientific Revolutions* (Chicago: University of Chicago Press, 1962, 1970, and 1996).

[6] There is a vast literature on Kuhn, the theory put forward in his seminal book, and the debate initiated by this work. For a summary of this literature, see the introduction in Wes Sharrock and Rupert Read, *Kuhn: Philosopher of Scientific Revolution* (Cambridge: Polity Press, 2002). See also Steve Fuller, *Thomas Kuhn: A Philosophical History for Our Time* (Chicago: University of Chicago Press, 2002) and *Kuhn vs. Popper* (Cambridge: Icon Books, 2003).

a legitimate protection of the purity and virtues of science. According to Kuhn's theory, the paradigm tends to outlive itself due to these protective mechanisms; the contradictions or anomalies have to build up to a point where the paradigm finally collapses. This results in a period of confusion with insufficient or nonexisting theories to explain the data available, which paves the way for "revolutionary science", gradually transforming into a new normal science. To simplify his theory, Kuhn concluded that general and well-known sociological and psychological mechanisms also were operating within scientific communities. As shown in many types of experiments, individuals tend to see what they expect to see and groups tend to develop and maintain consensus – the famous "groupthink".[7]

One of the key elements, and perhaps the most striking, is the resistance to new knowledge under the conditions that Kuhn described as normal science; that is, the periods when order prevails and when science is directed not towards new discoveries but rather to confirm the dominating theory. The dominating activity is what Kuhn labelled "mopping-up operations", easily recognised in other fields:

Mopping-up operations are what engage most scientists throughout their careers. They constitute what I am here calling normal science. Closely examined, whether historically or in the contemporary laboratory, that enterprise seems an attempt to force nature into the preformed and relatively inflexible box that the paradigm supplies. No part of the aim of normal science is to call forth new sorts of phenomena; indeed, those that will not fit the box are often not seen at all.[8]

The most important contribution of Kuhn's theory has perhaps been indirect in highlighting the institutional and conceptual context of knowledge production. Not even science – the profession with the most outspoken devotion to compassionate search for new knowledge and the critical reappraisal of common wisdom – can avoid getting trapped in the invisible net of normality or orthodoxy. Subsequently, new elements of the science-policy system have unintentionally entrenched normal science as the focus of peer review, evaluation, and priorities and forms of research funding.

The idea that the scientific community is a social entity among others and that scientific knowledge develops in a social and human context is hardly controversial today. The same is the case with the media, which

---

[7] For groupthink in intelligence, see Richard J. Heuer, *Psychology of Intelligence Analysis* (Washington: Center for the Study of Intelligence, 1999). A detailed discussion of groupthink at work is found in Rob Johnston, *Analytic Culture in the U.S. Intelligence Community: An Ethnographic Study* (Washington: Center for the Study of Intelligence, 2005).

[8] Kuhn, p. 24.

is generally regarded as the producer rather than the transmitter of news and the powerful creator of the frames of reference according to which the output is interpreted. That the social context also is relevant for knowledge production in intelligence is not a new insight either and constitutes a main theme in the literature, from Roberta Wohlstetter's classic work on Pearl Harbor[9] to the post–September 11 discourse. However, does Kuhn matter in this context? Is the behavior of intelligence communities similar to those scientific communities from which the theory of paradigms, normal science, and revolutionary change was formulated? If so, then why?

The structure of intelligence production and comprehension tradition-ally has been dominated by the pre-Kuhn concept of the intelligence cycle – the rational, linear process of demand, planning, collection, interpretation, analysis, and dissemination. Thus, problems in intelligence performance generally have been regarded as malfunctions in terms of guidance, organi-sation, training, and resources. However, the similarities between the intel-ligence failure literature and Kuhn's theory of the mindsets and modus operandi of the scientific community are striking.[10]

Because these cases of failure in function – especially early warning – are so arresting, it is not surprising that they have been so prominent in research on intelligence, a point made by Warner, Andrew, and others in this volume. The individual case in which the concept of paradigm has been employed most clearly to explain an analytic process is the failure of the Israeli intelligence community to assess the mounting flood of indications of war during the summer and autumn of 1973, culminating in the joint Egyptian–Syrian attack on October 6 and the October War. In its report on the intelligence failure, the commission headed by the High Court judge, Shimon Agranat, sought the major explanation in a phenomenon resem-bling Kuhn's paradigm: the overall assessment made by the research branch of the Israeli Defence Force intelligence, known as "the conception". Accord-ing to this explanation, war was impossible until the balance of power had shifted to the extent that the Arab forces could deny Israel air supremacy over the battle area and hit targets in the Israeli rear. The assessment behind the conception was reasonable enough. It was based on an almost complete intelligence picture of the military capability of the Egyptian and Syrian armed forces, as well as detailed insight into the operational intentions of the Egyptians, through Israeli access to the complete although not updated

---

[9] Roberta Wohlstetter, *Pearl Harbor: Warning and Decision* (Stanford, CA: Stanford Univer-sity Press, 1962).

[10] Wohlstetter; Ephraim Kam, *Surprise Attack: The Victim's Perspective* (Cambridge, MA: Harvard University Press, 1988) and Richard Betts, *Surprise Attack: Lessons for the Defense Planning* (Washington: Brookings Institute, 1982).

operational plan for the Suez front.[11] The major failure lay in the overall commonsense-based conclusion that because the combined Egyptian–Syrian forces were insufficient to defeat the Israeli forces and achieve the assumed territorial goals, there would be no attack. The assessment was wrong because it missed the possibility that war could have a political and symbolic aim rather than a military and territorial purpose. The assessment also missed that the Egyptians and Syrians could assess differently the balance of power and the operational options available and that this assessment, rather than the "objective" one, would guide their actions.[12]

During a prolonged warning period, Israeli intelligence received a stream of indications that war was approaching, but the overall assessment of the conception blocked all attempts for revision in a type of Catch-22: indications running contrary to the conception, by definition, must be either distorted or planted disinformation. The conception, thus, was virtually impossible to falsify through reinterpretation of the intelligence flow.[13] The intelligence flow was treated as the "anomalies" described by Kuhn and as observations running contrary to the prevailing theory either adjusted to fit the theory or discarded as simply wrong or unreliable (in the Israeli case, primarily as disinformation or noise created by the annual Egyptian exercise, thereby fitting the expected picture of "normal activity").

---

[11] The Israeli intelligence coverage came from SIGINT, ground and aerial observation, and the HUMINT network run by Mossad. The "crown jewel" was the Egyptian ambassador Ashraf Marwan, special advisor to President Anwar Sadat – a source who, among other things, supplied Mossad with the planning document for the Suez front, although not the updated version employed in the attack on 6 October 1973. Marwan died in London in 2007 under unclear circumstances. For the Israeli intelligence coverage and interpretations, see Uri Bar-Joseph, *The Watchman Fell Asleep: The Surprise of Yom Kippur and Its Sources* (New York: State University of New York Press, 2005). This is the latest and by far the most comprehensive study of the 1973 Israeli intelligence failure, drawing on recently declassified intelligence assessments in the period preceding the war. See also the classical work on the war by Chaim Herzog, *The War of Atonement* (London: Weidenfelt and Nicolson, 1975); Ephraim Kahana, "Early Warning versus Concept: The Case of the Yom Kippur War," *Intelligence and National Security*, 17, 2 (Summer 2002); P. R. Kumaraswamy (ed.), *Revisiting the Yom Kippur War* (London: Frank Cass, 2000); and Saad el Shazli, *The Crossing of the Suez* (San Francisco: American Mideast Research, 2003).

[12] This mistake is similar to the notorious failure of the CIA to predict the deployment of Soviet nuclear missiles in Cuba in 1962, an act that ran contrary to all assessments of Soviet behavior. See James G. Blight and David A. Welch, *Intelligence and the Cuban Missile Crisis* (London: Frank Cass, 1998).

[13] The conception finally collapsed in the early morning hours of October 6, with war less than 12 hours away, when Marwan contacted Mossad and gave positive confirmation that the war would start that day. The head of Israeli intelligence, General Zeira, later claimed that Marwan misled him by not giving the warning in time and that he was an Egyptian double agent planted to mislead the Israelis about the coming attack. See Bar-Joseph, cited previously.

In the Yom Kippur case, as well as in numerous other known or lesser known cases, the impact of a hierarchical and compartmentalised structure is visible. So is the impact of puzzle-solving and filling in of gaps, with no room for or incentive to question the very basis for the puzzle-solving, the prevailing theories, and supplying the world image and reference frame for groups as well as individuals.[14] There is a striking irony in the fact that the two systems explicitly designed for and tasked with the detection of new knowledge, science, and intelligence seem to display similar mechanisms working in the opposite direction. They *prevent* the detection and comprehension of new knowledge, whether on the validity of dominating scientific theories or on changes in a security environment of a type or to an extent not foreseen in forecasts or by common wisdom.

POST–COLD WAR: HERITAGE AND CHALLENGES

The four decades comprising the Cold War had a profound impact on intelligence as perceived and conducted by the great powers and their formal or informal allies – not only in terms of organisation, technology, and priorities but also in less obvious ways. The Cold War was a period that shaped and, to some extent, created intelligence as a profession, a craft, or an emerging science. Cold War intelligence *became* intelligence in much the same way that Cold War security *became* security. However, although this concept of security rapidly dissolved during the events of the 1990s, the concept of intelligence prevailed to a far greater extent and continued to do so even after the major challenges and shortcomings of warning and assessment concerning emerging new threats or reemerging old threats in new contexts.

The first major challenge was experienced by a number of European national-intelligence systems as a consequence of the disintegration of Yugoslavia and the subsequent humanitarian and political impact of the conflicts on the European Union and individual states. The intelligence demand mounted as the European nations were drawn into the monitoring and peacekeeping missions and the ongoing attempts to negotiate political

---

[14] In the Yom Kippur case, the conception was not just a creation of analysts, for it also was shared by intelligence consumers such as Chief of Staff General Elazar and Defence Minister Dayan. The close interaction in this intelligence–executive network is described by Bar-Joseph. Both Elazar and Dayan were consumers of the most significant flow of raw intelligence. The rather unfortunate analysts at lower levels, trying to question the conception, could thus be rebutted for their lack of insight into the complete intelligence picture. Few analysts, for instance, knew about Marwan or were trusted with reports supplied by him.

settlements. With increasing troop commitment on the ground, the European participants found that their intelligence systems were not capable of meeting the changing and unpredictable intelligence demand from a local crisis involving nonstate actors.

There was also a lack of understanding from all sides of the need for intelligence for the successful conduct of peace operations and humanitarian missions, most vividly demonstrated by events during the summer of 1995 with the Bosnian–Serb conquest of the Srebrenica enclave and subsequent expulsion of the populations and massive atrocities against the male population.[15] After Bosnia, it became obvious that the old pattern of "nonintelligence" peacekeeping under the blue flag of the United Nations (UN) was no longer feasible. Intelligence would become a crucial component not only for armed interventions but also for purely humanitarian missions, for the sake of both security and the accomplishment of the mission goals.[16]

Other more diffuse changes appeared at the national as well as multilateral level as a consequence of a broadened security agenda and subsequent intelligence needs. Some of these concerned sectors that previously had not worked in an intelligence-based mode and therefore lacked an intelligence culture in terms of both an intelligence system and an executive branch formulating intelligence needs and consuming intelligence output. The national-intelligence systems were faced with increasing anomalies in a number of areas. In Europe, organised crime spread rapidly with the opening of the borders, creating not only a nuisance for those at the receiving end but also a development that in the long run could undermine business, rule of law, and security for citizens and societies. The most profound intelligence response was establishment of the Europol criminal

---

[15] For an excellent overview of Western and UNPROFOR intelligence during the run-up to the Srebrenica massacre, see Cees Wiebes, *Intelligence and the War in Bosnia* (München: LIT Verlag 2003).

[16] Before Bosnia, UN forces did not have an intelligence function. Most national contingents, however, have one, usually disguised as "information". As Wiebes noted, this constituted a very rudimentary intelligence capacity, and there was no functioning intelligence process, especially beyond the national level. A complicating factor was that intelligence often followed national lines and priorities and was not primarily conducted for the sake of the international mission. Many accounts from the KFOR mission in Kosovo after 1999 emphasise that this pattern has not disappeared but rather increased with the influx of intelligence presence in the international missions, some heavily engaged in the surveillance of other contingents in the mission. Furthermore, the internal but often hidden competition among nations participating in multinational missions might even increase the problems of intelligence cooperation because intelligence can be used as a political instrument, granting and denying favours to others.

police intelligence-sharing system, which spurred the development of national police intelligence structures capable of supplying and using the shared intelligence.

With the Cold War over and a kind of lull perceived in the international system, the broader use of intelligence was contemplated in terms of support for both national decision making outside the traditional security domain and cooperation with various forms of nonstate actors, whether commercial or nongovernmental organisations. Although this cooperation surely had existed unofficially during the Cold War, it now appeared as a prospective new "market" for intelligence organisations in search of new missions – and new financing. Although this development generally did not go very far due to legal and security constraints, the discussion nevertheless was regarded as one of numerous signs of the eroding concept of the nation-state and the relevance and power of its institutions.

In retrospect, it is striking how limited the debate about post–Cold War changes in intelligence was during the 1990s.[17] Apart from a general scaling down of budgets, few major changes in the established structures appeared, as was discovered in the American context by the various post–September 11 investigations. The situation was no different in other Western countries, where the intelligence communities' main concern became the struggle to maintain competence and resist budget reductions. Terrorism was not a major issue and, more important, was not foreseen as one, at least not until well into the 1990s. If the September 11 attack in intelligence terms did not come as a lightning bolt from the blue, the massive impact on intelligence of the war on terrorism did, including in those countries with a long domestic experience in counterterrorism.[18]

If the 1990s were perceived as a lull, the first years of the new millennium were nothing of the sort. For the first time since the height of the Cold War, intelligence now emerged as a key element in national and international security. However, even more so, intelligence analysis – the ability of the

[17] Typical of this development is the Government Commission appointed in Sweden in 1996 to oversee the national-intelligence system after the Cold War. The task, however, was limited to defence intelligence only, leaving the security service and law enforcement outside of the oversight. Furthermore, the Commission was instructed to suggest improvements but not any organisational changes, something that guaranteed the preservation of the Cold War intelligence heritage. An interesting feature is that the finding, published in 1999, hardly discussed the role of intelligence for counterterrorism at all.

[18] Until the 7 July 2005, London bombings, British intelligence disregarded the possibility of domestically recruited terrorist cells and focused on the known al Qaeda–type infiltration missions. See "Report into the London Terrorist Attacks on 7 July 2005" (Intelligence and Security Committee, London, May 2006).

intelligence systems to make use of and comprehend the raw information they possessed or could collect – became a central issue. Problems of analysis that before September 11 had been, at best, the concern of a handful of specialists were suddenly transferred into the public domain through official investigations and media interest. In the course of a few years, intelligence analysis was more publicly discussed than during the entire Cold War.

For the intelligence communities, this was not uncomplicated because public scrutiny was focused on real or alleged failures of the surviving Cold War systems to deliver the timely and accurate assessments expected from them. In this respect, the misjudgement of the Iraqi possession of weapons of mass destruction (WMDs), spreading from the U.S. intelligence community to other Western agencies through the liaison structure, was far more damaging than the inability to predict the 2001 terrorist attacks. The Iraqi case displayed some cases of amazing incompetence as well as analytic entities unable to follow fundamental methods of source-criticism and hypothesis-testing. The image of thousands of analysts stuck under the streetlight determined to find the lost (or, rather, assumed) key was not a flattering one.

So, although intelligence in one sense rose as a key component in a hastily redefined security agenda, the underachievement in terms of foresight, comprehension, warning, and verification undercut both the public prestige and the self-esteem of intelligence as organisations and professions. Something utterly unforeseen had developed, a type of permanent intelligence crisis with a widening gap between expectations and performance.

But what was wrong? Why did a system and a profession that had developed over a half-century underachieve in this way? Was it just bad luck and awkward circumstances, or is there something fundamentally wrong not only with the organisation and priorities of intelligence but also with the very concept of intelligence, the way the problems are perceived or not perceived and solved or not solved?[19]

To answer these questions, it is necessary to reexamine Cold War intelligence and the more invisible heritage of the very concept or paradigm of intelligence established, developed, and confirmed in the course of a half-century.

---

[19] The failure of Western intelligence to predict the Afghanistan invasion in 1979 was not exactly a stunning success and neither was the inability of Soviet intelligence to assess the long-term consequences of the invasion. The permanent intelligence crisis is probably more a function of decreasing trust than decreasing performance; intelligence analysis is not less able to deal with anomalies, but the anomalies are perceived as more devastating and the response to the same kind of failures is different.

THE INTELLIGENCE CYCLE AND THE INSTITUTIONALISATION
OF "NORMAL SCIENCE" IN INTELLIGENCE

Let us return for a moment to where I started, with the failure of some
Swedish intelligence analysts to grasp the significance of the kind of phenomenon that Kuhn called anomalies – that is, observations and data that
do not correspond with the prevailing theory. This single instance is perhaps
not important as such, constituting no more than a footnote in the history
of Cold War intelligence. However, the underlying question, in endless vari-
ants, seems to accompany intelligence analysis in all times and contexts:
Why did the Swedish intelligence miss the boat (in every sense) when the
Storozevoy mutiny occurred, even though a mass of detailed raw intelligence was collected and, in principle, available? The answer appears to be
quite simple. The overall task of the intelligence community was equivalent
to the mopping-up operations of normal science. Here, as in most cases,
intelligence was the business of checking that everything proceeded as it had
been done in the past and was forecasted to continue in future. The night
watchmen, like rank-and-file researchers, were not supposed to think too
deeply about or ponder too much the unanswered and unasked questions;
if they did so anyway for one reason or another, they only brought trouble to
themselves.[20] The intelligence paradigm constituted an invisible intellectual
structure – a scheme according to which one could tell right from wrong
and relevant from irrelevant.

The intelligence cycle was in full swing, feeding the system with input
that was feasible, given the nature of the sources. For reasons of security
and divisions of labour, this input was divided among professional entities
that – for their own reasons of prestige, dislike, or simply neglect – did
not communicate in detail with one another. In the *Storozevoy* case, this
produced the familiar intelligence paradox, in which all the pieces existed
but were dispersed within the system, where they could be duly located in
the postmortem. However, because the pieces were not put together on the
current intelligence stage, no single professional entity could comprehend
the incomplete picture available, not even to the extent that its incomplete-
ness emerged. Air Force intelligence pondered the strange target practice of
the Brewer bombers, unaware of what had taken place on the surface below

---

[20] Pluralism is one of the fields in which goals and practice are mismatched and continue
to be so contrary to all intentions stated. An equally rare and depressing picture of the
intellectual working conditions of analysts is presented by Rob Johnston in his study of
the analytic culture in U.S. intelligence, cited previously. This is one of the cases in which
U.S. experiences are of more general than U.S.-specific relevance.

radar coverage. Navy intelligence was not concerned with the peculiarities of air tactics and training procedures.[21]

Cold War intelligence was not only a system dominated – or, rather, transcended – by the intelligence dimension of the bipolar world order. In that case, the post–Cold War challenges simply would have been an issue of new areas and new priorities, challenges difficult enough to address given the organisational inertia, the legacy of massive collections systems, and the competencies of existing personnel. However, Cold War intelligence was also an intelligence paradigm that had been institutionalised to an extent that made thinking and operating along other lines virtually impossible. The desperation emerging between the lines in the final chapters of the 9/11 Commission report illustrates this paramount impact of the normal science of intelligence: the problems are described in terms of innovation and imagination, but the only available tools are changes in the legal framework, in organisation, and in training. Although the intelligence cycle does not equal the paradigm, it is a key feature of it. As such, it is a concept that influences and probably limits every discussion on the intellectual aspects of intelligence.

The intelligence-cycle model is as old as intelligence as a function in organisations, first of all the military intelligence established and developed by the adversaries in the two World Wars. In this historical context, the intelligence cycle is simply a development of a traditional reporting procedure along a chain of command – a rigid structure enforced to ensure a timely and accurate flow of information and dispersion of orders. The intelligence cycle is still the model for intelligence at the field level, and there is probably little reason to change as long as military formations are organised and operate in traditional types of units. The same is true for other decentralised and standardised structures like customs intelligence and criminal police intelligence on the operational level. The main problem

---

[21] The R-130 radar station was solely an Air Force unit and its information was only fed into the air defence system. The Air Force and the Navy did run a joint low-level radar chain (in fact, two: one obsolescent and one with up-to-date technology), but because the probability of war was zero, the stations of the low-level chain were frequently closed down during weekends to reduce wear and tear and save money. A further twist of the *Storozevoy* story was provided by Jan Leijonhielm during the 2007 Stockholm conference. Leijonhielm, a former intelligence officer working with HUMINT collection in the mid-1970s, recalled that on the Monday when I first heard about "my Brewers", he had a meeting with a well-informed Estonian contact, who took for granted that his intelligence contact knew about the aborted mutiny. Leijonhielm immediately wrote a report on the matter, a report that presumably ended up in naval intelligence, discarded as the unreliable and wishful thinking of Baltic nationalists.

is that the intelligence cycle as a model and metaphor has come to cover every aspect of intelligence – on the national and multinational levels and on complex strategic issues that are remote from the tasks for which the intelligence-cycle model was designed and put into practice.

For years, there has been considerable debate about the feasibility of the intelligence-cycle model. Few who have pondered the matter would maintain that the model is a correct description of reality in an intelligence system. The cycle is a simplification – possibly an oversimplification – and real-world intelligence has to be understood in terms of a far more complex ad hoc model.[22]

However, refining and developing the model and adjusting it to the realities of intelligence work – although important from a perspective of professional self-reflection and historical case studies – might obscure the more fundamental aspect of thinking and problem-solving in intelligence. The cycle is not only a simplified model of a more complex reality (which it definitely is). It is also a model for intellectual activity that limits and perhaps even renders impossible precisely the type of imaginative analysis that appears as the only feasible way out of the current intelligence crisis.

The major problem related to the intelligence-cycle model is the reactive role assigned to analysis and the built-in process-oriented conception of analytic intelligence production. Perhaps no other feature has had such a broad impact on not only the organisational and legal structure of intelligence but also the very concept of intelligence, the perception of what intelligence is, how it should be conducted, and what constitutes best practice. It is tempting to look again at the scientific world in which a corresponding model hardly would be used to describe the methodological core of various disciplines. True enough, research is based on data collected in a planned and systematic manner, and the process is typically guided by an explicit or implicit research plan. The main differences are the extent to which the process is collection-driven in intelligence and the often poor methodological awareness and discussion of the analysis.[23] Furthermore, the planning and guidance that constitutes a central feature of the intelligence cycle – the demand that constitutes the very motive for the process model – makes

---

[22] See Herman and Treverton, cited previously.

[23] True enough, it could be argued that scientific research has a tendency to converge with intelligence analysis, not only in the obvious respect that research and scientific results increasingly are no longer presented and debated in the open domain but also in the structure of financing of research and the increased impact of vested interests.

conclusions running contrary to the intentions of the guidance not only difficult but also impossible as acts of insubordination.[24]

Of all the weaknesses of the Cold War intelligence paradigm, the hegemony of the intelligence-cycle model is probably the single most important factor in producing an intellectually inadequate concept of intelligence. While the "normal intelligence" supplied the communities with huge blinders, the adherence to the cycle tended to reduce intellectual creativity to information compilations, schematic interpretations, and unimaginative guesswork. With all its developed steering and guidance procedures, the cycle had the devastating consequence of blocking any development in the direction of "revolutionary intelligence" from within the system itself.[25]

Yet intelligence *outside* the intelligence cycle – is that possible? An increasingly critical debate about the impact of the intelligence-cycle model indicates that this should be the case. The question is how.

INTELLIGENCE ANALYSIS BEYOND THE COLD WAR HERITAGE

How is the inexplicable explained, the unknown understood? I attended a seminar on Central European security in Copenhagen in January 1990. The Berlin Wall had come down a few months earlier and the process towards German unification was rapidly proceeding. A colonel from the Danish defence headquarters spoke of the most familiar of all subjects in those days: the military balance on the central front. He noted that nothing actually had changed materially; the Soviet and East German divisions were still there. Then, to my amazement, he also stated that the wall coming down did not have much significance, that the Warsaw Pact was still in force, and that no significant change in the basic military situation in Central Europe thus could be expected in the foreseeable future. The colonel was, as were many other senior military intelligence officers, precise and clear in his judgement, an attitude that gave his ridiculous analysis of the transforming security situation a strange aura of trustworthiness.

---

[24] This effect of guidance and intelligence systems designed to serve decision makers is visible in the British and U.S. investigations into the Iraq WMD assessments. There are similar and growing problems in research, especially in heavily politicised and commercialised fields, in which certain results can become more or less impossible for researchers to publish if they wish to receive further funding and continue their career.

[25] Deborah G. Barger, in her research report, *Towards a Revolution in Intelligence Affairs* (Santa Monica, CA: RAND Corporation, 2005), noted with reference to the movement to reform U.S. intelligence: "The danger, then, would lie in the failure to recognize either the need for, or the possibility of, new or different roles and missions for intelligence in a world far different from the one in which U.S. centralized intelligence was created" (p. 2).

If the paradigms of normal science were to continue unchecked, no change would ever be possible. No major scientific breakthrough would occur, no wall would have come down, and no intelligence foresight would be possible – not even after the fact, when the world really *had* changed. However, as we know from experience, major scientific breakthroughs do occur and even the most stagnated and controlled systems break up. Foresight, however, remains a rare bird in this environment.

Aware of the problem of explaining why professionally closed scientific communities can produce the revolutions that – at least, temporarily – erase many of the "achievements" of normal science, Kuhn noted:

Because the unit of scientific achievement is the solved problem and because the group knows well which problems have already been solved, few scientists will easily be persuaded to adopt a viewpoint that again opens to question many problems that had previously been solved. Nature itself must first undermine professional security by making prior achievements seem problematic.[26]

However, this is not enough, not even when there is a new candidate, a new paradigm in-being at hand. First, the new candidate must offer a prospective solution to outstanding problems that cannot be solved in any other way. Second, the new candidate must preserve a relatively large part of the problem-solving ability of the earlier paradigm. Thus, scientific revolutions tend to embed past achievements.

Herein is perhaps the worst part of the post–Cold War inheritance for intelligence as a protoscience and profession. So many earlier achievements and proven techniques for problem-solving were rendered obsolete, useless, and even counterproductive. How could another pattern have been possible? And how should it be made possible in the future?

More analysts, better training, language skills, increased collection through legal access to information system, and interagency and bilateral intelligence liaison: in various degrees and forms, this is the reform program suggested to counter the new – or, rather, newly defined – threats from international terrorism, nonstate actors, states on the fringe of the international system, and development and flow of WMD technology and components.[27] This is all very well except for two details: the prescription

---

[26] Kuhn, p. 169.

[27] Examples of suggestions to reform and improve intelligence analysis are in Douglas Hart and Steven Simon, "Thinking Straight and Talking Straight: Problems of Intelligence Analysis," *Survival*, 48, 1 (Spring 2006); and David T. Moore, *Critical Thinking and Intelligence Analysis* (Washington: Joint Military Intelligence College, Occasional Paper 14, May 2006).

might be inadequate and the diagnosis might be wrong. A long historical perspective could teach both the practitioners and the users of intelligence that (1) the current threat, in the long run, is never the future threat; and (2) a system optimised to address current problems is bound to miss the gradual or sudden changes producing a new environment with new forms and combinations of threats and opportunities.

More analysts with better education will not necessarily lead to better intelligence output in this fundamental respect. It might improve the quality of individual analytic products, but it is not likely to alter the overall intellectual premises of intelligence analysis. If so, the reform, in the end, will produce only an increasing number of frustrated and disappointed analysts searching for a more promising intellectual environment and alternative career opportunities. The legal and technological development to increase collection of data related to individuals might improve coverage of objects and activities relevant for counterterrorism intelligence. However, this increased ability to collect is bound to produce simultaneously a new wave of "intelligence overkill": mass data of potential intelligence value, consuming vast human resources to interpret and comprehend, and, in the process, institutionalising one specific intelligence task with all subsequent development along the lines of normal-science orthodoxies.

In this respect, there is an appalling element of nonlearning from the Cold War experience. How could a new, focused, specialised, and goal-oriented intelligence system be expected to be able to detect the rise of new intelligence phenomena, new threats, or radical transformations of those under surveillance? How could a system so focused on puzzle-solving as the post–September 11security intelligence produce anything remotely resembling revolutionary science, an understanding of the previously unknown?

The most fundamental change in intelligence in the post–Cold War environment is therefore perhaps not the new demands emerging from a revised security agenda but rather the fact that the failures of the fundamental model of knowledge production in intelligence systems have become visible, undeniable, and – although on a limited scale – addressed. The 9/11 Commission report is probably the first major document on intelligence reform to mention the impact of imagination. Many of the recent attempts to describe the current state of intelligence are valid and the insights they provide are worth considering. Yet, they tend to miss the main point: the somewhat messy state of intelligence, with all the known and lesser-known cases of underperformance, is more a *symptom* than the cause.

We seem to be faced with a system that is extraordinarily unable to comprehend and react adequately to new and contradictory information. The irony in this is not minor because the intelligence structures are tasked with and expected to solve exactly this problem: to observe and pay attention to weak signals before they become obvious and to see the handwriting on the wall before it is visible to everyone. To describe it using another parallel: if science, with all the pitfalls caused by the tyranny of normal science, had operated as intelligence, few if any truly revolutionary scientific achievements would have been possible. Penicillin might still have been residue on laboratory glass plates.

Traditionally, the scientific community has tried to solve this problem with the instruments of openness, seminars, and the obligation to "share" data and their interpretation through the publication of scientific findings. The open culture, both locally and in a broader scientific community, had the explicit purpose of serving as a self-correcting mechanism.

My conclusion, therefore, is that intelligence analysis – at least, regarding issues that require creative thinking and imagination – cannot be expected to be accomplished within traditional intelligence organisations. Either these analytic tasks must be transferred to other institutions or structures more suited for them, or the intelligence organisations must undergo a far more profound transformation than hitherto contemplated.

Is failure the inescapable curse of intelligence analysis, a function of unrealistic expectations and overinflated organisational and professional self-images? Or, is it the twist of fate, the unpredictable nature of complex transformations and sudden events? Should intelligence analysis rather be transformed by scaling down the claims?

Possibly, because the ongoing trend to narrow the intellectual and cultural gap between policy makers and planners can be regarded as an attempt in this direction, to increase the awareness that an analyst does not possess the secret gifts of an oracle, that analysis of current intelligence is and must be written in water, and that there are better and less informed guesses but no secret formula by which the guess could be transformed into a prophecy.

Like science, intelligence analysis is about uncertainty. The similarities are sometimes striking, and it could be argued that there is a process of convergence where intelligence analysis increasingly relies not only on scientific output and competence. Intelligence analysis also relies on borrowed or transformed methods applied to specific intelligence problems, as illustrated by the expanding field of intelligence analysis on the proliferation of chemical, biological, radiological, and nuclear weapons. However, this field also illustrates the other side of the convergence: with an increasing role for science in early warning, prediction, and prescription over a wide range of political issues, science and research organisations are increasingly intelligence-oriented. This process constitutes a vital element in what could be called a social-intelligence revolution – the emergence of, if not intelligence-based, then at least intelligence-demanding societies.

Still, intelligence analysis is not information processing or analysis in general. Intelligence encompasses problems and challenges that are of a distinctly special character. Although scientists deal with uncertainty according to established and systematic methods, intelligence analysis is not always conducted under conditions allowing for the time and conditions typically available to researchers. Although a researcher would resist drawing premature conclusions, the intelligence analyst, depending on circumstances, has no choice but to make the best out of incomplete and inaccurate information or of inadequate time to comprehend an overwhelming wealth of information. Intelligence analysis is literally forced out into the no man's land of uncertainty, where assessments have to be made even if they cannot be substantiated.

That intelligence as a support for critical decision making – or, in the words of Francis Bacon, "the light of the state" – has to change, and continue to change profoundly, is hardly a controversial conclusion. But, can this be handled within the prevailing professional framework of the protoscience? Is not there a demand for new tasks and new questions as well as for new methods in the search for the answers? Or, to be more precise: Is it enough to redirect and reorganise intelligence? Is not the fundamental problem the way intelligence *thinks*? This leads to the ways that problems are formulated; hypotheses are generated and tested; and theories are employed, adapted, and developed to create comprehension. Instead of devil's advocates or occasional Team B exercises, intelligence analysis would probably need the step from protoscience to an applied science with an open culture in which competing interpretations are the norm, not the (barely tolerated) exception. *Open* in this respect should not be confused with *unclassified* because *open* simply refers to the nature of the analytic process.

There is no point in instructing a noninnovative intellectual environment to become innovative. The orthodoxy is embedded in the intelligence culture and no imagination will emerge unless this culture is transformed, probably to an extent that institutions and individuals would rather not imagine. The main intellectual and structural challenge lies not only in the difference between the better-informed and the less-informed guesses but also, ultimately, between the innovative guesses and the guesswork not even contemplated. If there is an emerging science of intelligence somewhere ahead, it is hoped that the main component will be a radically improved ability for innovative thinking, for dealing with, learning from, and utilising anomalies for the benefit of the guesswork.

PART 2

RESEARCH ON NEW CHALLENGES,
METHODS, AND THREATS

SIX

On Counterterrorism and Intelligence

Neal A. Pollard[1]

Counterterrorism is an intelligence war. The intelligence community (IC) plays a central role in counterterrorism in at least three key ways. Counterterrorism relies on intelligence to (1) understand the threat, (2) give warning of adversaries' intentions and capabilities, and (3) find and disrupt the adversary. In these roles, intelligence provides counterterrorism forces with targets and opportunities to attack terrorist capabilities and processes, thereby achieving strategic objectives.

Measuring the effectiveness of counterterrorism strategy is critical to the success of the strategy in order to validate the strategy and consequent resource decisions, to ensure the effectiveness of the plans and underlying action, and to provide policy makers with insight into whether counterterrorism efforts are actually making a difference. Here, the IC plays a fourth key role, in collecting, processing, and analyzing data required to assess effectiveness and providing planners with information necessary to establish "metrics" and measure strategic effectiveness. There are models of assessment that provide ways to measure strategic effectiveness that also provide insight into what is needed from intelligence.

The nature of the terrorist threat, the demands of effective counterterrorism strategy, the role of intelligence in counterterrorism, and the need to measure strategic effectiveness all generate new requirements for intelligence. Research on intelligence tradecraft, tools, process, and policy can provide intelligence agencies with ways to transform their business and better fulfill their counterterrorism roles. There are opportunities for innovative research to improve intelligence for counterterrorism in three particular

---

[1] The views expressed in this chapter are solely those of the author and do not imply endorsement or otherwise represent the policies or views of the U.S. government or any of its departments or agencies.

areas: measuring strategic effectiveness, strategic intelligence and warning, and intelligence processing and analysis.

THE THREAT

The primary terrorist threat against the United States and its allies is al Qaeda, as characterized by the former U.S. Director of National Intelligence (DNI) and the previous Director of the U.S. National Counterterrorism Center,[2] as well as other senior U.S. counterterrorism officers.[3] Al Qaeda continues to develop capabilities to attack Western interests and remains the most serious threat to the American homeland and other nations allied with the United States. Its central leadership continues to plan and resource high-impact plots while it continues to solicit and push like-minded groups in regionally focused extremist Sunni communities to mimic al Qaeda's efforts and supplement its own capabilities globally.[4] Al Qaeda has "protected or regenerated key elements of its homeland attack capability, including: a safe haven in the Pakistan Federally Administered Tribal Areas (FATA), operational lieutenants, and its top leadership."[5] Al Qaeda's plotting will likely continue to focus on "prominent political, economic, and infrastructure targets, with the goal of inflicting mass casualties, visually dramatic destruction, significant economic aftershocks, and/or fear among the U.S. population."[6] Furthermore, intelligence assesses that al Qaeda will try to acquire and employ chemical, biological, radiological, or nuclear materials or weapons, and it would use them if al Qaeda were to develop a sufficient capability.[7]

The U.S. IC also assesses that al Qaeda will continue to enhance its capabilities to attack the U.S. homeland through greater cooperation with like-minded regional groups that can extend al Qaeda's global reach and access to resources, capabilities, and mobile recruits.[8] Thus, these types of

[2] J. Michael McConnell, Director of National Intelligence, "Statement for the Record, Senate Homeland Security and Governmental Affairs Committee Hearing on Confronting the Terrorist Threat to the Homeland: Six Years after 9/11, 10 September 2007"; VADM John Scott Redd, Director, National Counterterrorism Center, "Statement for the Record, Senate Homeland Security and Governmental Affairs Committee Hearing on Confronting the Terrorist Threat to the Homeland: Six Years after 9/11, 10 September 2007."
[3] Edward Gistaro and Michael Leiter, "Implications of the NIE: The Terrorism Threat to the Homeland," Statement for the Record, House Permanent Select Committee on Intelligence and House Armed Services Committee, 25 July 2007.
[4] McConnell and Redd, op. cit.
[5] Gistaro and Leiter, op. cit.
[6] Ibid.
[7] Ibid.
[8] Ibid.

groups, such as al Qaeda in Iraq (AQI), which openly profess allegiance to al Qaeda and declare intent to attack the U.S. homeland, are also significant terrorist threats. The efforts of al Qaeda and regional affiliates are made more effective through "the spread of radical – especially Salafi – Internet sites,"[9] as well as globalization trends and recent technological advances (in communications as well as mobility) that enable "small numbers of alienated people to find and connect with one another, justify and intensify their anger, and mobilize resources to attack."[10]

Finally, U.S. intelligence assesses that Lebanese Hizb'allah may be "more likely to consider attacking the American homeland over the next three years if it perceives the United States as posing a direct threat to the group or Iran."[11] At what point or under what conditions Hizb'allah might perceive such a direct threat remains an unknown. What types of actions, and by which states, would precipitate such a perception?

This is the threat environment that characterizes the war on terror. One must also consider the global strategic environment in which these adversaries flourish and compete with Western counterterrorism forces. As DNI Mike McConnell stated:

The end of the Cold War and the advance of globalization enabled the acceleration of threats stemming from international terrorism, weapons of mass destruction (WMD) proliferation, failed states, and illegal drug trafficking. These threats, among others, move at increasing speeds due to technology and across geographic and organizational boundaries, blurring the distinction between foreign and domestic, and between strategic and tactical events.[12]

Terrorist groups exploit the engines, trends, and underlying technologies of globalization – including cheap intercontinental travel, transnational commerce, and global information and communications technology – to increase their productivity, much like other legitimate and illegitimate transnational actors. The war on terror is really an effort to compete against specific transnational terrorist groups – namely, al Qaeda, its regional affiliates, and Lebanese Hizb'allah – by preventing these groups from exploiting globalization to acquire, weaponize, and deliver increasingly lethal technologies; executing effective operational concepts; and sustaining supporting processes. Success in these efforts would indicate progress in the war on terror.

---

[9] Ibid.
[10] Ibid.
[11] Ibid.
[12] McConnell and Redd, op. cit.

U.S. POLICY AND STRATEGY AGAINST TERRORISM

U.S. President George W. Bush stated two broad policy objectives as a strategic vision for prevailing against terrorist groups: "the defeat of violent extremism as a threat to our way of life as a free and open society; and the creation of a global environment inhospitable to violent extremists and all who support them."[13] The president's National Strategy to Combat Terrorism offered six efforts necessary to achieve this vision:

- Advance effective democracies as the long-term antidote to the ideology of terrorism.
- Prevent attacks by terrorist networks.
- Deny WMD to rogue states and terrorist allies who seek to use them.
- Deny terrorists the support and sanctuary of rogue states.
- Deny terrorists control of any nation they would use as a base and launching pad for terror.
- Lay the foundations and build the institutions and structures we need to carry the fight forward against terror and help ensure our ultimate success.[14]

These elements laid out in the National Strategy to Combat Terrorism are supported by a number of supporting goals, such as advancing effective democracy,[15] countering violent extremist ideology,[16] attacking terrorists and their capacity to operate (including leaders, personnel, weapons, funds, communications, and propaganda),[17] denying terrorists entry to the United States and disrupting their travel internationally,[18] defending potential targets of attack,[19] denying terrorists access to materials and expertise required to develop WMD,[20] and eliminating physical and cyber safe havens.[21]

Counterterrorism strategy and operations seek to achieve these goals by disrupting the key underlying capabilities and processes in the "terrorist life cycle": leadership and organization; recruitment; training and indoctrination; planning, targeting, preparation, and resourcing; operational planning and execution; and exploitation of attack. These elements are similar to a

---

[13] The White House, "National Strategy for Combating Terrorism," September 2006, p. 7.
[14] Ibid., p. 1.
[15] Ibid., p. 9.
[16] Ibid.
[17] Ibid., p. 11.
[18] Ibid., p. 13.
[19] Ibid.
[20] Ibid., p. 14.
[21] Ibid., pp. 16–17.

factory assembly-line process with key stations along the way, and a core set of capabilities and processes supports each stage of the life cycle.[22] These stages might not necessarily be linear and are adapted to the size, scope, and complexity of the terrorist group. Nevertheless, a group's ability to grow, adapt, and wage an effective global (or even sustained regional) terrorist campaign depends on its ability to conduct these life-cycle processes. Consequently, a group's ability to sustain this life cycle and carry out its functional processes depends on key capabilities.

Counterterrorism strategy thus focuses on undermining five elemental capabilities and processes that support the terrorist life cycle and dramatically increase terrorist groups' effectiveness, resiliency, global reach, and lethality, as follows:

- *Ideological and operational leadership*: The "thought leaders" of the group's ideological underpinnings that provide fodder for recruitment and indoctrination and the top tier of leaders that drive the group's planning, preparation, training, targeting, and tradecraft.
- *Financial sources and infrastructure*: Especially the processes and channels of clandestine collection, transfer, and disbursement and methods to obtain sponsorship and supporting funds.
- *Safe havens*: Specific pieces of real estate where groups find sanctuary – by the grace of willing states or failed states too weak to counter the group's activities – so the group can conduct training, indoctrination, and exercises in group cohesion that results in, among other things, terrorist operatives meeting each other and exchanging familiarity, trust, and future contact information.
- *Adaptation and employment of critical technologies*: Obviously, capabilities and processes to acquire, weaponize, and deliver WMD such as nuclear, chemical, and biological weapons. Here, strategy can focus on opportunities on all three of these stages – acquisition, weaponization, and delivery of technologies – seeking to raise the hurdles in each stage. However, this strategic objective includes disruption of adaptation and innovative use of infrastructure technologies (e.g., for communication, surveillance, propaganda, and exploitation of terrorist attack).
- *Mobility*: The ability to move personnel and materiel across borders undetected, exploiting engines of globalization such as cheap intercontinental travel, seams in immigration control, and pervasive information technology.

---

[22] Raphael Perl, "Combating Terrorism: The Challenge of Measuring Effectiveness," CRS Report for Congress (RL33160), November 23, 2005 (updated March 12, 2007).

These are the five areas that can most effectively transform a terrorist group from a "homegrown," or localized, marginal threat to a sustained globalized threat able to disrupt or degrade strategic national interests. Attacking these capabilities and processes can produce measurable strategic effects against a terrorist group. Intelligence collection and analysis should emphasize reporting on terrorist groups' capabilities and processes in these five areas, as well as the effectiveness of counterterrorism efforts to undermine these capabilities and processes.

INTELLIGENCE REQUIREMENTS FOR COUNTERTERRORISM

Counterterrorism strategy and plans – that is, how the nation applies ways and means toward counterterrorism ends – apply all instruments of national power to disrupt specific terrorist groups' plans, intentions, and capabilities. This requires close interaction with the IC – itself an instrument of national power, reliant on clear strategy and objectives for effectiveness against a different challenge than traditional warfare. In traditional warfare, neutralizing the adversary is often regarded as more of a challenge than finding and engaging that foe; strategy usually reflected this. In counterterrorism, the opposite is true: the challenge is in finding and fixing targets of terrorists and support activities, driving our knowledge of terrorist groups from the strategic to the operational and tactical, after which rendering them harmless is usually less of a challenge but can carry strategic effects.

Intelligence requirements for counterterrorism array across a matrix of strategic, operational, and tactical analytical utility and offensive and defensive measures and actions. Strategic defense requires intelligence-analysis support for identifying long-term strategic vulnerabilities, how vulnerabilities might arise over time, or methods by which policy makers might receive strategic warning and reduce vulnerabilities to terrorist attack and future terrorist capabilities.[23] Operational defense requires intelligence to provide insight into how terrorists exploit globalization and leverage their capabilities, build networks of support, secure safe havens, establish training regimes, or adapt and employ technology. Tactical defense requires intelligence that can warn of planned attacks or movement of terrorist personnel or materiel.[24]

---

[23] This strategic–tactical breakdown of intelligence support to counterterrorism missions is a part of the U.S. IC's "Analytic Framework for Counterterrorism," described by VADM J. Scott Redd in his testimony, cited previously (McConnell and Redd, op. cit.). The author has added the additional element of operational intelligence support.

[24] McConnell and Redd, op. cit.

Table 6.1. *Levels of intelligence requirements and insights*

	Strategic	Operational	Tactical
Defense	Reduce long-term vulnerabilities to emerging terrorist capabilities	Identify terrorist exploitation of globalized infrastructure	Warn of attacks or terrorist movements
Offense	Counter violent extremist ideology	Disrupt transnational financing network	Capture or kill terrorist leaders

Strategic offense implicates intelligence requirements to support guidance to national policy for long-term efforts, such as countering violent extremist ideology,[25] anticipating the rise of specific terrorist groups and movements, and anticipating strategic surprise, such as a quantum leap in terrorist employment of critical technologies. Operational offense implicates intelligence requirements for targeting and disrupting key terrorist capabilities, processes, and infrastructure that support the viability of terrorist groups, such as safe havens, financial infrastructure and networks, mobility capabilities, leadership and command channels, and avenues of sponsorship. Tactical offense implicates intelligence requirements to support direct, tactical action to disrupt terrorist individuals and cells,[26] such as apprehension of a terrorist, disruption of an attack, or seizure of finances or materiel from a specific network. These various levels of intelligence requirements, and the insight they yield in support of specific actions, are summarized in Table 6.1.

The consequent goal of intelligence operations and analysis is to drive warning of the threat across this matrix – from strategic to operational or even tactical, and from defensive to offensive – to array resources effectively, support action against the threat, provide targets, and assess effectiveness. Strategic warning is "timely analytic perception and effective communication to policy officials of important changes in the level or character of threats to national security that require re-evaluation of U.S. readiness to deter or limit damage."[27] Strategic warning provides the necessary context and understanding to drive counterterrorism warning and actions to operational levels (responsive to the likelihood that an enemy will attack or change mechanisms for inflicting damage) or tactical levels ("when, where,

[25] Ibid.
[26] Ibid.
[27] Jack Davis, "Improving CIA Analytic Performance: Strategic Warning," *Sherman Kent Center for Intelligence Analysis Occasional Papers*, 1, 1 (September 2002), p. 3.

and how" of a specific incident, perpetrator, target, timing, or modality of attack[28]). Strategic intelligence – that is, that which is necessary to make and execute strategy[29] – is also critical to the formulation and execution of counterterrorism strategy (discussed previously). Measuring effectiveness of counterterrorism strategy and actions is also necessary for effective, adaptive counterterrorism strategy. Here, the IC has a role in providing intelligence across all three levels to help define metrics and measure the effectiveness of counterterrorism strategy. This requires developing appropriate mechanisms to craft metrics and measure effectiveness, identify and derive data to support metrics, and bridge counterterrorism planners with the IC. These mechanisms do not yet exist at the strategic level, frustrated in part because counterterrorism-intelligence challenges are very different from those around which the IC was designed.

In the past 60 years, the environment for collecting and analyzing intelligence has changed as much as the adversaries and our competition with them. Intelligence requirements have thus changed. Counterterrorism officers must have access to timely and accurate information on the adversary in order to:

- identify rapidly both immediate and long-term threats
- identify individuals involved in terrorist activities
- implement information-driven and risk-based detection, prevention, deterrence, attribution, response, protection, and emergency-management efforts.[30]

The primary targets of intelligence for counterterrorism are nonstate actors: terrorist groups and their leaders, suppliers, sponsors, and facilitators. This is a dramatic shift from the origins of the modern U.S. IC, which was built to focus on states – namely, the Soviet Union and Warsaw Pact states – during the Cold War.

The requirements for intelligence during the Cold War are different than those for the current war. During the Cold War, enemy forces were easy to find and observe but difficult to neutralize, and they operated almost exclusively overseas. Intelligence during the Cold War focused on orders of battle, numbers, strength, and movement of war-fighting materiel, intentions of

[28] Jack Davis, "Strategic Warning: If Surprise Is Inevitable, What Role for Analysts?" *Sherman Kent Center for Intelligence Analysis Occasional Papers, 2,* 1 (January 2003), p. 3.
[29] John G. Heidenrich, "The State of Strategic Intelligence: The Intelligence Community's Neglect of Strategic Intelligence." *Studies in Intelligence, 51,* 2 (2007), p. 16.
[30] McConnell and Redd, op. cit.

leaders, and punctuated activity of force movements or even regional conflicts during otherwise vacuums of hostile activity. During the Cold War, intelligence gave priority to strategic indications and warning (I&W) of hostile intent or action, changes in war-fighting or intelligence capabilities, and long-term plans. Tactical activity would be obvious or, at least, significantly easier to obtain than strategic I&W (e.g., tanks moving through the Fulda Gap, fueling of liquid-propelled rockets, or sudden activity in the Soviet Black Sea fleet). The "steady state" of normalcy was, simply, nothing happening.

Intelligence for counterterrorism is almost completely the opposite. With this war, enemy forces are easy to neutralize, once found. Finding them is the challenge: terrorists are less organized than a nation-state, their "forces" are smaller and more diffuse in number, and they hide among civilians and legitimate global activity. It is difficult to track terrorists because they move through the ordinary channels of globalization and legitimate commerce. Terrorists live, travel, work, study, and attack from within the borders of the United States and other target countries. Terrorist groups generally do not mask their intentions, capabilities, or long-term plans, but they do project their intentions to multiple audiences, making it difficult to parse their real intentions and frustrating efforts to drive strategic intelligence to tactical opportunities for action.

For instance, although terrorist ideological and operational leaders often broadcast their strategic intentions and grand designs in excruciating detail and flowery justifications, terrorist leaders offer complex layers of explanation behind their intentions, aimed at communicating multiple messages to multiple audiences: their adherents, their perceived "constituency," and the societies they target for attack. Even then, intentions are often cloudy: two examples that stand out are Lebanese Hizb'allah and terrorist groups acquiring and adapting critical technologies such as WMD. The question of Hizb'allah's intentions is critical to understanding what type of threat – to the group or to Iran – Hizb'allah would deem sufficiently "existential" to attack the U.S. homeland (as discussed previously). The question of a terrorist group's intention to acquire, weaponize, and deliver WMD will always be shrouded in some secrecy and will be among the most difficult information to collect against any terrorist group, given the risks and costs associated with WMD activity of any sort. These two issues pose difficult intelligence questions of both intention and capability.

Other questions of capability, such as terrorist "orders of battle," numbers, and strength of terrorist groups, might be tactically interesting but rarely compelling in determining the overall strategic posture of an asymmetric terrorist threat. Movement of terrorist personnel and materiel can be a compelling strategic indicator, but this movement is clandestine within a very open and crowded environment. Thus, it is the clandestine channels themselves and methods of exploitation that are of strategic interest more than their "forces" and materiel. Terrorists are more opportunists than strategists, and their orders of battle and plans frequently make use of opportunities rather than long-term development or acquisition mechanisms. Tactical I&W is a priority for intelligence, to interdict all phases of the terrorist-attack life cycle: leadership, recruitment, training, indoctrination, planning, preparing, operationally executing, and exploiting the attack. These tactical activities are clandestine, however, and tactical I&W will remain difficult to obtain. Terrorist activities do not occur in vacuums of hostile activity but rather are constant but faint signals of activity hidden within the persistent stream of noise that characterizes legitimate global commerce and movement. The steady state of normalcy is constant "chatter."

These differences present an overall intelligence challenge arguably more difficult to manage now than during the Cold War for a number of reasons. Terrorists blend in with civilian populations and commerce,[31] and they rely on surprise, small organizational cells, and intense secrecy of operations and communications to achieve their tactical ends.[32] The terrorist threat is less "bounded" or discrete than the Soviet Union or other states (i.e., by fewer geographic, political, or operational constraints). Terrorist groups are more reactive to U.S. policies and counterterrorism efforts, as opposed to being subject to deliberative, independent strategic considerations, thus making their actions less determinate and predictable. Events that create, drive, or result from terrorist groups (and thus change the threat environment) unfold and affect threat dynamics more rapidly than events that affected the Soviet Union and the Cold War balance of power. Finally, information and data about terrorist groups, activities, and processes are scattered, difficult to isolate, and must be plucked from countless sources in broader information bases with lower quality and less context (e.g., in the "sea of noise" that characterizes the daily transactions of globalization).[33]

---

[31] See, generally, Bruce Hoffman, *Inside Terrorism* (London: Victor Gollancz, 1998).

[32] Grant Wardlaw, *Political Terrorism: Theory, Tactics, and Counter-Measures* (Cambridge: Cambridge University Press, 1989), pp. 131–6.

[33] Warren Fishbein and Gregory Treverton, "Making Sense of Transnational Threats," *Sherman Kent Center for Intelligence Analysis Occasional Papers*, 3, 1 (October 2004), p. 8.

This latter characteristic reflects the environment in which the threat operates. "The same networks that allow the free flow of commerce and communication can also carry [terrorists] from one continent to another."[34] Counterterrorism requires information from the IC to find terrorists in the sea of globalization's noise. This means collecting and processing vast amounts of open-source information underlying the engines and transactions of globalization – most of which is legitimate – and distinguishing terrorist activity from this noise. The purpose of collecting this information will not be for disrupting these engines and transactions but rather for gaining understanding of how terrorist groups exploit globalization; how they incorporate capabilities, processes, and technologies into the stages of their "life cycle"; and how this information can be used to "map out" a terrorist group's network, infrastructure, and supporting capabilities and processes.

However, intelligence agencies do not have the configuration, manpower, or funds to observe the multitude of urban settings and globalized infrastructures – encompassing thousands of shady or illegal channels – through which terrorists move money, people, weapons, and plans.

The U.S. IC is not configured to meet counterterrorism requirements because it is not informed by them. Counterterrorism planning, operations, and intelligence personnel rely on one another to be effective. Counterterrorism planners require that intelligence drive knowledge of the threat from strategic to operational or tactical, from general to specific, and from static to actionable, after which decisions and options for action become clearer. To accomplish this, the IC must orient its collection and analysis around those strategic capabilities and processes that give specific terrorist groups increased resiliency, global reach, and lethality (described previously).

From this collection and analysis, the IC must provide information on terrorist capabilities, processes, history, concepts of operations, and trends that can assist counterterrorism planners to understand the adversary and the nature of the competition, derive strategic objectives that direct disruption of terrorist groups, and measure the effectiveness of counterterrorism strategy. Strategic objectives, in turn, will feed the IC with further collection and analysis requirements, which, once fulfilled, will provide counterterrorism forces with opportunities and targets to achieve those objectives. At this point, counterterrorism planners require data and information from the IC to measure the effectiveness of counterterrorism efforts – for instance,

---

[34] Richard N. Haass, "Supporting U.S. Foreign Policy in the Post-9/11 World," *Studies in Intelligence,* 46, 3 (2002), p. 18.

whether counterterrorism forces are effectively and favorably upsetting the balance among terrorist and counterterrorist capabilities, processes, and concepts of operation. Insight into this balance would thus help planners refine counterterrorism strategy, generating additional intelligence requirements – and the cycle begins anew.

A mechanism is required that supports this cycle by bridging the counterterrorism planning and IC, developing metrics and concepts to measure effectiveness, and providing a feedback link between intelligence and counterterrorism planning. Such a mechanism would facilitate the development of metrics around clear objectives, define clear end-states and conditions of victory, identify possible data sources to populate metrics, and communicate this information and additional requirements to the IC for collection and analysis. This mechanism would also help frame the context and requirements for strategic intelligence and warning: the starting point of understanding a terrorist adversary.

MEASURING EFFECTIVENESS: A NEW CHALLENGE FOR INTELLIGENCE

An effective strategy to win the war on terror requires the ability to measure progress. Measuring progress is important to understand success or failure to achieve strategic ends; thus, it is important to crafting an effective strategy and then calibrating it as a war evolves. The methodology of strategic net assessment, refined during the Cold War, offers insights into measuring strategic progress against terrorist groups. This methodology also offers insights into bridging more effectively counterterrorism planning and intelligence. Finally, the concepts that underlie strategic net assessment identify important questions for strategic intelligence and warning for counterterrorism.

Strategic net assessment was pioneered by the U.S. Office of the Secretary of Defense Director of Net Assessment under Andrew Marshall. Strategic net assessments weigh politico-military balances between adversaries, describing the nature of the competition across geographic and functional areas.[35] For counterterrorism, a strategic net assessment would help strategists and planners to understand the adversary and nature of the competition as a set of "balances" – that is, terrorist-group capabilities and processes balanced, somewhat symmetrically, against counterterrorist capabilities and processes – and to identify opportunities and strategic objectives to influence

---

[35] See, generally, Eliot Cohen, "Net Assessment: An American Approach," John M. Olin Institute for Strategic Studies, Harvard University Center for International Affairs, 1990, p. 4.

these balances favorably, as well as to measure that influence. Strategic net assessments are thus useful for counterterrorism in that they aggregate and assess the net progress against a specific terrorist adversary, across a number of varying, multidisciplinary competitions and levels of operation. Eliot Cohen, a noted military strategist and net-assessment advocate, offered a template for strategic net assessment.[36] Elements of his template, described herein, highlight some of the key questions and benefits that this methodology could offer counterterrorism planning and intelligence as a mechanism to develop and frame strategic intelligence and warning, measure effectiveness, and bridge the counterterrorism planning and ICs.

How Do We Measure?

Measuring effectiveness first requires establishing "metrics." A *metric* has been defined as a criterion against which to measure an outcome, and it consists of two parts: a "yardstick" of what to measure (i.e., territory, body counts, or some other indicator of progress against a terrorist group), and a "threshold" on the yardstick to mark the point when success is considered achieved – that is, the strategic objective.[37] Once these metrics are established, information is required about the outcome of the competition to determine whether one side of the conflict has been successful at reaching the relevant threshold on the yardstick, and – most important – how and why; that is, what specifically did counterterrorist forces do that caused them to reach the desired threshold (i.e., the causal link)?

From this basis, one may ask more useful questions, such as: Is the government doing the best it can, with the resources at its command, consistent with its stated policy objectives? Are these the appropriate policy or strategic objectives to sustain an effective competition against specific terrorist groups in specific modes of competition? These questions are answered by appraising the balance between terrorist and counterterrorist capabilities and processes – that is, measuring the erosion of terrorist capabilities and capacity, the effectiveness of counterterrorist capabilities, and how the two measurements match up over time as the net effect of an ongoing competition. The IC is accustomed to asking such questions about foreign adversaries. However, this approach examines the capabilities and processes of both terrorist groups (i.e., "Red" forces) and counterterrorism forces (i.e., "Blue" forces), appraising the balance between the two across a number of competitions. Bureaucratically, the IC is unaccustomed to examining

---

[36] See, generally, Cohen, op. cit.

[37] D. P. Johnson and D. Tierney, *Failing to Win: Perceptions of Victory and Defeat in International Politics* (Cambridge: Harvard University Press, 2006), p. 23.

Blue forces or conducting such an assessment of balances (a challenge discussed subsequently).

Defining thresholds, yardsticks, and causality is important but relies heavily on what information can be extracted and observed. This poses several questions that directly implicate intelligence: What indices or yardsticks might be used as indicators or trends to chart progress toward a desirable threshold or end goal? What end goals best serve national strategic objectives? What data sets can be extracted, observed, and used to populate those indices? How does one draw a causal link between counterterrorism actions taken and favorable changes or trends in indices? In what timelines should one reasonably expect counterterrorism actions to cause favorable trends (e.g., one might expect to see progress in attacking terrorist capacity sooner than in countering violent extremist ideology)? How can one aggregate various outcomes of competition to an overall strategic picture of net progress toward "victory" or "defeat"? Structuring metrics to answer these questions requires joint collaboration between counterterrorism planners (who must use Blue forces to meet strategic objectives, thresholds, and yardsticks) and intelligence officers (who provide the information and insight on Red forces to populate the metrics).

How Should We Think About the Balance?

This question gets to the heart of describing the fundamentals of the terrorist adversary and the competition and therefore addresses a range of complex issues. Two subsets of issues emerge in this inquiry that provide a context for strategic intelligence and warning for counterterrorism. First, what are the politics of the area or functional subject under consideration? For instance, what objectives do the two adversaries (i.e., Blue and Red) have in each region or function? What constraints exist in domestic or regional politics that shape each side's capabilities or preferred strategies? Second, what are the standards of comparison between the two adversaries for each of these issues? What are the symmetries and consequent measures of effectiveness that can indicate progress of one adversary against the capabilities and objectives of the other in that particular region or function? As Cohen pointed out, a thoughtful discussion of *which* measures to focus on – that is, which questions to ask – can be almost as useful as the ensuing analysis that applies them.[38] These are the fundamental questions for strategic intelligence and warning. Again, the IC has been configured to answer only such questions on Red forces.

---

[38] Cohen, p. 13.

This highlights a unique element that distinguishes strategic net assessment as a bridge between counterterrorism planning and intelligence: "[net assessment] requires extensive consideration of measures of effectiveness, and frequently the use of several such measures side by side."[39] For example, one must consider the technical effectiveness of each side's (i.e., Blue and Red) given capabilities and how each side *can* use them, as well as the operational styles and strategic requirements of using those capabilities – for example, *how* and *why* and *under what circumstances* either side *would* use them.

For example, considering the competition with al Qaeda, the regional competition would be described differently, for instance, in Pakistan's FATA than in Gaza. This presents interesting challenges in accounting for al Qaeda's mobility and transnational nature, as well as in accounting for how regional affiliates such as AQI or Jemaah Islamiya change both al Qaeda's capabilities, regionally and globally, and the regional political dynamic. That must account for the organic capabilities of regional affiliates themselves, in addition to how those affiliates extend al Qaeda's global capabilities and reach and which counterterrorism options are available (and would be effective) in this context.

Trends

Strategic net assessments examine long-term trends and patterns of behavior, extending up to 20 years in the past and attempting to look forward 5 or 10 years. This is important because it gives decision makers a sense of the long-term directions, habits, and investments of an adversary, as well as our own reactions and successes or failures against him. These insights, derived from trends, are important to understanding an adversary's "personality" – that is, its ideological pedigree and characteristics that influence its choices and decision making at all levels across the terrorist life cycle. Long-term trends provide insight into other elements of a group's strategic personality useful for strategic planning because this strategic personality influences many decisions across the terrorist life cycle: the group's goals and objectives, investments and use of resources, target selection, recruitment and training strategies, choices of weapons and concepts of operations, propaganda strategies and venues, tradecraft peculiarities, persistence against specific targets, preoccupation with critical technologies, types of rogue or failing states that a group will likely seek for safe haven, possible responses to disruption of certain logistical or financial channels, and so on.

[39] Ibid., p. 14.

This need for trends imposes requirements for strategic intelligence, which can provide counterterrorism planners with important objectives for effective strategy. However, like strategic intelligence, such long-term trends and considerations often are drowned out by the crowded, urgent clamor of a decision maker's daily inbox. The primacy of the urgent over the important is a refrain familiar to the IC and one that has led to a weakening of the practice of strategic intelligence.[40] A mechanism such as strategic net assessment can perhaps reverse this weakening – given its focus on the strategic balance between Blue and Red – yielding a product that is both reliant as a customer on strategic intelligence and warning and critical to effective counterterrorism strategy and planning. For example, trends can help identify how the balance between Red and Blue changes over time as terrorist groups adapt; as counterterrorist capabilities or processes become stronger; as terrorist leadership changes direction or objectives; and as political will supporting both sides increases or diminishes, limiting or expanding the options and support available to either side. Here, research in intelligence and long-term trends can provide some helpful examples and insights (discussed in the next section).

Concepts of Operation

Different military organizations fight differently, and assessments of terrorist groups must get beyond simple counting of an adversary's tanks, aircraft, artillery pieces, and so forth. It is important to understand how each side in a competition operates its forces and then "to speculate as intelligently as possible about the significance of those facts."[41] Understanding and countering a terrorist group requires "a thorough understanding of an opponent's style of warfare, and an effort to see how it interacts with one's own."[42] Again, these are questions of both intelligence for Red forces and counterterrorism planning for Blue forces.

This highlights a primary challenge of assessing terrorist groups: that there are no simple, relevant quantitative measures such as tanks, artillery pieces, or aircraft to count. Each terrorist group fights differently, with different preferences on how to apply technology, how to target, and how to modulate their use of violence (e.g., how lethal to calibrate their attacks). To assess the attack capabilities of a terrorist group, we must begin with concepts of operation, how both concepts and technology direct a group's approach to battle and how the decision-making process results in specific targets,

---

[40] See, generally, Heidenrich, op. cit.
[41] Cohen, p. 15.
[42] Ibid.

weapons, and operational strategies. More important, different groups seek different objectives and perceive differently their supposed constituencies (i.e., potential recruits and supporters as well as the broader "viewing" audience). This directly affects how lethal a specific terrorist group intends to be with a specific attack against a specific target: too much violence might alienate perceived supporters, stymie recruitment efforts, or provoke a counterproductive counterterrorism response; too little violence might undermine the group's credibility, deter supporters, or even go unnoticed by media oversaturated with violence.

These calculations consequently affect a range of terrorist decisions supporting their concepts of operations – from recruitment strategies to weapons and targeting to operational planning to exploitation strategies after the attack – and counterterrorist strategies must account for this full range of variables or, as Cohen termed it, the "culture" or personality of the group's decision making.[43] This includes accounting for how a terrorist group's concept of operations interacts with the organizational routines, preferences, and decision-making culture of counterterrorism forces, seeking to identify and measure the balance between adversaries' capabilities, but how an action or decision by one side produces a reaction by the other side. As discussed previously, terrorist groups are highly sensitive to the society and the culture they attack as well as the society and culture they purport to represent, and they calibrate their concepts of operations based on both perspectives. This makes it more difficult to collect and analyze intelligence on terrorist groups and also requires that one consider Blue counterterrorism capabilities and trends and their interaction with Red forces. Assessments should consider how this dynamic affects the overall balance and competition and where one side's capabilities and processes reflect perceived strengths and weaknesses in the adversary.

This is perhaps the most difficult aspect of a strategic net assessment for terrorism: understanding how the terrorist adversary truly perceives the balance, beyond grand statements of infidel weaknesses. Groups such as al Qaeda believe they can prevail against the United States, and this belief is likely based on something more than simply "Allah is on our side." Here, intelligence can provide valuable insights for counterterrorism planners and assessors, if the IC understands the requirements.

Scenarios

In the "traditional" strategic net assessment, scenarios were used as "prewar images" of a potential war, as base cases of wartime possibilities, which

[43] Ibid.

analysts would explore to determine potential adversary match-ups and outcomes, thus allowing for contingency planning.[44] Scenarios and "alternative assessments" (discussed herein) have often served as useful tools for strengthening strategic intelligence and warning. A range of scenarios is also useful for strategic net assessment, to understand the variety of conflict possibilities – if only to increase the decision maker's resilience to cope with unexpected events in real wartime.[45] This is especially important to counterterrorism decision making, given the unlikelihood that decision makers will receive tactical warning of a specific attack.

A fight against a terrorist group does not offer the traditional "campaign" around which one can devise a canonical scenario of this type. Nevertheless, scenarios are useful for counterterrorism strategic net assessments to provide decision makers and commanders with the opportunity to think through the assumptions underlying the construction of the scenario. The scenarios would be speculative descriptions of how terrorist and counterterrorism strategies and operations (including targets and use of specific weapons) would play out against a specific geopolitical environment (including a larger conflict, a civil war, or a natural disaster), against a specific spectacular terrorist attack, or against a specific U.S. or Allied action. These scenarios are useful for exploring assumptions about which terrorist groups would seek which types of targets, where, with what type of weapons and operations, and in pursuit of which objectives. Of course, counterterrorism planners will never capture the entire range of possible terrorist operations and attacks across the terrorist life cycle of any given group – the permutations of targets, operations, support processes, and uses of technology are too numerous. However, the use of a wide range of scenarios to inform a strategic net assessment can compensate for the difficulty of forecasting by exploring the domain of possible futures and the subsequent range of possible options for action, reactions, and consequent effects. This provides maximum flexibility for plans, planners, and the planning process because plans rarely survive first contact with the enemy.

PRACTICAL CHALLENGES AND OPPORTUNITIES FOR INTELLIGENCE RESEARCH

Cohen noted data issues that pose practical problems for strategic net assessment. These problems are both bureaucratic and substantive, and

---

[44] Cohen, p. 18.
[45] Ibid.

they underscore broader challenges for how the IC must orient to support counterterrorism, particularly in three areas: (1) measuring effectiveness of counterterrorism strategy, (2) strategic intelligence and warning, and (3) intelligence processing and analysis. There are opportunities to help resolve these challenges for research in intelligence tradecraft, tools, processes, and policy.

Measuring Effectiveness of Counterterrorism Strategy

The IC is not accustomed to providing information on both Blue and Red forces. This function is necessary to measure the effectiveness of counter-terrorism strategy. A strategic net assessor is not only a "voracious con-sumer of data, but a demanding, and sometimes even an irritating one,"[46] requiring data on Blue and Red forces. This involves significant and sensitive input from both the operational and the analytical communities. Organi-zationally, this is problematic for the governments, perhaps especially the U.S. government: the war on terror requires the government to apply all instruments of national power across virtually every department or agency of the government. However, no single office or agency has been respon-sible for examining both the capabilities of terrorist threats (traditionally, the responsibility of the IC) and the capabilities of U.S. forces to counter terrorism (traditionally, the responsibility of each department or agency); therefore, no single agency or office will have insight into all the relevant information. Indeed, U.S. intelligence was enjoined from domestic activity, which became translated into an exclusive focus on enemies "over there."

Relevant information will be disparate and distributed throughout the vast, possibly reluctant bureaucracy of the entire government. Departments and agencies will be understandably reluctant to provide data on their respective capabilities if the results of an assessment cause departments or agencies to lose missions, programs, or budgets. As Cohen described:

In order to perform its task properly, [the strategic net assessor] needs access to tightly held information about one's own forces, their plans, readiness levels, and capabilities, which can be even harder to obtain within a government than information about an opponent. One's own ... forces may as a matter of principle be quite unhappy about providing such information to a civilian agency. ... They may see it ... as a potential supplier of bureaucratic dynamite to organizational rivals.[47]

---

[46] Cohen, p. 20.
[47] Cohen, p. 20.

Currently, the U.S. National Counterterrorism Center (NCTC) maintains the statutory responsibility for both counterterrorism intelligence and "strategic operational planning":

NCTC serves as the primary organization in the United States Government for integrating and analyzing all intelligence pertaining to terrorism possessed or acquired by the United States Government (except purely domestic terrorism).... NCTC also serves as the primary organization for strategic operational planning for counterterrorism. Operating under the policy direction of the President of the United States... NCTC provides a full-time interagency forum and process to plan, integrate, assign lead operational roles and responsibilities, and measure the effectiveness of strategic operational counterterrorism activities of the U.S. Government.[48]

Public policy research into bureaucratic process and organizational effectiveness might examine how the NCTC performs this mission – as a central focus for both counterterrorism intelligence (Red forces) and strategic planning (Blue forces) – and how it could be positioned to drive a process such as strategic net assessment. In particular, as the Obama administration convenes its National Security Council (NSC) staff and designs its basic policy-planning processes, it should consider how to use the NCTC effectively and empower it as a forum to bridge counterterrorism policy, strategy, planning, and intelligence. Many of the research opportunities described herein also might provide tools to increase the NCTC's effectiveness in this role.

Measuring the effectiveness of counterterrorism strategy also poses substantive challenges. Strategic net assessments, for instance, use as a baseline and context the global distribution of effective power – military, political, and economic. The meaning of "global distribution" and "effective power" in a competition against terrorist groups is more ambiguous and subject to different measurements than during the Cold War against a conservative and stable opponent. As DNI McConnell testified, counterterrorism planners must consider the global strategic environment in which terrorists flourish. Terrorists exploit the engines, trends, and underlying technologies of globalization and turn them into capabilities in their own right, able to drive strategic trends to tactical advantage (e.g., wielding mass communications) very quickly. This poses challenges of redefining "strategic intelligence" and "strategic warning": What is strategic intelligence in globalization, where cheap and widely available technologies, used daily by legitimate actors, can also provide strategic capability to terrorist groups? What data would

[48] From www.nctc.gov, available at www.nctc.gov/about_us/what_we_do.html.

indicate a strategic shift in terrorist groups' exploitation of globalization, thereby providing strategic warning?

Measuring effectiveness is complicated by substantive data challenges as well. Data requirements cannot be fixed without concrete, measurable objectives and end-states expressed in strategy. Once measurable objectives and end-states are fixed in strategy, then trends can be identified for observation by the IC, which can then provide insight into what indices might be used as indicators (i.e., thresholds on yardsticks) to chart progress toward strategic end-states. Once these indices are identified, then three questions arise: What data sets can be measured and used to populate those indices? How can one draw causal links between counterterrorism actions taken and favorable changes or trends in indices? In what timelines is it reasonable to expect counterterrorism actions to cause favorable trends?

These questions differ across the range of competitions that underlie the "balance" between terrorist groups and counterterrorist forces. However, there is research that might provide insight into which data and metrics can be used to measure this balance and thus target counterterrorism strategy. Much research has been produced exploring the notion of "soft power," notably described by Joseph Nye in his research on how the United States should wield soft power – it is this soft power that international actors can derive from globalization.[49] Other research has described how illegitimate transnational actors exploit specific engines of globalization to increase their effectiveness.[50] This research can help intelligence officers and counterterrorism planners identify and develop innovative metrics to measure "power" and its global distribution; identify and measure how terrorist groups exploit globalization to produce strategic capabilities and effects; identify which data sources are available to measure this exploitation; and how such data can be collected and incorporated into strategic intelligence, warning, and measures of effectiveness.

Research into specific strategic competitions between terrorist groups and counterterrorist forces might also provide insight into meaningful metrics

---

[49] See, for example, Joseph Nye, *The Paradox of American Power: Why the World's Only Superpower Can't Go It Alone* (Oxford: Oxford University Press, 2002); Joseph Nye, *Soft Power: The Means to Success in World Politics* (Cambridge: Perseus, 2004); A. T. Kearney, "Measuring Globalization: Economic Reversals, Forward Momentum," *Foreign Policy, 54* (March/April 2004), p. 141.

[50] See Moises Naim, *Illicit: How Smugglers, Traffickers, and Copycats Are Hijacking the Global Economy* (New York: Doubleday, 2005); Neal A. Pollard, "Globalization's Bastards: Illegitimate Non-State Actors in International Law," *Law Enforcement and Low Intensity Conflict, 11,* 2/3 (Winter 2004), pp. 215–16; and Moisés Naím, "The Five Wars of Globalization," *Foreign Policy* (January-February 2003), pp. 29–33.

and available data sources. An example of such a strategic competition is
a terrorist group's capability for ideological leadership versus counterterrorism efforts to undermine the effectiveness of that leadership in pursuit
of the strategic objective of countering violent extremist ideology. Insight
into a group's personality has implications for counterterrorism strategy
aiming to disrupt ideological leadership. Insights derived from long-term
trends can provide insight into a terrorist group's "ideological soul" as well
as possible points of leverage and fissures among extremist leaders that can
be exploited by tracking the ideological pedigree of a group's leadership.
For example, the Combating Terrorism Center at the United States Military Academy (USMA) produced the "first systematic mapping" of modern
jihadi ideology. Its conclusions stated a number of interesting trends: for
example, evidence indicates that al Qaeda ideologues, Osama bin Laden and
Ayman al-Zawahri, have exerted relatively little influence over the movement's intellectual foundation. These ideologues have less opportunity to
influence the next generation of Islamic militants than other ideologists
such as certain Saudi and Jordanian clerics. Western governments have neither the credibility nor local expertise necessary to mitigate the popularity
of Salafism, but the diffusion and spread of ideology on the Internet could
lead to opportunities to exploit divisions within an ideological movement.[51]
USMA subsequently published a report titled "Cracks in the Foundation:
Leadership Schisms in al-Qa'ida from 1989–2006," which chronicled the
implications for strategy specifically aimed at creating fissures among the
ideological leadership of groups.[52]

Similarly, there are research opportunities to understand how terrorist groups transform the technologies and processes of globalization into
"capabilities"; that is, how do terrorists weaponize globalization to support
ideological and operational leadership, safe havens, mobility, financing, and
so forth? For example, continuing the analysis of ideological leadership:
How do terrorists weaponize globalization to wield ideological leadership
in a "War of Ideas," producing strategic effects using Web sites, viral marketing, blogs, YouTube, flash mobs, Short Message Service (SMS) messages,
or 24-hour multimedia news reporting?

For the IC to support strategic net assessment and leverage research into
terrorist exploitation of globalization, it will have to overcome two other

[51] Mark Mazzetti, "Qaeda Leaders Losing Sway over Militants, Study Finds," *The New York Times* (November 15, 2006), available at www.nytimes.com/2006/11/15/washington/15terror.html?_r=1&oref=slogin.
[52] USMA Combating Terrorism Center, "Cracks in the Foundation," available at www.ctc.usma.edu/aq/aq3.asp.

challenges: (1) redefining strategic intelligence and warning for counter-terrorism, and (2) processing and analyzing the mass of data available on terrorists' movements through globalization's sea of noise.

Strategic Intelligence and Warning

Producing useful intelligence is more difficult for counterterrorism than it was during the Cold War. This holds for strategic intelligence, which is critical for both warning and measuring effectiveness of counterterrorism strategy. These difficulties are compounded by the previously described primacy of the policy maker's inbox. Nevertheless, there are at least three sets of opportunities in intelligence research that suggest tradecraft and tools to improve strategic intelligence and warning for counterterrorism.

First, the research community should take the opportunity to redefine strategic intelligence and warning in the context of counterterrorism. These concepts of intelligence, much like the organization of the IC, still reflect the requirements of the Cold War.[53] Ignorance of their meaning has bred ignorance of the utility of their products, with too much focus on tactical issues (i.e., the inbox). Research has found that, post–Cold War, strategic intelligence has atrophied in the U.S. IC due to many factors, including ignorance of its utility against modern threats as well as responsiveness to intelligence customers more preoccupied with tactical intelligence and warning.[54] Research and analytical training on clear definitions of strate-gic intelligence and warning, its role in counterterrorism, and its utility to senior policy makers (e.g., an office of strategic net assessment for coun-terterrorism) would contribute to the institutionalization of strategic intel-ligence and warning and its embrace by senior and middle managers of the IC.

Second, there are research opportunities to institutionalize strategic intel-ligence and warning throughout the counterterrorism community, through tradecraft and processes that will support its development and benefit to consumers. Skill sets for tactical and strategic warning are often not in the same location, much less intelligence producers and counterterrorism plan-ners. Tools and tradecraft can link these communities. Research on intelli-gence has produced recommendations to institutionalize strategic warning, expand resources dedicated to it, and reconstitute it as a collaborative gov-ernmental responsibility – as opposed to an intelligence function – by

---

[53] Heidenrich, op. cit.
[54] Heidenrich, op. cit.

engaging the policy community more directly in the strategic-warning process.[55] Recommendations to achieve these goals include the following:

- Clarify the warning mission to place primacy on avoidance or limitation of damage, as opposed to avoiding surprise.
- Increase resources for strategic warning (on the theory that a government adequately prepared to respond to threats that receives no warning of a specific incident is better able to limit damage than a government that receives warning but is unable to respond).
- Strengthen strategic warning as part of "alternative analysis," including assessment of the following factors:
  - evidence and inference that support alternative views about what drives the situation (key variables)
  - similar tough-minded probing about the most likely path of future development of these key variables or drivers
  - triggering events or developments that could set off the alternative dynamics and paths
  - signposts or indicators that would signal increased or decreased danger for the United States.[56]

This latter recommendation builds on proven practices of alternative assessments – for example, "contrarian" techniques (i.e., Devil's Advocacy, Team A/Team B, and Red Teaming) and "contingent" techniques (i.e., "What If?" analysis and alternative scenarios).[57] The IC, as well as other public and private organizations, has developed tools to cope with uncertainty through rigorous self-review to help avert "failures of imagination"; these tools have come to be known collectively as "alternative analysis" or "structured argumentation."[58] Alternative-analysis techniques and tools help analysts and policy makers "stretch their thinking by broadening the array of outcomes considered – examining alternatives – or by challenging underlying assumptions that may constrain thinking."[59]

Opportunities for research into alternative assessment tradecraft and tools will move it from episodic and supplemental to institutionalized and influential in the policy process. Institutionalizing alternative analysis requires tradecraft that helps overcome hurdles such as drains on analytic

---

[55] Davis, 2003, p. 6.
[56] Davis, 2003, pp. 10–11.
[57] Fishbein and Treverton, p. 6. See also Davis, 2002, p. 7.
[58] Fishbein and Treverton, p. 1.
[59] Ibid.

resources, undermining group cohesion on controversial issues, appearance of politicization, and ability to convey subtleties to policy makers who need clear judgments and options for action.[60] Tradecraft can assist here by institutionalizing alternative analytical approaches, such as:

> ... sense-making: a process through which organizations – vice individuals – comprehend the complex environment with which they must contend. It is a continuous, iterative, largely informal effort to understand, or "make sense" of what is going on in the external environment that is relevant to the organization's goals and needs.[61]

Concepts such as "intuitive decision making" and sense-making can be combined into a framework for "categorizing the residual thought processes of intelligence analysts ... this process involves the application of expertise, imagination, and conversation – and the benefit of intuition – within intelligence analytic organizations to identify changes in existing patterns or the emergence of new patterns, without systematic consideration of alternative hypotheses."[62] These processes must be "continual" and institutionalized[63] and would provide clear benefit to processes for measuring the effectiveness of counterterrorism strategy (e.g., strategic net assessment).

Another promising area for tradecraft to accomplish institutionalization and benefit the practice of strategic net assessment is through research into techniques for evaluating the authenticity and diagnosticity of information:

> Regarding authenticity, use of denial and deception (D&D) is usually central to the planning of U.S. adversaries, because of its effectiveness in compensating for other power weaknesses. From obsessive operational security to distractive reports about planned attacks overseas, D&D probably increased the odds for success for the 11 September terrorists. The Intelligence Community has made important strides in understanding how a less powerful opponent can use D&D against the United States. The main frontier for improving warning analysis is conversion of this awareness into practical analytic tradecraft for identifying and countering an adversary's manipulation of intelligence and open source information.
>
> Regarding diagnosticity, the rapid expansion of both classified and open source information can be a burden as well as a benefit to the warning analyst. More than ever, powerful yet practical tradecraft is needed to distill information that serves as reliable "signal" from the mass of collected information that is distracting "noise." Sharper analyst insight on what new information is central to reducing uncertainty must then be used to rationalize intelligence and open source collection efforts.[64]

[60] Fishbein and Treverton, p. 8.
[61] Fishbein and Treverton, pp. 15–16.
[62] Fishbein and Treverton, p. 16.
[63] Fishbein and Treverton, p. 19.
[64] Davis, 2003, pp. 11–12.

Third, there are research opportunities in technology to develop tools that structure this "noise" of data and make alternative assessments creative, collaborative, counterintuitive, and consumer-friendly – all of which are necessary to an effective alternative process for intelligence sense-making.[65] The much-maligned Total Information Awareness (TIA) program, funded in 2002 by the Defense Advanced Research Projects Agency (DARPA) and cancelled in 2004 by the U.S. Congress, specifically sought to develop collaboration, automation, and cognitive-aid technologies that:

(1) increase information coverage by an order of magnitude, and affords easy future scaling; (2) provide focused warnings within an hour after a triggering event occurs or an evidence threshold is passed; (3) can automatically queue analysts based on partial pattern matches and has patterns that cover 90% of all previously known foreign terrorist attacks; and, (4) support collaboration, analytical reasoning, and information sharing so that analysts can hypothesize, test, and propose theories and mitigating strategies about possible futures, so decision-makers can effectively evaluate the impact of current or future policies and prospective courses of action . . .
  [These technologies will] support collaborative work by cross-organizational teams of intelligence and policy analysts and operators as they develop models and simulations to aid in understanding the terrorist threat, generate a complete set of plausible alternative futures, and produce options to deal proactively with these threats and scenarios. The challenges such teams face include the need to work faster, overcome human cognitive limitations and biases when attempting to understand complicated, complex, and uncertain situations, deal with deliberate deception, create explanations and options that are persuasive for the decision maker, break down the information and procedural stovepipes that existing organizations have built, harness diversity as a tool to deal with complexity and uncertainty, and automate that which can effectively be accomplished by machines so that people have more time for analysis and thinking. . . . [These technologies] aid the human intellect as teams collaborate to build models of existing threats, generate a rich set of threat scenarios, perform formal risk analysis, and develop options to counter them.[66]

These tools thus envisioned benefits for strategic intelligence and warning, strategic net assessment, and counterterrorism planning and decision making. The progeny of programs like TIA – developing tools for data mining, aggregation, visualization, and reasoning – seeks to allow analysts and decision makers to explore different implications of data and trends, to understand the extent to which hypotheses are supported or refuted by available data, and to identify critical gaps in data that might support alternative

[65] Fishbein and Treverton, pp. 19–23.
[66] Defense Advanced Research Projects Agency, Broad Agency Announcement 02–08 Information Awareness Proposer Information Pamphlet 2 (2002) available at www.eps.gov/EPSData/ODA/Synopses/4965/BAA02–08/IAPIP.doc, pp. 22–3.

hypotheses. To be sure, these functions are performed now by analysts, but this is an inefficient use of analysts' time. Some of these functions can be performed more efficiently by technology, reducing analysts' time researching and compiling data from myriad data bases, as well as generating hypotheses implicated by the data. If these tasks are effectively accomplished by technology, then more analysts' time can be spent focusing on those tasks that only a human can perform: tasks involving judgment, intuition, experience, and imagination. This holds the potential for an increase in the effectiveness of intelligence analysis.

Intelligence Processing and Analysis

Virtually every intelligence challenge described previously confronts the same formidable data challenges because of the sea of noise in which terrorists operate. Research into data-mining and aggregation technologies holds great promise in helping counterterrorism intelligence and planning officers to find the terrorist signal in that noise through more effective processing and analysis of intelligence. However, intelligence agencies will have difficulty applying these innovative technologies against the terrorist threat, particularly as the threat moves through the United States and the European Union (physically or, even more problematically, through cyberspace), until key questions in privacy policy are resolved. Here, policy research into privacy can benefit counterterrorism.

As the former director of DARPA's Information Awareness Office remarked, "The amount of data available to the federal government far exceeds the human capacity to analyze it. This has long been the case, but since 9/11 the need for better tools to help America fight the war against terror has become more urgent."[67] The IC cannot rely to the same degree it did in the Cold War on finding a relatively few rich sources of intelligence that will provide insight into capabilities, tactics, and plans of the adversary. All traditional intelligence-collection methods remain important, but understanding the terrorists and predicting their actions requires us to rely more on making sense of many small pieces of information.

Research into data mining and aggregation, pattern analysis, and "non-obvious link awareness" offers potential to make sense of this mass of data.[68]

---

[67] John M. Poindexter, "Finding the Face of Terror in Data," *The New York Times* (September 10, 2003).

[68] See Neal A. Pollard, "Competing with Terrorists in Cyberspace," *Mapping Terrorism Research: State of the Art, Gaps, and Future Direction*, Magnus Ranstorp (ed.) (London: Routledge, 2007), p. 240.

These technologies include data mining to extract data and patterns from massive amounts of data spread across disparate data bases, "evidence combination" to merge different sources of data and support analysts' reasoning and testing of hypotheses, "natural language" technologies for translating and extracting information from spoken-word transmissions, image and video processing, and data-visualization technologies to portray massive amounts of data in intuitive visual formats.[69] The potential of these research opportunities arises from a provocative hypothesis: if one can track terrorists' transactions and processes, one can track, anticipate, and interdict terrorists across the terrorist life cycle.

Terrorists exploit globalization. More to the point, terrorists transact, and these transactions create records and leave footprints in cyberspace. When terrorists exploit the engines and processes of globalization, they are consumers: they buy products and services, travel, communicate, send and receive money, apply for and present passports, drive cars, rent hotel rooms, and conduct surveillance on their targets. In virtually all cases, terrorists have left detectable clues in transactions, generally found after the attack.[70] The hypothesis underlying the use of data mining, aggregation, and pattern recognition is described accordingly:

> The research into data search and pattern recognition technologies is based on the idea that terrorist planning activities or a likely terrorist attack could be uncovered by searching for indications of terrorist activities in vast quantities of transaction data. Terrorists must engage in certain transactions to coordinate and conduct attacks against Americans, and these transactions form patterns that may be detectable.[71]

Data-mining and automated data-analysis technologies can be powerful processing and analysis tools for meeting the intelligence requirements described previously. To be sure, intuition, continual hypothesizing, and competitive analysis remain critical parts of the analytic process. However, these tools can assist analysts, planners, and assessors by automating some low-level functions. These tools can thus help prioritize attention and provide clues about where to focus, thereby freeing analysts and investigators to engage in the analysis that requires human judgment.[72] In addition,

[69] National Research Council, *Information Technology for Counterterrorism: Immediate Actions and Future Possibilities* (Washington: National Academies Press, 2003), pp. 63–71.

[70] Pollard, 2007, op. cit., p. 240.

[71] Defense Advanced Research Projects Agency, *Defense Advanced Research Projects Agency's Information Awareness Office and Total Information Awareness Project*, available at www.darpa.mil/iao/iaotia.pdf.

[72] Mary De Rosa, *Data Mining and Data Analysis for Counterterrorism* (Washington: CSIS Press, 2004), pp. 5–6.

data-mining and related techniques are useful tools for some early analysis and sorting tasks that would be impossible for human analysts. They can find links, patterns, and anomalies in masses of data that humans could never detect without this assistance,[73] which can drive further human inquiry.

The technology challenge in data mining and aggregation is to demonstrate that these tools can (1) identify sets of transactions that, when analyzed together, portend terrorist activity; (2) locate those transactions in a vastly larger set of all transactions conducted worldwide; and (3) distinguish between transactions that truly indicate terrorist activity and those that are similar but innocent (the so-called false-positive problem). The policy challenge in data mining and aggregation arises from the fact that information about terrorist activity is largely mixed in with data about innocent people.

Technology opportunities, such as TIA, have been shut down by policy makers because of unresolved policy issues such as privacy. Mary DeRosa summarized this policy problem with data mining:

> The potential benefits of data-mining and automated data-analysis techniques, as tools for counterterrorism, are significant. Moreover – and this is often misunderstood – these techniques do not permit the government any greater access to personal data; they can only operate on data that the government already has. But they can make private data more useful, and that is what causes controversy.... There is significant public unease about whether current protections for privacy are adequate to address the potential consequences of this government use.... Nor is there typically public debate or discussion before they are adopted.[74]

There is an opportunity for research into public policy on privacy to drive such a public debate. The practice of intelligence frequently conflicts with the values of a free and open society. "Given the limited applicability of current privacy laws to the modern digital environment, resolving this conflict will require the adoption of new policies for collection, access, use, disclosure and retention of information, and for redress and oversight."[75]

There are fundamental questions about privacy that should be addressed as the United States and other democracies practice intelligence in an era of globalization with globalized threats. The U.S. Supreme Court has held that privacy is guaranteed around those personal areas where one has a reasonable expectation that society is prepared to accept. Yet, what is a reasonable expectation of privacy with respect to information that people freely give

---

[73] Ibid.
[74] DeRosa, p. 14.
[75] James Jay Carafano and Paul Rosenzweig, *Winning the Long War: Lessons from the Cold War for Defeating Terrorism and Preserving Freedom* (Washington: Heritage Books, 2005), p. 113.

to third parties (e.g., Web sites, rental-car companies, and airlines)? If a surveillance technology gives false positives, what are the consequences or harm of false positives, and what rate is unacceptable? Do data mining and aggregation really pose a qualitatively different level of intrusion? How much data must be aggregated before privacy is violated? Can technology also protect privacy interests – for example, through data anonymization? If so, what level of anonymization is sufficient, and what is the best way to guarantee and oversee it? What constitutes personally identifiable information? How much of it should be available to government and under what circumstances? What are the long-term effects on public policy of data aggregation?

Technology opportunities have been missed because these policy questions remain unanswered. These questions can be answered, however, and privacy can be modernized effectively. Security and privacy are not mutually exclusive and addressing challenges of privacy can reconcile the imperatives of counterterrorism and intelligence with the values of representative democracy and an open society. America has two significant advantages over terrorism: (1) the capabilities and resources of advanced technology, and (2) the values and resiliency of liberal democracy. One advantage need not erode the other.

SEVEN

Technical Collection in the Post–September 11 World

Jeffrey T. Richelson

A quarter-century ago, Wilhelm Agrell reflected on the impact of technical collection – which initially consisted of overhead photographic reconnaissance and communications intelligence (COMINT) – on national intelligence. On the positive side, it made it possible for the most advanced countries to get "an almost complete picture of the strength, deployment, and activity of foreign military forces." The negative, for Agrell, was an overemphasis on what could be counted. Intelligence became "concentrated on evaluation and comparison of military strength based exclusively on numerical factors."[1]

Yet, since the fall of communism and since 11 September 2001, research has not really asked similar questions about the impact of technical collection. To be sure, the highly classified nature of some collection makes it difficult for outsiders to judge the effects on policy outcomes. It is possible, however, to come to the kind of judgments Agrell rendered about the impact of technical collection on the practice of intelligence. So far, however, more serious research has not moved much beyond the post–September 11 conventional wisdom that the change in intelligence's target renders technical collection less effective. Terrorists, it is thought, are small and fleet – networked enough not to depend on large fixed facilities that can be monitored from space and nimble enough to shift to forms of communication, such as couriers, that cannot be intercepted by satellite systems.

This chapter assesses research on technical collection, looking across the various "INTs" and, in particular, probing that conventional wisdom. Its aim is to begin to fill the gap by systematically considering the value of the various forms of technical collection in the post–September 11 world

---

[1] Wilhelm Agrell, "Beyond Cloak and Dagger," in Wilhelm Agrell and Bo Huldt (eds.), *Clio Goes Spying: Eight Essays on the History of Intelligence* (Lund: Lund Studies in International History 17, 1983), pp. 184–5.

in an unclassified public assessment. Such an evaluation needs to examine the value of such collection activities against the full range of targets that exist in the post–September 11 world. The chapter concludes with the area where technical collection, if not new, then is newly important: at home, in monitoring domestic communications in the fight against terror and in employing satellite imagery in support of law enforcement and border security. The chapter raises issues of the legal basis for those activities – an issue that David Omand takes up in Chapter Ten, with respect to communications intercepts, in another way.

THE GROWING IMPORTANCE OF TECHNICAL COLLECTION

It almost goes without saying after the Cold War how valuable technical collectors became, driven by advancing technology, the nature of the target, and adversaries' efforts at denial and deception. In Chapter Three, Christopher Andrew underscores how important, in particular, signals intelligence (SIGINT) was during hot war and cold. That process of increasing value as a component of intelligence capabilities, particularly for major powers, followed the development of radio communications and airplanes in the early 20th century. For the remainder of the century, technical collection increased in importance – the result of increased technical capabilities and the nature of the target. Intercept and code-breaking capabilities grew substantially between World War I and World War II, as did those of the aircraft employed for photographic reconnaissance.

The span of the Cold War featured a quantum leap in technical-collection capabilities. Imagery, electronic signals, and other signals could be gathered from space, air, land, sea, and underwater. With regard to imagery, satellites were able to produce ever more precise images, remain in orbit for longer periods, and eventually transmit their images in real time. In addition, their repertoire grew from being able to produce photographs only during daylight to being able to obtain images at night (through infrared sensors and radar) and in the presence of cloud cover (through radar). Major advances also took place in SIGINT and measurement and signature intelligence (MASINT) fields.

The utility of technical collection in the Cold War was *also* a product of the primary targets – the military, particularly strategic military, forces of the Soviet Union and then China. Those nations would build many facilities for the production of fissile material and nuclear weapons, deploy missiles, establish early-warning and air-defense facilities, maintain large navies, and build airfields for bombers and fighters across their territories. Imagery satellites and other technical-collection assets were ideal for monitoring their construction and status. Electronic-intelligence (ELINT) assets, both aerospace and ground – such as those that intercepted telemetry – played a major role in determining the capabilities of missiles and other targeted systems. MASINT systems, such as the Defense Support Program satellites and numerous radar systems, provided valuable intelligence on foreign missile and space systems.

In addition, a third variable in determining the value of technical-collection systems during the Cold War and the decade prior to September 11 was denial and deception – the inclination to attempt it, the quality of foreign denial and deception efforts, and the capabilities of the United States and other nations to see through such efforts.

Even during the Cold War, however, there were those in the United States who argued that the nation was overreliant on technical collection systems and under-investing in human intelligence (HUMINT) – that is, traditional espionage. Director of Central Intelligence Stansfield Turner (1977–81) was a particularly popular whipping boy in this regard. Often, it was claimed that human spies were unmatched in reporting the intentions of foreign leaders, despite the historical evidence that COMINT was also of significant value in revealing intentions.[2]

The value of technical collection was questioned further in the first decade after the collapse of the Soviet Union – as the smaller, often very covert weapons of mass destruction (WMD) programs of rogue states became primary targets for the intelligence communities of the United States and several other nations. At the same time, there was increasing emphasis on intelligence support for military operations during the Clinton administration. As a result, technical-collection resources would be in great demand and considerable effort would be made, and continues to be made, to establish direct "sensor-to-shooter" links.

By the late 1990s, imagery obtained by satellites and U-2 aircraft could be transmitted directly or via relay to theater forces – employing relay satellites, mobile ground stations (on land and sea), and theater imagery-transmission systems. Similarly, SIGINT from U-2s could be transmitted, via satellite, across the world. In addition, Army- and Navy-operated mobile terminals could obtain infrared intelligence from Defense Support Program satellites.[3]

---

[2] Stansfield Turner, *Secrecy and Democracy: The CIA in Transition* (Boston: Houghton Mifflin, 1985), p. 207.

[3] See Jeffrey T. Richelson, *The U.S. Intelligence Community* (Boulder, CO: Westview, 1999), pp. 170–3, 193; Jeffrey T. Richelson, *America's Space Sentinels: DSP Satellites and National Security* (Lawrence, KS: University Press of Kansas, 1999), pp. 189–91.

In March 2008 congressional testimony, the director of the National Reconnaissance Office (NRO) noted a number of "support to the warfighter" initiatives undertaken by the NRO. Included was the Threat Human Intelligence Reporting Evaluation Analysis and Display System (THREADS), which takes HUMINT reports and searches data bases of NRO satellite-system data to find relevant information. According to the NRO director, "Forward-deployed units have successfully used THREADS to piece together information leading to the capture or death of enemy forces in Iraq and Afghanistan."[4]

However, the terrorist attacks of 11 September 2001, seemed to renew and reinvigorate the case for devoting far more attention and resources to HUMINT and less to technical collection. The choice was often depicted as a choice between expensive "spies in the sky" and agents on the ground.

Al Qaeda and other terrorist groups have no airfields, missile silos, or air defenses to target with imagery sensors or intercept equipment. Terrorist training facilities could still be spotted, but they might well be empty when cruise missiles arrived to destroy them – as they were when the United States responded to al Qaeda's 1998 bombing of its embassies in Dar-es-Salaam, Tanzania, and in Nairobi, Kenya. The conversations of terrorists could be intercepted – but not as extensively as those of foreign governments that could not regularly and extensively resort to couriers or other forms of radio silence. Humans, at least potentially, could infiltrate terrorist groups and report on the whereabouts of key personnel, and – more important – on the plans for upcoming attacks. This conventional wisdom renders an assessment across the technical disciplines all the more necessary.

Imagery after September 11

In early 2001, the *International Journal of Intelligence and Counterintelligence* published an article by reporter John M. Diamond titled "Re-examining Problems and Prospects in U.S. Imagery Intelligence."[5] Diamond's article focused on the satellite-imagery component of U.S. overhead-imagery operations. He noted and examined the efforts to "redesign and redefine" U.S. satellite-imagery capabilities to enhance their ability to support military

---

[4] Scott Large, Director of the National Reconnaissance Office, "Statement for the Record," House Armed Services Committee Subcommittee on Strategic Forces Joint Hearing, Fiscal Defense Authorization Act Budget Request and Status for Space Activities, March 5, 2008, pp. 3–6.

[5] John M. Diamond, "Re-examining Problems and Prospects in U.S. Imagery Intelligence," *International Journal of Intelligence and Counterintelligence*, 14, 1 (Spring 2001), 1–24.

operations and the existence of gaps (including the failure to provide warning of India's 1998 nuclear tests and North Korea's 1998 Taepo-Dong missile tests), as well as the budgetary constraints facing the NRO, responsible for spy-satellite development, in the post–Cold War era.

Diamond reached the following five key conclusions:

1. The space-imagery community had not clearly laid out a forward path that had unanimous support within the intelligence community and congressional oversight committees.
2. The current space-imagery architecture had not demonstrated an ability to contribute decisively with regard to terrorism and weapons proliferation – "the nation's most important national security areas."
3. The primary mission of imagery intelligence (IMINT) is moving away from its Cold War strategic mission and toward a real-time battlefield support role.
4. The IMINT system in use today is essentially the same as the system used during the Cold War.
5. Among sophisticated adversaries, development of denial and deception skills appears to be outpacing advancements in satellite reconnaissance.[6]

Diamond's work was a prelude to trying to assess the value of imagery – at least, satellite imagery – in the first years of the new century.

To be sure, the circumstances changed radically by the end of 2001. In any case, subsequent to the September 11 attacks, some observers complained (as others had in the past) that too much confidence in the value of technical collection, particularly satellite collection, had caused the intelligence community to spend too much on satellites and too little on recruiting necessary human sources. Patrick Radden Keefe wrote that "Satellites provided an effective means of monitoring cold-war enemies, but where the Soviets were a big and lumbering target, America's terrorist adversaries are small and fleet. A satellite that passes briefly overhead during its orbit may not be able to catch an arms deal in a village square or a convoy in the desert."[7] He also wrote that "rogue countries like North Korea and Iran . . . know the United States already has more than 100 military and intelligence satellites in orbit; they aren't going to be foolish enough to conduct suspicious activities in open sight. Their nuclear programs are underground and in buildings, because they assume the United States is watching." Another observer and

---

[6] Ibid., pp. 2–3.
[7] Patrick Radden Keefe, "A Shortsighted Eye in the Sky," *The New York Times*, February 5, 2005, p. A17.

critic of the U.S. intelligence community Amy Zegart argued that "old Cold War spending patterns continued to favor technical [collection], which was well suited for detecting the location of Soviet warheads, over human intelligence efforts better suited for penetrating terrorist groups on the ground." Ted Gup wrote that "satellites are fine for tracking troop movements, but a fast-moving cell of terrorists, or a training camp consisting of little more than tents and rifle ranges, can easily elude an eye in the sky."[8]

It is certainly easy to make a case that the relative value of overhead-imagery collection is less significant in an era when terrorism is the priority target than when Soviet strategic nuclear forces were the priority target. Clearly, keeping track of missile-silo and nuclear-reactor construction, activities at airfields, monitoring nuclear-testing sites operated by acknowledged nuclear powers, identifying radar- and ground-based intercept facilities, and counting the number of bombers and fighters at military airfields were missions that could be best accomplished by satellites continually circling the globe. Such large, fixed facilities can be imaged repeatedly and a wealth of intelligence extracted from the visible-light, infrared, and radar images produced by U.S., French, Japanese, Israeli, and other nations' imagery satellites. In contrast, the small-scale activities associated with terrorist groups will be far more difficult to detect with satellites.

However, any assessment of the value of imagery in the post–September 11 world must consider the full range of targets (and the priorities attached to those targets), the different types of overhead-imagery systems, the impact of denial and deception measures, and the need to be able to shift intelligence-collection assets to deal with unexpected reporting requirements, including those generated by a crisis.

The terrorist target, specifically al Qaeda and its affiliates, is considered – at least, by the United States – to be at the top of the priority list. Specific components of that target include the identities and whereabouts of terrorist leaders and other high-value personnel (i.e., those with important financial and logistical jobs), training facilities, communications links or procedures, *jihadist* Web sites, locations at which bombs or WMD are being assembled, and, of course, the intentions and plans (at any stage of development) of terrorist groups desiring to attack the United States or its interests.

Also of high priority are the nuclear programs of rogue states – Iran and North Korea – as well as states that might be endeavoring to join the nuclear club. Included in that group may be a number of Arab states, some friendly

[8] Keefe, "A Shortsighted Eye in the Sky"; Amy Zegart, "September 11 and the Adaptation Failure of U.S. Intelligence Agencies," *International Security, 29*, 4 (Spring 2005), pp. 78–111 at p. 107; and Ted Gup, "Clueless in Langley," *Mother Jones*, January/February 2002, pp. 33–7.

to the United States (e.g., Egypt and Turkey) and others that are not (e.g., Syria).[9] Elements of information needed about existing or potential nuclear-weapons programs include the intentions of national leaders; details of procurement activities; identities and activities of scientists and technicians who are or might be participating in nuclear-weapons activities; and the location, purpose, and output of facilities known or suspected to be involved in a nuclear-weapons program. Such facilities may include those involved in mining and processing, in various stages of the production of fissile material, in weapons design and assembly, and in testing of finished devices. Similar information is required with regard to other WMD programs that those countries may be pursuing.

Examples of post–September 11 satellite imagery clearly of use in monitoring the activities of rogue regimes include the following:

- In May 2002, it was reported that U.S. imaging satellites detected that Iranian military forces had moved additional air-defense missiles to the vicinity of the Bushehr nuclear reactor.[10]
- In July 2002, U.S. imagery satellites detected activity at an Iraqi factory near Taji associated with Iraq's biological-weapons program.[11]
- In January 2003, it was reported that American satellites spotted trucks at the Yongbyon nuclear facility in North Korea that appeared to be moving eight thousand nuclear fuel rods out of storage.[12]
- In April 2005, U.S. imagery satellites detected the digging of a tunnel – similar to the one used by Pakistan in its 1998 nuclear tests – in the northern Kilju region of North Korea, which was considered a possible nuclear test site.[13]

Although terrorism and rogue nations may be at the top of the priority list in the post–September 11 world, they are not the only targets of interest

---

[9] Bob Drogin and Borzou Daragahi, "Arabs Make Plans for a Future with Nuclear Power," *Los Angeles Times*, May 26, 2007, pp. A1, A6–A7. Syria has been suggested as the possible fourth (unidentified) nation that was interested in the nuclear-weapons–related material being sold by A. Q. Khan. See Gordon Corera, *Shopping for Bombs: Nuclear Proliferation, Global Insecurity, and the Rise and Fall of the A. Q. Khan Network* (New York: Oxford, 2006), p. 235.

[10] Bill Gertz and Rowan Scarborough, "Inside the Ring," *Washington Times*, May 10, 2002, p. A10.

[11] Bill Gertz, "Iraqis 'Moving Stuff' at Germ Plant," *Washington Times*, August 14, 2002, pp. A1, A18.

[12] David E. Sanger and Eric Schmitt, "Satellites Said to See Activity at North Korean Nuclear Site," *The New York Times*, January 31, 2003, pp. A1, A10.

[13] David E. Sanger and William J. Broad, "U.S. Cites Signs of Korean Steps to Nuclear Test," *The New York Times*, May 6, 2005, pp. A1, A6.

to the United States or other nations. Military developments within several countries remain significant subjects for reporting and analysis. China has undertaken a significant military-modernization campaign – including conventional weaponry, strategic nuclear weaponry, space and counterspace, and information warfare. In addition to the testing, construction, and deployment of weaponry, the United States is concerned with how that weaponry might affect Chinese actions vis-à-vis Taiwan.[14]

Although Russia is no longer the concern that the Soviet Union had been, the growing hostility that emanated from Moscow during the tenure of President Vladimir Putin, along with the fact that Russia still possesses a rather considerable nuclear arsenal, requires that the U.S. intelligence community continue to monitor military developments in that nation – such as the May 2007 test of the RS-24 intercontinental ballistic missile (ICBM). The missile is intended to replace Soviet-era ICBMs and provide a means to counter any U.S. missile-defense system.[15]

Military developments in a host of other nations – India, Pakistan, and Israel, among others – also remain of great interest to the United States (and several other countries). Those developments include both the development and deployment of weapons systems (including various forms of WMD) and indications that some of those systems may be readied for a preemptive attack. In addition, nonmilitary developments such as humanitarian crises (e.g., Rwanda in the 1990s and Sudan today) will also be of concern to international and regional actors.

Moreover, although satellites comprise the preeminent imagery system, they are not the only such overhead system factor. Satellites are the most expensive form of imagery platforms, and they can provide both the greatest volume of coverage and the widest geographic access. The laws of physics guarantee that a satellite can be placed in an orbit that will allow repeated coverage of any target of interest beneath the satellite's path – at least until a nation develops and employs an antisatellite capability. Until then, satellites have an invulnerability not possessed by manned aircraft and unmanned aerial vehicles (UAVs). Their ability to operate for years also guarantees that a large file of imagery can be accumulated for any target.

The array of sensors carried on imagery satellites also permits images to be obtained during a variety of conditions. The United States operates three types of imagery satellites. The Enhanced Crystal System (i.e., advanced

---

[14] Office of the Secretary of Defense, *Military Power of the People's Republic of China, 2007*, 2007.

[15] "Russia Says New ICBM Could Overcome U.S. Defense," *Space News*, June 4, 2007, p. 8.

KH-11) satellites, in the absence of cloud cover, can obtain imagery in visible-light and darkness – the latter due to its Dragon infrared imagery sensor. Misty stealth satellites are also equipped with visible-light and infrared sensors; Onyx radar imagery satellites can produce imagery day or night and in the presence of cloud cover.[16] Other Western nations also operate satellite systems with one or more of those capabilities. Japan operates radar and optical satellites; France deploys Helios satellites with visible-light and infrared sensors; and Germany and Italy orbit radar imagery satellites.[17] The ability of some of those satellites, including all U.S. satellites, to operate in near real time also ensures a minimum time period between the acquisition of target imagery and its availability to an imagery interpreter.

However, satellites are not the only systems for the collection of overhead imagery. Aircraft such as the U-2 spy plane predated satellites and continue to be used extensively in the almost 50 years since the first successful satellite reconnaissance mission. The U-2 planes can carry an array of imagery sensors, although not all at once. U-2s that fly between 65,000 and 73,000 feet can carry visible-light, infrared, or radar sensors. The U-2 is only one of many aircraft still used to conduct overhead imagery missions by the United States; P-3 Orions, F-18s, and RC-7s are also part of the aerial-imagery fleet.[18]

Aerial-imagery systems can supplement the coverage of satellites, provide a quick-reaction capability, and produce imagery that can be more widely distributed than satellite imagery under current security policy. In addition, although satellite coverage of a particular area can be limited to the territory rotating under the satellite's orbit, aircraft can fly a route that focuses on a particular region or territory between any two points within its range – an ideal capability for monitoring troop or refugee movements.

Today, several key UAV programs are in operation or development. The GNAT 750-45, better known as the Predator, is an advanced version of the UAVs flown over Bosnia by the Central Intelligence Agency (CIA) in 1994. The original version of the Predator, the RQ-1, had a range of approximately 450 miles and a maximum altitude of 25,000 feet. It carried electro-optical and infrared imagery systems as well as synthetic-aperture radar. In the

---

[16] The MISTY program was canceled in June 2007. How long the satellite orbited in 1999 will remain operational, assuming it still is, is not known – even by those operating it.

[17] Jeffrey T. Richelson, *The U.S. Intelligence Community*, fifth edition (Boulder, CO: Westview, 2007), pp. 177–81; Peter B. De Selding, "European Space-Based Reconnaissance Takes Off," *Space News*, June 11, 2007, p. 13; "Japan Intel Satellite Malfunctions in Orbit," *Space News*, April 2, 2007, p. 3.

[18] Richelson, *The U.S. Intelligence Community*, pp. 187–91.

aftermath of September 11, the U.S. Air Force and the CIA completed the arming of Predators with Hellfire missiles to eliminate the delay between detecting a target and attempting to destroy it. The armed version of the Predator, designated the MQ-1, carries the Multi-Spectral Targeting System, which integrates the electro-optical, infrared, laser designator, and laser illuminator into a single sensor package.

Other UAVs for reconnaissance purposes include the advanced Global Hawk (RQ-4A). These vehicles have a 3,000-nautical-mile (nm) radius and carry electro-optical, infrared, and synthetic-aperture radar–moving-target indicator sensors. They can stay on station for 24 hours (if flown to maximum radius) at an altitude of 65,000 feet. In that time, they can image 40,000 square nm or obtain 1,900 2-kilometer-square images. Data can be transmitted to ground stations below or relay satellites above for relay to the United States and other locations.[19]

Such overhead capabilities, although impressive, still face significant challenges in monitoring not only terrorist activity but also the WMD activities of rogue states and other nations of concern because those programs are smaller and more covert than the massive programs conducted by the Soviet Union and China. The denial and deception activities of foreign governments are of sufficient concern that the U.S. intelligence community has a standing committee to address the issue.

The denial and deception techniques facing major U.S. and other overhead-imagery systems include the construction of underground facilities. Indeed, since 1997, the U.S. intelligence community has operated an Underground Facilities Analysis Center (UFAC), staffed with analysts from a variety of agencies. In 1994, a member of the Los Alamos National Laboratory (LANL) made a presentation at the NRO on a LANL-developed technique known as Geological Assessment Methodology for Underground Targets (GAMUT), which reportedly "showed results for an underground target of great interest in a foreign country."[20]

In 1998, India devoted significant attention to conducting preparations for its nuclear test in ways that avoided creating warning signs of its plans.

---

[19] Aeronautical Systems Center, U.S. Air Force Fact Sheet, "Global Hawk," December 2002; David A. Fulghum, "Global Hawk UAVs to Remain Unarmed," *Aviation Week & Space Technology*, April 15, 2002, pp. 20–1.

[20] Scott Robertson, "Collaboration Is Cornerstone of UFAC," *Pathfinder*, May/June 2007, pp. 21–2; "Brunish Gives Talk on LANL's GAMUT at the National Reconnaissance Office," available at www.ees.lanl.gov/News/news.sub.shtml, accessed July 23, 2004. Jeffrey T. Richelson, "Unearthing Secrets," *C⁴ISR Journal*, August 2008, pp. 28–30.

It conducted operations at night to reduce the number of imagery satellites that could detect its activities and eliminated signs of its preparations by the time daylight arrived.[21]

In reaching an assessment of overhead imagery, there are instances when such systems either provided significant warning of terrorist actions or could have. Satellite images obtained, but overlooked, before the September 1984 terrorist bombing on the U.S. Embassy annex in Beirut showed that a mock-up of the annex and its defenses had been built and used to practice driving trucks through them.[22]

UAVs, such as the Predator, have also allowed the tracking of terrorists as well as their targeted killing – as the result of Predators being armed with Hellfire missiles. An apparent Predator attack killed a former Taliban commander, Nek Mohammed, along with five others in South Waziristan in June 2004. On May 10, 2005, Haithem al-Yemeni, a potential successor to al Qaeda operations chief, Abu Faraj al-Libi – who had been captured a week earlier – was killed in Pakistan by a Hellfire missile. In December 2005, a Hellfire missile killed Hamza Rabia – identified by American officials as al Qaeda's chief of international operations – at a safehouse located in Asorai in Western Pakistan.[23] What satellites can do only in the world of the television series *24*, UAVs can do in the real world.

Finally, overhead-imagery systems can include a variety of smaller systems – such as micro-UAVs that are difficult to track and can serve not only figuratively but literally as a "fly on the wall." These systems have a long lineage. In the 1970s, the CIA developed the Dragonfly Insectothopter – an insect-sized UAV. Another project from the late 1960s, the Aquiline, involved development of a UAV with photographic sensors and disguised as a condor.[24]

One attempt has been made to evaluate the utility of a particular type of overhead-imagery system against a specific target. An article authored by Li Bin of the Institute of International Studies at Beijing's Tsinghua University examined the ability of a space radar system to track Chinese

[21] Jeffrey T. Richelson, *Spying on the Bomb: American Nuclear Intelligence from Nazi Germany to North Korea and Iran* (New York: W. W. Norton, 2006), pp. 427–35.
[22] Stansfield Turner, "Intelligence for a New World Order," *Foreign Affairs*, Fall 1991, pp. 153–66.
[23] "Airstrike by U.S. Draws Protests from Pakistanis," *The New York Times*, January 15, 2006, pp. 1, 4; Josh Meyer, "CIA Expands Use of Drones in Terror War," *Los Angeles Times*, January 29, 2006, pp. A1, A28–A29.
[24] Jeffrey T. Richelson, *The Wizards of Langley: Inside the CIA's Directorate of Science and Technology* (Boulder, CO: Westview, 2001), p. 148.

strategic mobile missiles.[25] Li analyzed the maneuverability, capabilities, and survivability of Chinese DF-31 mobile missiles along with the ability of the proposed U.S. space radar system to track them on a consistent basis. Li examined possible defensive strategies that China might adopt to reduce the vulnerability of the missiles to detection and destruction in a war. Specifically, he considered various alternative constellations of space radar satellites; satellites with different capabilities; and issues concerned with detection such as sight block (i.e., the blocking of a satellite's view of the target due to obstacles), radial speed, and stealth, as well as evasion strategies. Li concluded that their survivability would not be guaranteed in a war but also questioned how effectively a space radar system could keep track of their movements.

SIGINT after September 11

Compared to imagery, there are many more means of collecting SIGINT – a category that encompasses both COMINT and ELINT.[26] As with imagery, satellites contribute a significant part of the take. The United States, even before the collapse of the Soviet Union, maintained the world's largest and most diverse constellation of SIGINT satellites. Unlike imagery, where recent years have seen a large number of countries orbit high-resolution IMINT spacecraft as well as a number of commercial high-resolution satellite imagery ventures – the number of nations operating SIGINT satellites remains small, with France as the only newcomer on the horizon.

The constellation has included satellites in three different orbits. In 1960, the U.S. Navy orbited the first ELINT satellite – the Galactic Background and Radiation (GRAB) satellite – whose primary target was Soviet radar systems. In 1962, the U.S. Air Force began launching its own "ferret" satellites to monitor Soviet radars. All of these satellites operated in low-earth orbit – with a maximum altitude of 500 nm or lower. In recent years, a result of a consolidation of U.S. ocean surveillance ELINT and ferret programs, current ELINT satellites have operated in slightly higher orbits but well under 1,000 nm.[27]

---

[25] Li Bin, "Tracking Chinese Strategic Mobile Missiles," *Science and Global Security*, 15, 1 (January–April) 2007, pp. 1–30.

[26] Electronic intelligence includes intelligence derived from the interception of signals from radars, from missiles during test flights (telemetry), and other signals concerning the performance of aircraft, space systems, and other military vehicles.

[27] Dwayne Day, "Early American Ferret and Radar Satellites," *Spaceflight*, 43, July 2001, pp. 288–93.

Two other classes of SIGINT satellites have far higher maximum altitudes. Since 1968, the United States has orbited geosynchronous SIGINT satellites. One subclass of these satellites (the first generation of which was designated Canyon) operated between 19,000 and 23,000 miles and circled the globe at a speed that matched the targets beneath it. Another subclass (the first generation of which was named Rhyolite) operated in geostationary orbit at 22,300 miles above the earth. Follow-on systems for each subclass are operating today – each capable of monitoring both communications that leak into space and missile telemetry.[28]

The third class of U.S. SIGINT satellites are those that operate in highly elliptical Molniya orbit, with an inclination of about 63 degrees, and that reach as far as 24,000 miles above the earth (over the higher latitudes of the Northern Hemisphere) and as close as 240 miles (over the lower latitudes of the Southern Hemisphere). The first generation, designated Jumpseat, was replaced by the Trumpet generation, which apparently is in the process of being replaced by a new generation.[29]

Other major SIGINT-collection systems have included aircraft – a capability possessed by several nations and usually based on reconfigured aircraft originally designed for other purposes. The United States operates several SIGINT-collection aircraft, some originally developed and operated against Cold War targets (e.g., Soviet missile testing). These include Air Force RC-135s, Navy EP-3s, and Army RC-12 Guardrail aircraft, all of which have been used for both COMINT purposes and to gather scientific and technical intelligence. Both the Combat Sent version of the RC-135 and the EP-3 have been used to gather data on foreign radar systems.[30]

During the Cold War, the United States, its allies, and the Soviet Union operated numerous ground stations to gather SIGINT. The stations may have consisted of various antenna arrays, including circular-disposed antenna arrays with a diameter equivalent to several football fields that intercepted both strategic and tactical high-frequency communications bouncing off the atmosphere. Other stations consisted of satellite dishes to intercept satellite traffic – in some cases military traffic, in other cases civilian traffic. In the immediate post–Cold War era, the UKUSA Echelon program, which involved the exchange of intelligence obtained from

---

[28] Christopher Anson Pike, "CANYON, RHYOLITE, and AQUACADE: U.S. Signals Intelligence Satellites in the 1970s," *Spaceflight*, 37, 11, November 1995, pp. 381–3.

[29] Jeffrey T. Richelson, *The U.S. Intelligence Community*, fifth edition (Boulder, CO: Westview, 2007), pp. 219–20.

[30] Ibid., pp. 221–7.

intercepting civilian satellite (essentially, Intelsat) traffic, became the object of controversy in Europe.[31]

Finally, with regard to traditional types of SIGINT-collection platforms – are the surface ships and submarines, the former operated by several countries. Surface ships can lurk outside a nation's territorial waters and monitor communications along that nation's periphery. Submarines can operate more covertly, remaining underneath the surface but raising an antenna up through the water to intercept communications or monitor the telemetry from a missile test.[32] These systems can still provide intelligence on subjects of concern in the post–September 11 world.

Examples of intercepts from the pre–September 11 world are relevant because intercepts of similar material would be of interest today – and nothing in the post–September 11 world would necessarily prevent the intercepts from being obtained. In 1968, intercepted voice communications in the Beijing Military Region indicated a field exercise involving the 4th Armored Division. In 1980, U.S. intercepts of Soviet communications led to fear that the Soviets were about to invade Iran. COMINT played a significant role in preparing a 1982 study on Indian heavy water shortages. In 1983, intercepts allowed the United States to piece together the details concerning the sinking of a Soviet submarine in the North Pacific. In 1988, intercepted Iraqi military communications led U.S. officials to conclude that Iraq had used chemical weapons in its war with Iran. After the Iraqi invasion of Kuwait in August 1990, COMINT and other intelligence reports indicated that Saudi leaders were considering an attempt to pay off Saddam Hussein. Intercepts of Chinese diplomatic communications in 1996 and thereafter raised the question of whether the People's Republic of China had attempted to funnel money to American politicians for use in their campaigns. In 1998, intercepts revealed that the Russian foreign intelligence service had facilitated the sale of Russian missile technology to Iran. The following year, COMINT showed that high-ranking Yugoslavian officials had ordered an attack on the village of Racak in Kosovo, which resulted in the massacre of 45 unarmed Albanian civilians.[33]

---

[31] Jeffrey T. Richelson, "Desperately Seeking Signals," *Bulletin of the Atomic Scientists*, March/April 2000, pp. 47–51.

[32] Richelson, *The U.S. Intelligence Community*, pp. 233–5.

[33] Defense Intelligence Agency, *Soviet and People's Republic of China Nuclear Weapons Employment Policy and Strategy*, March 1972, p. II-B-5; [author deleted], "Indian Heavy Water Shortages," [from an undetermined NSA publication], October 1982; George C. Wilson, "Soviet Nuclear Sub Reported Sunk," *Washington Post*, August 11, 1983, p. A9;

Whether SIGINT can "deliver the goods" with respect to terrorism has been questioned. Ted Gup asserted that "those who monitor intercepts can easily be outwitted. Bin Laden and others appear to have used the United States' eavesdropping capacity to send intelligence agencies on wild-goose chases. In addition, the crushing volume of data often precludes analysts' ability to find the key messages until after the fact – after the attack. Such technology may be useful as a tool in gathering evidence, but it comes as little comfort to the bereaved."[34]

A similar view was expressed in 1997 by the U.S. Defense Science Board, which concluded that "because of the very high security consciousness of transnational groups, there is generally insufficient, verifiable information available about transnational adversary operation, membership, and other important details."[35]

Whether such views are borne out by the facts was the subject of Matthew Aid's 2003 article, "All Glory Is Fleeting: SIGINT and the Fight against International Terrorism."[36] Aid noted the incidents that would seem to support such pessimistic views. Most prominent are the National Security Agency (NSA) intercepts of September 10, 2001, in which the individuals being monitored made the statements "The big match is about to begin" and "Tomorrow was 'zero hour'" – statements that even if processed on the day they were intercepted rather than after September 11 were lacking any specifics about the location or nature of the planned attacks. Aid also noted, consistent with Gup's final observation, that intercepts obtained after the 1998 Kenya and Tanzania embassy bombings provided evidence

David B. Ottaway, "Iraq Said to Have Expelled High-Level U.S. Diplomat," *Washington Post*, November 17, 1988, p. A-33; George J. Church, "Destination Haiti," *Time*, September 26, 1994, pp. 21–6; Christopher Andrew, *For the President's Eyes Only: Secret Intelligence and the American Presidency from Washington to Bush* (New York: HarperCollins, 1995), p. 520; David Johnston, "U.S. Agency Secretly Monitored Chinese in '96 on Political Gifts," *The New York Times*, March 13, 1997, pp. A1, A25; Nora Boustany and Brian Duffy, "A Top U.S. Official May Have Given Sensitive Data to Israel," *Washington Post*, May 7, 1997, pp. A1, A28; Russell Watson and John Barry, "Our Target Was Terror," *Newsweek*, August 31, 1998, pp. 24–9; Matthew M. Aid, "The Time of Troubles: The U.S. National Security Agency in the Twenty-First Century," *Intelligence and National Security*, 15, 3 (Autumn 2000), pp. 1–2; Matthew M. Aid, "All Glory Is Fleeting: SIGINT and the Fight Against International Terrorism," *Intelligence and National Security*, 18, 4 (Winter 2003), pp. 72–120.

[34] Gup, "Clueless in Langley."

[35] Office of the Under Secretary of Defense for Acquisition & Technology, *The Defense Science Board 1997 Summer Study Task Force on DoD Responses to Transnational Threats, Volume I: Final Report*, October 1997, p. C-2.

[36] Matthew M. Aid, "All Glory Is Fleeting: SIGINT and the Fight against International Terrorism," *Intelligence and National Security*, 18, 4 (Winter 2003), pp. 72–120.

that the attacks had been perpetrated by al Qaeda. Similarly, NSA intercepts reporting that an attack was planned in the region where the USS *Cole* was operating were not received until after the attack.[37]

Yet, Aid also noted in a section of his article titled "The Fallacy of High-Tech Terrorism" that many of the assumptions concerning the difficulty of employing SIGINT resources against the terrorist target are incorrect. For instance, SIGINT has been a viable means of gathering data on terrorist activities because of the absence of landline telephone service in Afghanistan (forcing the use of satellite telephones), along with the willingness of many bin Laden subordinates to continue speaking on satellite and cellular phones even after bin Laden himself stopped using them to communicate.[38]

Most important, Aid cited a number of cases – both before and after September 11 – in which COMINT was instrumental in actually preventing planned terrorist attacks and apprehending terrorists. Pre–September 11 terrorist plots disrupted or terrorists apprehended, due in whole or in part to COMINT, include the following:

- a planned al Qaeda attack on American overseas diplomatic or military establishments, including the Prince Sultan Air Base in Saudi Arabia (1998)
- a planned attack on U.S. military installations in Saudi Arabia (June 2001)
- a planned attack on U.S. diplomatic facilities in Paris (about June 2001).[39]

Post–September 11 SIGINT successes related to terrorism include the following:

- the location and arrest of bin Laden lieutenant, Abu Zubaida, along with 19 al Qaeda operatives (March 2002)
- the arrest of Sheik Ahmed Salim, wanted for his role in the 1998 embassy bombings (July 2002)
- the arrest of Ramzi Binashibh, one of the al Qaeda planners for September 11 (September 2002)
- the arrest of September 11 mastermind, Khalid Sheikh Muhammad (March 2003).[40]

[37] Ibid., pp. 88, 91, 93.
[38] Ibid., pp. 84–5.
[39] Ibid., pp. 88, 92.
[40] Ibid., p. 105.

Aid also noted that only part of the SIGINT effort involves remote SIGINT systems (e.g., satellites, aircraft, and large ground stations). Another important part of the SIGINT effort against the terrorist target is clandestine SIGINT. As Aid let Gregory Treverton explain:

SIGINT will need to get closer to the signals in which it is interested. During the high Cold War, the Soviet Union sent many of its phone calls through microwave relay stations. Since private telephones were relatively few, intercepting those conversations with satellites yielded important insights into economic production and sometimes into military movements or lines of command. Now, though, with hundreds of communications bundled into fiber optic lines, there is less for satellites to intercept. If SIGINT is to intercept those signals, it will have to tap into particular communications lines in specific places. It will have to collect keystrokes straight from a personal computer, before software encrypts the message.[41]

Clandestine SIGINT, or CLANSIG in the trade, includes the type of operations that Treverton described and more. Such operations have a long lineage, conducted by the CIA and more recently by the joint CIA–NSA unit known as the Special Collection Service (SCS), which also conducts embassy-based eavesdropping operations.[42] In 1965, the CIA planted a nuclear-powered device on the summit of Nanda Devi in Garhwal, India. The device was intended to monitor the telemetry of Chinese missile tests from the Shuangchengzi test center in north-central China. After it was swept away in an avalanche, a second device was placed in 1967 on the summit of the neighboring 22,400-foot Nanda Kot. That device remained in place for a year before being removed.[43]

Another high-risk operation occurred in 1999, when a team of CIA officers from the SCS covertly entered southeastern Afghanistan to install a remote-controlled SIGINT collection system near a group of al Qaeda camps near the town of Khost.[44]

The need for expanding CLANSIG operations in concert with the CIA's operations directorate was noted in April 1999 by the NSA's deputy director of operations, who wrote that "our relationship with CIA is absolutely vital

---

[41] Ibid., p. 106, citing Gregory F. Treverton, "Intelligence Crisis," *Government Executive,* November 1, 2001, available at www.govexec.com/features/1101/1101s1.htm.

[42] The United Kingdom operates a similar unit: the Special Projects Activity. See Scott Ritter, *Iraq Confidential: The Untold Story of the Intelligence Conspiracy to Undermine the UN and Overthrow Saddam Hussein* (New York: Nation Books, 2005), p. 135.

[43] Jeffrey T. Richelson, *The Wizards of Langley: Inside the CIA's Directorate of Science and Technology* (Boulder, CO: Westview, 2001), p. 93.

[44] Matthew M. Aid, "All Glory Is Fleeting: SIGINT and the Fight against International Terrorism," *Intelligence and National Security, 18,* 4 (Winter 2003), pp. 72–120 at p. 90; Barton Gellman, "Broad Effort Launched After '98 Attacks," *Washington Post,* December 19, 2001, pp. A1, A26.

to our future success" and that "it is essential that NSA and CIA put our relationship on a sound basis tuned to the needs and realities of the next century. There are many things of great importance to our country that can only be achieved by NSA and CIA acting together."[45]

In addition, the U.S. Joint Special Operations Command Intelligence Support Activity conducts CLANSIG along with clandestine HUMINT operations. Britain's Special Reconnaissance Regiment may also conduct CLANSIG in addition to clandestine HUMINT.[46]

MASINT after September 11

IMINT and SIGINT trace their identities as collection disciplines back to at least the early 20th century. By contrast, the use of the term *measurement and signature intelligence* (i.e., MASINT) as a category encompassing a number of distinct collection activities is far more recent. The U.S. intelligence community first classified MASINT as a formal intelligence discipline in 1986.[47] MASINT is officially defined as follows:

... technically derived intelligence (excluding traditional imagery and signal intelligence) that, when collected, processed, and analyzed, results in intelligence that locates, tracks, identifies, or describes the signatures (distinctive characteristics) of fixed or dynamic target sources.[48]

Given this definition, MASINT includes all remote technical collection other than SIGINT and traditional IMINT, which includes visible – light, radar, and infrared – but not multispectral, hyperspectral, or ultraspectral imagery. MASINT's scope and diversity is indicated by the identification of its various components:

- radar (line of sight, bistatic, over-the-horizon)
- radio frequency (wideband electromagnetic pulse, unintentional radiation)
- geophysical (acoustic, seismic, magnetic)

[45] James R. Taylor, Deputy Director of Operations, National Security Agency, "Thoughts on Strategic Issues for the Institution," April 9, 1999.
[46] Michael Smith, *The Killer Elite: The Inside Story of America's Most Secret Special Operations Team* (London: Weidenfeld and Nicolson, 2006); BBC News, "Special Forces Regiment Created," May 4, 2005.
[47] U.S. Congress, House Permanent Select Committee on Intelligence, *IC 21: Intelligence Community in the 21st Century* (Washington: U.S. Government Printing Office, 1996), p. 149.
[48] Department of Defense Instruction Number 5105.58, "Management of Measurement and Signature Intelligence (MASINT)," February 9, 1993, p. 1.

- nuclear radiation (X-ray, gamma ray, neutron)
- materials (effluents, particulates, debris)
- electro-optical and infrared
- multispectral, hyperspectral, and ultraspectral imagery.[49]

Some MASINT systems and missions are well known, even if not thought of in terms of MASINT collection: Defense Support Program satellites with nonimaging infrared sensors that provide intelligence on foreign missile launches and atmospheric nuclear detonations; Global Positioning System satellites equipped with sensors that detect gamma rays and X-rays from nuclear detonations; aircraft such as the Cobra Ball version of the RC-135, which carries infrared sensors; radars that can be used to identify and track foreign missiles; ground stations that can detect seismic signals produced by nuclear detonations; and the Navy's Sound Surveillance System of underwater hydrophones that has been used to identify and track foreign submarines.[50]

Other applications, particularly tactical ones, are less commonly recognized. The collection of electro-optical spectral signatures from an aircraft's exhaust, the determination of the aircraft's radar cross-section, and the gathering of its acoustic signatures all can be used to collect varied data – range, speed, acceleration, climb rate, stability, turn radius, tactics, and proficiency – that would be useful in combat. These data can be loaded into an air-defense system to aid in targeting such aircraft.[51]

As is the case with IMINT and SIGINT, most MASINT systems were developed with Cold War targets in mind, such as Soviet and Chinese strategic missiles and submarines and Soviet and Chinese nuclear testing. No attempt has been made to examine the value of such systems in the post–September 11 world. The most recent attempt to examine the varieties of MASINT and its applications appeared in an article published in the summer of 2001.[52] However, as with imagery and SIGINT, some of those systems still have substantial value – against the targets they were originally envisioned

---

[49] Ibid., p. 2; John L. Morris, "MASINT: Progress and Impact, Brief to NMIA," November 19, 1996, Slide 1; Daniel B. Sibbet, "MASINT: Intelligence for the 1990s," *American Intelligence Journal* (Summer/Fall 1990), pp. 23–6. Also see John Morris, "The Nature and Applications of Measurement and Signature Intelligence," *American Intelligence Journal*, Winter 1999–2000, pp. 81–4; John Macartney, "John, How Should We Explain MASINT," *Intelligencer*, Summer 2001, pp. 28–34.

[50] Jeffrey T. Richelson, "MASINT: The New Kid in Town," *International Journal of Intelligence and Counterintelligence*, 14, 2 (Summer 2001), pp. 149–92.

[51] Morris, "MASINT: Progress and Impact, Slide 8"; Capt. Chadwick T. Hawley, "MASINT: Supporting the Warfighter Today and Tomorrow!," *Communiqué*, May 1996, p. 14.

[52] Richelson, "MASINT: The New Kid in Town."

as operating against as well as targets whose importance has increased in recent years.

Russian and Chinese missile and space activities can be monitored using Defense Support Program satellites; the Cobra Judy ship-based radar; the Cobra Dane radar on Shemya Island, Alaska; and the Cobra Ball aircraft. Most of those systems also can be employed to monitor the missile tests of other nations, including nations with which the United States has friendly relations (e.g., India) as well as rogue nations (e.g., Iran and North Korea). Seismic systems provided data to help estimate the yields of Russian and Chinese nuclear tests prior to the 1996 signing of the Comprehensive Test Ban Treaty, of Indian and Pakistani nuclear tests in 1998, and of North Korea's nuclear test in October 2006. Those data were instrumental in the assessment that the latter test's yield was significantly smaller than the North Koreans expected. In addition, aerial samples obtained by a WC-135 Constant Phoenix aircraft helped confirm that the North Korean event was indeed a nuclear test.[53]

As with SIGINT, MASINT also is not limited to remote collection. In cases going back to the Cold War, MASINT sensors were installed on mobile platforms. Sometime prior to 1961, U.S. or British intelligence agents attached Geiger counters to railway lines running to the Soviet Union so that the radioactivity of transports could be measured. Another operation, betrayed to the Soviet Union around 1985, was designated Absorb. It entailed the secret placement of radiation-detection devices in cargoes traveling on the Trans-Siberian railroad to pick up radiation emitted from missiles in the vicinity of the train tracks – radiation that could be used to determine the number of warheads on each missile.[54] A more recently developed mobile MASINT system is "Charlie," a robot fish that is capable of scooping up water that can then be analyzed for signs of nuclear activity.[55]

Clandestine MASINT also includes stationary or emplaced sensors that may have the same purpose as those installed on spacecraft, aircraft, ships, or other mobile platforms. However, placing them covertly in a single location rather than on mobile platforms offers two advantages. First, their proximity to the target may increase the value of the intelligence they produce.

---

[53] Jeffrey T. Richelson, *Spying on the Bomb: American Nuclear Intelligence from Nazi Germany to Iran and North Korea* (New York: W. W. Norton, 2007), p. 560.

[54] Paul Madrell, *Spying on Science: Western Intelligence in Divided Germany 1945–1961* (London: Oxford University Press, 2006), p. 152; Pete Earley, *Confessions of a Spy: The Real Story of Aldrich Ames* (New York: Putnam, 1997), pp. 19, 117, 197.

[55] Ted Bridis, "The CIA Dept. of Quirky Tricks," *Washington Post*, December 31, 2003, p. A17.

In many cases, a mobile platform operating from a distance could not produce the necessary intelligence. Second, emplaced sensors can continuously monitor a facility or activity. East Germany was a target of emplaced-sensor operations. In one operation, nuclear-detection equipment was installed in a series of posts on an East German road. The equipment transmitted its data to an antenna on a pile of rubble in West Berlin. In another operation, seismic-monitoring devices were placed underground near a road. The data they transmitted (to a satellite) allowed intelligence analysts to differentiate between seven different weight classes (e.g., jeep, passenger car, truck, or tank).[56]

Some of the most exotic emplaced sensors were those used in an attempt to monitor various Soviet weapons programs. One was a round device camouflaged as a tree stump and was discovered near a military facility that could transmit the data collected to a satellite. Another looked like a tree branch and was discovered in the late 1980s near a military airfield. According to a 1990 Soviet publication, it was an "automatic device for gathering intelligence on the parameters of the optronic control systems and laser sights used in the Air Force." The publication stated that the "optronic sensor enables it to receive scattered radiation from laser sights or missile control systems. The received laser beams are transformed into a numerical code and recorded by the electronic memory." The data could then be transmitted to a satellite.[57]

However, such sensors, even if developed long ago, are also of value against post–Cold War and post–September 11 targets. During the Cold War, the CIA's Directorate of Science and Technology developed a "Seismic Intruder Detection Device" that was designed to blend in with the terrain. It can detect movement of people, animals, or objects up to approximately 1,000 feet away; is fueled by tiny power cells; and has a built-in antenna. The transmitter relays data from the device via coded impulses.[58]

In 1994, it was reported that the Defense Intelligence Agency was developing Unattended Ground Sensors (UGS) and Unattended MASINT Sensors (UMS) (the latter codenamed Steel Rattler), which employed imagery and acoustic sensors to covertly monitor activity around critical targets such as North Korean nuclear facilities. UGS/UMS can be used to monitor nuclear-power plants, deeply buried bunkers, mobile missile-launch

---

[56] Interview; "Seismic Sensors," *Intelligence Newsletter*, January 17, 1990, p. 2.

[57] Lt. Gen. Nikolai Brusnitsin, *Openness and Espionage* (Moscow, 1990), p. 15; NBC, *Inside the KGB: Narration and Shooting Script*, May 1993, p. 39.

[58] "Seismic Intruder Detection Device," available at www.cia.gov/about-cia/cia-museum, accessed May 14, 2007.

sites, and weapons-manufacturing facilities. A high-speed digital signal-processor board inside the UGS can handle both the processing for the acoustic sensor and the image compression for the imager.[59]

Emplaced sensors also can be used to provide warning of approaching enemy troops rather than intelligence on foreign military activities and nuclear developments. In 2005, it was reported that "the U.S. military is developing miniature electronic sensors disguised as rocks that can be dropped from an aircraft and used to help detect the sound of approaching enemy combatants." It was expected that the devices, no larger than golf balls and employing tiny silicon chips and radio-frequency identification technology, would be able to detect the sound of a human footfall at 20 to 30 feet. The devices were expected to be ready for use by early 2007.[60]

Installation of these sensors, as with some CLANSIG sensors, involves joint operations with HUMINT – and represents another example of the artificial divide often exhibited in discussions of HUMINT versus technical collection. In his memoir of his time as director of Central Intelligence, Admiral Stansfield Turner recalled the "very risky planting of a sensing device to monitor a secret activity in a hostile country. The case officer had to do the placement himself, escaping surveillance and proceeding undetected to a location so unusual that had he been found he would have undoubtedly paid with his life."[61]

Human sources are also sometimes required to gather up the raw material of effluents or debris that cannot be snatched out of the atmosphere for MASINT analysis – a practice rooted in the Cold War, even World War II, but still relevant in today's attempts to gather intelligence about the WMD programs of rogue and other states of interest. In the earliest days of the American nuclear-intelligence effort, J. Robert Oppenheimer suggested that American agents be asked to gather samples of water from the Rhine River, analysis of which would reveal the presence of a reactor on its shores, if one existed. In 1954, a Latvian agent of the British Secret Intelligence Service was instructed to go to the region east of the Urals and procure a water sample from a river where it was believed, incorrectly, that a reactor was located.[62]

More recently, the 1998 U.S. strike against the El Shifa pharmaceutical plant in Khartoum, Sudan, was justified by the analysis of a soil sample

---

[59] Barbara Starr, "Super Sensors Will Eye the New Proliferation Frontier," *Jane's Defence Weekly*, June 4, 1994, p. 19.

[60] Jeremy Grant, "U.S. Military 'Rocks' Spy World," available at www.FT.com, accessed May 26, 2005.

[61] Turner, *Secrecy and Democracy*, pp. 59–60.

[62] Madrell, *Spying on Science*, p. 116.

obtained by a human source that was judged to contain a VX nerve-gas precursor – a judgment subsequently questioned but also vociferously defended by two former Clinton administration senior counterterrorism officials.[63]

In two other cases, almost 50 years apart, human sources inadvertently collected particles useful for analyzing nuclear activities of great concern at each time in history. In the 1950s, a CIA officer obtained a fur hat that had been worn by a German who had recently lived in Tomsk. The hat was turned over to U.S. nuclear intelligence analysts, who concluded that its exterior contained 50 parts per billion of uranium that was, without a doubt, slightly enriched in U-235. The analysts were able to eliminate the possibility that the uranium came from fallout or from a reactor. Tests for plutonium, radio-iodine, and separated lithium all came back with negative results. The hat was consistent with the hypothesis that somewhere in the Tomsk area, there was a uranium-enrichment plant.[64]

In April 2004, the U.S. intelligence community increased its estimate of the North Korean arsenal to eight nuclear bombs based on the conclusion that all eight thousand fuel rods withdrawn from the reactor in Yongbyon had been reprocessed. Among the evidence used in reaching that conclusion were traces of plutonium by-products – such as americium found on clothing worn by members of an unofficial U.S. delegation that visited Yongbyon – that were evaluated to indicate how recently the plutonium had been processed.[65]

Several recent articles have explored the utility of MASINT in the post–September 11 world, including a late 2001 article, "An Assessment of Antineutrino Detection as a Tool for Monitoring Nuclear Explosions," and the more recent, "Estimation of Electromagnetic Radiation Emitted from Centrifuges."[66] The authors of the first article noted that "the antineutrino is the only real-time inherently nuclear signature from a fission explosion that propagates great distances through air, water, and ground." They went on to consider the size and sensitivity of existing antineutrino detectors and

[63] Vernon Loeb, "Drug Plant Attack on Target, Says CIA Chief," *Washington Post*, October 21, 1999, p. A27; Daniel Benjamin and Steven Simon, *The Age of Sacred Terror* (New York: Random House, 2002), pp. 259, 355–6.

[64] Henry S. Lowenhaupt, "Mission to Birch Woods," *Studies in Intelligence*, 12, 4 (Fall 1968), pp. 1–12.

[65] Glenn Kessler, "N. Korea Nuclear Estimate to Rise," *Washington Post*, April 28, 2004, pp. A1, A16.

[66] Adam Bernstein, Todd West, and Vipin Gupta, "An Assessment of Antineutrino Detection as a Tool for Monitoring Nuclear Explosions," *Science and Global Security*, 9, 3 (2001), pp. 235–55; and B. Habib, "Estimation of the Electromagnetic Radiation Emitted from a Small Centrifuge Plant," *Science and Global Security*, 15, 1 (2007), pp. 31–48.

to examine the conditions under which they would be effective detectors of nuclear explosions. The second article focused on a model that estimates the strength of electromagnetic radiation emitted from a centrifuge as a function of distance from the plant and, therefore, the ability to detect plant operations.

TECHNICAL COLLECTION AND DOMESTIC TARGETS: THE TSP AND NAO

In December 2005, *The New York Times* disclosed that under a directive from President Bush, the NSA had been conducting wiretaps directed at Americans in pursuit of counterterrorism investigations without having first obtained warrants from the Foreign Intelligence Surveillance Court (FISC), as other administrations had done since the passage of the Foreign Intelligence Surveillance Act (FISA) in 1978. The program, probably known to a select few by a classified codename, became known to the public as the "Terrorist Surveillance Program" (TSP), based on President Bush's description of the activity.[67]

It is not surprising that there has been no systematic evaluation of the TSP. There are yearly reports on the warrants issued by the FISC but certainly no evaluation of what those warrants yielded – with respect to either counterintelligence or counterterrorism investigations. There have been assertions, reported in the press and originating with the Federal Bureau of Investigation (FBI), that the TSP produced few worthwhile leads.[68] Whether such complaints actually reflect a program of dubious value or simply an FBI mindset that dislikes sifting through masses of data for a piece of precious intelligence is not clear.

Apart from organizational concerns, any attempt to assess the value of domestic COMINT programs such as the TSP would be complicated. If it could ever be made, the assessment would have to consider the alternative uses of the resources employed, the extent to which the monitoring actually prevented terrorist attacks, and the value of such prevention. The metric of attacks prevented would be especially valuable, if it could be implemented, because it would contrast sharply with traditional evaluation of collection systems, in which the value may be judged important in intelligence terms

[67] James Risen and Eric Lichtblau, "Bush Lets U.S. Spy on Callers without Courts," *The New York Times,* December 16, 2005, p. 1; Eric Lichtblau, *Bush's Law: The Remaking of American Justice* (New York: Pantheon, 2008), pp. 223–4.
[68] Lowell Bergman, Eric Lichtblau, Scott Shane, and Don Van Natta Jr., "Spy Agency Data after Sept. 11 Led F.B.I. to Dead Ends," *The New York Times,* January 17, 2006, pp. A1, A12.

but almost always stops well short of anything as concrete as preventing an attack. Preventing just one significant attack might be enough warrant the program being judged effective.

Most systematic treatments of the TSP have focused not on its effectiveness but rather its legality, including articles in law journals, legal opinions from the Department of Justice and the NSA, and articles and books both pro and con. For instance, in December 2006, the NSA director, General Keith Alexander, wrote to the Senate Judiciary Committee chairman and attached a set of responses to questions raised at recent hearings. Among Alexander's justifications for the legality of the TSP was the argument that President Bush possessed the same inherent authority to authorize national-security wiretaps that other presidents had in the pre–FISA era and that submitting requests to FISA was an option, not a requirement. That view was echoed by Richard Posner in various articles and books, as well as by John Yoo, the former Justice Department official who was instrumental in formulating such arguments.[69]

Even before *The New York Times* December 2005 disclosure of the TSP, articles in legal journals confronted some of the issues involved in electronic surveillance post–September 11. The April 2003 issue of the *George Washington Law Review* carried an article by a law student, David Hardin, with the subtitle, "The Unconstitutionality of the USA PATRIOT Act Amendments to FISA under the Fourth Amendment." Specifically, Hardin challenged the constitutionality of the portion of the USA PATRIOT Act that permitted a relaxed probable-cause standard for FISA warrants when "a significant purpose" rather than "the purpose" of the surveillance is to collect foreign intelligence.[70]

Later that year, Nola K. Breglio, writing in the *Yale Law Journal*, expressed a similar concern over the consequences of the USA PATRIOT Act relaxation of restrictions on the issuance of FISA warrants. She argued that a FISA warrant had become little more than a standard warrant issued for criminal investigations – but issued in secret with no requirement to establish probable cause of criminal activity. She suggested requiring prosecutors

---

[69] Keith B. Alexander, Director, National Security Agency, Letter to Honorable Arlen Specter, December 19, 2006, w/attachment: Response to Questions, pp. 2–3; John Yoo, *War by Other Means: An Insider's Account of the War on Terror* (New York: Atlantic Monthly Press, 2006), p. 85. Also see Department of Justice, *Legal Authorities Supporting the Activities of the National Security Agency Described by the President*, January 19, 2006.

[70] David Hardin, "The Fuss over Two Small Words: The Unconstitutionality of the USA PATRIOT Act Amendments to FISA under the Fourth Amendment," *George Washington Law Review, 71*, 2 (April 2003), pp. 291–345.

to notify the targets of electronic surveillance after its conclusion and relying on regular courts to guarantee the reasonableness of searches if challenged.[71]

An article by a law professor, John Cary Sims, published in the aftermath of *The New York Times* disclosure, appeared in the *Hastings Constitutional Law Quarterly* with the title, "What NSA is Doing . . . and Why It's Illegal." After 35 pages of analysis, Sims concluded that "it appears that the core violation being committed is the targeting of international calls involving United States persons in the United States who appear to have had at least some contact with someone connected to al Qaeda, but where it is uncertain that the FISC would find that there is probable cause to believe that the potential target is an agent of a foreign power." He argued that FISA "plainly requires a warrant in the situation described" and that neither the post-September 11 Authorization for the Use of Military Force legislation nor the "inherent constitutional authority" theory is valid.[72]

A somewhat less intense controversy – but a controversy nonetheless – followed the disclosure in August 2007 by the *Wall Street Journal* that the United States was planning to expand its use of reconnaissance satellites to image targets within the United States in support of "civil agencies" – that is, agencies outside the Department of Defense and intelligence community – that may have domestic or foreign missions or both.[73]

For well over three decades, U.S. imagery satellites had been employed to image domestic targets in pursuit of a variety of objectives – including calibration on behalf of the NRO as well as disaster relief (i.e., hurricanes, floods, and earthquakes), mapping, and environmental protection in support of civil agencies. In 1975, a Civil Applications Committee (CAC) was established to vet requests from civil agencies for overhead coverage.[74]

The controversy that began in 2007 stemmed from the *Wall Street Journal* disclosure that the CAC was to be replaced by a National Applications Office (NAO) residing within the Department of Homeland Security (DHS), a move that reflected the intent of using reconnaissance satellites in support of law enforcement and border security missions. As a result of congressional objections, the new office did not become operational on 1 October

---

[71] Nola K. Broglio, "Leaving FISA Behind: The Need to Return to Warrantless Foreign Intelligence Surveillance," *Yale Law Journal, 113*, 1 (October 2003), pp. 179–217 at pp. 179–81.

[72] John Cary Sims, "What NSA Is Doing. . . . and Why It's Illegal," *Hastings Constitutional Law Quarterly, 33*, 2 & 3 (Winter–Spring) 2006, pp. 101–36.

[73] Robert Block, "U.S. to Expand Domestic Use of Spy Satellites," *Wall Street Journal*, August 15, 2007, pp. A1, A9.

[74] See Jeffrey T. Richelson (ed.), National Security Archive Electronic Briefing Book # 229, *U.S. Reconnaissance Satellites: Domestic Targets*, April 11, 2008.

2007, as planned. In April 2008, the DHS had not fully alleviated the privacy and civil liberties concerns of key members of the House Committee on Homeland Security, although Secretary of Homeland Security Michael Chertoff announced that the office would soon be ready to "go warm."[75]

Of course, in the absence of any operational activity, any evaluation of the utility of overhead imagery or MASINT for law enforcement and border security purposes would be, at most, theoretical.[76] Although there has been no such analysis, some authors, as with the TSP, examined the legal issues involved in the use of reconnaissance satellites for the full range of homeland-security activities.

One analysis that predates the plan to establish the NAO is Patrick Korody's "Satellite Surveillance within U.S. Borders." Korody examined various uses of classified satellite imagery for domestic purposes beyond disaster relief, including security for the 2002 Winter Olympics in Salt Lake City and Ronald Reagan's funeral procession. He reviewed spy-satellite technology (U.S., foreign, and commercial), legal issues involving satellite surveillance – including the implications of U.S. Supreme Court decisions (e.g., the *Katz* and *Kyllo* decisions) concerning searches based on other types of technologies – and the impact of the public availability of satellite technology on government authority to conduct overhead searches without a warrant. Korody argued that "a regulatory oversight framework should be established that balances law enforcement needs with society's privacy expectation that everyday activities will not be monitored without a level of justification."[77]

A more recent analysis was conducted by two staff members of the Congressional Research Service.[78] In addition to providing some background, the authors examined current policies and legal considerations. Those considerations included constitutional rights (including the distinction between searches and nonsearches and the question of reasonable warrantless searches), the statutory authorities and restrictions to be found in the National Security Act and Posse Commitatus Act, and executive-branch authorities (including those derived from the Executive Order on intelligence activities and Department of Defense directives).

[75] Spencer S. Hsu, "Administration Set to Use New Spy Program in U.S.," *Washington Post*, April 12, 2008, p. A3.
[76] The February 2008 NAO charter specifies that the NAO would not be involved in the use of satellites for domestic COMINT collection.
[77] Patrick Korody, "Satellite Surveillance within U.S. Borders," *Ohio State Law Journal*, 65, 4 (2004), pp. 1627–62.
[78] Richard A. Best, Jr., and Jennifer K. Elsea, Congressional Research Service, *Satellite Surveillance: Domestic Issues*, March 21, 2008.

FINAL THOUGHTS

The debate is about the legality and propriety of the domestic uses of technical collection. Serious research on the impact of that monitoring would not settle the debate but rather would enrich it. By the same token, there has been much reporting that researchers can use to assess the success and failures of technical collection in areas of interest to policy makers: events detected (or not) by satellite imagery, SIGINT, or various types of MASINT. However, with the exception of the four articles noted previously – one with respect to imagery, one with respect to SIGINT, and two with respect to MASINT – there appears to have been little systematic research on the value of technical collection in the post–September 11 world. What there has been are broad statements without real analysis that stress the need to devote more resources to HUMINT and fewer resources to expensive satellite systems – often packaged with remarks about the necessity of HUMINT for determining adversaries' intentions.

However, the research agenda for evaluating the role of technical collection in the post–September 11 world should be based on more than general criticism – sometimes as a matter of faith – of spending money on satellite systems that could be used to fund more extensive HUMINT operations.

A necessary component for any proper evaluation is consideration of the full range of post–September 11 targets. Some Cold War targets completely disappeared in the decade between the collapse of the Soviet Union and the terrorist attacks of September11, 2001 – for example, Soviet military bases in Eastern Europe. However, others rooted in the earliest years of the Cold War – such as Russian strategic forces – have survived, although with lower priority. Other targets have *grown* in importance (in contrast to having suddenly appeared) in recent years – terrorism and the WMD programs of rogue states being the most notable. For this reason, an evaluation of the full range of targets and priorities attached to them is required to properly assess the value of technical collection in the post–September 11 era.

It is also necessary to consider the full range of technical-collection systems available for gathering intelligence against targets of importance – including, of course, the terrorist target. Therefore, it is necessary to consider all forms of technical-collection disciplines (not just imagery), the varied forms of remote technical collection within each discipline (i.e., space, air, ground, sea, and underwater), and the utility of clandestine technical-collection activities in gathering data that remote technical-collection activities (or HUMINT) cannot gather or gather as well. Thus, what imagery satellites cannot do – such as monitor a target for continuously long periods – imagery UAVs can, and that capability has made them an important asset in combating terrorism. The UAV-launched Hellfire missiles most assuredly killed more key terrorists than CIA agents did on the ground, at least as far as is known publicly. Although satellites and aircraft may not be able to intercept a conversation between two terrorists in a remote part of Pakistan, an eavesdropping system installed covertly by members of the SCS or Special Projects Activity might be able to do just that.

Finally, it is necessary to have a dynamic view of the value of any form of collection. As the last two decades have demonstrated, some targets considered of great importance one year may be of no importance five years later, and the importance of others may grow dramatically. Collection activities cannot be funded simply on the basis of today's target; resources also must be allocated on the basis of the projected importance of certain targets. In addition, resource allocation must consider the possible or likely development of new technologies that allow technical-collection systems to do what they could not do in the past – just as geosynchronous eavesdropping satellites were able to access Soviet missile telemetry that other technical-collection systems could not, and radar-imaging satellites were able to provide imagery that other satellites could not in the presence of cloud cover. Tomorrow's innovations, funded today, may include dramatic breakthroughs that allow future technical-collection systems to access targets that today's systems cannot.

PART 3

INTELLIGENCE, POLITICS, AND OVERSIGHT

EIGHT

The Intelligence–Policy Maker Relationship and the Politicization of Intelligence

Olav Riste

The relationship between intelligence and policy making has been a matter of concern ever since the establishment of intelligence agencies as we now know them. The debate on the particular but related problem of politicization of intelligence has a shorter history. The phenomenon itself is not new. Before World War II, when intelligence was mostly collected by agents in the field, the fragmentary picture that resulted provided ample opportunity for policy makers to draw their own conclusions based on their own knowledge, fixed ideas, or prejudices. However, as intelligence during and after the war became a profession, with an increasingly sophisticated array of technical means of collection and analysis, the intelligence agencies and their products acquired a status which meant they could not so easily be bypassed in the policy-making process. In authoritarian regimes, this was not a problem; there, politicization permeated the entire intelligence process. Thus, for example, the KGB leadership in 1984 instructed its agents that their "chief task is to help to frustrate the aggressive intentions of American imperialism."[1]

In democratic systems, however, the leeway for simply rejecting intelligence analysts' products in favor of policy-maker preferences became narrower. Policy makers then had to resort to other and sometimes more devious ways of bypassing intelligence that they did not agree with or that did not fit with their policy choices. Thus, politicization of intelligence became an issue. This chapter addresses the issue through the recent debates in the United States and Britain about whether intelligence was politicized in the run-up to the 2003 war against Iraq. It locates that episode, however, in

---

[1] Christopher Andrew and Oleg Gordievsky, *Comrade Kryuchkov's Instructions: Top Secret Files on KGB Operations, 1975–1985* (Stanford, CA: Stanford University Press, 1993), p. 10.

the wider research on relationships between intelligence and its political consumers – and masters.

DEFINING POLITICIZATION

What, then, is *politicization*? The *Oxford English Dictionary* defines it as "The action or process of rendering political or of establishing upon a political basis; the fact of being politicized." This is too general to be particularly helpful to an understanding of the problem as it applies to the intelligence process. Attempts by intelligence scholars to define politicization of intelligence vary in length and complexity, although most will agree with a basic definition of *politicization* as "a process that fabricates or distorts information to serve policy preferences or vested interests."[2] Thus characterized, politicization is obviously a bad thing. In Richard Betts's typology, that definition covers politicization in its purest form, so to speak, defined as "the top-down variety, whereby policy makers are seen to dictate intelligence conclusions." A variant of this is given by Harry Howe Ransom: "When preferred policies dominate decision making, overt or subtle pressures are applied on intelligence systems, resulting in self-fulfilling intelligence prophecies, or 'intelligence to please' that distorts reality."[3]

Betts mentioned two somewhat milder forms of politicization.[4] First, there is what he called "a bottom-up coloration of products by the unconscious biases of the working analysts who produce intelligence analyses." Because no examples are offered, any discussion of this phenomenon becomes difficult. Betts referred in general to recurring suspicions that analysts in the military intelligence agencies are prone to "hawkish dispositions" and analysts in the Central Intelligence Agency (CIA) and the State Department have "dovish inclinations." However, in the more notorious cases of such divergences, as in the "bomber gap" and "missile gap" controversies in the 1950s, such institutional biases were a product of the paucity

---

[2] Richard K. Betts, "Politicization of Intelligence: Costs and Benefits," in Richard K. Betts and Thomas G. Mahnken, *Paradoxes of Strategic Intelligence: Essays in Honour of Michael I. Handel* (London and Portland, OR: Frank Cass, 2003), p. 59. Betts refers to this definition as the "prevalent conception behind the pejorative connotation," implying that his own view – as suggested by the title of his essay – is somewhat different.

[3] Harry Howe Ransom, "The Politicization of Intelligence," in Stephen J. Cimbala, *Intelligence and Intelligence Policy in a Democratic Society* (Dobbs Ferry, NY: Transnational, 1987), p. 26. Gregory Treverton has expanded on this type by distinguishing between "direct pressure from senior policy officials" and the more subtle "question-asking," where "the nature of the question takes the analysis a good way . . . to the frame in which the answer will lie." Gregory F. Treverton, unpublished manuscript, "Intelligence between 'Politicization' and Irrelevance," dated 15 December 2006, p. 3.

[4] Richard K. Betts, op. cit., pp. 61–2.

of reliable information rather than the result of a deliberate distortion of information for political purposes. Second is "the shaping of intelligence products by analysts' managers, acting in their capacity as editors or institutional brokers, in ways that original drafters consider to be inconsistent with evidence and motivated by policy concerns." Another form of politicization often mentioned is "cherry-picking," defined by Gregory F. Treverton as a process in which "policy officials see a range of assessments and pick their favorite."[5] That definition could be broadened to include the public use of such "favorites" in policy makers' speeches in support of their policy. Because assessments are classified, the analysts are generally precluded from publicly correcting the policy makers' version. This again is but one aspect of the larger problem of the selective "publicization" of intelligence to promote a certain policy, first studied by Glenn P. Hastedt with examples from the Nixon through the Reagan administrations – an issue to which I return.[6]

One particular form of politicization seems missing from most lists: the politically motivated establishment of separate and competing organs of intelligence collection and analysis. A stark example of this is the setting up of the Office of Special Plans (OSP) in the Pentagon in September 2002 by the neoconservative Undersecretary of Defense, Douglas Feith. Its purpose was to second-guess the CIA in regard to Iraqi weapons of mass destruction (WMD), based on information from back-channel meetings with foreign citizens such as the Iraqi exile, Ahmed Chalabi, and his agents. The information that the OSP collected was then "stovepiped" to the White House outside of established intelligence-review safeguards. According to an inquiry initiated by Senator Carl Levin and conducted by the Senate Armed Services Committee Minority Staff, the OSP also provided information purporting to prove a relationship between Saddam Hussein's Iraq and al Qaeda.

The non-IC or "alternative" intelligence analysis conducted by the DOD neatly fit the Administration's desire to build a strong case for an invasion of Iraq to overthrow the Saddam regime, particularly given the fact that the usual source of intelligence analysis, the IC, was sceptical about the existence of a close or cooperative relationship between Iraq and al Qaeda.[7]

---

[5] Gregory F. Treverton, unpublished manuscript, "Intelligence between 'Politicization' and Irrelevance," p. 3.

[6] Glenn P. Hastedt, "The New Context of Intelligence Estimating: Politicization or Publicizing?," in Stephen J. Cimbala (ed.), *Intelligence and Intelligence Policy in a Democratic Society* (Dobbs Ferry, NY: Transnational, 1987).

[7] Accessed from http://www.levin.senate.gov/newsroom/supporting/2004/102104inquiry report.pdpdf, p. 6.

Betts mentioned the OSP in a 2004 article in *Foreign Affairs*, but referred to it somewhat mildly as "an abuse of good procedure – especially if it is true, as critics have charged, the OSP's products were presented at the highest political level as if they had equal standing with the collectively agreed conclusion of the regular intelligence agencies."[8]

The recently retired Director of National Intelligence (DNI), Mike McConnell, however, in an interview in November 2006 before he had returned to active duty, was more forthright. Referring to Secretary Rumsfeld, Vice President Cheney, and President Bush, he said that he had been "unimpressed with many aspects of the Bush administration and its conduct of the war on terror, particularly what he felt was a politicized use of intelligence and lead-up to the war." Asked about this after having been appointed DNI, he was more specific: "What I was taking greatest exception to was to have a secondary unit established in the Pentagon to reinterpret information."[9]

The examples demonstrate that the debate on what constitutes politicization is not marked by either clarity or consensus. Partly this is due to the presence on the one hand of a grey zone between what is clearly politicization and, on the other hand, a situation in which the policy maker exercises his prerogative of choosing a policy in disregard of intelligence assessments. Perhaps that is why the recently published *Handbook of Intelligence Studies*, in which a galaxy of intelligence scholars reviews the field of intelligence in all its aspects, curiously has no entry for *politicization* in its index. We must therefore approach the problem by going to the wider question of the relationship between intelligence and policy makers and how that relationship has developed empirically since World War II.

THE INTELLIGENCE–POLICY RELATIONSHIP

In the *Handbook of Intelligence Studies*, an essay by Richard Russell entitled "Achieving All-Source Fusion in the Intelligence Community," identifies what he calls "two major schools of thought on intelligence-policy relations."[10] One is the Sherman Kent school, named after the doyen of

---

[8] Richard K. Betts, "The New Politics of Intelligence," *Foreign Affairs*, 83, 3 (May–June 2004), p. 5.

[9] As quoted in the transcript of an interview on NBC's "Meet the Press" on 22 July 2007, accessed from ww.dni.gov/Interviews/20070722_interview.pdf.

[10] Richard E. Russell, "Achieving All-Source Fusion in the Intelligence Community," in Loch K. Johnson (ed.) *Handbook of Intelligence Studies* (London and New York: Routledge, 2007) p. 195.

intelligence analysts who laid the groundwork for the American concept of National Intelligence Estimates (NIEs). The other school is often referred to as the Robert Gates school, which takes its name from the man who, after more than 20 years as intelligence analyst and manager, finally acceded to the post of Director of Central Intelligence (DCI) in 1991.

Intelligence experts of the old school, such as the veterans of the defunct Board of National Estimates (BNE) of the CIA, tended to regard intelligence analysis as an academic or, at least, intellectual discipline that should be untainted by politics. One expert, in a statement to the Senate Select Committee on Intelligence, acknowledged that there is "a natural tension between intelligence and policy." He then went on to say:

If the policy-intelligence relationship is to work, there must be mutual respect, trust, civility, and also a certain distance. Intelligence people must provide honest and best judgments, and avoid intrusion on decision making or attempts to influence it. Policy makers must assume the integrity of the intelligence provided and avoid attempts to get materials suited to their taste. When intelligence people are told, as happened in recent years, that they were expected "to get on the team," then a sound intelligence-policy relationship has in effect broken down.[11]

The author of that statement, John W. Huizenga, had joined the CIA from the State Department's Bureau of Intelligence and Research – better known by its initials INR – in 1952. After serving as a staff member, he became a member of the BNE in early 1961. He was its chairman from the end of the 1960s until 1973, when William Colby abolished the Office of National Estimates (ONE). Hence, for 15 years, Huizenga served an institution firmly imbued with the leadership of that icon of intelligence analysis, Sherman Kent, whose ideal was that of "dispassionate objectivity." On the relationship between intelligence and the policy maker, Sherman Kent once wrote:

Let things be such that if our policy-making master is to disregard our knowledge and wisdom, he will never do so because our work was inaccurate, incomplete, or patently biased. Let him disregard us only when he must pay greater heed to someone else. And let him be uncomfortable – thoroughly uncomfortable – about his decision to heed this other.[12]

---

[11] Statement to the Senate Intelligence Committee, (1975) by John W. Huizenga, the last chairman of the Board of National Estimates. Undated manuscript, in this author's possession.

[12] Sherman Kent, "Estimates and Influence," essay probably written in the early 1960s, published in the summer of 1968 issue of the CIA journal *Studies in Intelligence*, and republished in Donald P. Steury (ed.), *Sherman Kent and the Board of National Estimates: Collected Essays* (Washington: History Staff, Center for the Study of Intelligence, CIA, 1994), p. 34.

This avowedly elitist scholarly approach to the role of intelligence came under increasing pressure from policy makers from the late 1960s, climaxing in then–National Security Advisor Henry Kissinger's complaint that when reading the BNE's products, he had to "fight his way through 'Talmudic' documents to find their real meaning." In Donald Steury's somewhat blunt words, "the reverse (sic) of Sherman Kent's coin of detached objectivity was irrelevance."

There were deeper forces at work against the BNE's estimates at the time, however. The ONE's position on the Vietnam War was at odds with that of the administration. After Richard Nixon entered the White House in January 1969, "in the mood of a general occupying an enemy town,"[13] the CIA was high on the list of institutions that would come under fire from the new administration. The central issue during the next six years was the CIA's estimates of Soviet capabilities and intentions. Here, the NIEs had fairly consistently presented a more "dovish" picture than that of Washington's more hardline cold warriors. A foretaste of the dispute came already in 1969 on the question of whether the new Soviet SS-9 intercontinental ballistic missile (ICBM) was a Multiple Reentry Vehicle (MRV) with just three warheads or a Multiple Independently Targetable Reentry Vehicle (MIRV) – a missile whose warheads were independently targetable. If the latter, it would indicate that the Soviet Union had developed a first-strike capability. As a former Chief of CIA's History Staff wrote:

The issue revolved around the Nixon administration's determination to build a U.S. anti-ballistic missile (ABM) system, which an SS-9 first-strike threat would justify. A mid-1969 CIA memorandum updating the most recent Soviet strategic weapons National Intelligence Estimate repeated the long-standing position that the Soviet Union was not seeking first-strike ability. An outraged Secretary of Defense Melvin Laird accused the CIA of an attack on the Nixon administration's ABM policy. DCI Richard Helms reluctantly gave in to Laird's insistence and – to the intense chagrin of the Board of Estimates – withdrew the offending paragraph.[14]

During the early 1970s, the CIA was under attack on several fronts, both in regard to Vietnam and on account of its subversive involvement in Chilean politics. In 1971, President Nixon asked James Schlesinger to prepare a critique of U.S. intelligence. His findings were, in the words of one close observer, "searching and scorching" and included complaints that the ONE

---

[13] Thomas Powers, *The Man Who Kept the Secrets: Richard Helms and the CIA* (NY: Knopf 1979), p. 254.

[14] J. K. McDonald, "How Much Did Intelligence Matter in the Cold War?," in Michael Herman, J. K. McDonald, and Vojtech Mastny, *Did Intelligence Matter in the Cold War?* (Oslo: Norwegian Institute for Defence Studies, *Forsvarsstudier* No. 1, 2006), p. 54.

had become "too ivory towered."[15] William Colby, who took over as DCI in 1973, was determined to improve the Agency's standing with both the White House and Congress. He was also "by temperament and choice a covert political operator, impatient with the caution and painstaking procedure of traditional intelligence collection."[16] Conscious of the criticism of the BNE's estimates as being too academic with its "on the one hand" and "on the other hand" musings, he proceeded to abolish the ONE, replacing it with a system of National Intelligence Officers (NIOs). However, as Steury concluded in his introduction to the collected essays of Sherman Kent:

By seeking to provide more relevant or "engaged" intelligence analysis, the system that replaced the Office of National Estimates brought new problems: charges of "politicization" replaced those of policy irrelevance, while the effort to keep up with current reporting increasingly interfered with the kind of in-depth research that drove the estimates.[17]

The fiercest assault against the Agency was still to come. In 1976, after Nixon had resigned over Watergate and Gerald Ford had taken over the White House, a group of conservative hardliners on the President's Foreign Intelligence Advisory Board decided on a confrontation with what they saw as the dovish inclination of the CIA's analyses of Soviet capabilities and intentions. In this, they had the support of Ford's Chief of Staff Richard Cheney as well as Secretary of Defense Donald Rumsfeld. Thus was born the "Team A/Team B exercise," in which Team B would be given full access to the CIA's strategic intelligence on the Soviet Union. This concept of a conservative counteranalysis exercise had been opposed by Colby as an inappropriate intrusion into the integrity of the Agency's analytical product. However, his newly appointed successor as DCI, George H. W. Bush, decided to go along with what he saw as merely an intellectual challenge to the CIA's official assessments – an alternative view.

With hardliners such as Richard Pipes, Harvard professor of Russian history, and Paul Nitze, the founder that year of the "Committee on the Present Danger," it is hardly surprising that Team B produced a distinctly worst-case scenario of what the Soviet Union was up to. In a later assessment, Strobe Talbott wrote: "Bush allowed a panel of outsiders, deliberately stacked with hard-liners, to second-guess the agency's findings. Not surprisingly, the result was a depiction of Soviet intentions and capabilities that

---

[15] Harald P. Ford, "The U.S. Government's Experience with Intelligence Analysis: Pluses and Minuses," in *Intelligence and National Security*, 10, 4, p. 40.
[16] Powers, p. 359.
[17] Steury, p. xxv.

seemed extreme at the time and looks ludicrous in retrospect."[18] Christopher Andrew suggested that the impact of the B Team exercise "may have made agency analysts more conscious of the dangers of underestimating Soviet strength, but it did not persuade them that the Soviet Union intended to use its military might to secure global dominance."[19]

Two factors explain why the remainder of the Cold War period passed without further major clashes between the administration and the intelligence community. First, during the early years of Ronald Reagan's administration – often referred to as the "New Cold War" – the East–West tensions fuelled by the Soviet occupation of Afghanistan, Reagan's "evil empire" speech, and an intensified arms race left little room for dovish estimates of Soviet capabilities and intentions. Second, with William J. Casey as the new DCI and Robert Gates as his deputy, the top tiers of the CIA and the administration had similar worldviews. According to Loch Johnson, Gates confirmed to him Casey's tendency of "bending intelligence reports toward a conservative position consistent with policy pronouncements from the White House, notably with respect to Latin America." Later, with George H. W. Bush in the White House, "senior officials of the NSC wanted to hear only negative appraisals about the possibilities for reform in the USSR, suiting their predilections that Moscow was hopelessly committed to Communism. They are said to have received precisely those kinds of evaluations from a few senior CIA managers, even though lower-level analysts were arguing quite the opposite."[20] This is of interest also as showing that politicization can occur at two levels, both between the administration and the intelligence community and between the higher and lower levels within each agency.

The rumblings of resentment by senior and veteran analysts, at what they saw as politicization of intelligence during the Reagan years, burst into the open in the 1991 Senate hearings for confirmation of Robert Gates as DCI. One of them, as quoted by Betts, claimed that Gates, as head of the Directorate of Intelligence, had politicized intelligence in order to provide support for the extreme anti-Soviet policies of the administration by "the imposition of intelligence judgments, often over the protests of the consensus in the Directorate of Intelligence," or by "suppression of intelligence that didn't support the Casey agenda." In turn, Gates himself

---

[18] *Strobe Talbott,* "America Abroad: The Case Against Gates," *Time Magazine,* 14 October 1991.

[19] Christopher Andrew, *For the President's Eyes Only* (London: Harper Collins, 1996), p. 423.

[20] Loch F. Johnson, "Preface to a Theory of Strategic Intelligence," in *International Journal of Intelligence and Counter-Intelligence, 16* (2003), pp. 654–5.

and his partisans sharpened their criticism of the Sherman Kent school as being a prescription for irrelevance and saw their own approach – in Betts's words – "not as politicization but as contextualization."[21] Analysts needed to be closer to the policy makers to know what is on their minds and produce analysis that was sensitive to the policy context and the range of options available in order to be at all useful.

POLITICIZATION AND THE 2003 INVASION OF IRAQ

Any scholarly investigation of the occurrence of politicization of intelligence requires extensive access to primary sources, which is why research into the Cold War period tends to be exclusively concerned with the United States. None of the other major players in the intelligence world has had the number of official public or semi-public inquiries into the organization and performance of its intelligence community that the United States has experienced. A recent monograph from the CIA's Center for the Study of Intelligence reviews no less than 13 such studies prior to the 9/11 Commission.[22]

However, we now know much more about the intelligence process than before due to the spate of official investigations and inquiries sparked off by what are widely regarded as intelligence failures. In the United States, the shock of the 11 September 2001 terrorist attacks led to the establishment of the "National Commission on Terrorist Attacks upon the United States," which published its report in 2004.[23] In July 2004, a report from the Senate Select Committee on Intelligence regarding intelligence assessments about Iraq was published.[24] It was followed in March 2005 by a special report to the president on U.S. intelligence capabilities regarding WMD.[25] In the United Kingdom, there was an inquiry led by Lord Hutton into the circumstances that led to the suicide of Dr. David Kelly. Dr. Kelly was one of the British Ministry of Defence's leading experts on WMD and was alleged to be the source of media claims about pressure by No. 10 Downing Street on the

---

[21] Richard Betts, op. cit., p. 61.

[22] Michael Warner and J. K. McDonald, *U.S. Intelligence Community Reform since 1947* (Washington: Center for the Study of Intelligence, 2005).

[23] "Final Report of the National Commission on Terrorist Attacks upon the United States," authorized edition published in August 2004 as *The 9/11 Commission Report* (NY and London: W. W. Norton, undated).

[24] U.S. Senate, Select Committee on Intelligence, *Report on the U.S. Intelligence Community's Prewar Intelligence Assessments on Iraq*, 7 July 2004. Hereafter referred to as the Senate Intelligence Committee report.

[25] *Report by The Commission on the Intelligence Capabilities of the United States regarding Weapons of Mass Destruction*, 31 March 2005. Hereafter referred to as the Silberman/Robb report.

British intelligence community.[26] While that inquiry was still going on, the Intelligence and Security Committee of Parliament published a critical report on British intelligence relating to Iraqi WMD. Finally, in July 2004, a Committee of Privy Counsellors led by former Cabinet Secretary Lord (Robin) Butler published a major report entitled, "Review of Intelligence on Weapons of Mass Destruction."[27]

The 9/11 Commission need not be of concern here because it was only concerned with intelligence failures as such and only marginally touched on the role of politicians. Rather, the focus here is on the several investigations of the intelligence process preceding the attack on Iraq in 2003. The reason for that is that intelligence came to play such a major part in the public debate as to whether or not to go to war, in the United Kingdom as well as in the United States. At the center of that debate was the publication, by both countries, of an intelligence "dossier," or report giving the intelligence "findings" or assessments that purportedly provided the reasons for going to war. The avowed purpose was to give the public better information about the perceived threat from WMD that Saddam Hussein's Iraq either possessed or was in the process of acquiring and, therefore, to strengthen the case for stronger sanctions against the regime. The way in which those dossiers came into being is therefore central to the question of alleged politicization of intelligence and merits closer study.

THE BRITISH GOVERNMENT'S DOSSIER OF SEPTEMBER 2002

The initial reason for deciding to publish an official account of the British government's assessment of the situation in regard to Iraqi WMD was, according to the Butler report, to "inform public understanding of the case for stronger action (although not necessarily military action) to enforce Iraqi compliance with its obligations. . . . "[28] It is worth noting the words *the case for stronger action.* Britain, together with the United States, had been a consistent advocate in the United Nations (UN) Security Council for maintaining the pressure against Saddam Hussein, whereas the other permanent members of the Council had wavered in their support. The purpose of

---

[26] Lord Hutton's report was published in January 2004. Before that, however, the verbatim reports on the hearings had been available on the Internet, hereafter referred to as the Hutton Inquiry Web site.

[27] *Review of Intelligence on Weapons of Mass Destruction. Report of a Committee of Privy Councillors* (London: The Stationery Office, July 2004), para. 313. Hereafter cited as the Butler report.

[28] The Butler report, para. 313.

publishing such an account therefore was not so much to convince the public that Iraq had developed or was developing WMD. The consensus among the public and the media, in Britain and internationally, was that Saddam had developed or was developing such weapons. What the British government needed was to convince the public that those weapons represented such a serious threat that stronger and more determined action, in one form or another, was urgently necessary. When seen against the many reports that Iraq was still actively trying to undermine the UN sanctions regime and was unwilling to allow inspectors into the country to search for WMD, and in view of the weakening support in public opinion and among the members of the Security Council for maintaining and enforcing sanctions, it is perfectly understandable that the British government wished to convince its own people that the sanctions policy against Iraq was both right and necessary. Shortly before the British government went public with its own assessment, the case for action was strengthened by the publication on 8 September 2002 of a report compiled by the highly regarded International Institute for Strategic Studies (IISS). Presented as an objective, dispassionate assessment, the IISS concluded that "The retention of WMD capacities by Iraq is self-evidently the core objective of the regime, for it has sacrificed all other domestic and foreign policy goals to this singular aim." More specifically, the IISS report stated:

A reasonable net assessment is that Iraq has no nuclear weapons but could build one quickly if it acquired sufficient fissile material. It has extensive biological weapons capabilities and a smaller chemical weapons stockpile. It has a small force of ballistic missiles with a range of 650km, that are capable of delivering CBW [Chemical and Biological Weapons] warheads, and has prepared other delivery methods for CBW, including manned aircraft and UAVs [Unmanned Aerial Vehicles]. Sooner or later, it seems likely that the current Iraqi regime will eventually achieve its objectives.[29]

In September, Tony Blair decided to recall Parliament for 24 September and commissioned a dossier to be ready before that date. It was also decided that the dossier should be published and that it should draw mainly on material from intelligence – in itself an unprecedented event. Against that background, the two senior intelligence officials – Sir David Omand as the Security and Intelligence Coordinator in the Cabinet Office and John Scarlett as Chairman of the Joint Intelligence Committee (JIC) – decided that the JIC would take the responsibility for production of the dossier. According to the Butler report, they made that decision "to ensure that its content

---

[29] IISS Press Release, 8 September 2002.

properly reflected the judgements of the intelligence community.... "[30] However, ministers and senior officials have also adduced another motive: "... a Government document that claimed to be underpinned by intelligence would have been met with immediate scepticism unless it was evident that the JIC had endorsed its content."[31] The decision by the chairman of the JIC to take responsibility for the dossier enabled the Prime Minister to state, in his foreword to the published dossier, that it was "based, in large part, on the work of the Joint Intelligence Committee (JIC)."

The 50-page dossier, entitled "Iraq's Weapons of Mass Destruction: The Assessment of the British Government," was published on 24 September 2002, to coincide with the special session of Parliament. It did not at that time arouse much debate. Its prose was cautiously factual, even somewhat dull, and it did not in itself point to any particular policy option, such as war. When asked whether he thought the dossier was making a case for war, Hans Blix, chairman of the UN weapons inspectors in Iraq, was clear: "No, it was not. I saw it as a case for inspection."[32] Prime Minister Blair, in his foreword, was more specific, demanding "that the inspectors must be allowed back to do their job properly; and that if he [Saddam Hussein] refuses, or if he makes it impossible for them to do their job, as he has done in the past, the international community will have to act." However, Blair's foreword was also quite adamant about what the dossier amounted to:

What I believe the assessed intelligence has established beyond doubt is that Saddam has continued to produce chemical and biological weapons, that he continues in his efforts to develop nuclear weapons, and that he has been able to extend the range of his ballistic missile programme.

Every element of that statement reflected what was written in the JIC summary. However, whereas the JIC, in its summary of the dossier, presented its conclusions as "judgments," Blair saw them as being "beyond doubt."

A thorough investigation of the semantic process that intelligence undergoes before it is presented to the public is clearly not possible without full access to the intermediate stages between what is called "raw intelligence" and the finished product. However, the Butler report came as close as anyone could in pointing to the problems and pitfalls inherent in that process. First is the permanent, often overstated but perfectly legitimate concern of the intelligence community not to reveal its "sources and methods." Second

---

[30] The Butler report, para. 320.
[31] Ibid., para. 321.
[32] Ibid., para. 317.

is the balancing act between, on the one hand, revealing the inherent limitations of intelligence products – given the uncertainty of both the source material and its analysis – and, on the other hand, the need to provide assessments that are sufficiently clear for their political masters to act on. Then, as the Butler report stated:

Intelligence assessment is necessarily based heavily on judgment, relying on such material as intelligence has provided. It is not simply a matter of reporting this material but of presenting the judgments that flow from it to an experienced readership. Explaining those judgments to a wider public audience is a very different and difficult presentational task.[33]

In other words, when reporting intelligence assessments to the regular recipients of such reports, such as cabinet ministers and senior officials, a more academic "on the one hand" and "on the other hand" style – full of reservations and footnotes or "caveats" – can be used. However, such language can easily confuse the general public. Thus, the Butler report, comparing the dossier with an assessment produced by the JIC for internal consumption two weeks earlier on 9 September, noted that in the dossier "points were run together and caveats on the intelligence were dropped. The most significant difference was the omission of warnings included in JIC assessments about the limited intelligence base on which some aspects of those assessments were being made."[34] To give just one example of the effect of such presentational problems in the 24 September dossier, taken from the Butler report: the 9 September assessment made the following statement concerning Iraq's chemical and biological weapons:

Intelligence remains limited and Saddam's own unpredictability complicates judgments about Iraqi use of these weapons. Much of this paper is necessarily based on judgment and assessment.

In the published dossier, those caveats were reduced to the blindingly obvious statement that "This intelligence cannot tell us about everything."[35]

THE DEBATE ON THE BRITISH DOSSIER

The debate on the British government's September 2002 dossier developed in two stages. In the first stage, during the early months of 2003, criticism

---

[33] Ibid., para. 327.
[34] Ibid., para. 330.
[35] Ibid., p. 81.

of the government was triggered by two separate events: (1) the government's publication in February of another paper on Iraqi WMD, which soon became roundly condemned as a clumsy Cabinet Office effort to bolster the government's case; and (2) the allegation by a BBC reporter that the September dossier had been "sexed up" by the Prime Minister's "spin doctors." That allegation brought to the forefront Dr. David Kelly, the Defense Ministry expert on WMD claimed by the BBC as its source, who then committed suicide. His death led to an official inquiry chaired by Lord Hutton, whose detailed public hearings, recorded verbatim on the Internet, produced a mass of new information on the process that led to the September dossier.[36]

The second stage of the debate on the September dossier began in earnest with the July 2004 publication of the report by a committee chaired by Lord Butler,[37] whose remit was to review the performance of the British intelligence community in the events leading up to the war in Iraq. Although couched in impeccably balanced and moderate language, the Butler report revealed that the September dossier had failed to reflect the considerable uncertainties surrounding the judgments of the JIC – that the JIC, so to speak, had sexed up its product beyond what was warranted by the "raw intelligence." Even more damaging to the reputation of British intelligence was the revelation that three of the five human intelligence (HUMINT) sources – on which the famous Secret Intelligence Service (SIS) had relied – were, in fact, unreliable.[38] In particular, the Butler report reinforced the conclusion of Parliament's Intelligence and Security Committee report, published in September 2003,[39] that the dossier's most alarming claim had been misleading. This was the claim that the "Iraqi military are able to deploy these [chemical and biological weapons] within 45 minutes of a decision to do so," which the Prime Minister's foreword interpreted as meaning that some of the weapons could be "ready within 45 minutes of an order to use them." Although the intelligence report, in fact, referred only to battlefield

---

[36] Available at www.the-hutton-inquiry.org.uk/content/transcripts.

[37] Robin Butler (Baron Butler of Rockwell) was Secretary to the Cabinet Office and head of the U.K. Home Civil Service 1988–98.

[38] Butler report, para. 434–6.

[39] Intelligence and Security Committee, *Iraqi Weapons of Mass Destruction – Intelligence and Assessments* (HMSO, London, 9 September 2003), esp. p. 7: "As the 45 minutes claim was new to its readers, the context of the intelligence and any assessment needed to be explained. The fact that it was assessed to refer to battlefield chemical and biological munitions and their movements on the battlefield, not to any other form of chemical or biological attack, should have been highlighted in the dossier."

weapons, the wording in the dossier was widely believed to mean that the weapons in question could hit British bases in Cyprus.

To summarize, the Intelligence and Security Committee's report and particularly the Butler report amounted to a fairly severe indictment of the performance of MI6 (i.e., the SIS), for failing to exercise sufficiently critical judgment of its sources. Less severe but still very critical was the Butler report's conclusions on the JIC's authorship of the September dossier. On the way from JIC assessments to the dossier, "warnings were lost about the limited intelligence base on which some of these assessments were being made." This "left with readers the impression that there was fuller and firmer intelligence behind the judgments than was the case.... We conclude that it was a serious weakness that the JIC's warnings on the limitations of the intelligence underlying its judgments were not made sufficiently clear in the dossier."[40] In British civil service understatement, "serious weakness" is strong language indeed.

Were the errors for which SIS and JIC were criticized due to political pressure? Were they a result of the British government and its "spin doctors" leaning on the intelligence community to produce the type of results that would serve their political purposes? The JIC chairman, the parliamentary Intelligence and Security Committee, the report from the Hutton inquiry, and the Butler report all answered those questions in the negative. The Committee concluded: "We are content that the JIC has not been subjected to political pressures, and that its independence and impartiality has not been compromised in any way. The dossier was not 'sexed up' by Alastair Campbell or anyone else."[41]

However, the fact that strong judgments were formed on the basis of uncertain intelligence and that those judgments all went in the "worst-case" direction still requires an explanation. One of the first analyses to suggest an explanation was an article by Martin Woollacott in the *Guardian Weekly* in February 2004, titled "Spies Obsessed by Saddam; Mistrust Led to Iraq Intelligence Failures." With reference to the Hutton inquiry into the death of Dr. Kelly, Woollacott wrote:

In Britain the Hutton report's rejection of the argument that the available intelligence was exaggerated by politicians may have let the government off too lightly. But it

---

[40] Butler report, para. 464–5.

[41] Intelligence and Security Committee, *Iraqi Weapons of Mass Destruction – Intelligence and Assessments* (HMSO, London, 9 September 2003), p. 42. Alastair Campbell was Tony Blair's Press and Communications Officer and figured prominently in allegations of political interference in the production of the dossier.

does have the virtue of showing that the government and intelligence services had essentially the same mindset on Iraq. That mindset was exemplified by Dr. David Kelly himself. Dr. Kelly believed that Saddam almost certainly had some limited stocks of chemical and biological weapons, some capacity to restart production, some very limited means of delivery, and some hidden but very scaled down research programs.[42]

A veteran of the British intelligence community Michael Herman recently refined that analysis by bringing in the concepts of "groupthink" and "prevailing wisdom": "Most of the world was convinced that Saddam Hussein was concealing operational WMD weapons, and intelligence was locked into the process of creating and confirming this conviction."[43] The British government wanted a strong document to support its case for increasing the pressure on Saddam. There was a revealing moment in the Hutton inquiry when the questioner read an e-mail from someone in the Cabinet Office to the intelligence agencies during the drafting of the September dossier. It stated that "No. 10 through the Chairman wants the document to be as strong as possible within the bounds of available intelligence. This is therefore a last (!) call for any items that agencies think can and should be included." When asked about this e-mail, a member of the JIC replied that "you have to remember that the Joint Intelligence Committee itself was anxious to produce as strong a document as possible, consistent with the protection of intelligence sources and methods."[44] Seen in the context of the Butler report's criticism of the dossier's lack of caveats about the uncertainties of the underlying intelligence, this suggests that the JIC, in fact, had adopted the Cabinet's political agenda.

THE UNITED STATES DOSSIER, OCTOBER 2002

Ever since the new year 2002 began, the U.S. military had been working on war plans for Iraq. However, President Bush's stock answer when questioned by reporters about Iraq was that he had no war plan on his desk. Then, on 5 August 2002, Secretary of State Colin Powell met privately with the president. After pointing out the many risks inherent in any unilateral action by the United States, Powell brought up an alternative: "You can still make a pitch for a coalition or UN action to do what needs to be done." Bush was already scheduled to speak to the UN General Assembly on

---

[42] In the *Guardian Weekly*, 5–11 February 2004.
[43] Paper given to the British Intelligence and Security Association at the University of Warwick, December 2004, quoted by permission of the author.
[44] Hutton Inquiry Transcripts, Section 162.

12 September. Powell now argued for using that speech not only to make a statement about U.S. policy toward Iraq but also to make a serious attempt to internationalize the issue.

Bush himself had not yet taken a public stand on whether Saddam actually had WMD. In the "axis of evil" State of the Union speech on 29 January 2002, the talk was of the three states in question "*seeking* weapons of mass destruction." On 16 August, speaking to reporters, Bush said that Saddam "desires" such weapons. Vice President Dick Cheney, however, went further, with a speech that also seemed virtually to preempt the effect of any appeal to the UN. In an address to the Veterans of Foreign Wars on 26 August, Cheney declared that a "return of the inspectors would provide no assurance whatsoever of his [Saddam's] compliance with UN resolutions.... Simply stated, there is no doubt that Saddam Hussein now has weapons of mass destruction [and] there is no doubt that he is amassing them to use against our friends, against our allies and against us." [45] In a classic "worst-case" warning, Cheney highlighted the scenario of Saddam in possession of nuclear weapons:

Armed with an arsenal of these weapons of terror, and seated atop 10 percent of the world's oil reserves, Saddam Hussein could then be expected to seek domination of the entire Middle East, take control of a great proportion of the world's energy supplies, directly threaten America's friends throughout the region, and subject the United States or any other nation to nuclear blackmail.[46]

Such statements can be seen as confirming the impression, brought back from Washington and reported to a No. 10 Downing Street meeting on 23 July 2002 by the head of SIS, that "the intelligence and facts were being fixed around the policy (...) Bush wanted to remove Saddam, through military action, justified by the conjunction of terrorism and WMD."[47]

On 7 September, after a meeting with Blair, Bush then followed suit: Speaking to reporters together with Blair, he said: "Saddam Hussein possesses weapons of mass destruction." The next morning, *The New York Times*, in a front-page story headlined "U.S. Says Hussein Intensifies Quest for A-Bomb Parts," which came to dominate the TV talk shows that day, reported on Iraq's attempts to buy aluminium tubes that could be used in centrifuges to enrich uranium for a bomb.[48] Appearing on CNN, National Security Advisor Condoleezza Rice asserted that the tubes in question "were

---

[45] Bob Woodward, *Plan of Attack* (New York: Simon & Schuster, 2004) p. 164.
[46] Quoted in David Barstow's exhaustive study, "How the White House Embraced Disputed Arms Intelligence," *The New York Times*, 3 October 2004.
[47] "The Secret Downing Street Memo," in *The Sunday Times*, 1 May 2005.
[48] Woodward, pp. 178–9.

only really suited for nuclear weapons programs."[49] From then on, President Bush's own statements left no opening for doubt about Saddam's possession of biological and chemical weapons as well as his attempts to obtain the wherewithal to make nuclear weapons.

In contrast to the situation in Britain and Europe, there was little or no public demand in the United States for the administration to prove its case against Iraqi WMD. However, for the American Congress and preferably also the UN Security Council to authorize military action, more was needed. In the wake of President Bush's "conversion" to certainty about Iraq's possession of WMD, therefore, the chairman of the Senate Select Committee on Intelligence, Senator Robert Graham, formally requested on 11 September that the CIA provide a new intelligence estimate on Iraq. As Bob Woodward noted in his book, the CIA had until then "never declared categorically that it believed Saddam possessed weapons of mass destruction."[50] Consistent with the president's statements before 7 September, U.S. estimates – as well as DCI George Tenet's testimony to the Senate Select Committee on Intelligence on 6 February 2002 – claimed only that Iraq was seeking WMD. Now, against the background of the recent assertive statements by Cheney and Bush, Tenet "did agree reluctantly to do a rushed National Intelligence Estimate (NIE) on Iraq's WMD capability."[51] The work on the NIE took three weeks, resulting in a top-secret, 92-page document ultimately approved by the National Foreign Intelligence Board. A 25-page unclassified dossier, entitled "Iraq's Weapons of Mass Destruction," was issued for public consumption two days later. This document was not a sanitized version of the top-secret NIE, however; it was a white paper that the CIA's Office of Near East and South Asia had been working on since the spring, in response to a request from the National Security Council. Only the "Key Judgments" part of the dossier was a declassified version of its counterpart in the NIE where, like in the British case, the "caveats" had been eliminated.[52]

Comparing the British dossier to its CIA counterpart, it is impossible not to be struck by the ominously peremptory tone of the latter. At the top of its

---

[49] Barstow, cited previously.

[50] Woodward p. 194.

[51] Woodward, pp. 194–5. See also George Tenet, *At the Center of the Storm* (New York: Harper Collins 2007), p. 322.

[52] Senate Intelligence Committee report, pp. 286–8. According to Tenet, "In an effort to meld the white paper and the NIE, analysts took the Key Judgments from the NIE, declassified them, and stuck them in front of the white paper." George Tenet, *At the Center of the Storm*, p. 334.

"Key Judgments," it stated simply that "Baghdad has chemical and biological weapons." On nuclear weapons, it stated: "If Baghdad acquires sufficient
weapons-grade fissile material from abroad, it could make a nuclear weapon
within a year." It singled out the aluminium tubes as particularly significant:
"All intelligence experts agree that Iraq is seeking nuclear weapons and that
these tubes could be used in a centrifuge enrichment program. Most intelligence specialists assess this to be the intended use, but some believe that
these tubes are probably intended for conventional weapons programs."
Less certain but potentially more alarming was the judgment that Iraq was
developing an unmanned aerial vehicle (UAV) "that most analysts believe
probably is intended to deliver biological warfare agents.... Baghdad's
UAVs – especially if used for delivery of chemical and biological (CBW)
agents – could threaten Iraq's neighbors, U.S. forces in the Persian Gulf,
and the United States if brought close to, or into, the U.S. Homeland."[53]
Seldom has a serious intelligence estimate built a worst-case scenario on
such tenuous hypotheses.

The two-page "Key Judgments" were followed by more than 20 pages
of "Discussion." Here, the certainties and alarming prospects were inter-
spersed with qualifications and reservations, even suggesting that the intelligence basis for the judgments was limited in some cases. One remarkable
paragraph deserves to be quoted:

> *Limited insight* into activities since 1998 *clearly show* that Baghdad has used the
> absence of UN inspectors to repair and expand dual-use and dedicated missile-
> development facilities and to increase its ability to produce WMD.[54]

Information that has since become available has revealed that some of the
intelligence agencies distanced themselves from the NIE on some points. The
U.S. Air Force Director for Intelligence, Surveillance, and Reconnaissance
disagreed with the judgment on UAVs, stating that the UAVs probably
had "a primary role of reconnaissance."[55] Both the Department of Energy
intelligence unit and the State Department INR disputed the judgment that
the infamous aluminium tubes were intended for uranium enrichment;[56]
however, those dissenting opinions were buried in the top-secret NIE and
not shared with the public.

---

[53] All quotes in this paragraph are from the 'Key Judgments' that formed pp. 1–2 of the U.S.
Dossier.
[54] CIA, *Iraq's Weapons of Mass Destruction Programs*, p. 5. Emphasis added.
[55] 110th Congress, Senate Select Committee on Intelligence, *Report on whether Public Statements regarding Iraq by U.S. Government Officials were substantiated by Intelligence Information, June 2008. P. 53.*
[56] Ibid., p. 7–8.

THE DEBATE ON THE U.S. DOSSIER

A scathing verdict on the U.S. intelligence community's October 2002 NIE was delivered by the Senate Select Committee on Intelligence in its nearly 500-page report, published – with many deletions – in July 2004. The Committee's overall conclusions could hardly be more devastating:

Most of the major key judgments in the Intelligence Community's October 2002 National Intelligence Estimate (NIE), *Iraq's Continuing Programs for Weapons of Mass Destruction*, either overstated, or were not supported by, the underlying intelligence reporting. A series of failures, particularly in the analytic tradecraft, led to the mischaracterization of the intelligence.[57]

That condemnation applied to the judgments about nuclear, chemical, and biological weapons. Only the assessments concerning development of ballistic missiles were found to be reasonable and accurate. The Senate Select Committee on Intelligence's explanation for such a massive intelligence failure was similar to that in the Butler report on the failures of British intelligence. It had been a case of groupthink permeated by received wisdom.

Later, in March 2005, yet another critical report was issued under the long title of "The Commission on the Intelligence Capabilities of the United States Regarding Weapons of Mass Destruction." That Commission, chaired by Judge Laurence H. Silberman and Senator Charles S. Robb, had a wider remit than the Senate Select Committee on Intelligence in that it also studied the cases of Iran and North Korea. However, most of what it had to say about the latter has been excised from the 500-page report. On the matter of Iraq, it did not add much to what the Senate Select Committee on Intelligence has already reported, except concerning biological weapons.

On the much discussed question of political pressure on the intelligence analysts to come up with answers that suited the policy makers, the Senate Select Committee on Intelligence – like its British counterpart – concluded that it found no evidence of such pressure. However, a closely related question – that is, whether statements by government officials accurately reflected the intelligence available to them – was deferred by the Committee for later study. That much delayed "later study" finally appeared in June 2008.[58] Although appended by a number of "additional and minority views," the gist of it, as reported by the *New York Times*, was that "President

[57] Senate Intelligence Committee report, July 2004, p. 14.
[58] See note 54.

Bush and his aides built the public case for war against Iraq by exaggerating available intelligence and by ignoring disagreements among spy agencies about Iraq's weapons programs and Saddam Hussein's links to al Qaeda."[59] The Silberman–Robb commission, for its part, had simply stated that it was "not authorized" to look into the question of political pressure. However, it added the following admission: "It is hard to deny that intelligence analysts worked in an environment that did not encourage scepticism about the conventional wisdom." Thus, in the U.S. case, much more than in the U.K. case, the indirect pressure on the intelligence community of peremptory statements and conclusions by senior officials such as Vice President Cheney must have played an important part in the formation of the groupthink. Step by step, the publicly stated opinions of their political masters became steadily more difficult to gainsay. However, the intelligence community also allowed itself to be used politically.

Citing DCI Tenet's prominent role in Secretary of State Powell's presentation to the UN Security Council, and also the U.S. dossier of October 2002, Paul R. Pillar in an article in *Foreign Affairs* described how the CIA's intelligence managers let the intelligence community be "pulled over the line into policy advocacy – not so much for what it said as by its conspicuous role in the administration's public case for war."[60] As for Powell's misbegotten speech to the UN Security Council, Tenet's explanation for the CIA's role is a curious one:

We had two undesirable options from which to pick. We could let the administration write its own script, knowing that they might easily mischaracterize complex intelligence information, or we could jump in and help craft the speech ourselves. . . . We had a number of senior intelligence professionals assigned to check the accuracy of what was being said against the intelligence reporting, and others charged with examining the reliability of the sources. . . . Despite our efforts, a lot of flawed information still made its way into the speech.[61]

The fact that, in this case as well as in the two dossiers, the "mischaracterization of complex intelligence information" was done by intelligence officers can be seen to strengthen the groupthink theory of what went wrong. However, when groupthink is fomented by preemptive assertions and more or less subtle pressures by policy makers, then politicization has to be at least part of the explanation.

---

[59] *The New York Times*, 6 June 2008: "Bush overstated Iraq Evidence, Senators Report."
[60] Pillar, p. 20.
[61] George Tenet, *At the Center of the Storm*, pp. 372–3.

DEBATING POLITICIZATION

The debate among intelligence scholars as well as practitioners about politicization of intelligence for some time has been proceeding on several different levels. One debate has been concerned with the more mundane question of drawing the line between what is and what is not politicization. Here, the practitioners tend to adhere to a fairly wide definition. Not only blatant distortions of intelligence, but also more or less subtle pressures to make analysts adjust their conclusions to serve policy, are subsumed under the rubric of politicization by intelligence officials, sometimes in order to defend their profession when charged with intelligence failures. One clear example of this is Pillar, who was the CIA's NIO for the Near East and South Asia from 2000 to 2005. In his hard-hitting article in *Foreign Affairs,* he wrote:

In the wake of the Iraq war, it has become clear that official intelligence analysis was not relied on in making even the most significant national security decisions, that intelligence was misused publicly to justify decisions already made, that damaging ill will developed between policy makers and intelligence officers, and that the intelligence community's own work was politicized.[62]

Intelligence scholars are less clear when trying to determine whether concrete cases constitute politicization. Focusing on the role of intelligence managers, Betts, with an argument that illustrates the definitional quandary, appeared to defend them from accusations of politicization if what they were doing was "using their managerial discretion to improve the rigor and relevance of analytical products." It is in that context that he also introduced his concept of politicization as something that "can operate unconsciously from the bottom-up, if analysts let their own policy biases contaminate their writing."[63] Granted that bias can occur everywhere, that groupthink occurs in the best of intelligence agencies, and that complete objectivity is a chimera, it still requires a mental leap to accept that an unconscious bias can fall within the category of politicization as generally defined. Moreover, groupthink, or the development of prevailing wisdom, as discussed in the Butler report and by Herman,[64] is a phenomenon which is likely to affect both analysts and policy makers. Attempts over the years to institutionalize "red cells" or "devil's advocates" attest to the recognition of that particular danger in the "bottom-up" estimating process. However, in this writer's

---

[62] Pillar, p. 15.
[63] Betts, p. 70.
[64] Michael Herman, "Intelligence and the Iraqi Threat. British Joint Intelligence after Butler," in *RUSI Journal,* August 2004.

opinion, such prevailing wisdom is more often than not a "top-bottom" product, shaped by intelligence managers and policy makers.

In a thoughtful essay on "Reports, Politics, and Intelligence Failures," Robert Jervis[65] appears to discount many of the most current allegations about politicization in the run-up to the invasion of Iraq. He thus accepted the gist of both the Butler report and the report of the Senate Select Committee on Intelligence in the matter but stressed that, in some cases, "the line between distortion and legitimate emphasis is hard to draw." Jervis also had some important caveats. First, he noted that the reports "skip over some practices that could be included under the rubric of politicization, most obviously that leaders in the U.S. and U.K. gave inaccurate accounts about intelligence in order to garner political support." Looking at the practice of cherry-picking (i.e., "highlighting reports that support the policy to the exclusion of contradictory ones that may be more numerous and better established") and stove-piping (i.e., "the delivery of selected raw intelligence to policy-makers, bypassing intelligence analysts who could critically evaluate it"), Jervis considered that such practices can be defended as being within the prerogatives of top officials to reach their own conclusions. However, he added the important caveat that if such practices are used to justify policies to the public, they must not imply that their conclusions have the backing of the intelligence community.

In Jervis's nuanced conclusion, he noted that there was general acceptance by both the public and the intelligence agencies that Saddam Hussein's regime, with his WMD programs, constituted a serious threat. This created:

an atmosphere that was not conducive to critical analysis and that encouraged judgments of excessive certainty and eroded subtleties and nuances. Analysts and intelligence managers knew that any suggestion that Saddam's capabilities were limited would immediately draw hostile fire from their superiors. In this political climate it would have been hard for anyone to ask if the conventional wisdom about Saddam's WMD programs should be reexamined.... It is also possible that the desire to avoid the painful value trade-off between pleasing policy makers and following professional standards created what psychologists call 'motivated bias' in favor of producing estimates that would support, or at least not undermine, policy.[66]

A different debate takes up the more general issue of the relationship between intelligence and policy making. Here, the point of departure is the

[65] Robert Jervis, "Reports, Politics, and Intelligence Failures: The Case of Iraq," in *Journal of Strategic Studies*, 29, 1 (February 2006), pp. 3–52.
[66] Ibid., p. 36.

Sherman Kent school versus the Robert Gates school. In his brief discussion
of the merits or otherwise of the two schools, Russell, in his chapter in the
Handbook of Intelligence Studies mentioned previously, came down on the
side of the Gates school, albeit with some reservations. Russell's conclusion
was that the Kent school's pitfall of irrelevance is a more serious danger than
the risks of political subservience run by the Gates school's advocates:

> At the risk of stating the obvious, the Intelligence Community does not exist as
> an end of itself, but as a collection of institutions purposefully designed to serve
> national interests as articulated by policy makers supported by the American public.
> A strict adherence to the Kent school runs too great a risk of sanctioning an
> Intelligence Community that justifies its existence in terms of its own internal
> processes rather than the intelligence products that are relevant to the interests of
> the policy makers trying to advance national political interests. In the final analysis,
> the ideal intelligence-policy relationship is a pendulum swing towards the Gates
> school and away from the Kent school.[67]

What seems lacking here is a discussion of what is meant by *irrelevance*.
Relevance is a relative concept, determined in the eye of the beholder. It is
difficult to imagine a self-respecting intelligence agency producing papers,
studies, or assessments of total irrelevance in response to the requirements
of its political masters; such an agency would quickly consign itself to
oblivion. *Usefulness* might be a better term, but it is a double-edged sword.
To the politicians and senior officials, who are supposed to absorb and, if
necessary, react to its products, intelligence in the scholarly shape presented
by the estimates of the Sherman Kent school may have appeared as an
unwelcome addition to all the paperwork they were supposed to handle,
especially if the information went against their preconceived ideas. The
estimates, however, would become useful tools if the intelligence could be
used to support the policy that they favored and wished to push through.
This question of usefulness brings us to what Loch Johnson called the
marketing of intelligence:

> The challenge during this end phase of the intelligence process is to match informa-
> tion with the needs of the policy makers. Intelligence collectors and analysts need to
> know what late-breaking information ("current intelligence") their customers seek
> in their efforts to extinguish the hottest of the in-box fires. Long-range, in-depth
> information ("research intelligence") is important too.... Lengthy NIEs are seldom
> read word for word by busy senior officials; but like encyclopedias, which are not
> read from cover to cover either, they are available as detailed resources.

Clearly, both "research intelligence" and "current intelligence" must be
and have been provided by the intelligence agencies. The CIA, from the

[67] Russell, cited previously, p. 195.

beginning, was well aware that the most senior officials seldom if ever bothered or had the time to read the lengthy assessments or estimates that were produced for them. To remedy this, the CIA already by Harry Truman's presidency had begun to produce brief daily summaries of international events (called "the Daily") that were distributed to the president and other senior officials. In 1961, President Kennedy instituted a daily summary of all-source intelligence reports called the "President's Intelligence Check List" (PICL). These daily reports would then be points of discussion during the oral briefings by the DCI or senior analysts. The current variant is called the President's Daily Brief (PDB).

Another proponent of a closer relationship between intelligence analysts and policy makers is Richard N. Haass. In an article in *Studies in Intelligence*, he took as his point of departure Robert Bowie's definition of intelligence as "knowledge and analysis designed to assist action" and added as his own comment: "Information and insights that do not 'assist action' remain lifeless."[68] Seemingly aligning himself with the Robert Gates school, he wrote:

I appreciate the tradition in the Intelligence Community that insists that analysis should be insulated from policy making in order to prevent politicization. But, in my experience, an even greater danger to intelligence analysis is irrelevancy. The Intelligence Community's products can be less relevant than it should be because analysts do not understand what is really on the policy maker's mind, so they address the wrong questions – or, when they have the right questions, their intelligence fails to have the impact that it should because their answers do not reach the policy maker in a timely fashion or digestible form.

Having said that, however, Haass distanced himself from the dangerous ground entered by Betts by going on to encourage the analysts to protect their integrity:

Intelligence analysts should . . . resist allowing fears of losing influence with a policy maker lead then to check their analytic swing. If analysts do not use their access to give unvarnished assessments for fear of jeopardizing access, then what is the purpose of the access to begin with? Policy makers tend to appreciate timely candor because it is always better to confront an unpleasant development sooner rather than later, if only to have more time to formulate a response to it.[69]

If we look to Britain, the Sherman Kent school's ideal of scholarly objectivity was for a long time the hallmark of the "high table" of its intelligence

[68] Richard N. Haass, "Supporting U.S. Foreign Policy in the Post–9/11 World," in *Studies in Intelligence*, 46, 3 (2002), p. 11.
[69] Ibid., p. 12.

machinery – the JIC. In the words of John Scarlett, its previous chairman: "It . . . has a long tradition of providing independent, objective advice, drawing on all sources, including the most secret sources, to the Government. . . . "[70] A more down-to-earth view from the chairman of the JIC from 1985 to 1992 holds that intelligence and policy:

> should be close but distinct. Too distinct and assessments become an in-growing, self-regarding activity producing little or no work of interest to the decision-makers. . . . Too close a link and policy begins to play back on estimates, producing the answers the policy makers would like. . . . The analysts become courtiers, whereas their proper function is to report their findings, almost always unpalatable, without fear or favor. The best arrangement is intelligence and policy in separate but adjoining rooms, with communicating doors and thin partition walls, as in cheap hotels.[71]

Clearly, the trend in both countries has been to bring the process of intelligence assessment closer to the policy makers. However, in Britain, this has been accomplished by way of an expansion of the membership of the JIC so that it came to appear as a "forum of mixed intelligence chiefs and senior policy people, acting in an intelligence mode."[72] This combination of intelligence heads and senior policy officials is mirrored in the composition of its supporting organs. Since 1968, the JIC has been supported by an Assessments Staff, "staffed in the main by normal secondments from elsewhere in the public sphere, including policy departments with a strong Foreign Office element among them"[73] and located in the Cabinet Office's Intelligence and Security Secretariat, whose head is the chairman of the JIC. Recent reforms have meant a considerable increase in the size of the Assessments Staff and the appointment of a Professional Head of Intelligence Analysis. Draft assessments are then subject to formal interdepartmental scrutiny in Current Intelligence Groups, composed of experts from government departments as well as from the intelligence agencies. According to a former insider, this may suggest that "the most powerful voices tend to be those who are in a sense 'amateurs' – professional diplomats, senior service officers and other Whitehall officials, either as JIC members or on secondment to the Assessments Staff – rather than career intelligence professionals."[74] There

---

[70] Hutton Inquiry Web site, Hearing Transcripts, section 80.

[71] Percy Cradock, *Know Your Enemy*, p. 296.

[72] Michael Herman, "Intelligence and the Iraqi Threat: British Joint Intelligence after Butler," in *RUSI Journal*, August 2004.

[73] Ibid.

[74] Michael Herman, "The Role of the British Intelligence Committee: An Historical Perspective," in L. C. Jenssen and O. Riste (eds.), *Intelligence in the Cold War: Organisation, Role, and International Cooperation* (Oslo: Norwegian Institute for Defence Studies, 2001), p. 37.

is, further, a specialized multiagency unit with the self-explanatory name of Joint Terrorism Analysis Center (JTAC), likewise staffed by members of the three intelligence agencies together with representatives from relevant departments.[75]

In the United States, the CIA's BNE, whose products were often criticized as being too "academic" with their detailed "on the one hand" and "on the other hand" assessments, was – as we have seen – in the 1970s replaced by a number of NIOs who form the National Intelligence Council, reporting their estimates to the DCI. Since 2004, the DNI has replaced the DCI as the chief national intelligence officer. The estimates are then formally approved by the National Intelligence Board, composed of the heads of the 16 intelligence agencies and headed by the DNI. Although the old ideals of objectivity and dispassionate analysis are still held in high regard, the American system is such that the estimate "was and is the Director's estimate, and its findings are his"[76] – and it is the DNI who reports to the White House.

Thus, the crucial nexus in the relationship between the intelligence agencies and the policy makers in the United States is embodied in the person of the DNI, who is the president's principal advisor on intelligence matters as well as being the head of the intelligence community. This "fusion" of the world of intelligence and the world of politics in the person of an "intelligence manager" may have been a necessary development, given the multitude of agencies that comprise the intelligence community. However, it increases the risk of politicization of the third form as described by Betts: "the shaping of intelligence products by analysts' managers . . . in ways that original drafters consider to be inconsistent with evidence and motivated by policy concerns." That risk increases if the manager – for example, DCI Tenet – is not an intelligence professional. Betts seemed on dangerous ground when he expressed understanding for managers who "know that there are times and issues when it serves no purpose to fall on their swords, and when it is more sensible to live to fight another day – even if it means caving in on a hopeless issue."[77]

POLITICIZATION – FUTURE PROSPECTS

This chapter has been concerned primarily with strategic intelligence, a discipline developed through the years of the Cold War, whose principles and problems are still with us despite being pushed backstage by the pervasive threat of terrorism. Strategic intelligence, in the main, aims to measure

[75] Booklet *National Intelligence Machinery* (London: The Stationery Office, 2006).
[76] Sherman Kent, as quoted in the Senate Intelligence Committee report, p. 10.
[77] Betts, cited previously, p. 63.

and analyze the capabilities and intentions of hostile or potentially hostile state actors, and it has a time frame that includes more long-term perspectives. Strategic intelligence plays for high stakes because intelligence failure may endanger the survival of one's own state. A prescription for improving strategic intelligence, as suggested herein, would seem to require a closer relationship between the intelligence community and the policy makers but one imbued with the mutual respect and understanding suggested in this chapter's introductory quotation from Huizenga's 1970 statement to the Senate Select Committee on Intelligence. In that better world, analysts – when meeting the policy makers – would defend and not veer from their analyses and the policy makers would appreciate the analysts' "timely candor" even if at the end of the day they decided on a policy that, in Sherman Kent's words, disregards the analysts "because he must pay greater heed to someone else." For although it is the intelligence analyst's duty to present his analysis as dispassionately and objectively as possible, it is within the policy maker's prerogatives and even duties to reach his own conclusions, as Jervis reminded us.[78]

In June 2007, the DNI issued a directive on "Analytical Standards," one of the points of which stated: "Analysts and managers should provide objective assessments informed by available information that are not distorted or altered with the intent of supporting or advocating a particular policy, political viewpoint, or audience."[79] A worthy aim – in many ways reminiscent of the ideals of the Sherman Kent school.

The problem with that injunction is that the intelligence analyst's world and the policy maker's world are fundamentally different. It is tempting to speak of two cultures, or what L. Keith Gardiner called "the intelligence-policy disconnects."[80] It is worth thinking about some of the crucial distinctions that Gardiner sees between the two worlds:

- On balance, policy makers enjoy possessing and using power. They tend to be decisive and confident. They are also fundamentally comfortable with themselves, and they are not particularly self-critical or willing

---

[78] Jervis, p. 34.

[79] DNI, "Analytical Standards," Intelligence Community Directive No. 203, 21 June 2007. Accessed from www.fas.org/irp/dni/icd/icd-203.pdf.

[80] L. Keith Gardiner, "Dealing with Intelligence–Policy Disconnects," in H. Bradford Westerfield (ed.), *Inside CIA's Private World: Declassified Articles from the Agency's Internal Journal 1955–1992* (New Haven, CT, and London: Yale University Press, 1995). This article by the veteran reformer-analyst, L. Keith Gardiner, was first published in the CIA's in-house journal *Studies in Intelligence* in 1989 and was one of four articles chosen by Westerfield to cast light on the relationship between analysis and its consumers.

to accept criticism. Analysts tend to distrust power and those who enjoy exercising it. They are usually more comfortable with criticism, especially in giving it. Basically, they have questioning personalities.

- Whenever possible, policy makers make hard decisions quickly. Though they often are too busy to do everything they need to do, this frequently occurs because they are more comfortable being active rather than being more contemplative. Analysts, however, are given to extensive examination of an issue, in part because they would prefer to avoid decisions that call for action.
- Policy makers dislike ambiguity and complexity because these qualities impede decision making. Analysts, however, believe that the real world *is* ambiguous and uncertain, and they see their primary role as reflecting it as faithfully as possible. Oversimplification is something to be avoided.

In each of these cases of disconnect, the spectre of politicization can be seen to lurk in the shadows, depending on which stage the process of political decision making has reached. Gardiner saw three such stages. In the first stage, a political issue may exist but is not urgent; hence, the policy maker has not engaged with it and is uninterested in any analysis of it. In the second stage, the issue has become relevant, but no decision has been made about how to address it. At this stage, the policy maker is open to factual intelligence as well as analysis. In the third stage, the policy maker has more or less decided what to do about the issue, but no hard decision has been reached about how to proceed. Then, the policy maker's interest in information and analysis is limited to the implications of his proposed course of action, and he tends to resist analysis that might advise against his decision. In the final stage, implementation, the only analysis of interest to him is that which supports his plan of action. It is in the third and final stages that politicization may occur, especially if the proposed action is controversial.

Gardiner's article contains several suggestions for overcoming the chasm between the two worlds, with the need to put analysts in closer contact with policy makers as his most important recommendation. However, he acknowledged the risk that this would lead to analysis becoming politicized. So, even in that better world suggested by Haass and with the improvements in intelligence–policy-maker relationships proposed by Gardiner, politicization is bound to recur from time to time, especially when hotly debated policy choices arise. Perhaps the greatest danger lies in a particular legacy from the debate on the Iraq war, which Hastedt focused on in an article entitled, "Public Intelligence: Leaks as Policy Instruments – The Case of the Iraq War." Hastedt's concern is about what happens when the normally highly secret intelligence "goes public" and becomes part of the debate over the conduct of foreign policy. "Secret intelligence becomes public intelligence through unauthorized leaking of secret intelligence, the sanitized release of secret material, or public reference to sources and analyses."[81] Hastedt is especially concerned with what he called "orchestrated intelligence." Although not invented in the run-up to the Iraq war, as Hastedt demonstrated through numerous examples, it became a dominant feature as the policy makers in the United States, as well as in the United Kingdom, were trying to build up support for the Iraq war.

The ubiquitous references in public speeches to what "our sources tell us," as well as the sanitized release of "dossiers" purporting to be authorized versions of actual intelligence assessments, may well have let "the genie out of the bottle." In our brave new media-dominated world, the reporters and the public are not likely to be satisfied with mere leaks of snippets of intelligence, and they will insist on knowing also the dissents and alternative conclusions of the intelligence community. Will the senior managers of the intelligence community and their political masters be able in the future to resist those demands? Greater openness about intelligence is, on the face of it, a good thing. However, much will have to remain secret. How can the public then be certain that what it is told is not "orchestrated" to serve a political purpose? As a recent example, the DNI in July 2007 released what was called a "National Intelligence Estimate" on "The Terrorist Threat to the U.S. Homeland." However, what was published was, in fact, just one and a half pages of "Key Judgments." Is the public to assume that those judgments are the unanimous verdict of all the analysts, agencies, and other organs of the intelligence community that participated in the nine-month production process? Are some judgments more certain than others? What were the dissents and alternative analyses that the analysts had apparently been encouraged to register during the process, or the reactions of the two outside experts that were highlighted in the complete text of the NIE?

Ultimately, the best insurance against overt politicization of intelligence is for the intelligence community to demonstrate independence and integrity, by standing by its assessments even when they are at variance with the public assertions of its political masters. An encouraging pointer in that direction was the November 2007 release by the Office of the DNI of "Key Judgments"

---

[81] Glenn Hastedt, "Public Intelligence: Leaks as Policy Instruments – The Case of the Iraq War," in *Intelligence and National Security*, 20, 3 (September 2005), p. 421.

from a new NIE on "Iran: Nuclear Intentions and Capabilities."[82] That NIE was, it said, "an extensive reexamination" of its assessment of the same issues in May 2005 – an assessment on which President George W. Bush had built much of his case against Iran. Not only that – the new NIE appeared to pull the rug from under some of the most dire warnings about the Iranian nuclear threat contained in speeches and statements coming from the White House. When some hardline commentators hinted that the new NIE had the odor of politicization in reverse, the Principal Deputy DNI felt sufficiently provoked to declare emphatically that "the task of the Intelligence Community is to produce objective, ground truth analysis. We feel confident in our analytic tradecraft and resulting analysis in this estimate."[83]

In the fight against terrorism, intelligence is, more than ever, the "first line of defense." What has changed is that because the terrorist threat directly affects every citizen, the measures taken by governments for their defense – measures affecting people's daily life such as their freedom of movement and their civic rights, in general – are determined by intelligence assessments of the imminence of the threat. Here, we need to be aware that politicization can also occur in the way intelligence is used to warn against the terrorist threat. One legacy of the instances of politicization in the run-up to the Iraq war could be seen in the occasional suspicion that policy makers in the United States, but also in the United Kingdom, have used warnings about terrorist threats to bolster their image as protectors of the nation. This makes it doubly important that intelligence in the fight against terrorism can be trusted – that its integrity, as Sir David Omand discusses in Chapter Ten, is not open to question.

---

[82] National Intelligence Estimate, November 2007. Accessed from the DNI Web site.

[83] Statement by Principal Deputy Director of National Intelligence, Dr. Donald M. Kerr, 8 December 2007. Accessed from the DNI Web site.

NINE

Oversight of Intelligence: A Comparative Approach

Wolfgang Krieger

Intelligence oversight, defined as a special control of intelligence services by national parliaments, is a fairly new function in the development of modern governance as is also research into that function. It reaches back only to the 1970s in the United States and to the 1990s in Britain. To be sure, there are some exceptions. The Netherlands established a specific parliamentary control in 1952; Germany (then West Germany) did so in 1956. France, one of Europe's oldest parliamentary democracies, passed its first extensive legislation in 2007.[1]

Parliaments, however, are not alone in checking on what intelligence services do. Primary responsibility for their proper functioning lies with the executive. Governments are politically responsible to parliaments and to the public for what intelligence does or fails to do. Yet, they face a difficult-to-resolve dilemma. Due to extremely tight security requirements, only a small number of government ministers and officials are in a position to monitor continuously and systematically the potentially most dangerous and most controversial intelligence operations. Because these are the same people who also give the orders, they are understandably reluctant to burrow deeply into intelligence failures of one sort or another. As a result, the most powerful oversight instrument is also the most unlikely to do the job rigorously. Typically, it takes an intelligence "scandal", revealed by the press to the public, to get parliaments and executive overseers to act.[2]

---

[1] France established a special intelligence-oversight mechanism for wiretapping in 1991 and for the control of secret funds in 2002.

[2] Loch K. Johnson, "Lawmakers and Spies – Congressional Oversight of Intelligence in the United States", in Wolbert K. Smidt et al. (eds.), *Geheimhaltung und Transparenz: Demokratische Kontrolle der Geheimdienste I internationalen Vergleich* (Berlin: LIT, 2007); Loch K. Johnson, "A Shock Theory of Congressional Accountability for Intelligence", in Loch K. Johnson (ed.), *Handbook of Intelligence Studies* (New York: Routledge, 2007), pp. 343–60.

In some cases, the judiciary becomes involved in pinpointing intelligence failure and forcing the executive to make needed changes. Thus, intelligence oversight is a concern for all three of the classical branches of state power, of which parliament is merely the most frequently discussed. All in all, it is a complex web of institutional responsibilities which, in most democracies, has undergone important changes within the last decade or two.

This chapter explores the key issues involved and the institutional "solutions" found in a select number of countries. In that sense, it compares how different countries exercise a critical intelligence function. It is not a comparison of intelligence systems, as Michael Warner frames them in Chapter Two; however, focusing on oversight does illuminate broader differences in systems across countries. Indeed, this chapter sets out from the assumption that there are no generic solutions to oversight. We speak of global threats, such as terrorism, organised crime, and weapons of mass destruction (WMD) proliferation which affect all liberal democracies in similar ways, but their intelligence services occupy very different places in the politics of different states. For this reason, oversight practices are difficult to compare. Yet, there is much cross-border institutional learning and much pressure, particularly in the European Union (EU) and in the context of international humanitarian operations, to make intelligence services – and, by extension, intelligence oversight – more compatible.

SCANDALS AND THE EMERGENCE OF OVERSIGHT

The existing national systems emerged not so much by design as by a haphazard process of trial and error, mostly driven by intelligence "scandals", technological change, and the changing security environments after the end of the Cold War in 1991 and 11 September 2001. Essentially, the systems respond to widespread fears about two dangers. One concerns the extent to which civil rights are being threatened by the possibilities of clandestine surveillance which modern technology, particularly modern electronics, puts at the disposal of security agencies. From this perspective, the increasing importance of intelligence and the continuing growth of its resources are viewed as a threat.

The other concern is directed primarily at international terrorism and crime but also at environmental crises and various side effects of "globalisation", such as mass migration, global diseases, and spillover effects from regional conflicts (mostly in Africa and Southwestern Asia). As soon as public debates focus on those threats, there is a demand for more protection by the state, including more security provided by intelligence. To reconcile those two highly divergent demands, a consensus has emerged in support of more oversight. In this way, it is generally assumed, civil liberties can be better protected and intelligence can be made more effective at the same time.

How valid is this assumption? In thinking that more oversight will make intelligence services less dangerous to their own citizens and more effective against domestic as well as external threats, we take a leap of faith. We think we know what intelligence actually does and how it is used by governments. Indeed, until recently, much of the literature on the subject was marked by this type of optimism.[3] This is particularly true of comparative studies of oversight, which hold out the promise that by institutional fine-tuning, intelligence can be made safe for democracies just as armed forces, by a drawn-out historical process, have been placed under increasing democratic control. As its name indicates, the Geneva-based Centre for the Democratic Control of Armed Forces (DCAF) sets out from this assumption. It has produced a number of important studies on the subject, specialising in defining rules and models of oversight which can be applied particularly to the postcommunist democracies of Central and Eastern Europe.

Recently, however, a series of inquiries launched into the intelligence background and politics surrounding both September 11 and the Iraq war have thrown cold water on this optimism. How could September 11 happen in a country like the United States which already had the most extensive as well as intrusive parliamentary oversight system (plus a vintage National Security Council system)? How could Congress overlook for so long the structural and even technical problems which came to light in the September 11 reports? In Britain, the intelligence management by the political leadership became the focus of several inquiries into how intelligence was handled both before and during the Iraq war. Although Britain has a more limited parliamentary watchdog committee than the United States, British intelligence management, including executive oversight, has generally been given very high marks. Yet, it failed to prevent a number of grave misjudgements and mishandlings of intelligence.

It may be that oversight is better suited for keeping tabs on the day-to-day workings of intelligence services than for managing such exceptional cases

---

[3] See, for instance, Hans Born (ed.), *Democratic Control of Intelligence Services: Containing Rogue Elephants* (Aldershot: Ashgate, 2007); Hans Born (ed.), *Who's Watching the Spies? Establishing Intelligence Service Accountability* (Washington: Potomac Books, 2005); Hans Born and Ian Leigh, *Making Intelligence Accountable: Legal Standards and Best Practice for Oversight of Intelligence Agencies* (Oslo, WK: Parliament of Norway, 2005); Marvin C. Ott, "Partnership and the Decline of Intelligence Oversight", *International Journal of Intelligence and Counter-Intelligence*, 16 (2003), 69–94; Peter Gill, *Policing Politics: Security Intelligence and the Liberal Democratic State* (London: Routledge/Curzon, 1994).

as September 11 and the Iraq war. However, from a close reading of those official reports, a rather subtle picture emerges which sees intelligence as *sui generis* among the tools of government and which suggests that certain parts of the oversight system are perhaps inherently ill-suited to prevent certain types of failures in the intelligence cycle. It may well be impossible to give executive oversight leverage over executive behavior with respect to intelligence policy. Although for different reasons, parliaments also may not be ideally suited to provide oversight. This experience makes for more sympathy for the hesitation with which legislatures had treated intelligence in the past.

Generally speaking, national parliaments regulate government activities by passing legislation which defines their scope and by controlling individual budgets down to line items. However, such control is difficult to exercise in the realm of intelligence, where operations and capabilities must be kept secret from the general public and even from most or all parliamentarians. Therefore, until the 1980s or even 1990s, intelligence services operated on the basis of executive orders rather than laws. Their finances were often not subject to parliamentary scrutiny. In other words, lawmakers for a long time had practiced a mixture of benign neglect and postmortem review. Only major intelligence disasters, such as the Dreyfus affair in France or the Japanese attack on Pearl Harbor, led to major parliamentary inquiries. Intelligence was considered an area of state activity that was limited to the executive. Parliaments restricted themselves to providing close control of other functions of domestic and foreign security policy, particularly of the military and law enforcement agencies, hoping that intelligence as an ancillary function would somehow follow those same guidelines.

In those days, even executive oversight was performed with a certain hesitation. It consisted of little more than a reporting routine in which the chiefs of intelligence agencies, from time to time, gave oral reports to their responsible government ministers. Except in wartime, a head of military intelligence did not usually talk to anyone beyond the level of top military commanders or staff officers. Only after the vast expansion of peacetime intelligence did governments see a need for more complex management structures and procedures about which, alas, the scholarly literature has little to say.

Why this earlier neglect of executive oversight? Quite likely, there was a certain desire to maintain "plausible denial" – that is, the possibility to deny that a particular intelligence operation had actually been ordered or at least cleared in advance by the political leadership. Another reason may be that in stable democracies, the political leadership did not feel threatened by intelligence, except perhaps by domestic intelligence services which tended to keep dossiers on prominent persons. In France, for example, the police prefect of Paris historically wielded much political power by "knowing the dossiers" of the mighty.[4] Military intelligence was another matter, however. From the late 19th century, it became a professionalised specialty firmly anchored within the general staff system, whereas traditional peacetime foreign intelligence primarily addressed spying on foreign embassies and their messaging traffic. Both were considered subjects for narrow specialists and of no relevance to ordinary democratic politics.

Judiciary oversight also developed rather slowly. The behavior of the French judges in the Dreyfus affair is just the most prominent example that comes to mind. It shows an incredible submissiveness to the political executive as well as to the military. Even a half-century later, the judiciary could be a most ineffective instrument when it came to intelligence, as John E. Haynes and Harvey Klehr showed in their recent book about early Cold War communist espionage in the United States. During the late 1940s and throughout the 1950s, U.S. prosecutors were faced with the choice of having to make public some very sensitive intelligence information or letting their suspects get away in the hope of neutralising a larger espionage network or operation.[5]

The problem was that most evidence deriving from intelligence was barred from being used in court. In the end, only a small fraction of the 180 identified Soviet spies working inside the U.S. federal government were indicted for treason.[6] In some of those trials, the only way to punish the spies was to entangle them in contradictory testimony or to trap them with the help of other procedural tricks. Thus, the failure of U.S. intelligence and other security agencies who hired, promoted, and in some cases even protected Soviet spies could not be laid out in court, which, tragically, gave people like Senator Joseph McCarthy the chance to use the issue in a grossly distorted manner.[7] The small number of actual convictions made many Americans at the time and most historians to this very day believe that Soviet subversion could not possibly have been a serious problem.

Since then, the role of the judiciary has greatly changed. Additional legislation has helped to improve relations between law enforcement and

---

[4] Jean-Paul Brunet, *La police de l'ombre: Indicateurs et provocateurs dans la France contemporaine* (Paris: Seuil, 1990).

[5] John Earl Haynes and Harvey Klehr, *Early Cold War Spies: The Espionage Trials That Shaped American Politics* (New York: Cambridge University Press, 2006).

[6] The figure is taken from ibid., p. 83.

[7] Another consequence may well have been the disproportionate severity of the sentences passed on Ethel and Julius Rosenberg in 1951.

intelligence but, in the United States, the reliance on trial by jury still makes it difficult to prosecute certain types of intelligence-related cases. The constitutionally doubtful existence of the Guantanamo detention center and the equally doubtful practice of sending terrorist suspects all over the world for questioning (i.e., "special rendition") testify to this problem. In Europe, the courts have perhaps more effective ways of dealing with evidence derived from intelligence. It can be withheld from the public and, in certain cases, even from the defendants. Juries have much less prominent roles while judges are largely in control of the trial proceedings. In either case, however, judicial oversight remains difficult to accomplish in a satisfactory manner.

Finally, among democratic oversight institutions, there are the press and civil society organisations such as civil-rights groups. According to Loch Johnson, the press is frequently the real driver behind congressional intelligence oversight because members of Congress will not readily devote much time to intelligence (or anything else) unless they get rewarded by public attention.[8] The same principle is likely to apply elsewhere. Indeed, the media are not so different than the politicians. They, too, only pay attention to intelligence if they can turn it into an issue which quite literally sells. Few journalists actually specialise in intelligence and develop the expertise needed to make an assessment of a related news item or piece of information. No sports editor of a provincial newspaper would tolerate the type of nonsense which one can find in "serious" newspapers on the subject of intelligence.

CRITICAL ISSUES IN OVERSIGHT

What are the principal concerns in intelligence oversight? Authors differ somewhat on this point. The Dutch historian Cees Wiebes identified six major areas: (1) legality, (2) effectiveness, (3) efficiency, (4) budgeting and accounting, (5) conformity with human rights treaties and conventions, and (6) policy and administration.[9] In a recent volume from the Geneva-based DCAF, Marina Caparini grouped those concerns into two main areas: efficacy and propriety.[10]

---

[8] Johnson, "Lawmakers and Spies", cited previously.
[9] Cees Wiebes, "The Netherlands" in Smidt, *Geheimhaltung und Transparenz*, pp. 106–28, 120.
[10] Marina Caparini, "Controlling and Overseeing Intelligence Services in Democratic States", in Hans Born and Marina Caparini (eds.), *Democratic Control of Intelligence Services: Containing Rogue Elephants* (London: Ashgate, 2007), p. 9.

Efficacy has several dimensions. One is about the extent to which an intelligence service is able to meet the expectations of its customers – that is, the government departments that assign particular tasks. The military leadership will wish to know everything about the strategic capabilities and intentions of its potential enemies. The interior minister and his law enforcement agencies will wish to know about potential domestic dangers, such as organised crime, terrorism, and subversive political forces which seek to overthrow the liberal democratic order of the state. Efficiency, a more narrowly focussed concept, concerns the relationship between achieving those goals and the resources applied. Are we getting our money's worth? Is the money being properly budgeted and accounted for? These are the classical questions asked by parliament, which, in turn, needs to convince the voters that they are receiving the best possible value for the tax money spent on intelligence.

How does one reasonably measure the effectiveness of an intelligence service? What can reasonably be expected and how much security provided by intelligence can a nation afford? The logic of these questions reminds us of the debates on military capabilities. "How much is enough?" was a widely discussed question during the heyday of the nuclear-arms race. No comparable debates have taken place with respect to intelligence, although various parliamentary figures or political parties at times have suggested that too much is being spent. The end of the Cold War produced a few such debates and parliamentary motions. There was a brief interlude in the early 1990s when foreign intelligence appeared to have run out of work. However, the cruel manifestations of Islamist terrorism soon resulted in restored funding levels that permitted substantial expansions of staffs and equipment. In the United States, intelligence reform went hand in hand with a massive expansion; in France and Germany, vast construction projects for intelligence headquarters in Paris and Berlin are sure signs of the new importance that intelligence holds for the political leadership.

However, in the context of oversight, the question remains an open one: How much intelligence is actually needed? One has only to relate the wealth of individual nations to their intelligence budgets to realise that there appears to be no obvious answer. Unlike the expenditures for police forces or the judiciary, which are roughly proportionate among states of comparable wealth, there are huge differences when it comes to the relative size of intelligence budgets. The greatest differences can be seen in foreign and military intelligence, which makes it obvious that intelligence serves very different kinds of foreign and security policies. As an imperial superpower, the United States sets very different kinds of goals from such regional powers as Germany or Italy, which have only limited ambitions.[11]

When it comes to propriety – that is, specific ethical and legal standards which are to be imposed on intelligence agencies – the differences between states are much smaller. Essentially, they concern where states strike the balance between the commitment to civil and human rights, on the one hand, and the tolerance for "inevitable" infractions of those principles on the other, whereby *inevitable* is defined as being tolerable in the "national interest." To be sure, observers have been aware of this dilemma for a long time; however, the recent urge to expand oversight marks a major change in expectations about how the specific potential for misuse of power associated with the practice of intelligence will be monitored and policed. Previously, the hope had been that the "dirty work" of intelligence would go largely unnoticed by the public and, if revealed, would be viewed as a necessary evil. Now, there is widespread fear that the high-tech tools of intelligence pose an imminent threat to the liberal body politic, along with the hope, or assumption, that this challenge can be met by bringing all "necessary" intelligence operations within the boundaries of the law and under the immediate control of oversight institutions, especially that of parliament. This is the logic behind the burst of security legislation which lawmakers passed all over the world in the wake of September 11. It remains to be added that there has been an important shift in the definition of what is "necessary", expanding traditional definitions of national interest by such "new" concerns as international terrorism, WMD proliferation, and humanitarian intervention.

Stated briefly, the new enthusiasm for intelligence oversight is fuelled by pessimism in some respects and optimism in others. On the pessimistic side, global Jeremiah prophecies have come to dominate the political agenda in the rich democracies – from the "clash of civilisations" to "global warming". However, at the same time, there have been rapid advances of legalism; that is, the belief that all public life (and, indeed, much of our private life) can and should be brought under the roof of law-centred institutions, making the written and minutely defined law into a type of secular deity.

To be sure, there remains some pragmatism in this new brand of intelligence politics. It is mainly feared that intelligence services will threaten the civil rights of their own nationals and that their potential for manipulating

[11] To my knowledge, no reliable calculations have been undertaken which make intelligence-personnel figures comparable across national borders. The model to be followed would be the statistics of military personnel (and equipment) published annually by the International Institute of Strategic Studies (*Military Balance*) in London.

state power may be used in the interest or to the detriment of particular political parties, ethnic and religious communities, and private businesses at home. When it comes to illegal or unethical intelligence operations targeted at foreign nationals or groups or governments, the situation is very different.

The world outside has generally received much less attention, except for a few unusual cases such as the public outcry over the "family jewels" of the CIA – including plans to assassinate Fidel Castro – which were investigated by the Church and Pike committees in 1975–6. However, this happened during a massive crisis of public confidence in American political institutions and elites brought on by the American defeat in Vietnam and the fall of the Nixon presidency. Moreover, it is worth noting that the public outcry in 1974–5 started with the disclosure of potentially improper or even illegal surveillance programs targeted at Americans – by the Federal Bureau of Investigation (FBI) counterintelligence program as well as various domestic CIA programs.[12] Thus, it remains true that foreigners have always been of secondary concern to the overseers of intelligence and, indeed, to the democratic public at large.

PROBING NATIONAL DIFFERENCES: THE DUTCH AND FRENCH CASES

How did those changes in intelligence oversight actually occur? How can one account for the noticeable differences among the rich democracies with respect to oversight? The Netherlands, which boasts the oldest parliamentary oversight committee for intelligence, is a good place to start looking for the answers. The Dutch have produced one of the most extensive oversight regimes in Europe and, incidentally, one of the most active scholarly communities in intelligence studies.[13] As early as 1952, the parliament's Second Chamber (or lower house) set up a Standing Committee on the Intelligence and Security Services. It consisted of the heads of the five leading political parties, although later only four parties were represented. In

---

[12] There is a vast literature on these committees and their findings. Frederick A. O. Schwartz, Jr., "The Church Committee and a New Era of Intelligence Oversight", *Intelligence and National Security*, 22, 2 (2007); Harry Howe Ransom, "A Half-Century of Spy-Watching", in Loch K. Johnson (ed.), *Strategic Intelligence*, vol. 5: *Intelligence and Accountability* (Westport, CT: Praeger, 2007); and Michael Warner and J. Kenneth MacDonald, *Intelligence Community Reform Studies since 1947* (Washington: Center for the Study of Intelligence, 2005). A somewhat redacted version of the CIA's "family jewels" report was recently declassified and is available from the CSI Web site under the key words *family jewels*.

[13] An excellent summary is found in Wiebes, "The Netherlands", cited previously.

2003, the leader of the Socialist Party stopped attending the meetings after the minister of defence refused to share intelligence information on Iraq. A year later, membership was widened again by opening it to the leaders of all political parties represented in parliament.

This composition is typical of parliaments elected by proportional representation, which usually leads to coalition rather than single-party governments. It reflects the fear that intelligence services might be misused by one or several political parties to gain an advantage over others. By restricting the membership to the leaders of the dominating political parties, the Standing Committee followed not only a form of consensus politics which has characterised the Netherlands since the reestablishment of Dutch democracy in 1945. It also responded to what during the Cold War was a tricky problem in virtually all West European parliaments: How to keep the communist members of parliament from participating in intelligence oversight?

From publicly available sources, including its annual reports since 1967, it is impossible to get more than a sketchy impression of the actual proceedings of this committee.[14] It receives briefings from intelligence officials and their responsible ministers. The frequency of the meetings has increased considerably since the sudden rise of Islamist terrorism during the 1990s and since the Netherlands began to participate in multinational military missions in the Balkans as well as outside of Europe. However, the committee suffers from a weakness shared by many other similar bodies around Europe – the lack of both staff and a research arm.

Since 2002, an independent oversight commission has existed in the Netherlands, one that has not only a secretariat and a small research unit but also a mandate – based on the 2002 Intelligence and Security Services Act – to call witnesses and draw on experts, even under oath. The commission can request the cooperation of intelligence services and their ministerial supervisors, and it can make unannounced visits to their offices. However, this new commission advises the responsible minister; it is thus closer to the executive than to parliamentary oversight.

Both the Dutch intelligence services and their ministerial management have undergone a number of sweeping changes since 1945. Essentially, there is a division between military intelligence, which operates under the defence department, and "general intelligence", which is supervised by the minister of the Interior and Kingdom Relations.[15] A separate foreign intelligence

---

[14] The 2004 report is available in English from the civilian intelligence agency at www.aivd. nl/contents/pages/43523/annualreport2004_aivd.pdf.

[15] The interior minister is also responsible for Dutch overseas territories (hence, "Kingdom Relations").

service was founded in 1946 but was then discontinued in 1994 after several major overhauls had failed to resolve its ongoing management problems. Apparently, the service could not cope with the volume of incoming information and fell victim to competition with the foreign ministry over various foreign-policy issues.[16] Its tasks were subsequently handed over to military and domestic intelligence. Eventually, in 2003, a separate SIGINT service was founded. In 2005, the Defence Institute for Security and Intelligence was established in an effort to improve training and quality control of the intelligence product.

The ministerial management of Dutch intelligence went through a long gestation of institutional trial and error. The intelligence-coordinating committee, established in 1948 and chaired by the prime minister, was soon replaced by a coordinator working under the prime minister and, in 1976, by a cabinet subcommittee for intelligence. In 2003, a national security council was established in which key ministers, including the minister for immigration and integration, sit together with the intelligence chiefs. In parallel, the intelligence coordinator chairs a committee of intelligence and law enforcement officials that discusses the "nuts and bolts" – that is, the especially security-sensitive issues and information. A national ombudsman for the intelligence and security services, who handles complaints from civilians, and the general accounting office, which supervises the spending of secret funds, round out the picture of Dutch intelligence oversight.

As a general conclusion, it is clear that the Dutch parliament, at best, has performed a reactive oversight of sorts and that for many years, cabinet ministers apparently did not spend much time on oversight either. A much-improved structure evolved from the needs of managing military missions abroad and the awareness – painfully brought home by the murder of Dutch filmmaker, Theo van Gogh, in November 2004 by an Islamist fanatic – that the Netherlands could no longer rely confidently on what had long been considered an exceptionally successful integration policy. Suddenly, intelligence was seen as a critical part of a more aggressive national-security policy. Oversight was now more about intelligence efficacy than anything else.

The French case is somewhat the opposite of the Dutch case. Although French presidents and their ministers have long had a deep interest in intelligence matters, executive oversight often was concerned with efficacy even at the price of sacrificing propriety, whereas parliament for a long time

[16] Cees Wiebes, *Intelligence and the War in Bosnia 1992–1995* (Münster: LIT, 2003), pp. 94–5; and Bob de Graaf and Cees Wiebes, *Villa Maarheeze: De geschiedenis van de inlichtiningendienst buitenland* (Den Haag: SdU, 1999).

played only a minor role, leaving much of the watchdog function to the press.

In the early postwar years, France, like most West European states, did not put its intelligence services on a statutory basis. Instead, guidance was provided by government decrees. As a result, parliament had no role in defining what intelligence could and should do. It was seen as a prerogative of the government; even today, reference is made to the *outils régaliens* (i.e., instruments of the king) deriving from the original *secret du roi* (i.e., the king's secret). This language appears in an article by the current director of the French Directorate-General for External Security (DGSE) (i.e., the foreign intelligence service) and published in 2006 – 136 years after the final collapse of the French monarchy![17] Even during the 1980s and 1990s, when a number of European states passed specific legislation in which they redefined their intelligence services, France kept to the habit of reform by executive order, still leaving parliament out of the picture. In 1999, however, the defence committee of the Assemblée Nationale adopted a legislative proposal for an oversight committee. Although this proposal was not immediately followed up, an amendment to the budget authorisation law for 2002 provided for a special oversight committee to control "secret funds".[18] This group consists of four members: two nominated by each of the presidents of the two houses of parliament (i.e., Assemblée and Sénat), and two other members from the Budget Control Office. The committee is chaired by one of the parliamentarians from the Assemblée. Its proceedings and report to the government are to be kept secret as are its reports to the chairs of the finance committees in each house. Parliamentarians have to be sworn to respect national defence secrets. To that extent, they lose part of their independence from the executive.

This was a breakthrough but one that covered only a small part of parliamentary oversight. To make the point that France was behind other Western democracies in this respect, the European foreign affairs committee of the French Sénat, published in March 2002 a study comparing parliamentary oversight at an international level.[19] Again, the message did not get across swiftly; it took until the summer of 2007 – following the election of President Nicholas Sarkozy and a new Assemblée – for a legislative proposal to be voted on by both houses.

---

[17] Pierre Brochand, "Les activités et les défis du Service", *ENA Hors les Murs*, no. 365 (Octobre 2006).

[18] The secret funds go mostly to the DGSE and total well below 10% of the DGSE annual budget.

[19] See www.senat.fr/lc/lc103/lc103_mono.pdf.

What changed the mind of French lawmakers? The needs of post–September 11 counterterrorism intelligence are the predominant reason given by Senator Serge Vinson, the rapporteur of the Sénat foreign affairs commission.[20] In his view, two points are now essential: a better public understanding and acceptance of intelligence and the development of a French "intelligence" culture.[21] His report sees a need to improve both the performance of intelligence services and the use that is being made of them in political decision making. In addition, the proponents of the legislation hope to improve the legal framework that surrounds intelligence. This includes such issues as the status of agents when involved in court cases but also wider concerns relating to the cooperation between law enforcement and intelligence. Because lawmakers will inevitably have a role in those reforms, closer communication with the world of intelligence is considered desirable.

As far as one can tell from the outside, the need for more communication with parliament and the wider public is now also shared within French intelligence circles. As DGSE director Brochand stated: "The doctrine of transparency, which is essentially about a much enhanced role of the media and of the courts of law (*médiatisation et juridiarisation*), cannot fail to weigh heavily on how intelligence functions".[22] That doctrine is now simply part of the *Zeitgeist*.

The core of France's much enlarged parliamentary oversight is a joint commission with four members from each house.[23] A "pluralist" composition is required, meaning some representation of the opposition parties. The commission's mandate specifically excludes all intelligence operations, past and present, and all liaison with foreign services. No intelligence officials below the director of a service can be called to testify. Secret information can be withheld if revealing it might endanger individuals or reveal methods. Thus, the commission's mandate is a fairly narrow one. Nevertheless, it marks a considerable gain for parliament, which explicitly does not give up its right to examine intelligence policy in other committees or, in special cases, to set up parliamentary inquiries. Even the committee addressing secret funds is left intact.

The commission is to deliver a secret annual report to the French president, the prime minister, and the president of each chamber of parliament.[24]

---

[20] Rapport législatif – Avis no. 339 (2006–2007) déposé le 20 Juin 2007, available at www.senat.fr.
[21] Implicitly, the model to be followed is Britain.
[22] Brochand, "Les activités", cited previously.
[23] It is composed of the chairs of the committees for defence and domestic security plus two members to be designated by the presidents of each chamber. For further details, see *Loi* no. 2007–1443, du 9 Octobre 2007, *Journal Officiel* no. 235 (10 Octobre 2007).
[24] The related parliamentary papers can be found on the Web site of each chamber.

The report will cover six intelligence services: three under the ministry of defence and three under the ministry of the interior. The report will not address other intelligence activities nor will it look into the top-level management structure, which currently consists of a special cabinet committee and a committee of high officials doing the actual planning and performing of executive oversight. The Sarkozy presidency has established a National Intelligence Council and the position of an intelligence advisor to the president, which are part of a far-reaching reform of French intelligence agencies and of the establishment of a national security council somewhat along the lines of the U.S. structure. This indicates that the institutional transition from the post-Soviet era to the post–September 11 era is still incomplete in France.

The oversight commission itself is an interesting construct of parliamentary work. France established the first bicameral committee of this type in 1979, dealing with EU policy. Five other committees are concerned with science and technology assessment, sustainable growth, and gender equality, among other issues. Clearly, the intelligence-oversight commission marks an important step in a larger reform agenda which is aimed at giving the French parliament more weight vis-à-vis the executive and finding a wider consensus among the political parties. With the French communists down to 4 percent of the Assemblée members, the Cold War fear of letting them in on state secrets is now only a faint memory.

THE GERMAN EXPERIENCE OF OVERSIGHT

The German oversight system – until 1990, the West German system – developed from a very different background. First, the scope of German intelligence was much narrower. Unlike Britain, France, or the Netherlands, Germany had no colonies and therefore became involved in neither postcolonial intelligence-gathering nor covert operations during what is usually described as the era of decolonisation. Instead, German intelligence was chiefly about finding information on Soviet and Warsaw Pact capabilities and intentions. Given that country's limited sovereignty, its security policy was restricted to the North Atlantic Treaty Organization (NATO) framework. The rest of German foreign policy did not reach far either, except for global business relations which, however, made little difference to Germany's foreign intelligence.

However, there was a special counterintelligence problem due to the geographical proximity of the Soviet Bloc, the close affiliation of East German intelligence (i.e., the "Stasi") with Soviet intelligence, and the shared German language. Although it was easy for the communist side to infiltrate any number of spies among the many thousands of Germans migrating annually from east to west, Western intelligence operations were made increasingly difficult by the fortifications, electric fences and, from August 1961, the Berlin Wall, which sealed off the Soviet Bloc.

Another highly unusual challenge derived from the peculiar origins of West German intelligence during the early and mid-1950s when the three Allied High Commissioners – American, British, and French – still oversaw all legislation, particularly in the sphere of security. The domestic-intelligence services were given a two-layered structure in which the Federal Office for the Protection of the Constitution (BfV) was paralleled by similar offices in each of the 11 states. Their activities were closely watched by the related permanent committees of the federal and state parliaments. Apart from their administrative structure and their carefully defined mandate, which explicitly excluded any police-type executive functions, the key concern among the three Allies was the choice of personnel.

These matters were particularly delicate when, in 1956, the foreign intelligence service, the *Bundesnachrichtendienst* (BND), was established in the context of West German rearmament under NATO tutelage. The BND had its origins in the "Gehlen organisation", a clandestine intelligence arm first set up in 1946 by the U.S. military and later (from 1949) managed by the CIA. It was staffed mostly by former Wehrmacht officers and performed a variety of intelligence functions, chiefly monitoring Soviet forces in Eastern Germany (and elsewhere in the emerging Eastern Bloc) as well as in the four-power city of Berlin. Another important task was to debrief the vast numbers of German POWs returning from Soviet captivity and refugees from Eastern Europe.

Although the BND was founded by executive order only, General Reinhard Gehlen, the head of the Gehlen organisation, quickly established contact with many key members of the federal parliament. The formal founding procedures of April 1956, therefore, were based on a consensus between the conservative-led government headed by Chancellor Konrad Adenauer and the main opposition party in the federal parliament, the Social Democrats. Immediately, an oversight group was established which consisted of the party leaders and was chaired by the chancellor. There was little in the way of formal procedures and, from the scant source materials available, it appears that during its first years, the group was principally concerned with two issues: (1) rumours that Gehlen, under the cover of counterintelligence, was providing Adenauer with "dirty stories" about the chancellor's political opponents; and (2) allegations that a number of former officials from the police and security apparatus of Heinrich Himmler, the notorious *Reichssicherheitshauptamt* (Reich Security Main Office), were being employed by Gehlen.[25]

The presence of ex-Nazi and even ex-SS officials in the BND was a highly sensitive issue. It appears that such people, in fact, were hired while Gehlen worked for the Americans – that is, before 1956 – and that they were chiefly employed in counterintelligence work for which neither Gehlen himself nor his former colleagues from Wehrmacht intelligence were qualified. The political problem involved was highlighted when the chief of West Germany's domestic intelligence (i.e., BfV), Dr. Otto John, defected to East Berlin in July 1954. At a press conference there, he denounced the presence of ex-Nazis in the BND. The intelligence risk involved in hiring such people became painfully obvious in 1961, when Heinz Felfe, the chief of the BND's counterintelligence department for Soviet affairs, and his associate, Hans Clemens, were arrested and eventually convicted of spying for the Soviets. Felfe, an ex-SS officer, had been recruited by Soviet intelligence in 1950 and by Gehlen in 1951.

In general, the German federal parliament did not show much interest in continuous oversight. Its control committee met infrequently. It preferred to deal with the BND in special parliamentary inquiries, set up to deal with the ever-growing number of BND scandals – for example, the "Spiegel affair" of late 1962. The scandal led to the dismissal of Defence Minister Franz Josef Strauss in what he believed was an intrigue by Gehlen. It also revealed serious gaps in executive oversight on the part of the chancellor's office. Another scandal was the "Traube affair" in 1977, triggered by a BfV wiretapping operation against nuclear-energy manager Klaus Traube which subsequently led to the dismissal of the secretary of the interior, Werner Maihofer.[26]

In the wake of the Traube case, a reinforced parliamentary oversight system was established and put on a statutory basis in 1978. A control commission was established, members of which were elected by parliament. Yet, parliament waited until 1989 to put the German intelligence services

[25] Stefanie Waske, "Mehr Liaison als Kontrolle: Die Kontrolle des BND durch Parlament und Regierung 1955–1978", (unpublished dissertation, Universität Marburg, 2007); for the Nazi personnel, see James H. Critchfield, *Partners at the Creation: The Men behind Postwar Germany's Defense and Intelligence Establishments* (Annapolis, MD: U.S. Naval Institute Press, 2003); Richard Breitman et al. (eds.), *U.S. Intelligence and the Nazis* (New York: Cambridge University Press, 2005); and Wolfgang Krieger, "U.S. Patronage of German Postwar Intelligence", in Johnson, *Handbook of Intelligence Studies*, pp. 91–102.
[26] Traube had a number of communist friends but was not a communist himself. The fact that he was of Jewish-German descent and lost both of his parents in the Holocaust further complicated matters.

on a statutory footing, which was in response to strong public pressure to restrict all governmental collection and use of personal data. It is obvious that intelligence services were among the potentially most dangerous obstacles to what was now called *informational self-determination*, a term first used in 1983 in a constitutional court decision concerned with the right of the German government to collect census data.

With some modifications made after German unification, a fairly extensive system of parliamentary oversight emerged in which the oversight commission enjoys far-reaching rights to cross-examine not only the political masters – in the case of the BND, the minister in charge of the chancellor's office and his intelligence coordinator tasked with the day-to-day work of executive oversight – but also agents from the services. The commission can request files and carry out on-site inspections. However, in the recent past, various leaks have seriously harmed its prestige. The efficacy of the commission's oversight work is called into question because it has no properly trained research staff.[27] In these circumstances, it could be argued that the wide-ranging mandate of the German intelligence oversight commission is a case of parliament biting off more than it can chew.[28]

BRITISH AND AMERICAN EXPERIENCES

The British case is particularly interesting for the way in which parliamentary oversight is being carefully limited. In 1994, when an act of parliament created the Intelligence and Security Committee (ISC), the three main intelligence services already had been put on a statutory basis. This was done in 1989 for the Security Service (i.e., domestic intelligence) and in 1994 for the Secret Intelligence Service (SIS) (i.e., foreign intelligence), as well as the Government Communications Headquarters (i.e., SIGINT). The ISC can only "examine the expenditure, administration, and policy" of those three agencies. Military intelligence, as well as all the offices, officials, and committees which provide executive guidance and oversight for intelligence, is left outside of ISC purview. In terms of composition and procedure, it is unlike normal parliamentary committees which can force a government

---

[27] Among the most serious breaches of secrecy is the release of a classified report ("Schäfer-Bericht", 2006) with insufficient deletions, which made it possible for any layperson to reconstruct the names of several BND agents. See Wilhelm Dietl, *Deckname Dali – ein BND-Agent packt aus* (Frankfurt am Main: Eichborn, 2007).

[28] For further references, see Eric Gujer, *Kampf an neuen Fronten: Wie sich der BND dem Terrorismus stellt* (Frankfurt am Main: Campus, 2006); and Wolfgang Krieger, "*Der Bundesnachrichtendienst in der deutschen Öffentlichkeit seit 1990*", *Journal for Intelligence, Propaganda and Security Studies*, 1, 1 (2007), 6–16.

department to produce official papers and to hear senior officials. The ISC is composed of members from both houses of parliament, but the selection is made by the prime minister, who only needs "to consult" the leader of the opposition in the process. Because the ISC reports to the prime minister, who subsequently presents an edited version of the reports before parliament, it is clear that the executive holds all the cards – at least, in a legalistic sense. The only real threat that the prime minister and his ministers face in this context is pressure from the press, which, in a sense, is co-equal to the ISC in oversight power.

The intelligence crisis around the WMD issue relating to the Iraq war illustrates this point quite well. The most hard-hitting investigations that were initiated to restore public confidence in the government's intelligence policy were not carried out by the ISC but rather by special ad hoc inquiries led by highly respected retired senior officials and generals. When the ISC's special report of September 2003 on the government's handling of the WMD issue took a rather cautious line in its conclusions, the nonparliamentary group under the chairmanship of Lord Butler did not mince its words. Its report of July 2004 not only voiced massive criticism but also made various recommendations for reforming the government's intelligence management.

The ISC can study various matters of intelligence planning and administration. It can make recommendations which render the services more efficient and more aware of legal sensitivities.[29] However, it cannot become involved in the planning and execution of intelligence operations, which are controlled exclusively by the responsible government departments and their ministers. As Michael Herman remarked, with typical British humour: "... there are few checks and balances against the use of intelligence as a prop for tyranny. It fits British assumptions that a dictatorship cannot happen here.... "[30]

By contrast, in the United States, all government activities are widely perceived as being inherently dangerous to the liberties of the "ordinary American". What Samuel Huntington called the "promise of disharmony" means that the U.S. government's efficiency often takes second place to controlling its propriety.[31] Indeed, intelligence oversight as practiced today began with a huge moral outcry in 1975 – the *annus horribilis* of U.S. intelligence politics – when *The New York Times* accused the intelligence

---

[29] Michael Herman, "Great Britain" Smidt, *Geheimhaltung und Transparenz*, pp. 99–100.

[30] Herman, "Great Britain", p. 100.

[31] Samuel Huntington, *American Politics: The Promise of Disharmony* (Cambridge, MA: Belknap Press, 1981).

community of having spied on domestic civil-rights organisations and of planning to assassinate foreign dictators, among them Fidel Castro. The subsequent congressional investigation reports – which are known by the names of the respective chairs in the Senate and House committees, Senator Frank Church of Idaho and Congressman Otis Pike of New York – opened a new chapter in congressional intelligence oversight. However, those investigations also protected the integrity of American intelligence machinery by agreeing to keep certain information secret despite the urge to publicise a considerable number of scandals which turned up in the course of the inquiry.[32]

Beyond the shock those scandals inflicted on the American public, one of the key questions remained essentially unanswered: Who was ultimately responsible for all those misdeeds? Most people seemed to like the idea that the CIA – and, by extension, the FBI and other agencies – had been "rogue elephants on a rampage", as Senator Church famously expressed it, but, in fact, the evidence pointed the other way. None of what was now termed to have been illegal, unethical, or both was actually done without the knowledge of the intelligence leadership and essentially without the more or less obvious consent of two Cold War presidents, Eisenhower and Kennedy (who were both dead at the time of the congressional inquiry). In that sense, executive oversight had worked tolerably well or, rather, as well as it was required by the government at the time. In the words of the Church Committee report, "On occasion, intelligence agencies concealed their programs from those in higher authority; more frequently, it was the senior officials themselves who, through pressure for results, created the climate within which the abuses occurred".[33]

Even three decades later, the president is shielded from taking personal responsibility by the fact that his daily intelligence brief cannot be released to congressional oversight proceedings. This became a heated issue when the question was raised about the precise intelligence that President Bush had been shown in the summer of 2001 – that is, weeks and days before the September 11 attacks.

The U.S. intelligence oversight system, which has been somewhat modified since its creation in the 1970s, differs most markedly from the European systems in three respects. First, the size of the U.S. intelligence community – with its 16 different agencies, enormous budgets, and literal worldwide deployment of assets – makes it difficult to compare the task of oversight in

---

[32] The published reports are now available on the Internet from various sources. Among them, see www.aarclibrary.org/publib/church/reports/contents.htm.

[33] Quoted in Schwarz, "The Church Committee", p. 290.

the United States to that of any other country. Second, a somewhat curious American attitude toward domestic intelligence before 1974 led to a situation in which not only the FBI but also the CIA, and other agencies as well, ran domestic intelligence programs – illegally in some cases – that would have been routine work in European democracies. The issue arose again in the inquiries into the September 11 terrorist attacks, which well may have succeeded because the United States had no proper domestic-intelligence organisation – for example, like the British MI-5 or the French Directorate of Territorial Security (DST). Remarkably, even the subsequent intelligence reforms, including the creation of the Department of Homeland Security, did not make Americans change their mind on this matter – although, in reality, the American government runs any number of intelligence operations and programs which are as intrusive on private citizens as any in other liberal democracies. President Bush's 2001 program for extensive domestic wiretapping without a court order is an obvious indication.[34] By enhancing the FBI's counterterrorism and counterintelligence programs, the United States largely dismantled the "wall" between intelligence and law enforcement – a step which most European democracies would be reluctant to take.

The third unusual feature is the shared decision making between executive and legislative on covert operations. Since the Hughes–Ryan Act was passed in December 1974, the president has had to give explicit orders for all covert operations and has had to report them to Congress. Since 1980, Congress must be informed *prior* to such operations. Further legislation in 1991 (i.e., the Intelligence Authorization Act) requires the president's written order (i.e., "presidential finding") to be placed before Congress intelligence-oversight committees – again, *before* the start of any operations. The inherent logic seems to be that covert operations are somewhat akin to making war on a foreign country and that launching them may well be the prelude to getting into a war. Therefore, they touch on the constitutional right of Congress to declare war. However, this constitutional logic obviously leads to a dilemma with respect to oversight because the same people in Congress who are supposed to oversee presidential policy in intelligence matters now become co-responsible for operational decisions. Among the practical consequences could well be some sort of "micromanagement" on the part of congressional oversight committees or lawmakers "going native", thus losing their critical distance vis-à-vis intelligence managers.

The list should perhaps be expanded by a fourth item that distinguishes the U.S. system: the availability of ample specialised staff working for the

---

[34] Those wiretaps were revealed to the press in December 2005.

oversight committees. This feature not only considers the far greater volume of work compared to other nations, it is also exemplary of the way in which Congress seeks to balance the far superior expertise that intelligence services have over their political masters as well as vis-à-vis their overseers.

SPECIAL OVERSIGHT FOR SPECIAL PURPOSES

Given the obvious imperfections of both executive and parliamentary intelligence oversight systems, a number of additional oversight instruments have emerged. The most widespread example is the special oversight regime which exists in most states for wiretapping and other forms of electronic surveillance, such as videotaping, acoustic surveillance, and surveillance of Internet traffic. The remote surveillance of fixed disks in personal computers by way of "Trojans" (or other malware) is a reality, although its legal framework is still highly questionable. The rapidly increasing numbers of telephone conversations carried over the Internet mark yet another technological challenge to not only surveillance technology but also legal propriety of surveillance measures and, by extension, intelligence oversight.

Typically, such operations cannot be carried out on the home territory without a court order or some type of authorisation from another body specifically established for this purpose. In the United States (in 1978), Congress legalised wiretaps when authorised by judicial warrant – or even without one, in national security cases. The Foreign Intelligence Surveillance Act (FISA) created a special court of seven judges to approve such measures and a three-member court to hear appeals. However, as the name indicates, the FISA does not squarely address the issue of spying on U.S. citizens. Moreover, its procedures are too cumbersome, which is why in response to September 11, President Bush ordered such surveillance measures outside the FISA framework.

In Europe, democratic states sought to cope with the situation by providing legal frameworks such as the "G-10-Kommission" of the German federal parliament, which was established in 1968 to authorise surveillance measures in certain well-defined circumstances. Originally, it consisted of five members who were elected by parliament but who did not have to be active parliamentarians. (One of them had to be an experienced lawyer or judge.[35]) Other European states had less rigorous oversight procedures or – like Britain – none at all until the European Human Rights Court passed a

---

[35] Its name refers to Article 10 in the German constitution, which deals with privacy. Today, the committee has four regular and four deputy members.

ruling in 1986 that wiretapping and similar measures could be ordered only on the basis of appropriate national legislation which, at the same time, provided for proper oversight and facilities for judicial appeal. Britain, France, and other countries subsequently adapted their legislative and institutional provisions accordingly, although many in Britain did not appreciate the fact that international law so obviously interfered with the sovereignty of the Westminster parliament. The issue was made even more painful by the fact that several citizens fighting against British policy in Northern Ireland won European court rulings against Britain in cases in which British police and intelligence had violated human rights during the "dark age of Irish terrorism".

As in the Dutch experience described previously, intelligence oversight may well be executed more efficiently and impartially by a special body of professionals than by parliamentarians. This model also has been followed by Norway. In Canada, the Security Intelligence Review Committee (SIRC) was established in 1984 to oversee operations of the Canadian Security Intelligence Service (CSIS), founded in the same year and based on the same act of parliament. This occurred after a series of scandals involving the Royal Canadian Mounted Police, which until then had carried out domestic-intelligence functions. SIRC investigates only past intelligence operations, which means it is not involved in concurrent oversight and decision making. It has full access to all CSIS files and it reports to the minister responsible for CSIS. Because the five members are privy councillors, appointed by the government with the consent of the parliamentary opposition, it is assumed that their investigations are independent. Their highly trained staff makes them effective.

The inspector general (IG) is another instrument for controlling the work of intelligence services. Within the U.S. federal bureaucracy, there are currently 57 IGs, including one inside the CIA, who are charged with preventing and identifying fraud, waste, and misconduct. All democracies have a special office or person responsible for checking the accounting of secret intelligence funds – either directly by a parliamentary committee, an accounting office, or a combination of the two. However, the appointment by the president with confirmation by the U.S. Senate makes the CIA IG (and his colleagues inside other major intelligence services) something of a specialty in the world of intelligence oversight.

However, because the IG reports to the president and to Congress, who jointly manage U.S. intelligence, ordinary citizens may require something else in terms of protection against impropriety of intelligence. Establishing the office of ombudsman, originally a Scandinavian institution, would be a way to process such complaints. However, few countries – among them, the Netherlands – have so far applied this idea to the world of intelligence. In Germany, there has been debate about how to handle complaints from intelligence-service staff. One possibility would be to follow the example of the Commissioner for the Armed Forces, who is elected directly by parliament and has the right as well as the duty to investigate individual complaints. The idea has not yet been accepted, however, presumably because the parliamentary-control commission does not wish to share its intelligence-oversight responsibilities. Neither has the idea caught on to make legal provisions for protecting whistle-blowers in the world of intelligence. The issue gained much publicity in the United States after September 11 when FBI officials let it be known that they had been on the heels of several of those terrorists but had been blocked by their superiors from continuing their investigations.

Surely, the whistle-blower model entails numerous pitfalls. For example, who should be authorised to receive such complaints, ones that most likely contain highly classified information? The price of not allowing for people to come forward is also well known; it is the press leak. Although few are likely to become as prominent as "Deep Throat" – the deputy FBI chief Mark Felt who leaked to the *Washington Post* his knowledge about the White House and CIA involvement of the 1974 Watergate break-in – the history of modern intelligence is filled with intelligence leaks. Indeed, the oversight role of the press depends largely on leaks of one sort or another, and parliamentary oversight bodies usually become energised in their wake. However, because leaks, by definition, cannot be counted on or brought under control, it is more likely that some type of whistle-blower arrangement will grow from the soaring concern over electronic surveillance, particularly when it targets Internet communication and data storage on private computers.[36]

In a way, all of those oversight instruments somehow fail to address a part of intelligence reality which is quite likely to expand in the coming years: the world of intelligence liaison. Originally, such cooperation took place in the context of coalition warfare – for example, during the two World Wars. Then, during the Cold War, various bilateral intelligence relationships – most famously the one between Britain and the United States – and multilateral networks such as NATO evolved between liberal democracies fighting Soviet and Chinese communism. Since September 11, liberal

[36] Hansjörg Geiger, "*Ein heimlicher Anwalt für die Bürge*", *Süddeutsche Zeitung* (18 September 2007), p. 2. Geiger was, consecutively, head of the BfV and the BND during the 1990s.

democracies have vastly expanded their cooperation with dictatorships of all types, particularly those opposed to Islamist terrorism.

As discussed previously, however, intelligence oversight systems typically exclude such cooperation from the range of intelligence activities to be watched by oversight bodies. The reason usually given is that the scrutiny of foreign-intelligence secrets is likely to lead to a freeze in those relationships and the loss of critical intelligence information. This is not to say that liaison issues are absent from public debates on intelligence oversight; one only needs to recall the controversial "Echelon" investigation by the European parliament or the controversy about U.S. "special rendition flights" across Europe and the alleged existence of secret U.S. interrogation centres in East European NATO states. Yet, it is true that such topics do not fit well into the regular workings of national oversight machinery, which is essentially targeting intelligence failure or wrongdoing within its own national boundaries.

For both political and legal reasons, the emerging common security policy of the EU plays a special role in this context. In 2006, the intelligence oversight committee of the Italian parliament invited its colleagues from around the EU to gather in Rome, hoping to establish a continuous dialogue on their respective experiences. The obvious goal of this dialogue is to harmonise intelligence policies, including oversight systems, along with military structures and policies. Such harmonisation appears to be necessary for both the collaboration among EU member states on international terrorism and crime and the growing number of joint humanitarian and military operations worldwide. There are now at least four EU institutions with an intelligence function which need to be controlled. Although they mostly coordinate and analyse intelligence gathered by national services, there is, as Björn Müller-Wille ably pointed out, a need for oversight – a need further complicated by the fact that the European Parliament is not a parliament in the true sense and that the EU Commission is not a democratic government in almost any sense.[37]

In conclusion, intelligence oversight has become a vivid subject of public debate due to three main developments. The first could be called the electronic revolution. As liberal democratic societies consign their communication infrastructure to those new technologies at a dizzying speed, intelligence-gathering becomes more intrusive and more difficult to control. The resulting fears among the public call for strong measures to bring

---

[37] Björn Müller-Wille, "Improving the Democratic Accountability of EU Intelligence", *Intelligence and National Security*, 21, 1 (2006).

this process under political and legal control – in other words, to expand the power of intelligence oversight, particularly with regard to propriety of intelligence practice at home.

The second development relates to the rapid expansion of international terrorism and crime which, similarly, makes the state look increasingly impotent in the face of those new threats. Improved intelligence oversight, it is hoped, would lead to more intelligence efficacy and thus to better protection of the citizens and their way of life.

Third, the end of the Cold War has somehow made intelligence less secret. While increasing their intelligence power, liberal democracies have called on their citizens to take an active part in fighting new security threats such as Islamist terrorism. A parallel might be with the investigative work of police detectives who depend heavily on support from ordinary citizens, typified by the pensioner walking his dog who notes "something suspicious" in his neighborhood. It is therefore logical that the borders between foreign and domestic intelligence, on the one hand, and intelligence and police, on the other, have blurred. Even the distinction between the military and the police has narrowed – for example, international peacemaking and peacekeeping missions. In other words, the place of intelligence has not only changed because of new challenges and new technologies but also because of a fundamental change in security architectures. As a result, intelligence has become more visible and less different from other state bureaucracies – at least among those dealing with security in one form or another.

In this perspective, the expansion of intelligence oversight can be seen as a process in which intelligence services are becoming more "normal" parts of government, subject to the same procedures of scrutiny as law enforcement and the military. Because the recasting of the security apparatus from its original Cold War configuration is still far from completion, it is difficult to predict how much intelligence oversight will expand. However, the general direction of this evolution seems clear enough. In the years to come, intelligence will be more "normal" and oversight will be more complex as well as more intrusive. Whether it will also be more effective seems far less certain than many people would like to think.

TEN

The Limits of Avowal: Secret Intelligence in an Age of Public Scrutiny

Sir David Omand

Compare these two quotations. First, testimony to the Congressional Oversight Committee from the Director of the Central Intelligence Agency (CIA)[1]: "We can't break the law.... You just can't go to that place.... I actually said fairly publicly to our workforce that, as director, I have to be certain that that which I'm asking a CIA officer to do is consistent with the Constitution, the laws and the international treaty obligations of the United States.... If I can't say that, I can't ask an officer to do it". Second, as put to the British author Bickham Sweet-Escott on his recruitment into the British Wartime Special Operations Executive: "I can't tell you what sort of a job it would be. All I can say is that if you join us, you mustn't be afraid of forgery, and you mustn't be afraid of murder".[2] The first quotation is from 2007, the second from 1940. Almost 70 years and a revolution in intelligence work separate these two attitudes. A question hangs over the quotations: Can the acknowledged, democratically accountable, independently overseen, and publicly Web-visible government intelligence agencies that we now have, operating to a strict ethical code, be expected to be able to collect worthwhile secret intelligence and engage in effective secret action?

The question is not academic. Academic analysis, however, should help answer the opening question. Were we to conclude that avowal, accountability, oversight, and ethics should have no place in the secret world, then we stand to pay a high price in terms of the risk that our security authorities will lack public backing from important sections of the community and may well fail as a result. Conversely, were we to conclude in the opposite

[1] Available at www.q-and-a.org/Transcript/?ProgramID=1123, Evidence, General Hayden, April 2007.
[2] Quoted in Bruce Page, David Leitch, and Philip Knightley, *The Philby Conspiracy* (New York: Doubleday, 1968), p. 135.

sense that for reasons of public morality, the modern world should hold no hiding place for secret sources and methods, then the terrorists will be able to operate largely unhindered by our security measures. To be able to answer the question positively is therefore important for national security. This chapter aims to show that this is currently the case for the United Kingdom. Additionally, because it is not self-evident that this confidence will continue to be justified, it is important in the course of this analysis to identify where additional strains may be expected to arise in the future from the demands that supporting counterterrorism is placing on the intelligence community.

I write from my experience of recent circumstances in the United Kingdom. In the past, the United Kingdom often has been discovered after the event – sometimes long afterwards – to have been the first to experience and apply new thinking in the world of intelligence. The United Kingdom operated an effective state intelligence system in great secrecy for centuries and yet was one of the first to recognize the need to involve the scientific community in its work, to avow publicly the existence of its most secret activities, and to open up new levels of intelligence interchange with law enforcement.[3] Every country, however, has its own particularities in the matter of secret intelligence and security arrangements, but there may be pointers here of more general value by looking at the factors that impelled the United Kingdom to acknowledge the existence of its secret agencies and to place them on a statutory footing with both parliamentary and judicial oversight.

In this quest, the research community has potentially much to offer the practitioner. Historical situational awareness[4] helps in the understanding of our present condition, and learning drawn from other debates such as heuristics, just-war theory,[5] and the literature on counterinsurgency[6] may help shape responses from the intelligence community. The study of intelligence can help unpack the traditional case for secrecy in the intelligence world and test the justification for maintaining the veil of secrecy over

---

[3] Sir David Omand, "Reflections on Secret Intelligence", in Peter Hennessy (ed.), *The New Protective State* (London: Continuum Books, 2007).

[4] R. J. Aldrich, "Policing the Past: Official History, Secrecy and British Intelligence since 1945", *English Historical Review*, CXIX, 483 (September 2004).

[5] Michael Walzer, *Just and Unjust Wars* (New York: Basic Books, 1977), and the up-to-date analysis in the collection of essays by Charles Reed and David Ryall (eds.), *The Price of Peace: Just War in the Twenty-First Century* (Cambridge: Cambridge University Press, 2007).

[6] Rupert Smith, *The Utility of Force* (London: Penguin Books, 2005).

intelligence sources and methods, while also helping governments under-stand what they should be doing now to retain public confidence in the methods of their intelligence community.

Because it is in relation to the work of the intelligence agencies in coun-tering terrorism that the fundamental question seems the most difficult to answer, I start by identifying what is special about their work on that target. I try to disentangle the complicated linkages that exist between the factors that make intelligence operations the key to successful counterterrorism, the necessary secrecy surrounding them, and yet the need for public con-fidence (including the confidence of Muslim communities) in their results and methods. To rephrase the opening question in a more pointed way: If we are to prevail against *jihadist* terrorism of the type inspired by al Qaeda (AQ), can we afford not to have secret agencies that are avowed accountable and independently overseen and crucially trusted to operate according to an accepted code of ethics? Far from it being a handicap, there is consid-erable value in being able to demonstrate that intelligence work in support of counterterrorism sits within an ethical framework based on respect for human rights.

THE ROLE OF THE INTELLIGENCE COMMUNITY IN COMBATING *JIHADIST* TERRORISM

Specific transatlantic flights are cancelled for fear they have been targeted for attack; concrete bollards appear outside public buildings to deter vehicle bombs; armoured vehicles surround the United Kingdom's main airport to counter a possible surface-to-air missile attack; in the early morning, armed police storm a house in a residential area looking for a chemical explosive device; air travellers are suddenly told that no liquids may be taken in hand luggage because of the risk of the components of peroxide-based explosives being smuggled on board – such events have become part of the everyday response to the growth of *jihadist* terrorism.

There is a common factor to the rationale behind these (real) examples of counterterrorist action: each rests on preemptive intelligence that was sufficiently well sourced that it could not be ignored, forcing the secu-rity authorities to act, to act quickly, and to act publicly. The publicity surrounding recent arrests, trials, and convictions of members and sup-porters of terrorist networks gave the public insights on the threat, as well as glimpses of the value of the intelligence effort going on under the surface, both domestically and overseas. Nevertheless, in each case, there were media stories questioning the quality of the intelligence behind the warnings, with commentators[7] (no doubt with the shadow from Iraq falling over their keyboards) directly challenging the veracity of police and government accounts and claiming that the threat was being talked up for political motives.

The skepticism around intelligence on weapons of mass destruction (WMD) in Saddam Hussein's Iraq – a theme that runs throughout the chapters in this book – has not yet dissipated, and it helps to undermine public trust in the intelligence case that governments adduce for counter-terrorist measures. Some of the measures adopted by the U.S. security and intelligence community, such as detention without trial, rendition, coercive interrogations, and targeted killings, have themselves raised controversy. What is clear is that the intelligence community is under scrutiny as never before – and pressure is increasing for more disclosure of details of their current work, following the unprecedented openness about the work of U.S.[8] and U.K.[9] communities in the reports from recent September 11 and Iraq-related inquiries on both sides of the Atlantic.

This intense scrutiny comes at a time when the intelligence agencies have been engaged in a massive reorientation of effort towards counterterrorism, coupled with major expansion of the effort to reverse the savings of the immediate post–Cold War years. The U.K. Security Service, for example, has doubled in size from its post–Cold War level. This expansion reflects a belief in the fundamental importance of good preemptive secret intelligence in counterterrorism strategy because it enables the authorities to:

- protect the public directly by preventing the criminal acts before they occur
- by lowering the level of violence, buy time for longer term measures addressing the roots of the current problems to take effect
- provide the leads for criminal investigations that will lead to prosecutions, thus reassuring the public, reducing the threat, and upholding the rule of law.

---

[7] For example, in the United Kingdom, Peter Oborne, *The Use and Abuse of Terror: The Construction of a False Narrative on the Domestic Terror Trail* (London: Centre for Policy Studies, 2006); and, for the United States, John Mueller, *Overblown: How Politicians and the Terrorism Industry Inflate National Security Threats and Why We Believe Them* (New York: Free Press, 2006).

[8] Formally, *Final Report of the Commission on the Intelligence Capabilities of the United States Regarding Weapons of Mass Destruction* (Washington, 2005), available at www.wmd.gov/report.

[9] Review of Intelligence on Weapons of Mass Destruction: Report of a Committee of Privy Counsellors, HC 898 (HM Stationary Office, 14 July 2004), available at www.butlerreview.org.uk/index.asp.

The dual task of defeating the ideology of the terrorists as well as frustrating their planned attacks imposes significant constraints on counterterrorist tactics as well as strategy. Given good preemptive secret intelligence, however, the security authorities can hope to achieve another important requirement of any sound counterterrorism strategy – namely, to operate in ways that reassure, do not alienate, the communities in which the terrorists seek support. Replace the bludgeon of state power – stop and search, pass laws, house-to-house searches, mass arrests – with the rapier or, if you prefer, the surgical scalpel.

What secret intelligence must illuminate are the three powerful forces that bin Laden and al-Zawahiri have created:

- *A compelling narrative of victimhood and fanatical religious righteousness, of which the highest form is martyrdom.* Having failed in their quasi-insurgencies in Egypt, Algeria, Indonesia, and elsewhere, the different groups of self-styled *jihadists* have turned from attacking their "own" governments to forming the common front (i.e., AQ) to attack the United States and its allies in order to force changes in their policies and reduce their influence in the Muslim world. We need intelligence assessment of how they now see the state of their campaign and especially the conditions under which we might expect AQ-inspired insurgencies to intensify.
- *Dispersed networks of radicalised violent extremists in many countries including the United Kingdom, which are able to conduct attacks themselves, or provide practical support to those who can.* As the then–Director General (DG) of the U.K. Security Service[10] stated publicly, "If the opinion polls conducted in the U.K. since July 2005 are only broadly accurate, over 100,000 of our citizens consider that the July 2005 attacks in London were justified". The tactical capabilities of such networks, such as countersurveillance and use of secret methods of communication and financing, are improving, potentially frustrating conventional law enforcement. The reasonable expectation is that intelligence agencies will be able to use their special skills and advanced techniques to penetrate and disrupt these networks.
- *A core of trained terrorists, of many different nationalities, able to inspire, plan, and mount complex terrorist operations against "the far enemy".* For this group, violent *jihad* against "the head of the snake" is a personal duty because, in their eyes, the policies of the United States and its allies

---

[10]   Dame Eliza Manningham-Buller, speech at Queen Mary College, 9 November 2006, available at www.mi5.gov.uk.

towards the Muslim world are incurably discriminatory and, at heart, colonial. At least one analyst[11] has concluded that AQ is reestablishing its capability and reach, an analysis that reinforces the case for the current North Atlantic Treaty Organization (NATO) military operations to prevent the Taliban undermining the government of Afghanistan, and other intelligence-led steps to prevent AQ from establishing secure bases elsewhere from which terrorists could operate.

Terrorists, of course, are criminals who need to be brought to justice through proper process and, if convicted, punished according to the law. However, they are unlikely to be neither deterred by penal sanctions nor preempted by conventional criminal investigation. Domestic criminal justice is necessary but is not, on its own, sufficient to protect the public adequately, at home or overseas, and neither will it bring this menace to an end; hence, the search for a comprehensive (i.e., military and civilian) national-security strategy in response, one that is informed by intelligence assessment and guided by preemptive intelligence reporting. For example, the single overarching U.K. national-security objective (set out in the U.K. government's 2008 White Paper[12]) is "protecting the United Kingdom and its interests, enabling its people to go about their daily lives freely and with confidence, in a more secure, stable, just, and prosperous world". Within that overall aim sits a specific counterterrorism objective[13] that can be paraphrased as: "working in partnership, to reduce the risk from international terrorism so that people can go about their daily lives, freely and with confidence." Much that is relevant to this present discussion is compressed into this short statement of aim. Let me unpack each phrase.

"Working in partnership" emphasises the point that counterterrorism involves the specialist intelligence, security, and law enforcement communities working closely together, blurring the traditional distinctions between the domestic space occupied by police and security authorities and "overseas" as the preserve of secret services. The experience of working on Irish terrorism, including the threat to Great Britain itself, undoubtedly led to closer relations with law enforcement than has been the case with most of the United Kingdom's close allies and partners and with most parts of civil government, as well as with industry and the academic world. "In partnership" also has a message for international cooperation and the recognition

---

[11] For example, Peter Bergen, "The Return of Al Qaida", *The New Republic*, 29 January 2007.
[12] *The National Security Strategy of the United Kingdom*, Cm 7291, March 2008.
[13] *Countering International Terrorism: The UK Strategy*, Cm 6888, July 2006.

that no nation, not even the most powerful, can create security against this threat unaided, and that how allies and partners behave matters.

"Reducing the risk" implies correctly that in the next few years, well-targeted counterterrorism action can measurably reduce the threat and the public's vulnerability to it. This places a huge responsibility on the intelligence community to generate preemptive intelligence. The phrasing also conveys the important message that although the risk can be reduced, there can be no assurance that there will be no further attacks. Nevertheless, the burden rests on the shoulders of the intelligence community which must brace itself for the inevitable charges of "intelligence failure" when the terrorists occasionally get through under the radar – another important reason for paying attention now to the issue of underlying public confidence in the structures and work of the intelligence community.

"So that people can go about their daily lives" sets the criterion against which success in countering terrorism can be measured. It represents the determination to deny the terrorists what they most seek in this phase of their campaign: global polarisation with a revolutionary consciousness developing across the world of Islam of an inevitable struggle against Western nations that are represented as being increasingly economically, culturally, and militarily hostile. This provides the context in which the extremists can preach violent *jihadism*, claiming that it has become the individual duty of Muslims to attack us with no limits on the form of their violence. This realisation, however, does place limits on the methods of the security authorities precisely because the terrorists want to expose the values of Western societies as fragile and hypocritical, suppressing civil rights at home and supporting apostate and repressive governments overseas. Their motives should be understood as the well-understood tactics of the revolutionary through the ages. The ability to go about daily life also means, therefore, not being tempted by the terrorists' excesses into overreaction.

"Freely" signals determination to maintain such rights as having straightforward access to our political representatives; to be able to cross London or, indeed, the Atlantic, without intrusive security or undue delay; and to transact business safely overseas or have goods shipped economically around the globe. It also means not to be rushed into disproportionate measures that would undermine our values or the rule of law or represent a retreat from simple freedoms we take for granted. There are considerable implications here for the intelligence community about such issues as the use of intelligence in criminal trials, the development of technologies such as data-mining of private information, and the sharing of intelligence between government agencies and internationally.

"With confidence" demonstrates our determination to not be intimidated into living our life under a shadow or letting political debate be dominated by a climate of fear. It means encouraging our minority communities to have confidence in the authorities in their upholding of the rule of law. It means commitment to human rights and, above all, involving the active support of the public at large. Thus, in pursuing its strategy, the government must constantly persuade the public to hold fast to that which we are defending from the barbarities of the terrorist: our values, liberties, freedoms, and rights, including the proper rule of law. It is illusory to imagine that the security of the majority can be secured at the expense of the rights of a minority. This also has fundamental implications for the limits that, in the interests of the success of the strategy itself, ought to be placed on the methods used by the intelligence community, to which we return in the next section.

CONSTRAINTS ON THE RESPONSE OF THE INTELLIGENCE COMMUNITY

The sought-for intelligence to help deliver such a strategic aim will come from two directions: (1) modern, professional intelligence collection using all the human and technical tradecraft of which we are capable; and (2) information volunteered from within the community in rejection of the extremists and their ideology.

To make possible the former, society needs to accept the necessity of intrusive surveillance and investigation, thereby gaining greater security, and accept that this may have to be at the expense of some aspects of privacy rights (the opposite conclusion, it must be said, to the current calls to curb the so-called surveillance society). It is a difficult choice but, following the logic outlined here, greatly preferable to suspending other human rights, tinkering with the rule of law, or derogating from fundamental human rights. Being able to demonstrate proper legal authorisation and oversight of the implications of such intrusive intelligence activity becomes important if the public at large is to be convinced of such a proposition.

The issues that arise over the difference between U.S. and U.K. legal authorities are fully discussed by Laura Donohue.[14] It was revealed only in 2004 that President Bush (acting, in the words of his then–Attorney General, "at the zenith of his powers") had in October 2001 secretly authorised the

---

[14] Laura K. Donohue, "Anglo-American Privacy and Surveillance", *The Journal of Criminal Law and Criminology*, Northwestern University School of Law, 96, 3 (Spring 2006).

interception of communications outside the framework of the 1978 Foreign Intelligence Surveillance Act (FISA).[15] Controversially using war powers, the Bush administration harnessed the capability of information technology to search large volumes of personal Internet communications and to examine international financial transactions carried by the international SWIFT system.

The intelligence value of advanced technology will increase further at the same time as its cost will continue to decrease. This advanced technology is particularly valuable in providing initial clues to the existence of covert networks, but the very effectiveness of these techniques is already rubbing up against legal constraints, feelings of invasion of individual privacy, and worries over the wider uses of such information.

Using those techniques means maintaining community confidence in the actions of the state, including the protection provided by the framework of human rights and the quality of justice. Good preemptive intelligence reassures the community by removing the extremists and disrupting potential attacks without having to fall back on the sort of blunt discriminatory measures that alienate moderate support within the community on which effective policing and counter terrorism depends. Conversely, segments of the public in the United Kingdom and elsewhere in Europe (in particular, in the Continental powers that have been subject to totalitarian or fascist regimes) are becoming concerned about what is alleged to be happening in their name by secret agencies involved in the so-called war on terror. Means as well as ends matter here.

Intelligence has been used to direct a combination of overt military force and covert means to strike at known locations of terrorist activity overseas in order to disrupt terrorist planning, training, and logistics and to disable terrorist leadership. Some of these counterterrorist operations raise fundamental questions about the use, outside of the battlefield, of intelligence to guide military or covert action against terrorists. "Targeted killing" is carried out by U.S. forces – for example, by precision-guided air strikes – it is assumed,[16] following determination by the American president that individual terrorists concerned may be killed, if located and if capture is not feasible.[17]

---

[15] Donohue, cited previously.

[16] See the full discussion of the U.S. experience in Philip B. Heymann and Juliette N. Kayyem, *Protecting Liberty in an Age of Terror*, BCSIA Studies in International Security (Cambridge, MA: The MIT Press, 2005).

[17] D. Krezmer, "Targeted Killing of Suspected Terrorists: Extra-Judicial Executions or Legitimate Means of Defence?", *European Journal of International Law, 16*, 2 (2005), 171–212.

The legal issues over the rules of engagement for use by military forces of such preemptive lethal force are considerable. What degree of intelligence confidence should be required before strikes are launched? We can expect the debate to quicken as the revolution in military affairs progresses with net-centric warfare creating real-time demands for target intelligence and collateral-damage assessments.

The U.K. intelligence community does not engage in assassination[18]: Is it therefore acceptable to pass actionable intelligence on to a country whose rules of engagement for dealing with terrorists is different from ours? What methods are ethically acceptable for detaining and interrogating those captured, given the U.K. Attorney General's judgement[19] that Guantanamo Bay "is unacceptable and that it is time that it should be closed; that it has become a symbol of injustice, a recruiting agent for terrorists. It is a symbol which the long American tradition of justice and liberty deserves to see removed at the earliest moment". What should be the rules for returning suspects to third countries who wish to interrogate them regarding allegations of involvement in terrorism?

Western governments, reasonably, are helping to develop the security and intelligence capability of governments overseas that are themselves suffering from terrorism. The current British policy is to accept information from any source that bears on our major interests while we also take all reasonable steps to promote overseas our views about acceptable interrogation methods. Can we sustain the position that, in return, British intelligence information should be passed to other countries if that information might lead to action by others that would be considered unacceptable by the United Kingdom?

THE ORIGINAL CASE FOR SECRECY

In almost all of the cases of controversy cited previously, the intelligence-related activities driving the action were meant to be kept from domestic public attention by using the blanket secrecy that executive power can impose. In some cases, such as the use of nonjudicial warrants, the U.S. government has vigorously defended in public its policies once exposed; in others, such as rendition, there remains the awkwardness of international

---

[18] Sir Dick White tightened up the rules for MI6 after the Crabb fiasco and specifically forbade assassination, as quoted by Christopher Andrew, *Secret Service* (London: Heinemann, 1985), p. 496.

[19] In a speech to the American Bar Association, September 2006.

embarrassment and legal action.[20] In her testimony before the 9/11 Commission, U.S. National Security Advisor Condoleezza Rice noted that America is allergic to domestic intelligence.[21] U.K. experience of counterterrorist operations in Northern Ireland in the early 1970s provides a lesson in the danger of allowing ends to justify means, using secrecy to cover intelligence activity that, once exposed, proved impossible for the government to justify. That was the case, for example, with the decision to introduce internment in 1971 and to accompany it by the selective "deep interrogation" of a small number of suspects using techniques later condemned by the European Court of Human Rights as cruel and degrading, and which then had to be banned. (A ban is still in force for U.K. Armed Forces and agencies, but the methods are similar to those in use by U.S. authorities in its war on terror.)

Accusations continue to be made[22] about British Army intelligence collusion with paramilitaries in Northern Ireland and whether running "participating informers" within terrorist organisations turned a blind eye to serious criminality in order to protect intelligence operations. Much damage was caused in Northern Ireland in the early days of the campaign through the alienation of moderate opinion by the revelations of the intelligence-gathering methods used (just as there has recently been damage to the U.S. ability to project "soft power" around the world from its recent choice of methods[23]). This bears out Stansfield Turner's advice:[24] "There is one overall test of the ethics of human intelligence activities. That is whether those approving them feel they could defend their decisions before the public if their actions became public". In other words, do not undertake activities that you would be ashamed to try and defend and which therefore rely only on the cloak of secrecy remaining intact.

So, at the heart of the issues we are considering, here lies the dilemma of how – consistent with operational security – the public can be reassured that there is sensible control of collection of secret intelligence and access to personal data, and that those they elect are not abusing their powers. A

---

[20] As uncovered by Stephen Grey, *Ghost Plane* (London: Hurst, 2007).
[21] Quoted in the essay by Henry R. Crumpton, in Jennifer Sims and Burton Gerber (eds.), *Transforming U.S. Intelligence* (Washington: Georgetown University Press, 2005).
[22] *The Guardian* newspaper front page of 10 April 2007 leads with "MI5 and MOD battle to keep Ulster secrets" in advance of four key inquiries "set to expose the full extent of security force collusion. . . . "
[23] The judgement of Professor Joseph Nye, Lecture to King's College London, 14 February 2007.
[24] Admiral Stansfield Turner, *Secrecy and Democracy* (London: Sidgwick and Jackson, 1986), p. 178.

legislative framework and oversight, both judicial and political by elected representatives, would seem necessary. It is self-evident that for this to be possible, there must be acceptance that the very existence of secret agencies is admitted and that their activity is to be subject to law (even if that law itself legitimises extraordinary behaviour such as domestic surveillance). However, in terms of our opening question, will this fatally erode the necessary secrecy that needs to surround such activity? Intelligence studies can shed light on this dilemma. From history, we can illustrate how some of these once-overriding reasons for secrecy have come to lose their original force while others remain as potent as ever.

Kings, princes, and rulers generally have always wanted secret means to keep abreast of – and thus be in a position to stifle – potential threats to their hold on power – a point that Michael Warner stresses in Chapter Two. In England, the methodical use of secret service money can be traced back to Tudor times when Henry VII set up his own personal intelligence service – directed, in fact, at his domestic enemies. The British accumulated considerable experience in combating external interference in domestic affairs through secret intelligence directed at uncovering networks of domestic sympathisers, monitoring foreign agents of influence (e.g., the Spanish Ambassador at the Court of St. James during the reign of James I), and tracing their means of finance and communication. Agents and double agents thrived during the Civil War: one of the finest mathematicians of the time, Professor John Wallis, having been recruited by Cromwell's Director of Intelligence, continued his cryptographic services in support of the Restoration Government – an early precursor of the later tradition that secret servants serve impartially the government of the day!

Moreover, during subsequent periods, in parallel with the development of British constitutional monarchy, a habit of mind formed that it was entirely legitimate for the government to use executive privilege – that is, the Royal Prerogative – to maintain a secret set of defenses for the state, valuable in countering the Jacobite revolt of 1715 and the insurgency of 1745 and in monitoring attempts by foreigners to foment internal troubles, either directly or by the influence of their revolutionary writings. Much later, the police Special Branch was charged with the surveillance of civilian "revolutionary movements".[25]

In the United Kingdom, the Security Service was created as part of the War Office in response to paranoia over alleged German espionage and sabotage in the years just before World War I. Subsequently, without any

[25] John Curry, *The Security Service 1908–1945* (London: PRO, 1999).

definite mandate, the Security Service assumed the role of countering the influence of any subversive movement, especially in the Armed Forces and Civil Service, that could threaten loyalty to the Crown and thus, in terms of the unwritten constitutional settlement, parliamentary democracy. The Security Service thus informed itself "at least in a general way in case such a movement may develop more serious aspects of the activities of such groups as. . . . Trotskyites, the Anarchists, the Scottish and Welsh National- ist movements, Jehovah's witnesses, Pacifist movements, Polish intrigues, the Palestinian terrorists, the Greek nationalists on Cyprus, and so on".[26] It is hardly surprising that great efforts were made to keep the entire enterprise hidden from the public. The Security Service's postwar activities in combat- ing the influence of international communism, however, lead to suspicions of many on the left that they were spied on for their domestic political beliefs and created a mythology relating to the extent of surveillance, leav- ing a continuing legacy of distrust colouring some of the reception to the present case for expansion of counterterrorist surveillance.

A second closely related explanation for the persistence of the secret agencies of government rests on the wish of governments and generals to steal a march on military opponents and to outwit foreign powers through seeing the back of their cards. Historical debate will continue as to how important secret sources have been in influencing key decisions, such as whether Nelson's crucial victory at the Battle of Copenhagen resulted from Canning's genuine advance intelligence of Napoleon's intention to draw Denmark into joining the blockade of Britain (an intelligence triumph) or from Canning falling victim to misinformation (another early dodgy dossier). We should not be surprised at the persistence over the centuries of the rationale in an uncertain world of having secret intelligence to maximise national bargaining power.

For the United Kingdom, resting particularly on the intelligence triumphs of World War II and the continuing collaboration with the close wartime allies, being professional about intelligence has been an important part of the national self-image as a significant modern player on a world stage. Even the ending of the Cold War – although it resulted in significant redundancy in the mix of intelligence capabilities, overseas bases, and personnel skills – did not diminish the desire of governments to reshape the intelligence com- munity to deliver new benefits (and, of course, matched by the instincts of self-preservation of the agencies themselves). Significant for our argument here, the switch to gathering intelligence on such obvious evils as terrorism,

---

[26] Ibid.

proliferation, narcotics, and serious and organised criminal gangs provided a "new target set" that could be more easily admitted to internationally[27] and, indeed, fitted a model of much wider international cooperation rather than the traditional secrecy of the maximising national advantage through intelligence oneupmanship.

A third reason for secret agency lies in the natural attraction for governments to have the capability to pursue in the dark policies that for one reason or another they could not afford to be seen to advocate in the light. The "secret agent" of modern times – to enable and promote such policies through confidential personal contacts and secret information – is a logical necessity of such thinking. The gradual organisation of secret agents into more formal structures, with organisational hierarchies and institutional learning about sources and methods, was inevitable given the rise of the Prussian general-staff structure and the spread across civil government of the Weberian bureaucratic model of organisation. The process was greatly accelerated by the pressures of World War I, although with room for the unconventional secret agent to operate, such as Sydney Reilly.[28]

The industrialisation of aspects of intelligence, introduced in World War II and developed to manage technical exploitation during the long Cold War, did not stifle the ability of the U.K. intelligence community to operate secretly in a mode that would have been recognisable to Walsingham (whose intelligence network by 1580 included agents in France, Spain, Germany, Italy, the Low Countries, and the Ottoman Empire). A recent example of the persistence of such tradecraft, chronicled in Lord Butler's report[29] on Intelligence on WMD and in the memoirs of the U.S. Director of Central Intelligence (DCI) George Tenet,[30] is the successful secret backchannel diplomacy conducted with Libya – that is, deploying the extensive U.S. and U.K. secret intelligence on its procurement activities to persuade the Libyans to come clean and disclose their WMD programmes. The demand for such secret agency will not lessen. In the context of counterterrorism in particular, the need increases for substantive overseas liaison with a wide

---

[27] The United Nations, previously unwilling to recognise the right of one member state to spy on another, has accepted the value of intelligence in combating terrorism, UNSC Resolution 1373, and the European Court of Human Rights has accepted that nations have the right to protect their economic well-being and national security.

[28] Fresh insights into this period of development of secret intelligence are given in Gill Bennett's biography of Desmond Morton, *Churchill's Man of Mystery* (London: Routledge, 2007).

[29] Review of Intelligence on Weapons of Mass Destruction, cited previously.

[30] George Tenet, *At the Center of the Storm: My Years at the CIA* (New York: Harper Press, 2007).

range of foreign security and intelligence services by professionals whose presence and provenance is acknowledged to their host governments. With some overseas regimes, it was – and still is – more effective to liaise with the security apparatus of the foreign court or power rather than its diplomatic or civil bureaucracy.

THE RISKS OF SECRECY

What were the secret agencies of past eras afraid might happen from exposure of their activity? How far should we be swayed by such arguments today? Here, too, research can be useful.

Part of the concern must have been fear of public disapproval of the very existence of secret service in a domestic context. Public concern about methods used in uncovering the doings of "foreigners" (including Feinians) and in protecting the Empire was never going to be widespread. However, as already noted, the gathering of domestic intelligence in a later era on left-wing activists with possible communist sympathies could have been genuinely divisive of the body politic. Only recently have the declassified files begun to reveal what, in fact, was done by the Security Service and police Special Branch in the 1950s and 1960s. Their countersubversion operations were designed to identify and remove from positions of potential access or influence those judged by the investigators to be unreliable or open to pressure. The files also reveal what was done by covert activity of bodies such as the Information Research Department of the Foreign Office working with the Secret Intelligence Service (SIS) in mounting covert operations of influence to counter Soviet propaganda and promote the Western point of view. There are lessons here for today in avoiding public misunderstanding, as we read that the U.K. government is establishing within the Counter-Terrorist Command of the Home Office "a research, information and communications unit in support of the struggle for ideas and values",[31] reporting to the Home Secretary, Foreign Secretary, and Secretary of State for Communities and Local Government.

Concerns about diplomatic embarrassment from exposure of systematic espionage are obvious and must have included fear of domestic pressure mounting to withdraw political and parliamentary support and finance. In recent times, this concern has no doubt lessened with the remarkable postimperial prominence of secret intelligence in British popular culture

---

[31] Statement by the Prime Minister, 29 March 2007, available at www.number10.gov. uk/output/Page11376.asp.

and an evident pride in the tradition of "the great game". (It has been estimated that half of the world's population has seen a James Bond film; as Christopher Andrew notes, Bond, a fictional spy, is far better known than any real one.)[32]

The dangers for the intelligence community of coming up against an excess of zeal in managing ethical foreign policy, however, can be seen in 1844 after the Mazzini affair when overzealous parliamentary committees of inquiry led to the abolition of both the Secret Office and the Deciphering Branch, which had been serving British interests since it opened in 1653 and was put on a legal footing by Parliament in 1670. As a result, Britain entered World War I without an effective signals intelligence (SIGINT) system, which had to be rapidly assembled from scratch in Room 40 of the Old Admiralty Building to help fight the war at sea and the German submarine campaign. There is an echo here of "gentlemen do not read each other's mail", as U.S. Secretary of State Stimson was alleged to have said in 1931 – an attitude that may have contributed to the relative underdevelopment at the start of World War II by the United States of intelligence from diplomatic interception.

For cryptanalysts, another fear was that revelation of the existence and scale of U.K. effort would alert potential targets to the ubiquitous listening ear or engender "*un certain fantasme d'écoute*".[33] One difficult lesson occurred when Prime Minister Baldwin in the House of Commons, under pressure to justify the 1927 raid on the offices of the Russian trade company ARCOS, revealed enough for Moscow to deduce that their ciphers were being read and made them secure, thereby firmly shutting out British intelligence. The SIGINT budget was secret – the major components of expenditure and staff numbers were hidden in different defence votes – because otherwise, visibility of the willingness of the U.K. government to fund such effort might be taken by potential targets as evidence that the enterprise was producing significant results. Thus, the strenuous postwar efforts to keep secret the wartime success of Bletchley Park until the aging of that remarkable generation led to an intense desire by some for recognition in their lifetime.[34] Once the conventions of secrecy were broken, the flood of

---

[32] Jeremy Black, *The Politics of James Bond: From Fleming's Novels to the Big Screen* (Westport, CT: Praeger, 2001), p xiii, cited by Peter Hennessy, cited previously.

[33] Peter Szendy, *Sur Ecoute, L'Esthetique de l'Espionnage* (Paris: Editions de Minuit, 2007) provides a postmodern structuralist analysis of this fear.

[34] F. W. Winterbotham, *The Ultra Secret: The Inside Story of Operation Ultra, Bletchley Park, and Enigma* (London: Weidenfeld, 1974); and J. C. Masterman, *The Double-Cross System* (New Haven, CT, and London: Yale University Books, 1972).

books and personal memoirs, some more reliable than others, poured out, leading to more synoptic accounts[35] and to the decision to allow the Official History of World War II to describe the use of SIGINT on an industrial scale,[36] as well as the active use of methods of strategic deception,[37] using captured and turned double agents.

The technology behind those wartime successes, in any case, was by then outdated, but the need for genuine secrecy over more recent technologies remained. A dramatic example was the sudden loss in 1998 of the ability of the SIGINT agencies to intercept bin Laden's satellite communications, a loss believed to follow revealing articles in U.S. newspapers. According to James Bamford, writing about the U.S. National Security Agency: "... the NSA lost all track of him. ... He may still use [satellite phones] occasionally to talk about something mundane, but he discovered that the transmitters can be used for homing".[38] We cannot afford such revelations in current efforts to monitor the communications of terrorists and proliferators. The risk of unauthorised disclosures by insiders on both sides of the Atlantic, however, will increase if there is continuing controversy about the ethical and even the legal basis on which operations are being conducted, a point to which I return herein.

Secrecy in the Cold War intelligence world was in tune with the prevailing attitude that the public did not need to know, certainly had no right to know, and was better off not knowing what was being done to protect it by the secret parts of the state. Nuclear deterrence depended crucially on convincing Soviet planners that they would not be able to achieve strategic surprise that would have left the Western nuclear powers with no other choice than to admit defeat or resort to suicidal escalation. At the same time, it was crucial to the working of deterrence that the potential opponent should not learn the details of these arrangements, other than knowing that they existed, they were obviously thorough, and they were well tested. Soviet attempts to obtain sensitive information on the vulnerabilities of the United Kingdom's posture had to be thwarted through the work of the Security Service and through counterintelligence operations to recruit agents in a position to know what the Soviet military and intelligence establishments were attempting to do. It was a logical consequence that the British public also had to be kept in the dark about what was being done in its name.

---

[35] See the works of David Kahn and James Bamford.

[36] F. H. Hinsley et al., *British Intelligence in the Second World War* (HMSO, 1988–93).

[37] Michael Howard, *British Intelligence in the Second World War*, vol. 5, *Strategic Deception* (HMSO, 1990).

[38] Available at archives.cnn.com/2001/US/09/20/inv.terrorist.search.

Despite recent Freedom of Information legislation, the habit of government secrecy in the United Kingdom is difficult to shake off. Different attitudes are needed today to build public understanding of and support for the role that security intelligence plays in uncovering terrorist networks and plots.

RECALIBRATING THE CASE

Some of the past arguments for the veil of secrecy may no longer have their old force, but what remains is the continuing genuine sensitivity of all intelligence communities about the detail of their work and the identity of their personnel being exposed. Rule number one of British intelligence-officer training was always: keep the agent's identity secret to avoid exposure to unnecessary risks.[39] Rule number two was: keep secret the identity of the case officer – which meant throughout the career because even the most senior officers managing the Security Service would once have been operational officers recruiting and running sources and obtaining information from those who might well have not known the true status of their interlocutor. Neither should we forget that secrecy brings its own mystique, which has value in the secret world. This remains the case despite the occasional exception in which the agent himself wishes vindication, as in the case of Vassily Mitrokhin, the KGB archivist (described by the FBI as "the most complete and extensive intelligence ever received from any source"[40]).

Technical intelligence and "national technical means" have also involved huge investments that could be put at risk by a careless security slip or hostile penetration, such as the exposure by George Blake of the Berlin tunnel (dug in the early 1950s for the then-vast cost of $6.7 million[41]). Even disclosure in specialised publications, through the power of the Internet search engines, can quickly come to notice.

The U.K. media has traditionally had a slightly more deferential attitude to official secrecy generally than that of the United States. An example was the news blackout agreed to between the Ministry of Defence in London and all major news organisations operating in the United Kingdom to not report on the presence of Prince Harry's operational duty in Afghanistan in order to reduce the risk to the prince and his regiment. The prince's tour was cut

---

[39] As taught to the novelist Graham Greene, quoted by Norman Sherry in *The Life of Graham Greene*, vol. 2 (London: Jonathan Cape, 1994).

[40] Christopher Andrew and Vasili Mitrokhin, *The Mitrokin Archive* (London: Allen Lane, The Penguin Press, 1999).

[41] See the declassified history of the U.S./U.K. Berlin tunnel operation available at www.fas.org/irp/cia/product/tunnel.pdf.

short when the U.S. Web site, the Drudge Report, broadcast the fact.[42] That disclosure was widely criticised in the United Kingdom, but it is nevertheless increasingly the case in the United Kingdom as well as the United States that an aggressive media, with many journalists now freelancers and dependent on selling stories, makes operational secrecy more difficult to maintain. Even in France, where the media has traditionally respected official requests for restraint in publication of sensitive material, the same wind is blowing, as seen, for example, in the revelations[43] related to past arms exports and government ministers.

Within the intelligence world, in particular, there will always be tension between the risk of genuinely sensitive operational material being disclosed and the value to the "brand" of having a strong professional reputation, as well as the advantages of recognition in governmental circles of the value of secret intelligence. A retired "C" (i.e., Chief of SIS) stated: "When we make the final approach and ask someone to help the British as an agent, as often as not they almost stand to attention".[44] Although Prime Minister Thatcher's files record her[45] 1984 view that "too much has been said and written about intelligence and less should be in future", she did agree in 1985 to the publication of the magisterial Official History of Intelligence in the Second World War[46] that set many records straight. As Sir Stephen Lander wrote,[47] this was the first chink in that formidable Thatcher armour on the subject of agency avowal. He added that to him, it now seems bizarre that the government persevered with the fiction for so long that government organisations which did not exist had office blocks in central London, hundreds of staff, and names that featured in the press with monotonous and usually sensationalist regularity.

The 1992 Waldegrave initiative in the United Kingdom led to the gradual release of intelligence files, including early Joint Intelligence Committee (JIC) assessments. The motivation we may suppose was, as Peter Hennessy expressed in the dictum often attributed to Lord Acton, that if secrecy prevents you writing your own history, only one thing is guaranteed – that it will

---

[42] The story is described at www.usatoday.com/life/people/2008-02-29-britain-prince_N. htm, accessed 21 April 2008.

[43] For example, the Elf Affair, www.iht.com/articles/2003/01/30/dumas_ed3_.php, accessed April 2008.

[44] Quoted by Peter Hennessy in W. G. Runciman (ed.), *Hutton and Butler: Lifting the Lid on the Workings of Power* (Oxford: Oxford University Press, 2004).

[45] Quoted by Sir Stephen Lander, The Hinsley Lecture 1993, St. John's College, Cambridge.

[46] Hinsley, op. cit.

[47] Lander, op. cit.

be written by your enemies.[48] Most recently, by reading the Butler[49] inquiry into the intelligence on WMD in Iraq, the public can see what a current JIC assessment looks like and can gain a sound understanding of the nature of modern intelligence from the masterly short essay written by the late Peter Freeman, historian of Government Communications Headquarters (GCHQ), which was incorporated into the Butler report.

However, the danger from all this public material is that historians and followers of intelligence matters will come to believe that the level of detail of what could at some distance of time be safely revealed of wartime days – and wartime technology – can also be revealed on much more recent times and capabilities. There has been a shortening of the expected time span of enforced secrecy creating real problems for the intelligence community when it comes to the intensive use of their various tradecrafts for counter-terrorism, on which lives of agents and the security of the public may well depend.

So, a major challenge for the intelligence community in both the United States and the United Kingdom is the problem of continuing to operate effectively in the modern public-information environment. This includes the intrusiveness of the media and the development of its own capabilities to acquire information by covert and unacknowledged means, whether by the investigative reporter, the undercover or sting operation, or the recruiting of networks of "agents" willing to provide unauthorised disclosures for payment or for sheer devilry. The challenge also must include political cultures in which the leaking of information for tactical gain or to acquire leverage by those who are not in a position to assess the sensitivity of the material has become all too common. In an Internet age, of course, any indiscretion is almost certain to become widely disseminated and picked up by the potential opponent. The intelligence agencies, nevertheless, have no option but to accept this new reality and learn to operate safely in it.

THE IMPACT OF AVOWAL AND OVERSIGHT ON THE U.K. INTELLIGENCE COMMUNITY

As previously argued, there was never any difficulty for the United Kingdom in accommodating secret agencies within the British unwritten constitution. The Royal Prerogative, as applied to the keeping of "the King's peace" and the confounding of the King's enemies, provided ample authority for the

---

[48] Peter Hennessy, The Hinsley Memorial Lecture 2005, St. John's College, Cambridge.
[49] Butler report, cited previously.

Crown and, thus, the Crown's ministers to fund a secret vote – which predated by several centuries the creation of actual secret services – as a device to provide parliamentary authorisation for secret activity without the usual scrutiny of the objects of expenditure. As Foreign Secretary Sir Edward Grey stated in 1906: "The Secrets of this fund are not to be revealed to common official eyes: it is my purdah lady veiled even from the lascivious gaze of grasping treasury clerks".[50] The external audit of the accounts of the secret agencies was entrusted to specially cleared auditors (now of the National Audit Office, itself accountable directly to Parliament) with only the Chairman of the Parliamentary Accounts Committee (by convention, a leading figure of the main opposition party in Parliament) and Deputy Chairman being briefed. The prime minister was regarded by Parliament as personally accountable for secret intelligence but was not routinely quizzed on the floor of the House. Foreign Secretary Austen Chamberlain informed the House of Commons in 1924: "It is of the essence of a Secret Service that it must be secret, and if you once begin disclosure it is perfectly obvious to me as to hon members opposite that there is no longer any Secret Service and you must do without it".[51]

This comfortable acceptance of secrecy occasionally was punctuated by scandals, not least the long-running story of the prewar Cambridge spies. By the 1980s, the structure of the U.K. intelligence community was increasingly visible to the public. The Franks Committee of Inquiry into intelligence failures before the Argentine invasion of the Falkland Islands lifted the lid on the working of the JIC. The banning of Trades Unions at GCHQ in 1984 by Prime Minister Thatcher led to unparalleled publicity about SIGINT. A different set of circumstances was also affecting the ability of that secretive organisation to shelter itself from public knowledge because the commercialisation of cryptography with public key systems (ironically, originally a GCHQ discovery[52]) on which modern commerce depends led to the rapid development of an academic literature and, indeed, university departments of cryptography. A succession of security scandals in Whitehall and in the intelligence agencies additionally revealed weaknesses, leading to an increasing number of questions being tabled in Parliament.

Against this swirl of publicity, the changing climate of legally enforceable human rights was causing increasing concern within intelligence-agency

---

[50] *The Foreign Office and the Secret Vote 1782–1909*, FCO Historical Branch Note No. 7, June 1994.

[51] Hansard, House of Commons fifth series, vol. CLXXIV, 15 December 1924, col. 674.

[52] The previously classified history of this remarkable feat can be found at www.cesg.gov.uk/site/publications/media/ellis.pdf.

circles. An adverse judgement in Europe (i.e., the Malone case[53]) risked severely restricting their ability to operate: a concurring Opinion on the case stated that "the mission of the Council of Europe and its organs is to prevent the establishment of systems and methods that would allow 'Big Brother' to become master of the citizen's private life" and "the continuing temptation facing public authorities to "'see into' the life of the citizen", words with considerable resonance in today's conditions.

In the 1980s, the case of *Hewitt, Harman v. United Kingdom* brought Security Service practice up against Article 5 of the European Convention on Human Rights (i.e., The Right to Respect for Private and Family Life, Home, and Correspondence). How could a citizen be assured that a balance was being struck between the needs of the state to protect itself and its citizens from perceived threats and the right of individuals and organisations to privacy, freedom of association, and freedom of expression? As David Bickford, Legal Advisor to the Security Service at the time, expressed it, "The only international forum in which this question has been decided is the European Court of Human Rights".[54]

In a series of cases ranging from *Leander v. Sweden, Klass v. Germany, V et al. v. Netherlands, Ludi v. Switzerland and Hewitt and Harman* (1) and (2), *Esbester and Christie v. United Kingdom*, and *Chahal v. United Kingdom*, the main questions were determined and the balances established. Broadly, the Court accepted in *Leander v. Sweden* that states may establish secret agencies to protect the interests of their economic well-being and national security. Within reason (i.e., the margin of appreciation), states can determine for themselves what those interests are. The states, however, must legislate to declare the existence of their secret agencies and to explain their functions and powers, including those explained in *Hewitt and Harman v. United Kingdom* concerning the obtaining and dissemination of information. Moreover, as stated in *Esbester and Christie v. United Kingdom* and *Ludi v. Switzerland*, the powers of any secret agency may only be exercised in proportion to the threat, and there must be independent effective oversight of the agencies and the exercise of their powers".[55] Effectively, the European Court was putting an end to the traditional British prerogative of secrecy around its Security Service.

According to a former DG of the U.K. Security Service,[56] we owe the decision to legislate to the diplomat Sir Anthony Duff, who was by then recalled from retirement to become DG of the Security Service. In

---

[53] *Malone v. United Kingdom*, 7 Eur. Ct. H.R. 14 (1985).
[54] David Bickford, lecture to Harvard Law School Forum, 15 April 1997.
[55] Bickford, op. cit.
[56] Lander, cited previously.

1987, – largely because of his own personal standing with Mrs. Thatcher following his role in the War Cabinet during the Falklands War – he was able to secure her acceptance of the need for legislation for the Security Service. That became the Security Service Act of 1989 that legislated the Service into existence, established a Tribunal supported by a Commissioner and able to investigate complaints from the public as well as review the issue to the Service of warrants for entry on or interference with property and for interception of telecommunications.

Despite avowal, the route to parliamentary oversight was not direct. In the words of the House of Commons Home Affairs Select Committee,[57] "In 1992, emboldened perhaps by the spirit of *glasnost* that prevailed elsewhere in the world, the then Home Affairs Committee asked the Home Secretary at the time, the Rt Hon Kenneth Clark MP, if it might take evidence from the then Director-General of the Security Service, Stella Rimington, whose responsibilities – theoretically at least – came within the Committee's remit. The answer was a firm 'no'". Only when it was pointed out that Rimington was already dining with certain favoured journalists did the Home Secretary relent. A private lunch was arranged at the Security Service headquarters between Rimington and six members of the Committee.

The Committee, however, took the view that a free lunch was no substitute for proper parliamentary scrutiny. In January 1993, it published a report concluding that the Security Service should be made subject to the normal departmental select committee structure. The government rejected this recommendation; the Committee, said the government, had paid "insufficient regard to the unique nature of the Security Service and to the personal nature of the Director-General's accountability to the Home Secretary".

The precedent of the Security Service Act, however, was eventually extended through the Intelligence Services Act 1994 to place the SIS and GCHQ on a comparable statutory basis and to establish the Intelligence and Security Committee (ISC) of parliamentarians to monitor the work of all three intelligence and security agencies.

Thus, for the first time, members of both Houses of Parliament were to be involved in the scrutiny of the expenditure, administration, and policy of the three U.K. secret agencies. The ISC has demonstrated since 1994 that it can investigate even very sensitive matters requiring access to highly secret information without compromising its security. ISC recommendations are almost always immediately accepted by the government. Building on this track record, by agreement with the government, its remit has expanded in

---

[57] Select Committee on Home Affairs, 3rd Report *Accountability of the Security Service*, 14 June 1999.

practice beyond the original legislation to cover not only the agencies but also the entire U.K. intelligence community, including the work of the JIC and its staff. The ISC investigations, such as those into intelligence relevant to the 2002 Bali terrorist bombing and the London bombings of July 2005, now extend beyond matters of agency administration. This has been welcomed by the agencies as providing a group of senior parliamentarians who could vouch for the integrity of the work of the agencies and, where necessary, recommend improvements without risking uncontrolled exposure of a wider audience.

For some observers,[58] the ISC suffers from the drawback that it is a statutory committee with members appointed by the prime minister, who has the final say (for security reasons) about which parts of its reports can be published. It can be fairly argued that the Committee's work would have greater external credibility if it enjoyed the privileges of a Select Committee of Parliament (as do most counterpart organisations in other countries) to write its own rules of procedure and have the power to "send for people and papers". Those optics have to be balanced against the major advantage it has over U.K. Select Committees in that official witnesses before the ISC give evidence on their own behalf; those in front of Select Committees do so on behalf of their minister,[59] leading inevitably to more cautious evidence from officials trying to protect their ministers and a political edge being put on questioning from the Committee. Change in this area is likely under Prime Minister Gordon Brown, but there may be a choice to be made in revising the arrangements between greater public credibility and greater effectiveness.

Another major innovation was the passing of the Regulation of Investigative Powers Act of 2000, which regulates all forms of intrusive surveillance and information-gathering by the intelligence agencies, the police, and other governmental departments involved in surveillance work such as revenue and customs. This Act[60] laid down the level of authority required for different classes of intrusion such as the acquisition of communications data (e.g., billing data), intrusive surveillance, use of covert human intelligence (HUMINT) sources (e.g., agents, informants, and undercover officers), interception of communications, and access to encrypted data. For each of these powers, the Act ensures that the law clearly covers the purposes

[58] Anthony Glees, Philip H. J. Davies, and John N. L. Morrison, *The Open Side of Secrecy* (London: Social Affairs Unit, 2007).
[59] Under the so-called Osmotherley Rules, a widely observed convention followed by successive governments.
[60] The operation of the Act is described in detail on the Home Office Web site, www/security.homeoffice.gov.uk/ripa/about-ripa.

for which they may be used, which authorities can use the powers, who should authorise each use of the power (with the most intrusive having to be warranted ex ante by a Secretary of State, typically the Home Secretary for operations in Great Britain), and the use that can be made of the material gained. The Act provides additionally for ex-post independent judicial oversight by commissioners (i.e., senior judges) and a means of redress for individuals.

It is difficult to overstate the overall impact in recent years on the U.K. agencies of this body of legislation, or its value relative to the demands of counterterrorism being discussed here, in creating a strictly law-abiding culture within the agencies while enabling them to carry out a full range of intelligence-gathering operations for authorised purposes. In the view of a former DG of the Security Service, Sir Stephen Lander, "It has been wholly beneficial (though that is not to say that scrutiny by MPs has always been entirely comfortable or that the need for additional due process has not been costly). We moved from a position that was based on the rather dubious assumption that if something was not expressly illegal then it was okay. We now had the assurance of statute law as opposed to the insecurity of the royal prerogative, under which much agency activity hitherto notionally took place. That change played a key part in the 1990s and beyond in making the agencies more self-confident and thus more effective". In terms of legal structures and oversight, the basic mechanisms thus seem to be in place – although not yet fully operational – to cope with the more difficult conditions that countering terrorism imposes.[61]

TAKING AN ETHICAL APPROACH

Oversight is therefore needed, but against which standards should the overseers oversee? Secret intelligence is information others want to stop one from having. It follows that the realm of intelligence operations has never been a zone in which the ethical rules that we might hope to govern our private conduct as individuals in society could fully apply – what Joseph Conrad, in his introduction to *The Secret Agent*,[62] called "the moral squalor of the tale". Finding out other people's secrets will involve breaking everyday moral rules, the equivalent of reading others' mail, listening at and

---

[61] One of the conclusions reached by Peter Gill regarding the U.K. Intelligence and Security Committee: Peter Gill, "Evaluating Oversight Committees: The UK ISC and the 'War on Terror', and Mark Pythian, "The British Experience with Intelligence Accountability", both in *Intelligence and National Security, 22*, 1 (February 2007).

[62] Conrad, J. (1907). *The Secret Agent* (London: Penguin Books, 1994).

peeping through keyholes, deliberately encouraging indiscretion, and inciting breaches of confidence, as well as masquerading as what one is not.

Much invaluable lifesaving intelligence comes from using modern information technology to sift through large quantities of personal information about the innocent as well as the suspect, and that, in turn, raises issues of individual privacy and distaste for state prying. In addition, effectiveness against global networks requires cooperation with secret services abroad; such liaisons will include countries whose methods we might regard as crude and ethically doubtful. Imagine intelligence chiefs having to persuade their minister using Machiavelli's argument[63] that "taking everything into account, he will find that some of the things that appear to be virtues will, if he practices them, ruin him and some of the things that appear to be wicked will bring him security and prosperity".

Are there no rules in this domain? As Sir Michael Quinlan stated it,[64] "Is this not quintessentially one where Machiavelli and realpolitik have to rule?"

In a recent article,[65] I suggested that the U.K. intelligence community is already governed by a combination of law, internal regulation, and implicit culture that I believe embodies ethical principles. I summarise these as six guidelines by analogy with just-war doctrine, as follows:

- There must be sufficient sustainable cause. Primary legislation should set down limits on what the intelligence machine can be used for and remove fears that the power of modern intelligence methods will become ubiquitous and thus seriously erode individual liberty.
- There must be integrity of motive, from collection all the way to presentation to the top of government, especially guarding against any perception of politicisation of collection, analysis, or reporting.
- The methods to be used must be proportionate to the harm to be prevented, and the absolute prohibition on torture must be upheld.
- There must be right authority, especially for highly intrusive operations. In the case of the United Kingdom, this involves ex-ante approval by a Secretary of State of the most intrusive operations, such as domestic wiretapping, and ex-post judicial oversight of the exercise of this authority, with recourse to an independent judicial tribunal if abuse is suspected by an individual.

---

[63] Machiavelli, *The Prince* (London: Penguin Books, 1961), translation by George Bull.

[64] Sir Michael Quinlan, "Just Intelligence: Prologemena to an Ethical Theory", *Intelligence and National Security, 22,* 1, February 2007.

[65] Sir David Omand, "Ethical Guidelines in Using Secret Intelligence for Public Security", *Cambridge Review of International Affairs, 19,* 4, December 2006.

- There must be a reasonable prospect of success, and authorisers must be vigilant over the risks of "collateral damage"; the use of intelligence to target military or paramilitary operations raises significant issues.
- Recourse to secret intelligence must be a last resort if there are other ways of obtaining the information. In particular, more use should be made of open sources.

Thus, to meet the first guideline, intended classes of intelligence targeting must be within the requirements drawn up annually by the JIC and submitted to ministers along with strategic guidelines for the development of future capability, always within the outer boundary set by Parliament in the legislation (described previously) that put the agencies on a statutory footing. For example, the functions of MI6 and GCHQ are legally restricted to being exercisable only[66] in the interests of national security, the economic well-being of the United Kingdom, or in support of the prevention or detection of serious crime.

The second guideline is a reminder of the importance of ensuring that there is integrity in presenting intelligence to customers. Whatever the arts of deception that may be deployed to acquire intelligence, the customer must have complete confidence in the integrity of the system that delivered it. The results must not be massaged to fit prejudices or prevailing orthodoxies. This point is clearly relevant to the issue identified previously relative to public trust in the intelligence behind counterterrorist measures and public warnings related to threats that are being uncovered by intelligence. The best chance of reducing the risk to the public is to follow the leads and uncover the entire conspiracy. Counterterrorist operations involve significant nerve on the part of the police and intelligence staff alike as they manage the risks involved. They have to be trusted to have as their sole motive the protection of the public, now and in the future, and not considerations of media presentation or political climate. This guideline is also linked to the need to make clear that there is no possibility of political authority being misused.

In what is probably the most sensitive area – the Security Service's intelligence-gathering at home – unlike in most areas of government,[67] the minister is not statutorily personally responsible and therefore cannot give operational directions. The statute[68] gives authority to direct domestic

---

[66] Intelligence Services Act 1994, available at www.opsi.gov.uk/acts/acts1994/Ukpga_19940013_en_1.htm.

[67] Under the "Carltona" principle, civil servants act using the authority of their minister who therefore retains responsibility for their actions in his name.

[68] The Security Service Act 1989.

activities to the DG, not the Secretary of State, in order to avoid any perception of the misuse of the power of their office by ministers for party-political or personal purposes. The Secretary of State, however, is accountable to Parliament (i.e., may be held to render an account rather than be held personally responsible) for the operations of the Security Service. Because the DG is appointed by the Secretary of State, a counterbalancing means of ultimate democratic control is provided.

The third guideline invites the continual application of the principle of proportionality: Is the impact of the specific intelligence-gathering operation proportionate to the seriousness of the business at hand? For a HUMINT operation, the impacts would include the nature of the agent recruitment and inducements, the physical risks involved, and the moral hazard to both agent and handler, particularly where the agent is a participating informant. No one in the U.K. community has 007 status; nor do agents have "get out of jail" cards.

For technical operations, the impact also must be judged in terms of the extent of intrusion, a principle that is built into the Regulation of Investigative Powers Act (RIPA) 2000 through differing levels of request and approval. In other words, the RIPA provides a test for those who approve operations of minimum necessary intrusion[69] comparable to the common-law doctrine of "minimum necessary force".

Most of the ethical problems associated with legislation to counter terrorism, including facilitating intelligence-gathering, center on how to arrive at the appropriate mix for the circumstance in question of individual categories of rights: on the one hand, the right to life and to be protected by the state from threats to oneself and one's family; on the other hand, the right to privacy of personal and family life. There is an obvious danger that security concerns are somehow thought to trump human rights, with any immediate security gain as having automatic primacy. It is a balancing act within rights that should be sought and not a trade-off between rights and something called security.

It is also a balancing act to ensure that long-term interests as well as immediate gains are suitably weighed. Governments will always want to apply utilitarian judgements in their balancing act, and they will find it easier to do so if they ensure that strategic as well as tactical considerations are included, thus avoiding the obvious trap of desirable security gains for the majority justifying actions that disproportionately affect a minority. For a struggle against terrorism that has to take place among the people – whose

---

[69] A term used by the late R. V. Jones in his *Reflections on Intelligence* (London: William Heinemann, 1989).

support is needed to sustain the campaign – that price could be too high. This underscores the sustainability part of the guideline, which is a difficult test in realpolitik as well as in ethics.

The fourth guideline is that there has to be the right authority over the intelligence activity in terms of a proper authorising process with accountability within a chain of command, and proper oversight from outside the intelligence community. For the sensitive category of intrusive operations, the U.K. public can take reassurance, mentioned previously, in that the relevant act, RIPA 2000, carefully calibrates both those who may request intrusive intelligence-gathering methods (e.g., telephone interception) and the level of seniority of those approving them. The position of the Secretary of State at the apex of approval for the warranting of the most intrusive operations provides him and the key officials in his department with insight into the day-to-day activities of the agencies. There is, however, no authority to authorise torture, whose prohibition remains an absolute, or interrogation methods that would contravene the United Kingdom's acceptance of the relevant international conventions.

The fifth guideline requires there to be a reasonable prospect for success of an intelligence operation before approval is given, with acceptable levels of risk if the operation were to be exposed. For many years (i.e., since the infamous Commander Crabb affair[70]), it has been the practice that the Foreign Office must be consulted about operations by any of the agencies where there are risks of diplomatic damage so that officials – or, in major cases, the Foreign Secretary himself – can judge whether to authorise the operation.

The final test proposed is that of last resort in the specific sense that there is no reasonable alternative way of acquiring the information from nonsecret sources and thus avoiding all the possible moral hazards and trade-offs that the collection of secret intelligence may involve.

CONCLUSION

Secret intelligence and secret agency are still essential components of statecraft, not least in providing public protection – the first duty of any government. In particular, public support and understanding for the existence and value of the work of secret agencies is needed, given the importance of preemptive intelligence in combating terrorism. This requires public

---

[70] This refers to the botched and fatal frogman operation of 19 April 1956 to inspect the hull of the Soviet cruiser *Ordzhonikidze* in Portsmouth Harbor that resulted in the resignation of the Chief of SIS.

confidence, through effective oversight, that the intelligence community is operating according to generally accepted principles of conduct, such as proportionality and right authority. However, it also requires that the sources and methods of the intelligence gatherers and assessors remain shielded from exposure in a world of increasing respect for human rights and concern for personal privacy and in a world of rapidly developing intrusive information technology.

My overall conclusion is that we can have confidence in answering the chapter's opening question in the affirmative for the United Kingdom, provided that the activities of the intelligence community continue to be conducted within the type of ethical framework described herein. Maintaining that position rests on the constant persuasion of the public to hold fast to that which we are defending from the barbarities of the terrorists: our values, liberties, freedoms, and rights, including the proper rule of law.

ELEVEN

The Science of Intelligence: Reflections on a Field That Never Was

Wilhelm Agrell and Gregory F. Treverton

In May 1939, a young British Ph.D. in physics from Oxford, R. V. Jones, was approached by a staff member of Sir Henry Tizard's Committee for the Scientific Survey of Air Defence. Britain was, in this period, ahead of most other nations in integrating the academic scientific community and defense research and development (R&D), as illustrated by the lead that the Royal Air Force enjoyed in radar technology over the main adversary, Germany. However, as war drew closer, the Committee had experienced a problem regarding intelligence or, rather, the lack of intelligence: the British services simply were unable to collect material that might provide any insight into German efforts to apply science in aerial warfare. Jones was offered the task of looking into this problem and he accepted – by coincidence, agreeing to start his new job on September 1, the fateful day that Germany invaded Poland.[1]

Jones's experience underscores the central theme of this book. Our purpose in surveying the state of research on intelligence is not only to suggest promising topics or even to promote better understanding by academics and others of what intelligence does – although later in the chapter we assemble some of the research suggestions that derive from the assessments of the book's chapters. Rather, our ultimate purpose is also to improve the practice of intelligence. The theme of this chapter as well as the book is that in the threat circumstances of the 21st century, intelligence needs to move beyond "established" practice to become an authentic profession. To do that, it needs to find ways to open itself to and ultimately embrace the importance of empirical studies and methodological self-reflection – not

---

[1] R. V. Jones, *Most Secret War: British Scientific Intelligence 1939–1945* (London: Coronet Books, 1979), p. 1.

as a peripheral matter but rather in the essential interest of intelligence itself.

ORIGINS OF THE MERGER THAT WAS NOT TO BE

In the years after 1939, the academy and the military merged on both sides of the war, as the academic community joined the national mobilizations of the warring parties, symbolized by names such as Fermi, Oppenheimer, and Szilard as well as von Braun and Heisenberg. In the process, the scientific world was split apart and, to a considerable extent, was to remain divided by the Cold War for a half-century. The wartime national mobilization of the academic community was focused on technological development, but many other aspects of warfare were also influenced by the influx of people with an academic background. Prominent among those domains was the rapidly developing field of intelligence. To some extent, the growing use of science in warfare and intelligence was, as in the case of R. V. Jones, simply two sides of the same coin: scientific development of means of warfare created the need for countermeasures, impossible without intelligence coverage of developments on the other side of the conflict – an interaction that would continue and permeate much of Cold War intelligence.

However, scientific and technological intelligence was only one of a wide range of tasks for rapidly expanding and transforming intelligence organizations. Foreign intelligence, cryptography, special operations, deception, and psychological warfare were tasks that demanded not only new agencies but also human resources with new competencies. In Britain, Bletchley Park, the Secret Intelligence Service (SIS), and the Security Service enlisted many young university graduates, many of them to experience – in the words of Michael Herman – "great wars."[2] Others, like Kim Philby, were engaged in their own silent war, possibly no less great for themselves but certainly not for their official employers once the truth dawned on them.

University people were not an uncomplicated type of recruits for intelligence, bringing along not only vital knowledge and competencies but also individualism, academic flamboyance, and ideological affiliations that in some cases could turn out to be devastating. Still, intelligence could not do without them, a fact most vividly displayed in cryptanalysis, where rank-and-file intelligence officers could accomplish no more than they could in other realms of scientific intelligence. As Commander Torkil Thorén, the first head of the successful Swedish communications

---

[2] Michael Herman at the Stockholm Intelligence Conference, May 2007.

intelligence (COMINT) agency, was alleged to have said, "Director is the only job I can handle in this agency."[3]

However, recruitment from the universities was not only a matter of adding specific competencies to fields or problems that could not be handled without those new competencies. The new recruits not only joined intelligence as specialists but also as intelligence officers, serving along with officers who had a more traditional background in the military, the diplomatic service, or the police. One obvious reason for this type of recruitment was the need for language skills in the accomplishment of a range of intelligence tasks, from human intelligence (HUMINT) collection to the study of open sources and the conduct of intelligence liaison and covert operations. The wartime Office of Strategic Services (OSS), as well as the SIS, needed people who not only spoke German but who also understood German society, culture, and mindset.

Sweden established a secret intelligence service for espionage, or HUMINT collection, and special operations in the autumn of 1939. Headed by a military officer, the majority of the small staff came from the universities. One of the recruits was Thede Palm, a doctor of theology who was fluent in German. He was assigned the task of interrogating travellers arriving on the regular ferry lines from Germany, seeking any observation with intelligence significance. Palm would take over as chief after the war and run secret intelligence for another 20 years.

Thus, languages, like physics and mathematics, were only additional supportive competencies to the conduct of intelligence. University graduates, whether in economics, classics, or theology, brought something else along in the bargain – a way to think, to deal with intellectual problems and structure information. Although not as immediately useful as the ability to read and speak German, the significance of this more general intellectual competency was soon obvious. It was no surprise that the Research and Analysis Branch of the OSS drew heavily on the academic competency of the mostly university-recruited staff. Also in its field operations, the OSS came to appreciate the value of an academic training. In his final report, Calvin Hoover, head of the OSS North Central European Division covering Germany, the Soviet Union, and Scandinavia, noted that from his experience, intelligence officers who lacked a university or college background did not perform well on missions. Those operatives often were left to solve or even formulate tasks on their own, without any detailed guidance from

---

[3] Sven Beckman, *Svenska kryptobedrifter* (Swedish Accomplishments in Cryptology), (Stockholm: Albert Bonniers Förlag, 1996), p. 167.

remote headquarters, and over unreliable and slow communications. It took the perspective gained by theoretical education to grasp the complexity of the conditions under which they had to operate, what type of information was needed, and the crucial distinction between gossip and hearsay on the one hand and information that could be proven and documented on the other.[4]

Hoover's remarks on recruitment reflect an insight that the scientific–intelligence interface went beyond the specific intelligence-related skills. As in the early development of operations analysis in support of warfare,[5] the scientific approach to complex problems emerged as a value in itself, even when it first seemed to interfere with the tradecraft that had been established in the military profession. Still, Hoover primarily referred to recruitment and selection, to the preferable educational background and personal qualifications of intelligence officers, and to the ability of individuals to perform well when out on their own.

The recruitment of R. V. Jones to British intelligence reflected a similar ambition to add a scientific perspective on the production and flow of intelligence. As he became familiar with the intelligence system, Jones went one step further, analyzing intelligence as scientific data and employing intelligence collection for the conduct of what could be labeled intelligence experiments. The first major intelligence problem of this type that Jones confronted was an indication of the existence of an unknown German beam-navigation system, employed in support of the escalating German air offensive against Britain in June 1940. Initially, Jones had only minimum information: a single Enigma decrypt of a Luftwaffe message mentioning the codename *Knickebein*, Kleve (a town in Western Germany), and the coordinates for a place in the Midlands. That the message referred to a

[4] Calvin B. Hoover, Final Report (no date), RG 226 (OSS), Entry 210 Box 436, National Archives, College Park, MD. As an example of inadequate educational background, Hoover referred to a report received by one of the OSS agents in Switzerland, who then in great excitement reported that he had learned the secret by which the Germans produced gasoline from coal. But, instead of a complicated industrial process, what he described was simply the principle of adding so many atoms of hydrogen to so many atoms of carbon, well known to any chemical engineer. This particular report was actually disseminated and, as Hoover remarked, "aroused considerable amusement from some of the agencies which received it."

[5] An early classic in this area was the RAND Corporation study of bomber-basing for the U.S. Air Force, which broadened the question from efficiency of location to survivability of the bomber force. See, for instance, Albert Wohlstetter, *Economic and Strategic Considerations in Air Base Location: A Preliminary Review* (Santa Monica, CA: The RAND Corporation, 29 December 1951), available at www.rand.org/about/history/wohlstetter/D1114/D1114.html.

beam-navigation system was simply one hypothesis among many; the main competing hypotheses believed that the references were to coordinates for radio navigation beacons that would be activated by a German fifth column in Britain or that it was simply a German hoax. Not only was there no confirmation from other intelligence sources that such a system existed, the possibility was also questioned on scientific grounds by Jones's senior colleagues. British scientists had not been able to accomplish beams narrow enough to serve as long-range navigation aids and therefore regarded such a system as not feasible.[6] Still, the intelligence significance of the beam-navigation-system hypothesis was obvious: if the Germans, in fact, possessed such a system, it would greatly enhance their ability to strike British targets at night and in bad weather. If this were indeed the case, the development of countermeasures would have top priority.

In fewer than 10 days, Jones reexamined existing intelligence files, initiated further collection, and finally staged an intelligence experiment to confirm or refute the beam hypothesis. Through renewed technical examination of a downed Heinkel-111 bomber, along with interrogation and subsequent eavesdropping of German aircrews,[7] Jones could establish that, indeed, the German bombers had a receiver for long-range beam navigation disguised in their normal blind-landing system. However, this still did not confirm the existence of a system in operation.

The final test, therefore, was an attempt to locate the beam itself. Jones engaged in some guesswork on probable frequencies based on notes found in a wrecked plane and additional Enigma decrypts. He also assumed that the most likely top-priority bombing target was the Rolls Royce aircraft-engine factory in Derby. On those speculations, a British aircraft was sent up to try to catch the beam. After three nights, the plane – probably one of the first airborne electronic intelligence (ELINT) missions in the history of intelligence – managed to locate two narrow intersecting beams from bearings that corresponded with the suspected stations of the *Knickebein* system.[8] Until the final confirmation, Jones knew that there was an element of uncertainty and that the discovery of beams in places other than over

---

[6] Jones, cited previously, Chapter 11.

[7] The technique of interrogating POWs individually and then allowing them to talk among themselves in a location with hidden microphones was used extensively by the British, especially with the German nuclear researchers captured at the end of the war.

[8] The codename *Knickebein* (i.e., crooked leg) referred to the specific configuration of the slightly V-shaped antenna. The Germans were, as Jones experienced, notorious in selecting revealing codenames. The successor of *Knickebein*, a one-beam system, was thus designated Wotan, after the one-eyed god in German mythology, illustrating the importance of knowledge about a broad cultural context in intelligence analysis.

likely German bombing targets would refute his hypothesis – meaning that he had led the intelligence system on a wild-goose chase and, in the process, consumed time and scarce resources at a most critical moment in the war.[9] The "Battle of the Beam" illustrates a rare case of an intellectual merger of science and intelligence in which scientific and intelligence methods were interlinked to solve an intelligence problem while displaying a high standard of rigor, methodological accountability, and innovative thinking.

CONSOLIDATING INTELLIGENCE AS A PROFESSION

The Cold War saw a massive consolidation and development of the intelligence profession but not along the methodological line displayed in the Battle of the Beam. The years of the amateurs were generally over as the intelligence organizations established themselves as a core component of national security – a component perceived as indispensable at various levels in the Cold War security system, ranging from long-term planning and arms development to disarmament negotiation, early warning, crisis management, and support for ongoing operations. However, the focus was firmly on the collection–dissemination process established during World War II that constituted the intelligence foundation of deterrence. Intelligence was – as Allen Dulles forcefully stated in his book, *The Craft of Intelligence* – an activity for professionals who knew the nature of their trade and focused on the collection and dissemination of vital information. Although addressing collection in two chapters, Dulles hardly mentioned analysis and instead referred to the task of compiling vital information.[10]

University graduates were still wanted and, in specific fields, badly needed. Technical collection and intelligence analysis became increasingly scientific enterprises, the former through the demands of advancing technology – the surveillance "arms race" in signals intelligence (SIGINT) and the rapid emergence of imagery intelligence (IMINT) – the latter by the recruitment of analysts with an academic background and knowledge in useful scientific disciplines. The best prospective analyst of intelligence on the Soviet economy had to be a researcher trained in economics. Following the mobilization of intelligence resources against terrorism, this academic influx in analysis has expanded further and changed focus, with specialities not previously regarded as relevant becoming top priority – ranging from experts on pathogens to Islam.

---

[9] Jones, cited previously, p. 148 ff.
[10] Allen Dulles, *The Craft of Intelligence* (New York: Harper & Row, 1963), p. 154.

However, outside of specific fields and events, such as the invention of photo-reconnaissance (to become IMINT) from space platforms in the 1950s,[11] few scientists had any "great wars" during the Cold War. Cold War intelligence, in the East as well as in the West, was a closed domain consisting of bureaucratic, compartmented agencies with limited or no breathing space. Intelligence, of course, could be a rewarding career in itself and sometimes a stepping-stone to a subsequent career in politics or public administration. However, this book on the state of research on intelligence has found, like others have, few testimonies of intelligence work that is perceived as *intellectually* rewarding in the academic sense, if for no other reason because of the limited or, in most cases, nonexistent possibility of publishing anything of significance for a subsequent academic career.

To be sure, development in the social sciences did not pass unnoticed by intelligence. Sherman Kent, himself an academic recruit to the OSS Research and Analysis Branch, acknowledged in his classic work on strategic intelligence published in 1949 the importance of development of the social sciences not only as a competency pool but also for the employment of scientific methods in a hypothesis-driven intelligence process.[12]

By using the output of the research community as well as recruiting specialists from its ranks, it could be argued that science and intelligence had, in fact, if not merged, then at least become increasingly linked to each other, with science as mainly an intellectual provider and intelligence as mainly a consumer in terms of both personnel and products.[13] However, contrary to all figures of recruitment and employment of academic knowledge and methods, this integration has had surprisingly limited impact on the intellectual nature of intelligence. To state it more bluntly, the intelligence profession has not generally become a science-based profession through this process; rather, it has become a semi-academic profession with an increasing segment of frustrated and dissatisfied staff members – which is something quite different. Within the profession, the mystique of intelligence analysis has been cultivated for a variety of reasons. The "craft" of intelligence is described as not one taught but rather as experienced. Intelligence could

---

[11] See Dwayne A. Day, John M. Logsdon, and Brian Latell (eds.), *Eye in the Sky: The Story of the Corona Spy Satellite* (Washington: Smithsonian Institution Press, 1998).

[12] Sherman Kent, *Strategic Intelligence for American World Policy* (Princeton, NJ: Princeton University Press, 1949).

[13] The academic influx in intelligence production is illustrated by the declassified CIA publication series, *Studies in Intelligence*, with issues that comb airy memoirs with articles that easily could have passed a blind test as papers in political science, international relations, or contemporary history.

be learned only through intelligence; outsiders, however gifted, remained outsiders, nonmembers of the secret guild.[14]

CRAFT, PRACTICE, OR PROFESSION?

If intelligence as an intellectual activity is not science-based, on what then is it based? In medicine, the answer would be "established practice."[15] A clinical treatment could be based on either scientific results, according to a common standard, or on experience, the way things have always been done and where outcomes have been monitored long enough to conclude that the treatment works. "Established practice" is an experience-based model that has an extensive background in the military profession, in policing, in education, and in farming, to mention just a few fields of experience-based human activity. However, as medicine illustrates, experience-based established practice is not enough and sometimes is disastrous, especially in fields with rapidly developing technologies and expanding knowledge.

A unique study by the ethnographer Rob Johnston provided ample, although somewhat discouraging, empirical support for this observation that established practice is not a good-enough model for intelligence. The aim of his study, commissioned shortly before the September 11 attacks and completed in the wake of the most debated failure of analytic tradecraft in the history of intelligence – the Iraqi WMD assessments – was to identify and describe conditions and factors that degraded intelligence analysis.[16] Although others had addressed the same questions before, no one had done so with the unique empirical material at Johnston's disposal. He was able to interview almost five hundred intelligence professionals, academics, and researchers throughout the U.S. intelligence community about their experience of analytic work, thereby providing not only a cross-section of experience in the U.S. intelligence context, but probably also the premises and problems of intelligence analysis more generally.

---

[14] For some further comments on perceptions of intelligence as profession, see Wilhelm Agrell, *When Everything Is Intelligence, Nothing Is Intelligence* (Washington: Central Intelligence Agency, Kent Center Occasional Papers, 2003).

[15] For a discussion of the scientific nature of medicine and the implications for intelligence, see Walter Laqueur, *World of Secrets: The Use and Limits of Intelligence* (London: Weidenfeld and Nicolson, 1985), p. 302 ff.; and Stephen Marrin, *Intelligence Analysis: Turning a Craft into a Profession*, Proceedings of the 2005 International Conference on Intelligence Analysis, McLean, VA, May 2005.

[16] Rob Johnston, *Analytic Culture in the U.S. Intelligence Community: An Ethnographic Study* (Washington: Central Intelligence Agency Center for the Study of Intelligence, 2005), p. xiii.

Johnston's major finding was the absence of a baseline, a standard analytic method. Instead, he found that the most common practice in intelligence analysis was to conduct limited brainstorming on the basis of previous analysis, thereby producing a bias toward confirming earlier views. The overriding principle in the process seemed to be managerial conservatism, with much more emphasis on avoiding errors than on imagining surprises. The analytic process stands out as driven by current intelligence, in much the same way outlined by Dulles almost a half-century earlier.[17] The focus on compilation is vividly illustrated by one of the analyst's comments quoted by Johnston: "People seem to have confused writing with analyzing. They figure that if you just go through the mechanics of writing something, then you must have analyzed it."[18]

In Johnston's opinion, this confusion, in turn, reflected the confusion of tradecraft and analysis. Although tradecraft certainly is relevant in operations, it can be a confusing and counterproductive concept for analysis, to the extent that the term connotes a lack of scientific method. To quote Johnston, "Tradecraft purposefully implies a mysterious process learned only by the initiated and acquired only through the elaborate rituals of professional indoctrination. It also implies that the methods and techniques of analysis are informal, idiosyncratic, unverifiable, and perhaps even unexplainable. 'Good' methods are simply those that survive, and then are passed on by 'good' analysts to novice analysts."[19]

Another observer from the outside 20 years earlier, Walter Laqueur, made a similar observation on the mystifying nature of intelligence. In the introduction to his account of the use of intelligence, *World of Secrets*, he referred to the kind advice he received from inside the intelligence community. Very politely, as he puts it, he was made aware of the fact that something of value in intelligence could only come from someone who, unlike Laqueur himself, had spent a lifetime in the profession, preferably at a high level. According to the Spanish proverb, "It is not the same to talk of bulls as to be in the bullring."[20]

Johnston and others who have tried to explore the intellectual nature of intelligence analysis have found the bullring surprisingly empty or, if not empty, then obscured not merely by secrecy but also by genuine methodological confusion.[21] There are traces neither of a hidden secret science

---

[17] See Foreword by Gregory F. Treverton in Johnston, cited previously.
[18] Johnston, cited previously, p. 15.
[19] Johnston, cited previously, p. 18.
[20] Laqueur, cited previously, p. ix ff.
[21] For instance, Gregory F. Treverton and C. Bryan Gabbard, *Assessing the Tradecraft of Intelligence Analysis* (Santa Monica, CA: The RAND Corporation, 2008).

nor the systematic employment or adaptation of methods employed in the open scientific culture. The secrecy surrounding sources and methods seems to have little relevance when it comes to the complex assessments and predictions that constitute the most demanding task of analysis.

Why has a half-century of debate about the importance of a scientific dimension in intelligence led to such remarkably meager results? The field has developed rapidly and is of undeniable importance: Why, then, did it not long ago transform in a scientific direction as an integral part of the process of professionalizing? Perhaps under the circumstances, the right question to ask is not what incentives there were for the development of a science of intelligence but rather why those incentives were lacking or pointed in another direction.

The first and most important of the incentives that were lacking derives perhaps from the self-image of the intelligence profession. The craft or mystery conception is not only a product of the absence of alternatives, of possible paths toward scientifically based analytic methods. The conception is also a powerful instrument for intelligence analysts and officials in drawing a sharp dividing line between insiders and outsiders – those "in the know" and those not in the know. The impact of this for self-esteem, professional identity, and political influence should not be underestimated. The notion of a secret tradecraft is a powerful instrument to avert external critics – a method that also can be observed in many academic controversies when interference from representatives of other disciplines is often not well received and is, almost by definition, regarded as ignorant and irrelevant. The transformation of intelligence analysis in the direction of overt, systematically employed, and verifiable methods would inevitably weaken the protective wall surrounding a craft and mystery. One of the most important aspects of the critical public debate about the performance of intelligence has been the penetration of this wall and therefore the possible weakening of this major negative incentive.

Yet, the unprecedented openness on analytic products and processes around the Iraqi WMD case also touched a second negative incentive: the impact of secrecy. As a phenomenon in intelligence, secrecy is both functional and dysfunctional; both an obvious necessity to protect sensitive sources, methods, and valuable intellectual property and an element in the intelligence mythology, employed to shield organizations and activities and to amplify the assumed significance of trivial information and assessments. The extensive employment of secrecy, intentionally or not, has blocked the intellectual development of intelligence analysis by drastically limiting the empirical basis for any such development. True, there is a growing scholarly literature on the history of intelligence based on documentary sources, but there is a vast time lag between the periods covered by historians and the everyday conduct of intelligence analysis. Furthermore, the documentary material available to historians is often incomplete and, in some cases, misleading due to prevailing secrecy.[22]

Intelligence cannot abandon secrecy for the sake of methodology. However, secrecy can be employed in a more selective way if the importance of empirical studies and methodological self-reflection is regarded not as an outside interest but rather as being in the interest of intelligence itself. Johnston's study is an interesting example of development in this direction – and the Central Intelligence Agency (CIA) Center for the Study of Intelligence deserves credit for sponsoring it – yet, it remains an example that would still be regarded with horror by most intelligence agencies around the world.

TALKING OF BULLS VERSUS BEING IN THE BULLRING

The negative incentives blocking the development of scientific methods and perspectives in intelligence cannot be ascribed to only the intelligence culture and the modus operandi of intelligence agencies. The wider political, public, and (not least) academic context has also enforced the intellectual isolation of intelligence. There has been little or no political interest in stimulating contacts over the university–intelligence divide. On the contrary: political self-preservation for long periods has been a strong incentive against any such enterprise. If hostile penetration of the intelligence agencies was a menace, academic penetration was only a variant. As for the academic communities themselves, there has been a widespread reluctance, sometimes developing into hostility – and not always without reason. Somewhat more trivial but no less important is a widespread lack of interest in intelligence matters from the academic disciplines concerned, which is partly due to academic priorities, partly due to ignorance and widespread misconceptions about "spying" (see Christopher Andrew's Chapter Three in this volume). Academic interest in intelligence matters will come about only to the extent that intelligence is perceived as an interesting and rewarding

---

[22] One example of this, further discussed in Wilhelm Agrell's Chapter One in this book, is the often referred-to case of the Israeli intelligence failure prior to the October War of 1973. Until the late 1990s, the interpretation of the case was based on false assumption. Because the existence of a centrally placed Israeli agent close to Egyptian President Sadat was unknown, "cognitive blindness" continued to be emphasized as an explanation of the Israeli failure.

field for research – a process now finally underway, although by no means on any grand scale. The rise of intelligence studies will not automatically transform intelligence analysis, but it can diminish ignorance on the part of the academy, along with some of the hang-ups in the fragile relationship between the two cultures.

The chapters of this volume provide a number of suggestions about research directions. Although all sorts of comparative work on intelligence are enriching, reaching beyond comparisons of agencies or functions (e.g., early warning) would be rewarding, as Michael Warner argues in Chapter Two. Construing intelligence as a *system* that is itself a dependent variable would beg for answers to questions about which characteristics of national regimes, interests, politics, and values would account for differences across nations in intelligence systems.

Surely, technology is one of the drivers of intelligence systems. In that sense, it is no accident that the wizardry of technical collection during the Cold War, especially for the major powers, drove them to empha- size those means, leading to what Wilhelm Agrell calls "bean counting" of what could be seen or heard. Now, the conventional wisdom holds that transnational targets like terrorists, small and nimble, are less susceptible to collection by technical means. In Chapter Seven, Jeffrey Richelson poses the question: Is that so? More broadly, how will this century's technolo- gies match intelligence's targets and how will intelligence be shaped in the process?

Although in different ways, Christopher Andrew and Jennifer Sims both suggest work on how intelligence affects outcomes in international politics. For Andrew, the historian, there are glaring historical gaps to be filled, espe- cially on the role of SIGINT during the Cold War and on the place of covert action in Soviet foreign policy. For Sims, who is more of a political scientist by inclination, the question is more general: How does intelligence, which seeks to provide nations (and other entities) with competitive advantage but also can increase transparency, bear on the central propositions of realist theories of international relations?

The change in the targets of intelligence, especially terrorism, will drive changes in how intelligence does its work and how it relates to both policy and policy makers. The implications of that change for intelligence and strategic planning constitute the theme of Neal Pollard's Chapter Six. In Chapter Five, Wilhelm Agrell discusses how the change in the targets of intelligence, in particular, has produced the need for nothing less than a paradigm shift in the practice of intelligence. That discussion takes him to Thomas Kuhn and revolutions in science. It also suggests the value of continuing to ask – as several studies already have – what intelligence might learn from transformations in military or business affairs.[23]

In Chapter Eight, Olav Riste addresses how the change affects intelligence's relationship to policy makers, asking whether the WMD affair, as carefully investigated in both the United States and Britain, bespeaks an increased danger of politicizing intelligence. In Chapter Nine, Wolfgang Krieger examines research on the oversight of intelligence, looking especially at differences between Europe and the United States. Both chapters suggest the value of continuing to examine cases and comparative studies, across nations and other domains or disciplines – ranging from medicine to law enforcement.

The change in target is also driving the need for intelligence to open up, in two senses. One sense is the openness, called for in this chapter, to scientific methods and empirical analysis as intelligence becomes a profession. The other is the sense that Sir David Omand writes about in Chapter Ten: If intelligence now needs to collect and analyze more at home, will not its methods have to be more transparent and accountable to the public? How can it accomplish this without telling its targets too much about how it does its work?

A RENEWED PERIOD OF CRISIS

Intelligence analysis or, to be more precise, the intellectual dimension of intelligence has entered a renewed period of crisis in the early 21st century, due first to a number of obvious or perceived intelligence failures, but also to wider skepticism about the ability of intelligence to deliver what has been expected – a skepticism often taken for granted and thus not addressed by intelligence organizations and their representatives.[24] As the Cold War sinks back into history, it becomes increasingly evident that the period probably was unique for intelligence, with remarkably stable frames of reference and, thus, limited fundamental challenges in a system optimized for and, on the whole, content with regular recounting of the beans. True, there were crises, but none ended in war or global disaster – an outcome that

---

[23] For instance, Deborah G. Barger, *Toward a Revolution in Intelligence Affairs* (Santa Monica, CA: RAND Corporation, 2005), available at www.rand.org/publications/TR/TR242/index. html.

[24] It is worth noticing that Laqueur, two decades ago, described national intelligence in terms of a structural crisis, created among other things by a widening gap between external unrealistic expectations and the ability of intelligence systems to deliver. See his book, cited previously, p. 9.

cannot be credited to the intelligence systems that often failed to foresee and comprehend events once the situation turned fluid.

Over the years, various analytic methods borrowed from statistics, political science, and psychology have been tested but with limited impact on the practice of intelligence analysis.[25] It is doubtful if any specific scientific method of the type discussed or tried would have averted the faulty assessments about WMD in the run-up to the 2003 Iraq war, a failure not only of the U.S. intelligence community but also of most Western intelligence services. Certainly, the recruitment of an academically trained analytic staff in itself did not help much. The impact of the intelligence culture, as illustrated by Johnston's study, is a more powerful factor than individual training and ambitions. Scientists in a nonscientific context do not perform well, which is an old lesson in science policy. The crucial aspect of the relationship between intelligence and science, therefore, is not recruitment and job satisfaction but rather the intellectual consequences of the intelligence culture.

Is there such a thing as a science of intelligence? The answer to this question is both no and yes. From an epistemological perspective, the answer must be negative. There is no proper description of this science, no literature on methods and applications – only a scattered and often inaccurate empirical output and no coherent ongoing internal debate over theories, methods, and the nature of the field. No academic area of study in that state could claim the status of a scientific field.

However, from another perspective, the answer is probably affirmative. What R. V. Jones employed in the Battle of the Beam in 1940, and again in the attempts to comprehend and disrupt the German V-weapons programs in 1943–4, was more than an application of scientific competence to intelligence; it was the systematic employment of a scientific approach to the type of analytic problems specific to intelligence. That this scientific approach should not have more general potential seems a dubious conclusion. Instead, the nondevelopment of this scientific perspective must be found elsewhere than in its lack of potential. The answer is to be found in the counterproductive elements within the intelligence culture discussed herein, as well as in historical circumstances supporting the status quo, particularly the long absence of the type of national emergency powerful enough to break the bonds of professional tradition. Called back to service once again by the aging Winston Churchill in the early 1950s, R. V. Jones

---

[25] For instance, FACTIONS and other similar methods in the "expected utility" family have been used in intelligence with powerful results. However, time and resource consuming, they have been regarded by analysts as occasional luxuries, not as regular features of analysis.

was to experience this stagnation himself. He found scientific intelligence profoundly transformed, with the fusion of the methods of science and the profession of intelligence – a fusion invented out of necessity and favorable circumstances – lost in a war of bureaucratic infighting.[26]

Intelligence analysis has the potential to become an applied science. Its purpose would be managing the uncertainty in assessments of threats and possibilities based on incomplete, unreliable, or uncertain data in a context in which demand requires those assessments irrespective of the limitations. Defined in these terms, intelligence analysis stands out as a genuine cross-disciplinary science in-being, with a theoretical basis and a set of methods not limited to any single subject matter or field of analysis but rather adapted to every specific application. There are no cases in which intelligence analysis can be studied at the meta-level; rather, all the cases and empirical evidence are to be found in the specific applications. The lack of methodological dialogue – or even interaction – among the different domains of intelligence analysis, such as strategic intelligence, traditional military intelligence, counterterrorism intelligence, law enforcement intelligence, and business intelligence, therefore stands out as a crucial obstacle to the development of a common understanding of and standard for the scientific basis of intelligence analysis.

Is there a need for this potential science of intelligence, the theoretical framework, and methods for uncertain assessments? From intelligence professionals, the answer has often been negative, in that professional experiences overshadow whatever possible virtues there might be to a scientific approach. As scientists have experienced in many other contexts, nonscientists have a tendency to disregard the importance of scientifically based methods. However, does the lack of a scientific approach in intelligence really matter? This question was seldom addressed during the Cold War and the "mid-war period" in the 1990s. Since September 11, there is a growing awareness of a fundamental limitation not only in the way intelligence is structured but also in the way the problem of intelligence assessments is handled. *Established practice* no longer suffices as a guarantee for correct assessments in an evolving threat environment; on the contrary, established practice and tradecraft can instead become the blueprint for groupthink and, hence, coming intelligence disasters.

A theory of intelligence, referred to by many but formulated by no one, might be helpful in understanding intelligence. However, it would not necessarily improve the *performance* of intelligence, at least not in a direct way.

---

[26] Jones, cited previously, Epilogue.

A theory of intelligence would be more helpful for the academics trying to make sense of intelligence systems and their role in society than for the practitioners, in much the same way that international-relations theory is of limited immediate use for those dealing with an international crisis. However, somewhere along the line, theory can indirectly affect practice through a more well-informed public debate, awareness and self-reflection among customers, and a decreasing ignorance in the academic world on the nature and problems of intelligence.

Index